PATRIOTISM

PATRIOTISM

edited by

IGOR PRIMORATZ

Humanity Books

An Imprint of Prometheus Books

59 John Glenn Drive
Amherst, New York 14228-2119

Published 2002 by Humanity Books, an imprint of Prometheus Books

Inquiries should be addressed to
Humanity Books
59 John Glenn Drive
Amherst, New York 14228–2119
VOICE: 716–691–0133, ext. 210
FAX: 716–691–0137
WWW.PROMETHEUSBOOKS.COM

13 12 11 10 09   5 4 3 2

Library of Congress Cataloging-in-Publication Data

Patriotism / edited by Igor Primoratz.
    p. cm.
Includes bibliographical references.
ISBN 1–57392–955–7
1. Patriotism. I. Primoratz, Igor.

JC329 .P365 2001
323.6'5—dc21   2001051717

Printed in the United States of America on acid-free paper

Contents

ACKNOWLEDGMENT

I would like to acknowledge with gratitude a grant from the Australian Research Council Special Research Centre for Applied Philosophy and Public Ethics, the University of Melbourne Division, which contributed to covering the publication costs of this anthology.

I.P.
Melbourne, December 2001

INTRODUCTION

*F*or a long time, patriotism was a neglected subject in philosophy. The prevailing view was that it may be of importance in social science, but that it raises no philosophical questions. But in the last two decades or so, philosophers have shown renewed interest in patriotism. The reasons for this are partly theoretical, and partly relate to recent political developments in some parts of the world.

One of the central debates in moral and political philosophy today is that between adherents of universalism and those who emphasize the moral (and, where appropriate, political) significance of local loyalties and identities; the value of particular, personal relationships; the binding force of special duties. In this context, patriotism is brought up as a central instance of the latter type of considerations. On the practical level, philosophers have been seeking to make a contribution to the understanding and evaluation of nationalism, which has unexpectedly reemerged as a central political and cultural influence in a number of conflict-ridden parts of the world. In this connection, patriotism is often discussed too. Indeed, some authors use the terms "nationalism" and "patriotism" in a very similar, if not identical sense, or assume that the moral status of the two attitudes must be the same.

However, both such indiscriminate usage and the assumption about the equal moral standing of nationalism and patriotism are misleading. In the search for clarity and discerning moral judgment, we should seek to acknowledge both the similarities and dissimilarities between the two. The latter may well be no less important than the former. They are significant enough to make patriotism an important moral and political issue in its own right.

This book offers a collection of writings of contemporary philosophers and political theorists on patriotism as an issue distinct from nationalism. Before introducing the reader to the main views and lines of argument advanced in these writings, some brief remarks on the meaning of "patriotism" are in order.

WHAT IS PATRIOTISM?

If we look it up in a dictionary, we will find that "patriotism" is "love of one's country." This definition is correct, but much too thin; it needs to be fleshed out if it is to be of any use in coming to grips with the moral and political significance of what the word stands for.

For one thing, it is important to spell out that the patriot's love of his country is a love expressed in action. It involves certain beliefs about and feelings for one's country; but the touchstone of one's patriotism is what one is prepared to do for it. Accordingly, we can say that patriotism is a certain type of concern for one's country and compatriots. Obviously, it must be *special* concern for our country and compatriots. To feel and show the same sort and degree of concern for them that we have for human beings in general would be something else altogether: humanitarianism, not patriotism. A patriot may or may not be a humanitarian too. But even if she is, her concern for her own country will be significantly greater than her concern for the rest of humanity: she will normally be willing to do more, to sacrifice more for the former than for the latter.

Moreover, historically, "patriotism" has been a political concept. As Mary G. Dietz shows in her account of the history of "patriotism" in the English-speaking world (chapter 11), when it first appeared in English, in the sixteenth century, "patriot" meant "compatriot": a person living in, or stemming from, one's own country. But the word soon took on an expressly political import, and came to refer to a person committed to a certain set of principles thought to constitute the distinctive political tradition of his country. And although the political content has changed over time, the political character of the concept has remained. The *patria* to which the patriot is committed is not only a geographical, but also a political entity. Those for whose welfare the patriot shows special concern are not merely inhabitants of his country, but also citizens of his polity. The special concern that defines patriotism is also a concern for one's own polity. This concern involves active participation in the political life of one's country, in which the common good is expressed and promoted. Normally, we would not describe an apolitical person as a patriot.

Just why does a patriot show special concern for her country? Is it because the country exhibits certain valuable traits, because it has special achievements in certain fields of human endeavor? Or is it simply because it is *her* country?

The first reply gives us *value-based* patriotism, while the second indicates what might be termed its *egocentric* variety. Each has both strong and weak points. The former appears reasonable; when asked why does he love his country, why is he more concerned for its welfare than for the welfare of the rest of humanity, the adherent of value-based patriotism will give his reasons: he will point out the values exhibited by his country, its distinctive merits and achievements. In doing so, he will be assuming certain standards of value which others can acknowledge as valid. Thus a German patriot can point out the immense German contribution to virtually all areas of culture, an American patriot can portray the United States as the embodiment of the ideals of liberty and democracy, and so on. However, it is difficult to resist the suspicion that this is but a superficial, if not merely apparent type of patriotism. For a patriot of this sort will, in consistency, have to grant that he ought to be no less concerned for the welfare of any other country which satisfies the same standards of value. It turns out that these values themselves, rather than his own country, are the object of his love, commitment, and concern.

In this respect, an adherent of egocentric patriotism would seem to be at an advantage. She loves her country as *her* country, rather than *a* country that lives up to certain standards of value. Her patriotism is not derived from some general values and merely focused on her country. It is rather directed at her country in an immediate, unconditional, stable way, because that country, and that country only, is *her* country. However, this type of patriotism may well strike us as unreflective, indeed irrational; we might be tempted to cite the words of J. B. Zimmerman that "the love of one's country . . . is in many cases no more than the love of an ass for its stall."[1]

Clearly, neither of the two answers will do by itself; the full account of the way a patriot relates to his country will have to include both of these partial replies, and the inevitable tension between them. We understand a patriot's love for his country and special concern for its welfare when we acknowledge that neither the fact of the merits and achievements of the country, nor the fact that it is *his* country, is in itself sufficient for patriotism, but that each is necessary. What is sufficient is the conjunction of the two. Patriotism appears as irrational and unintelligible if the *only* reason the patriot can adduce for his love and concern for his country is the fact that it is *his* country. We feel we can reasonably expect to hear something more, to be told about certain valuable traits, certain achievements of the country. But these traits and achievements will provide reasons for his patriotism because they are traits and achievements of *his* country, and not in themselves. If they happen to characterize a neighboring country too, that will not, and cannot, generate the same relationship to that country, since the country is not *his*.

Thus patriotism involves two equally important components, one general (the merits and achievements of a country), the other particular (the allegiance to *this* country). As a consequence, patriotism is vulnerable to questioning, revision, and even repudiation from two directions. The patriot may come to doubt that her country really exhibits valuable traits or has impressive merits; or she may come to the conclusion that the country is not truly *hers*.

Obviously, a *description* of patriotism would have to include such psychological and sociological phenomena as the patriot's identification with his country, the need to belong to a collectivity and to be a part of a wider

narrative, to be related to a past and a future that transcend the narrow confines of the individual's life and its paltry contents, and more. But for the
immediate purpose of providing the focus for the debate about the rights and
wrongs of patriotism, a mere *definition* should suffice. With this purpose in
mind, "patriotism" can be defined as love of one's country (and polity), motivated in part by the fact that it is one's country, and expressed in a special concern for its welfare and that of compatriots.

PATRIOTISM AND MORALITY

The moral standing of patriotism is a highly contentious issue. Some consider
it a morally unacceptable partiality to one's own country and compatriots, and
a source of many evils in social and political life. Others portray it as a morally
legitimate stance, or a duty, or a moral virtue. The extreme version of the
favorable view presents patriotic loyalty as the basic moral virtue and the
source of all genuine morality.

In the moral critique of patriotism two main lines of argument can be distinguished. One warns of its consequences. Authors such as Leo Tolstoy or
Emma Goldman portray patriotism as an unreasonable belief in the superiority
of one's own country, and the promotion of its interests at the expense of all
other countries. It is but egoism writ large, bound up with uncritical and
unlimited support of one's country, an aggressive stance toward other countries, and a tendency to militarism and jingoism. It makes for international tension and conflict, and much too often leads to war. If we really wish to put an
end to war and attain lasting world peace, we must overcome patriotism.[2]

Tolstoy provides a good example of the other main moral objection to
patriotism. Patriotism, he claims, is the very opposite of the central message of
both morality and religion: that of equality and fraternity of all human beings.[3]
This objection reflects a widely held view of moral judgment as universally
valid and impartial, a view shared by otherwise different, and even mutually
opposed ethical theories such as Kantianism and utilitarianism. Moral judgment is held to apply universally: to the person being judged, and to anyone
else who happens to be in the same circumstances. The moral point of view
enjoins respect for *every* rational being as an end in itself (Kant) or, alternatively, a consideration of the interests of *every* human being on an equal footing,
as the interests of *one* human being (the utilitarians). Patriotism is by definition
partial, and incompatible with moral universalism and impartialism. Morally
speaking, it is on a par with egoism: an arbitrary, morally unacceptable preference for a person or group simply because it is close to *me*, a judgment I will
not and cannot universalize in the way required by morality. My country is
more important to me than any other; and I am not willing to universalize the
judgment concerning my preference so as to allow for the preference of

strangers for the welfare of their countries. How can this be right? What magic is there in the pronoun "my," asks William Godwin, that should justify me in overturning the decisions of impartial truth?

Others defend patriotism by questioning the alleged universality and impartiality of all moral judgment. A good way to start is by displaying the context of Godwin's question. From the point of view of the common good, Godwin writes,

> the illustrious bishop of Cambray was of more worth than his valet, and there are few of us that would hesitate to pronounce, if his palace were in flames, and the life of only one of them could be preserved, which of the two ought to be preferred. . . . Suppose the valet had been my brother, my father or my benefactor. This would not alter the truth of the proposition. The life of Fénelon would still be more valuable than that of the valet; and justice, pure, unadulterated justice would still have preferred that which was more valuable. Justice would have taught me to save the life of Fénelon at the expense of the other. What magic is there in the pronoun "my", that should justify us in overturning the decisions of impartial truth?[4]

But this conclusion is surely absurd, and reason enough to reject any ethical theory that leads to it. Granted, the contribution of one of the leading minds of his time to the common good cannot be compared to the contribution of his valet. But is that reason enough for suppressing one's love for one's father or brother, or for ignoring one's duty of gratitude to one's father or benefactor, and leave him in flames, in order to save his employer, the great thinker and writer? Godwin's words show in a striking way that this understanding of the moral point of view as consistently universal and impartial is doubly wrong. It enjoins us to act in a way that is psychologically, humanly impossible. And it exempts us of all special moral duties, duties generated by particular, personal connections and relationships, for the sake of the most general duties we owe to every human being.

Some critics of this understanding of morality argue that morality is based just on such connections and relationships, and amounts to a set of loyalties to persons and to various groups which may be large or small, but are always limited. A moral consideration is generated by one's love for one's father, care for a friend, or concern for family, country, or nation. Such a consideration is irreducibly personal, and can be generalized only within a particular group. As Andrew Oldenquist writes in his seminal paper "Loyalties" (chapter 1), if we attend to our moral experience unencumbered by universalist prejudice, we readily see that "loyalties ground more of the principled, self-sacrificing, and other kinds of nonselfish behavior in which people engage than do moral principles and ideals" (p. 25). He attempts to show how our various loyalties, wide and narrow, define moral communities within which we are willing to universalize our moral judgments, act impartially, and promote the common good. And he turns the tables on the adherents of universalism and impartialism. The latter reject all particular loyalties, and tell us that morality obligates universally and impartially toward every human being, that moral obligation is owed to humanity. But the demand for impartiality is nothing but a demand for loyalty to an expanded group. Universalists are actually pleading for a particular loyalty: the loyalty to humanity (and not, say, to all beings who can suffer, or to all living beings). In doing so, they simply assume what needs to be established by argument: that the loyalty to one's species always has greater moral weight than loyalty to any other group, larger or smaller.

One of the particular loyalties Oldenquist wants to vindicate is the loyalty to one's country: considerations of patriotism are genuinely moral considerations, and they determine, in part, what we should do. He also offers a typology of patriotism, distinguishing "impartial patriotism," roughly equivalent to what I have called value-based patriotism, and thus neither a type of loyalty nor true patriotism; "loyalty patriotism," or patriotism proper; and "sports patriotism," modeled on a fan's loyalty to the team and inherently unstable, if not incoherent.

While Oldenquist argues that patriotism provides a prima facie moral reason for acting in a certain way, the other landmark defense of patriotism, Alasdair MacIntyre's lecture "Is Patriotism a Virtue?" (chapter 2), expressly endows patriotic loyalty with much greater moral weight. An individual, MacIntyre points out, can understand and adopt moral rules only in the particular version in which they are endorsed by his community. Moral rules are justified in terms of certain goods, but these goods, too, are always given as part and parcel of the way of life of a particular community. The individual becomes and remains a moral agent only when shaped and sustained as such by his community. Accordingly, MacIntyre argues, "my allegiance to the community and what it requires of me—even to the point of requiring me to die to sustain its life—could not meaningfully be contrasted with or counterposed to what morality required of me." Therefore "patriotism and those loyalties cognate to it are not just virtues but central virtues" (p. 50).

This, clearly, is not patriotism as but one of our many loyalties with differing contents and scope, which must compete with other loyalties and which sometimes wins, and at other times gives way. For MacIntyre, considerations of patriotism *always* have greater weight than other moral considerations. This includes those highly general considerations of justice between states and nations, as well as solidarity with *all* human beings, held to be paramount by moral universalists. Patriotism, MacIntyre says, may require that I support my country even when its cause is not just or good from a universal and impartial point of view. If my loyalty is not robust enough to override abstract justice or universal human solidarity, mine is not true patriotism, but merely its "emasculated" version.

Now this type of patriotism may well be thought too strong; we may be unwilling to accord patriotism so much moral weight that it overrides all other moral considerations. On the other hand, we may be just as unwilling to embrace the uncompromising version of universalism and impartialism, which would make us oblivious to the moral import of particular relationships and to special moral obligations. It is understandable that some philosophers have been trying for a middle-of-the-road position which would accommodate both the universal and the particular components of our moral experience, the impartial and the partial types of practical deliberation.

A good example of this approach is "Patriotism and 'Liberal' Morality" by Marcia Baron (chapter 3). Her central argument is that the conflict between impartiality and partiality is not as deep as it may appear. Morality allows for both types of considerations, but at different levels. At one level, one is often justified in taking into account one's particular attachments and commitments, including those to one's country. At another level, one can and should reflect on such attachments and commitments from a universal, impartial point of view, delineate their proper scope and determine their weight: for instance, "allow that with respect to certain matters and within limits, it is *good* for an American to judge as an American, and to put American interests first" (p. 64). In such a case, particularity and partiality are seen as legitimate and indeed valuable from a universal, impartial standpoint. This means that with respect to those matters and within the same limits, it is also good for a Mexican to judge as a Mexican and to put Mexico's interests first, and so forth. This, indeed, is how we think of our preferences for, and moral obligations to, our family, friends, or local community: the partiality involved is legitimate, and perhaps also valuable, not only for us, but for anyone.

For MacIntyre, the type of partiality in general, and patriotism in particular, that is at work only on level one of moral thinking and against the background of impartiality of level two, lacks content and substance. But from Baron's standpoint, MacIntyre's uncompromisingly particularistic type of patriotism appears as mindless and morally pernicious. Moreover, she finds unattractive the popular conception of patriotic loyalty which ties it to the country's might and its interests as defined by whatever government is in power. She argues for a different understanding of this loyalty: one that emphasizes the country's cultural and moral excellence. Such a conception has two advantages over both the popular understanding of patriotism and MacIntyre's account: it leaves room for criticism, even radical criticism, of one's own country, and does not make for division and conflict in international relations.

Another philosopher who has been defending a morally acceptable version of patriotism is Stephen Nathanson. In his "Defense of 'Moderate Patriotism'" (chapter 4), Nathanson too argues that impartiality required by morality allows for special obligations and particular attachments. The wording of the Ten Commandments, for instance, is for the most part impartial, but they also include "Honor *your* father and *your* mother." But he focuses on constraints which universal, impartial morality imposes on our special loyalties, and on patriotism in particular. Both the proponents of patriotism such as MacIntyre and its critics such as Tolstoy assume that true patriotism must be exclusive and unrestricted. If that were true, its critics would clearly carry the day. But it need not be so; loyalty to one's country can be constrained by moral rules that apply universally. Such patriotism, which Nathanson terms "moderate," encourages people to promote the interests of their country only in ways permitted by moral rules. It allows for some concern for the good of other countries. And unlike the conventional type of patriotism, defended by MacIntyre, which puts at least the "large interests" of one's country beyond questioning, moderate patriotism is conditional on the country's living up to certain basic moral standards. If the country fails this test, loyalty to it is no longer morally appropriate.[5]

Moderate patriotism may well be thought unexceptionable. Yet, if its defense is to be judged a success, will it not prove too much? Why not construct an argument along the same lines showing that a special concern for one's race is just as unexceptionable, as long as it is constrained by universal, impartial moral rules? This question is the subject of a lively debate between Nathanson and Paul Gomberg that followed in the wake of Nathanson's paper. Gomberg (chapter 5) argues that patriotism *is* like racism, and takes that to show that we must reject both. Nathanson (chapter 6) grants that there is a version of racial loyalty parallel to moderate patriotism, but draws the opposite conclusion: such loyalty is indeed morally acceptable. However, it should not be termed "moderate racism." For racism is inherently exclusive and thoroughly unsympathetic, if not downright hostile, to members of other races. In other words, racism is by definition extreme; "moderate racism" is a contradiction in terms.

The point about patriotism and racism is also taken up by David McCabe in "Patriotic Gore, Again" (chapter 7), in the context of a systematic critique of both extreme and moderate patriotism. McCabe displays certain weak points in some of the crucial moves in both Oldenquist's and MacIntyre's arguments for the extreme version. His main objection to the moderate version is that the requirements of concern for one's country and compatriots, when properly circumscribed by universal moral considerations, no longer differ very much from those included in universal, impartial morality. Consider, for instance, the issue of foreign aid. Given the drastic disparity between rich and poor countries, reasons of universal justice, or of human solidarity, may well rule out favoring one's own country, which has a comparatively high standard of living, over Third World countries mired in abject and chronic poverty. If this is granted, it turns out that universal morality leaves very little room for patriotic partiality.[6] But if, for all practical purposes, the difference between moderate patriotism and universal, impartial morality turns out to be very much a moot point, it is no longer clear why the former should be advanced as an improvement upon the latter.

Yet another way of accounting for patriotism is by integrating it into a rule-utilitarian theory of morality. The rule that we should show special concern for our country and compatriots, just like other rules concerning special attachments, is justified by the good consequences of adopting such a rule. For many reasons, we will do more good if we concentrate on promoting the interests of "our own" (family, local community, country) than if we keep concerning ourselves with the good of humanity as a whole. This approach is defended in Robert E. Goodin's paper "What Is So Special about Our Fellow Countrymen?" (chapter 8). There are two main versions of a rule-utilitarian account of patriotism: the mutual-benefit-society model and the assigned responsibility model. The first has some serious flaws; most damagingly, it implies that we need show no particular concern for those compatriots who were born handicapped and cannot contribute to society the way the rest of us do. Accordingly, Goodin opts for the second version, which justifies patriotism as a device for assigning our basic, general moral duties to particular agents. To be sure, patriotism conceived in this way is considerably less weighty than on alternative accounts; the answer to the question in the title of Goodin's paper turns out to be "not much, really."

The issue of aid to the needy, which figures prominently in the papers by McCabe and Goodin, is the subject of Richard W. Miller's "Cosmopolitan Respect and Patriotic Concern" (chapter 9). Once one acknowledges the moral significance of human poverty and deprivation, as one surely must, it is difficult to see how it could be circumscribed by one's country's borders. Yet a certain bias in favor of one's compatriots is widespread, if not universal. Moreover, it is widely considered morally unobjectionable and indeed required. This may not be true with respect to private aid, but is quite obvious with regard to aid provided by the state and financed through taxation. Miller focuses on tax-financed aid, and defends patriotic bias in this type of aid from the standpoint of moral universalism. To be sure, that cannot be the utilitarian type of universalism, which demands equal *concern* for all human beings. Equal concern for all is the point of departure for both Goodin and McCabe, although their arguments differ: Goodin defends a fairly weak type of patriotism, while McCabe argues that, in terms of moral guidance offered, morally acceptable patriotism hardly differs from universalist morality pure and simple. Miller opts for the Kantian type of universalism, which enjoins equal *respect*, rather than concern, for all humans. These are not the same, nor does the former require the latter: "I certainly regard the life of the girl who lives across the street as no less valuable than the life of my own daughter. But I am not equally concerned for her. For example, I am not willing to do as much for her" (p. 171). Universalism of respect is the basis of Miller's two-pronged argument for patriotic bias in state-provided and tax-financed aid to the needy. A policy of aiding the needy abroad instead of providing relief at home would seriously damage mutual respect and trust at home and alienate our disadvantaged compatriots. A degree of preference for the needy at home over those abroad is an important incentive for our disadvantaged compatriots to conform to the coercive institutions we help impose on them. By proffering it, we make sure that our polity does not degenerate into a system of unjust domination.

Assuming there is an acceptable version of patriotism, just what is its moral status? Oldenquist sees patriotic loyalty as providing a part of the answer to the question of what we ought to do. MacIntyre sets out to vindicate the virtue of patriotism, but presents it as the foundation of morality; accordingly, it cannot be an optional virtue, but must be one we ought to cultivate and exhibit. For these philosophers, then, patriotism is a duty. So it is in Goodin's rule-utilitarian account, albeit a less weighty one. McCabe, too, understands patriotism, whether extreme or moderate, as the claim that our relationship to compatriots generates special duties. And Miller argues for a duty to give preference to our compatriots in matters of state-provided and tax-financed aid to the needy. Baron and Nathanson, on the other hand, have been less clear on this point. Baron portrays the type of patriotism that is compatible with "liberal," i.e., universal and impartial morality, as good and a virtue; but the arguments she offers in its defense appear to ground only the thesis that patriotism is a morally permissible preference. A close reading of Nathanson's papers included in this volume, as well as of his book-length study of patriotism, displays some vacillation between three claims for moderate patriotism: that it is merely a morally permissible preference for one's own country, that it is a duty, and that it is an optional virtue or an ideal. But again, the arguments advanced seem to support only the first, comparatively modest claim.

My own paper (chapter 10) addresses this question. It includes brief comments on the rule-utilitarian rationale for the duty of patriotism. But for the most part I discuss a different type of argument for the claim that we have a duty to show special concern for our country and compatriots: one focusing on the concepts of positional obligations, membership, and identity. On this view, which has a distinctly communitarian flavor, patriotism is a positional obligation bound up with one's membership in a polity and constitutive of one's identity, rather like the obligations one has to one's family. The individual does not deliberately undertake such obligations, but rather finds she has them: finds that she was born into and belongs to *this* family, *this* country, *this* polity. I try to show that this line of argument does not succeed, and that most that can be said for patriotism is that it is morally allowed. It is neither a morally required stance, nor one that is optional, but morally valuable when adopted. Thus we have no good reason to condemn those who show no special concern for their country and compatriots, nor to judge those who do (other things equal) as morally better.

PATRIOTISM WITHOUT NATIONALISM

As I said at the outset, the renewed interest in patriotism as a topic in philosophy and political theory is due, in part, to the reemergence of nationalism as
an important and, much too often, dangerous and destructive influence in
some parts of the world. In view of this, and of the bad press nationalism has
had for almost a decade,[7] some authors have been emphasizing the distinction
between the two types of partiality, and attempting to vindicate (some version
of) patriotism as different from and untainted by "nationalism, patriotism's
bloody brother" (John H. Schaar). This is not an easy task. Ordinary usage
makes for conflation rather than distinction and dissociation, in more than one
way: for instance, as a result of the ambiguity of the word "nation," which is
used both in an ethnic and a political cum legal sense. Moreover, even if we
can sort out the concepts of patriotism and nationalism, the conceptual distinction may have only a limited purchase on reality. For *patria* is not only a
geographical, but also a political entity, a polity. And since so many states
today are nation-states, one's compatriots are more often than not members of
one's nation in the ethnic sense of the term too.

Yet, as Mary G. Dietz shows (chapter 11), the history of "patriotism" was
for the most part separate from that of "nationalism." The former can be traced
back to ancient Rome, while the latter is, on most accounts, a phenomenon of
the modern age. Dietz analyzes the transformation of the idea of patriotism in
modern times. When, in the late seventeenth century, "patriot" and "patriotism"
appeared in the mainstream of English political debates, they belonged to the
Whig side of the great divide and stood for liberty and the rights of subjects
against the throne. But by the late nineteenth century, against the background
of the ever stronger state power and the rise of nationalism, patriotic discourse
lost its original, critical bite, and got harnessed to the service of the nation-state.
As a result, it can no longer be easily distinguished and disconnected from the
rhetoric of nationalism. Dietz considers this a major loss, tantamount to "a
failure of citizenship." It indicates that "we have literally lost touch with history,
with a very real past in which real patriots held to a particular set of political
principles and their associated practices—to a conception of citizenship that
bears scant resemblance to modern nationalism" (p. 211).[8]

The task of detaching patriotism from nationalism has been undertaken,
for the most part, by political theorists rather than philosophers. Political theorists tend to accord less importance to the moral issue of partiality versus
impartiality. They focus on patriotism as an essentially political idea: the idea
of identification with and loyalty to the basic values and principles of one's
polity. Their main worry is whether patriotism, thus conceived, can replace
nationalism as the principle of unity of a healthy, stable, and prosperous polity.

In view of twentieth-century history, it was to be expected that German
intellectuals in particular should be suspicious of patriotism as long as it has not

been disentangled from nationalism. Jürgen Habermas is the most prominent among those who have tackled this issue. Writing in the wake of the reunification of Germany, he rejects the communitarian claim that free institutions and liberal political culture can be strong and effective only if they have taken deep root in a particular historical and cultural community, in a particular prepolitical form of life citizens can identify with. He brings up the examples of multicultural societies like Switzerland and the United States as proof that

> a political culture in which constitutional principles can take root need by no means depend on all citizens' sharing the same language or the same ethnic and cultural origins. A liberal political culture is only the common denominator for a *constitutional* patriotism (*Verfassungspatriotismus*) that heightens an awareness of both the diversity and the integrity of the different forms of life coexisting in a multicultural society.[9]

Habermas argues that by cultivating such constitutional patriotism, Germany and other prosperous liberal democracies of western Europe have a better chance of withstanding the temptations of "the chauvinism of affluence" that keeps out immigrants and asylum seekers. In his view, "the democratic right to self-determination includes the right to preserve one's own *political* culture, which forms a concrete context for rights of citizenship, but it does not include the right to self-assertion of a privileged *cultural* form of life."[10]

This project of a purely political patriotism is spelled out in Attracta Ingram's contribution (chapter 12). The project has been criticized as too abstract and out of touch with the realities of history and contemporary politics. Some have argued that to dispense with all prepolitical identities and attachments and ground the polity on voluntary commitment of citizens to its values and principles is to make their union "rescindable, defeasible, and insecure." Another criticism has been that a merely political collective identity is no identity at all, and that adherents of constitutional patriotism tacitly take for granted that certain prepolitical—cultural or ethnic—identities are already in place. Drawing on Habermas and Rawls, Ingram offers a defense of constitutional patriotism against these and some further objections.

While Ingram's paper addresses primarily the concerns raised by European integration, this volume also includes two statements of a distinctively American version of a purely political patriotism: John H. Schaar's plea for a "covenanted patriotism" (chapter 13) and Michael Walzer's essay on what it means to be a good citizen in America today (chapter 14). Schaar, too, is at pains to dissociate patriotism from nationalism, portraying the latter as inherently exclusive and aggressive. Patriotism or, more accurately, "natural patriotism" is, at its core, love of one's homeland and all the familiar things associated with it: its people, language, traditions, and memories. It involves the recognition that the individual has a patrimony, and enjoins both gratitude for that patrimony and a commitment to sustain it and help ensure its continuation. This type of patriotism is one of the basic human sentiments. However, it is not available to Americans. For Americans "were bonded together not by blood or religion, not by tradition or territory, not by the walls and traditions of a city, but by a political idea . . . by a covenant, by dedication to a set of principles and by an exchange of promises to uphold and advance certain commitments" (pp. 238–39). This distinctively American type of patriotism "transcends the parochial and primitive fraternities of blood and race, for it calls kin all those who accept the authority of the covenant," and is compatible with the most generous humanism (p. 241).

Walzer, too, acknowledges that American identity and any patriotic loy-alty it may generate must be essentially political. But his stand on patriotism is more cautious. Being American is a complex ideal. A citizen is expected to be loyal to America and to be willing to fight and die for it. She is invited to par-ticipate in political life, to do her part in the collective self-government of the republic. But that is to be done in a civil and tolerant way. The latter two requirements are of vital importance in a country such as the United States: a country whose citizens are mostly immigrants or descendants of immigrants, and whose population is accordingly extremely heterogeneous by virtually any standard. As a result, the American ideal of citizenship is not easy to teach or live up to. For political activism and patriotism require, and nurture, a certain zeal; they make for excitement and drama in public life. Civility and tolerance attenuate the strain, but do so only by undercutting the political and patriotic passions and attachments. Walzer does not propose to resolve this tension. He points out instead that "what exists today and what will always exist is some balance between them. But the balance has changed over the years: we are . . . more civil and less civically virtuous than Americans once were" (p. 267–68).[11]

On the face of it, the emphatically political conception of patriotism is gen-erous indeed. It is certainly an improvement upon both patriotism of the sort propounded by Oldenquist or MacIntyre and most versions of nationalism that are on offer. And yet, it is not clear that it succeeds in overcoming the parochial loyalties of blood and soil and supplanting nationality as the unifying force in a stable and successful liberal-democratic state.

In the final selection in this volume, Margaret Canovan takes a critical look at both main varieties of the "new patriotism": the more abstract version advocated by Habermas or Ingram, and the more "rooted" one, propounded by Schaar or Maurizio Viroli[12] (chapter 15). As she rightly reminds us, today, no less than before, state boundaries remain the touchstone of any attempt at combining universal principles with attachment to a particular polity. The issue may no longer be where the borders should be drawn, but rather how open they can be; but it is no less difficult to resolve. Advocates of the "new patriotism" must acknowledge that a people is a succession of generations, that a polity is an inheritance passed on from one generation to another, and that citizenship is, more often than not, an individual's birthright. Accordingly, "the principles of the constitution are not just liberal principles but . . . 'our' principles, handed down to us by our forefathers, biological or adopted" (p. 283). But if so, the "new patriots" cannot really mean some of the things they say: that a free republic should, or indeed could, keep its gates wide open to all those beyond its borders willing to commit themselves to those principles (Schaar, p. 241), or that its borders "cannot exclude needy strangers knocking at the gate when there is room for them inside" (Ingram, p. 223). Nor is it fair to suspect a country that fails to open its gates so wide of "chauvinism of affluence"; not doing so is merely a condition of a polity's continued existence.

The issue of immigration and refuge is just an instance, albeit a particularly topical and painful one, of the fundamental problem of reconciling universal moral and political principles with particular loyalties.[13] The "new patriotism" is more attractive than the more familiar variety; but it still fails to provide a convincing philosophical solution to that problem. But then, such a solution may be too much to try for in the first place. Canovan may also be right in saying that such issues can only be settled "by more or less messy political compromises" (p. 288).

Even if this is, in the end, all we can hope for when our commitment to humanity and universal justice comes into conflict with our attachment to our country and compatriots, our polity and fellow citizens, the views and arguments of the sort presented in this volume can still serve a useful purpose. They cannot resolve such issues for us in a straightforward and compelling way; but they certainly can, and should, provide some guidance in our search for compromises we can live with.

NOTES

1. Quoted in S. Nathanson, *Patriotism, Morality, and Peace* (Lanham, Md.: Rowman & Littlefield, 1993), p. 3.

2. See L. Tolstoy, "On Patriotism" and "Patriotism, or Peace?" in *Tolstoy's Writings on Civil Disobedience and Non-violence* (New York: New American Library, 1968); E. Goldman, "Patriotism: A Menace to Liberty," *Anarchism and Other Essays* (New York: Dover Publications, 1969).

3. Tolstoy, "On Patriotism," p. 75.

4. W. Godwin, *Enquiry concerning Political Justice*, ed. I. Kramnick (Harmondsworth: Penguin Books, 1976), pp. 169–70.

5. For a more detailed statement of Nathanson's account of moderate patriotism and a discussion of a number of related issues, see his book *Patriotism, Morality, and Peace*.

6. For Nathanson's discussion of the problems foreign aid poses for moderate patriotism, see his *Patriotism, Morality, and Peace*, chap. 13. For a wide range of views on the morality of foreign aid, see W. Aiken and H. LaFollette, *World Hunger and Morality*, 2d ed. (Upper Saddle River, N.J.: Prentice-Hall, 1996).

7. For a good sample of recent discussions of nationalism in philosophy and political theory see, for instance, J. Couture, K. Nielsen, and M. Seymour, eds., *Rethinking Nationalism* (Calgary: University of Calgary Press, 1996) (*Canadian Journal of Philosophy*, supplementary vol. 22).

8. For a detailed history of patriotism, which also focuses on its relation to nationalism, see M. Viroli, *For Love of Country: An Essay on Patriotism and Nationalism* (Oxford: Oxford University Press, 1995).

9. J. Habermas, "Citizenship and National Identity," *Between Facts and Norms: Contributions to a Discourse Theory of Law and Democracy*, trans. W. Rehg (Cambridge, Mass.: MIT Press, 1998), p. 500.

10. Ibid., p. 514.

11. See also M. Walzer, "What Does It Mean to Be an 'American'?" *Social Research* 57 (1990).

12. See Viroli, *For Love of Country*, pp. 1–17, 161–87.

13. For a range of views on ethical questions raised by migration, see B. Barry and R. E. Goodin, eds., *Free Movement: Ethical Issues in the Transnational Migration of People and of Money* (University Park, Pa.: Pennsylvania State University Press, 1992).

Chapter One
ANDREW OLDENQUIST

LOYALTIES

*M*ost recent philosophical writing about ethics accepts willingness to universalize on the basis of repeatable features as a necessary condition of an evaluative judgment. Given this condition, legal judgments, because they refer essentially to a particular jurisdiction and egoistic judgments, because they refer essentially to a particular person, are not evaluative judgments. Normative judgments based on loyalty to one's own family, community, or nation doubtless would be excluded for the same reason, were it not for the fact that philosophers generally neglect to discuss loyalties at all. Yet it is the most common thing in the world for a person to decide that he should (or should not) do so-and-so on grounds of loyalty to his friend, family, organization, community, country, or species. Indeed, it is likely that loyalties ground more of the principled, self-sacrificing, and other kinds of nonselfish behavior in which people engage than do moral principles and ideals. If this is true, Anglo-American philosophy has ignored an important area of the normative. American as well as Soviet society face grave problems concerning hooliganism (what we call vandalism and drunken rowdyism), noncaring, and alienation (in a sense I shall explain) that seem to be caused more by the absence of expected loyalties than by the absence of ordinary moral conscientiousness. Loyalty needs to be distinguished from both impersonal morality and self-interest, and it must be defended, if it can be, against the charge that loyalty is no more than a bias, a bigotry, and that whoever defends loyalty defends immorality. I shall make a somewhat radical suggestion about a way in which all of social morality may depend on loyalties and, in the light of this suggestion, defend obligations based on loyalties. I conclude by drawing some implications regarding the nature of and remedy for urban alienation.

From the *Journal of Philosophy* 79, no. 4 (1982): 173–93. Copyright © 1982 The Journal of Philosophy. Reprinted by permission of the *Journal of Philosophy*.

I. LOYALTY, SELF-INTEREST, AND IMPERSONAL MORALITY

If someone claims that he ought to protect child C because the child is blond, he judges in terms of an ideal or value, and he is committed, unless he finds other reasons, to protecting any child that is blond. So too, if he judges that he ought to attend to a small child about to do something dangerous, consistency requires a similar judgment in similar circumstances. If he judges that he ought to protect child C because the child is *his* child, the situation is radically different, since 'his child' does not name any repeatable feature in addition to that of being a child. If this is the reason (and if it counts as a reason at all) it is, in one important respect, a nonuniversalizable reason: he can without inconsistency deny that he has a similar obligation to George's exactly similar child, which he would not be able to do if he had based his judgment on some repeatable feature that was shared by his child and George's child. For, again, the *basis* of his judgment is that the child is his, not that it has a certain feature.

Let us at once clear away some possible confusions about universalizing. There are at least three ways to universalize "H ought to protect his own child":

(1) H ought to protect any similar child.
(2) Everybody similar to H ought to protect H's child.
(3) Everybody ought to protect his own child.

H might think consistency requires accepting (3); but, if his reason is that the child is his child, consistency does not require that he accept (1). Because his reason is simply that the child is his, and not that it has some protection-warranting feature ϕ, his normative judgment need not be universalized in way (1). He may go on to claim that *everyone* has a similar nonuniversalizable obligation to protect his or her own child ahead of other people's children.

The case is exactly analogous to the more familiar case of egoism. An egoist says, "I ought to look out for myself first," and he might feel required to be a universal egoist and also say, "Everybody ought to look out for himself first." But if he is an egoist at all, his reason for thinking he should perform some act is simply that it benefits himself, which is a reason that is not universalizable in way (1). For, however similar another person may be to him, his reason will not oblige him to benefit that other person, because it is not a matter of similarities. The logic of 'I should do it because it benefits *my* so-and-so' and 'I should do it because it benefits *me*' is the same.

Normative judgments based on egoism and normative judgments based on loyalties share the characteristic of containing uneliminable egocentric particulars. We can call such judgments "self-dependent" normative judgments. If I say that I ought to defend my country, I have a putative loyalty. But if I am willing to replace 'my country' with, e.g., 'a democratic country' or 'a Christian country,' I have not a loyalty but an ideal; in this case what I am committed to is a kind of thing, not some particular thing. If I am unwilling to replace 'my country' with a characterizing expression, I have a genuine loyalty and not an ideal; my normative judgment is self-dependent.

If we replicated an egoist, he still would be able to favor the particular that is himself, even though he and his replica are exactly alike. This is what it is to be an egoist, and it is what separates his position from that of social morality. He favors an entity that he picks out only by means of a singular term. But he cannot employ just any singular term. He cannot simply say that he values *this* more than *that* because he would have no intelligible ground for deciding *which* of them to favor. For the same reason he cannot say he values Max more than Harry, given that we understand these names as pure labels. He must say he favors *himself*, and then the bewilderment that attends his favoring a "this" over a "that" vanishes. All of this equally characterizes a person with a loyalty, requiring only that we substitute 'his country' (or whatever) for 'himself.' If the object of his loyalty is just a "this" or "that," his loyalty is unintelligible; if he employs a definite description he is not espousing loyalty but praising things that answer to the description; if he calls it "America" we must ask him whether 'America' functions like 'this' or like a disguised definite description. Only if he calls it "my country" is his position both intelligible and nonuniversalizable.

When I have loyalty toward something I have somehow come to view it as *mine*. It is an object of noninstrumental value to me in virtue (but not only in virtue) of its being mine, and I am disposed to feel pride when it prospers, shame when it declines, and anger or indignation when it is harmed. In general, people care about the objects of their loyalties, and they acknowledge obligations that they would not acknowledge were it not for their loyalties. Unlike the object of self-interest, an object of loyalty can be shared or "owned" by a number of people. In this case, I (and others) can speak of *our* family, community, country, etc., and not just of *my* family. Group loyalty toward a common object is not inappropriately called group egoism, or alternatively, tribal morality. When a person replaces egoism with group egoism he at once acquires *social* values. Thus the shift from "me first" to "mine first" (and hence to "ours first") is of the greatest moment: it is what makes society possible. Egoists cannot possess a noninstrumental common good; on this level egoists have no one to talk to. But group egoists (group loyalists) can share noninstrumental goods, such as a nation, a family, a neighborhood, or a philosophy department, and therefore can constitute a moral community. Nevertheless, we must not lose sight of the egoism in group egoism. An egoist puts first a particular person, not just a kind of person, and values that person more than he would an exact replica. In exactly the same way, a group egoist puts first a particular group, not just some set of group-defining features, and values that group more than he would another group with the same defining features. It is only because of this that we can distinguish group loyalty from a shared ideal.

Loyalty is neither egoism nor impersonal morality. It is not self-interested, because people can sacrifice, in the name of loyalty, their happiness and even their lives, and it probably is this element of potential self-sacrifice that makes most people classify motives of loyalty as moral motives. Moreover, reasons of loyalty have a general appeal among members of a society whereas a self-interested reason appeals only to the agent. But neither is loyalty impersonal morality, since an obligation of loyalty depends on viewing a thing as one's own. The terms of the logic of the reasons they provide, loyalties are a third category of the normative, distinct from both self-interest and impersonal morality. There is the morality of rules and relevant properties, of universalizable oughts and thou-shalt-nots. There is enlightened, rational egoism that fancies it can see that being a nice guy pays. And, different from these, but sharing features with each, are loyalties. Loyalties are part of what make our societal worlds go around, but they cannot be understood if we try to turn them into either impersonal duties or sophisticated egoism.

Should we conclude that group loyalty is just a bias, that it is the enemy of morality, and be done with it? Think of what tribalism in the form of racism and nationalism have brought upon the world. Before I take up the general question, in terms of a suggestion I wish to develop about the relation between loyalties and impersonal morality, it should be noted that racism is usually dependent on ignorance of the nature of race differences and on hostile, false claims about other races. Family, community, and civic loyalties seldom have those features. A loyalty, like any norm, can be rationally faulted if it depends on ignorance of facts. Moreover, it is not obviously correct to characterize racism as a loyalty, logically on all fours with patriotism or community loyalty. This is because racism is negative, being much more concerned with hatred of other races than with pride in one's own, whereas loyalty is positive and is primarily characterized by esteem and concern for the common good of one's group.

II. ARE WE ALL GROUP EGOISTS?

The suggestion I wish to make is the following. Our wide and narrow loyalties define moral communities or domains within which we are willing to universalize moral judgments, treat equals equally, protect the common good, and in other ways adopt the familiar machinery of impersonal morality. For example, if I believe that my family comes first when scarce resources or their safety is at stake, I am bound to universalize within my family: if one family member deserves a benefit so do the others unless some additional consideration applies to one but not to all of them. A loyalty defines a moral community in terms of a conception of a common good and a special committment to the members of the group who share this good. The members, along with certain conventional, institutional structures, and often a geographical location, together constitute the community that is the object of my loyalty. Those who share this common good comprise my tribe; the common good is its flourishing, and this is why we acknowledge a system of social morality whose purpose is the safety and flourishing of the tribe and which applies impartially to its members.

I belong simultaneously to many "tribes" or moral communities, some of which include my family as a part and some of which do not. If the good of humanity as a moral end is species loyalty and not a shared ideal, it will have the same logical features as family loyalty and national loyalty: *my* species may not differ in any relevant respect from the invading Andromedans, just as my child may not differ in any relevant respect from George's child, yet in each case I will treat similar cases similarly only within the domain of what I have come to view as mine.

Social morality is impersonal and impartial when it confines itself to *intratribal* considerations, as when a parent, facing no challenge to family loyalty itself, seeks to do the right thing when interests conflict within his or her family. But when the national good competes with the good of one's family, the latter appears as a naked loyalty, and the former as social morality that demands impartial consideration of family and nonfamily. So too, nationalism in turn is a mere loyalty from the wider perspective of utilitarianism, but takes the form of impersonal, social morality in internal matters, including clashes with nested, narrower loyalties such as community or civic loyalty. This complexity probably did not face primitive man and arises because modern man belongs to many tribes at once.

According to this scheme every loyalty has the double aspect of being a self-dependent value in *intersocietal* competition and of grounding a system of impersonal, social morality for adjudicating *intrasocietal* conflicts. For example, when an academic department chairman apportions benefits and duties within the department he is guided by the common good of the department, which is taken for granted; what become at issue are fairness and relevant differences, as part of a system of social morality operating within a miniature moral community. But if the dean wants to take away part of his budget and give it to the English Department, department loyalty is exposed and competes with what the dean calls the common good, i.e., the good of the college. A system of social morality that is grounded on group loyalty is not inappropriately called tribal morality, and the question arises whether or not all morality is tribal morality in this sense. If it were true that there was a widest loyalty and also true that wide loyalties were the best ones, we might envisage a hierarchy. As we shall see, neither of these two claims can be shown to be true or even plausible.

To claim that all morality is tribal morality is not to deny that we value certain qualities in themselves. A loyalist favors a particular group under a certain description. But the description must be significant and concern such things as language, geography, culture, and the major activities of our lives. The explanation of what we find significant lies with the environmental and evolutionary determinants of human sociality. Moreover, people do not feel proud of just *any* features their community or nation possesses. We value in themselves certain features of a family, community, or nation which enter into our definition of its "flourishing." Such things as freedom, rationality, happiness, power, diversity, and beauty, and detailed variants of these, seem to be valued for their own sakes and to play a role in whether I view some social unit as mine.

Consequently, a loyalist doesn't value something simply because it is his. It must have features that make it worth having, and it could deteriorate to the extent that shame ultimately kills his loyalty. But morality will still be tribal morality if *our* tribes count for more than other tribes with the same intrinsically valued features. It is tempting to say that, since two families, cities, or tribes never will be *exactly* alike (which is true enough), some of these differences must be ones I think "relevant." This, as we shall see, is most likely a mistake.

Are even Kantians tribal moralists? Let us grant that to a Kantian rational nature is valuable in itself, and ask instead whether there are always possible situations in which Kantians would be loyal to some rational beings and not others. This is a psychological question whose answer is not certain, but a plausible answer would be importantly relevant to the nature of human morality. Kant's Kingdom of Ends is the assemblage of rational beings each of which, ideally, treats every member (including itself) as an end and never a means. Beings who are not rational beings can be treated as mere means because Kant apparently had no conception of a still broader moral community. Kantians seem to value rational beings, not just "their" rational beings, and suggesting that Kantians are group egoists requires speculating about what they would say in hypothetical situations. Someone who knew only his own family, other individuals being solitary or machine-reared, might say that families were of intrinsic worth, recognizing a loyalty to his own family only when he encountered other families. A philosophical tribesman who knew only his own tribe might decide that tribe members comprised a "kingdom of ends," having worth that hermits, exiles, and animals lack; what is he to say when he discovers a dozen tribes, some in competition with his own? What if human space explorers were to encounter many rational civilizations, all competing for resources as do the different families and tribes we now encounter? I suspect that a Kantian would come to think in terms of *our* rational beings and *their* rational beings. Rationality might remain an intrinsic value and be subordinated to group egoism. A very wide loyalty looks more like a pure ideal than does a narrow loyalty because we haven't to decide what to think of competitors. On this view all morality is tribal morality and there will be as many systems of social morality as there are loyalties.

III. THE ETHICS OF PARTS AND WHOLES

Some of our loyalties are wide, some are narrow, and most of them are nested. I may be loyal to my community and also to my country, a wider domain that includes my community, and again to my species, a still wider domain. If we were to represent a person's system of loyalties by drawing concentric circles, we could think of the center point as the self, the "inward" logical limit on self-dependent morality. The ever larger circles would represent ever wider loyalties. Is there an "outer" limit as well as an "inward" one, such as one's species or the members of one's galaxy? I shall be defending the position that there is no outer limit to loyalty that rational thinking can discover, although there are psychological limits.

When a person's nested loyalties clash there is a problem regarding the relative authority of parts and wholes. Is it better or more rational to support my city to the disadvantage of my neighborhood, or to support my neighborhood to the disadvantage of my city? Am I a traitor to my neighborhood if I yield to the claims of some larger whole? In the political arena it is commonly argued that the conflict is unreal, the city saying that what is good for the whole is good for the part and the neighborhood saying that what is good for the part is good for the whole. Each argues that the rational interests of both parties are served by its position because any other kind of defense implies that someone must be sacrificed, which produces an irresolvable adversarial situation. These arguments are very often sophistical; it often is simply false that what is good for the whole is good for the part. What is good for Columbus may not be good for a neighborhood, what is good for America may not be good for Columbus or for General Motors, and what is good for the world may not be good for America. So too, going the other way.

Though it cannot reasonably be denied that the good of the whole often is incompatible with the good of a part or constitutive unit, utilitarians would argue that our duty is to Humanity and that doing what benefits your neighborhood or country is wrong if it prevents a greater good for a larger whole. On this view, the wider the loyalty, the greater the moral claim it has on us, and regional competition for resources or benefits would be justified only when it was the more efficient way to maximize the good of everyone. The utilitarian position seems to present a dilemma for those who wish to take loyalties seriously. Should university administrators, community leaders, mayors, or presidents always adopt the so-called impartial point of view regarding the allocation of goods? They often will be disloyal to their constituencies if they do, and they will be judged unethical, from the point of the "general good," if they do not. The utilitarian asks, rhetorically, "Does the mere fact that a university, community, or nation is *yours* add, even in the slightest degree, to the case for its deserving a benefit or advantage?"

There are two reasons why the utilitarian attack on loyalties is unconvincing. The first is that utilitarianism itself simply assumes that species loyalty is always the most demanding one. If it is claimed that it is the most demanding loyalty because it is the widest, this in turn implying that the most good and harm are at stake, the claim is incorrect. Wider conceptions of one's own kind can be in terms of rational beings, beings capable of suffering, living beings, and so on. If family loyalty and patriotism are biases, in the sense of valuing some particular group more highly than one otherwise would because it is one's own, so too is the claim that the greatest good is the greatest happiness of the greatest number of human beings. The argument should be familiar: if the elimination of human suffering is more important than the elimination of animal suffering, the ground is either a reasonless bias in favor of one's own species or some list of relevant features that warrants protecting beings with those features. But any list is bound to fail to protect humans invariably, because of what we might call "the problem of imperfect specimens." No matter what the list, some human cases of senility or mental defect will satisfy it less well than some gorillas or chimpanzees, and so we would be forced to justify using the human ahead of the chimp for medical experiments; such a position would not be a utilitarian one. Of course, someone might abandon the search for "relevant" features and just list the taxonomic differentia of humans; in that case we would be justified in saying the list was just a rationalization for species bias. The utilitarian cannot make his case by criticizing community loyalists or patriots for being in a similar position.

Second, it is not obvious that wider loyalties always take moral precedence over narrower ones. We are often told to look beyond our neighborhood, city, or country in the name of impartiality, and treat what we had hitherto favored as our own as just one among many neighborhoods, cities, or countries. But the demand for impartiality is never true impartiality, it is merely an invitation to give one's loyalty to a larger whole with which someone identifies; in other words, an invitation to join a larger tribe. If our first love is to some narrower group, this forced shift may render our moral concern weak and pallid. Equal moral concern for the whole of humanity or the whole of sentient nature is, for most of us, too diluted to be able to generate effective moral enthusiasm and too weak to outweigh narrower loyalties. If one thinks that the wider loyalty *must* carry greater moral weight just because it is wider, it is important to remember that it identifies one's kind under a different description than the narrower loyalty. The nature of the description as well as the size of the domain it encompasses determine how much I care about my kind under that description. This consideration by itself refutes the utilitarian claim that more is always better. I have extremely weak galaxy-member loyalty relative to species loyalty, and weak species loyalty relative to family loyalty. More is not always better because it is not always more of the same thing. Hence, without further argument it will not do to claim, in the name of speciesism, that nationalism, community loyalty, and family loyalty count for less because they count for fewer.

What this implies is the defensibility of the position that sometimes what benefits my family obligates me more than does a greater benefit to the whole of humanity; and also that a still greater benefit (or threat) to humanity might nevertheless obligate me on the side of humanity. It implies the acceptance of a world in which rational, moral people can have loyalties that are in limited competition with those of other people, for example, members of different families, communities, or nations. If this is so, the rational community leader is not always obliged to be a traitor: he need not accept the expressway that obliterates his neighborhood just because he sees that it is likely to produce a small, offsetting greater good for some larger whole. If he is intellectually honest with himself he admits that his own neighborhood counts more for him than do other people's neighborhoods. This is simply the equivalent, in microcosm, of the patriot who says that his own country counts more for him than do other people's countries and of the person who says that his own species counts more for him than other species. This conception of group loyalties does not imply "My community, right or wrong" or "My country, right or wrong," because each loyalty determines obligations only prima facie. Even if someone admits that, say, family loyalty is his strongest loyalty, it should not be forgotten that the good and harm at stake come in degrees. Such a person has no reason to deny that a small family sacrifice still can be outweighed when it is balanced against some great harm to be avoided (or good to be achieved) by his community or his country.

IV. PATRIOTISM

I wish to distinguish three types of patriotism: *impartial patriotism, sports patriotism*, and *loyalty patriotism*. As we shall see, impartial patriotism arises from the demands of wider loyalties, sports patriotism arises from pressure to universalize patriotic judgments. A case can be made that only loyalty patriotism should be called patriotism.

Loyalties are norms that define the domains within which we accept the moral machinery of universalizable reasons and relevant differences. This machinery makes moral argument, hence the possibility of persuasion, possible; the naked declaration of a loyalty makes it impossible. Consequently, whatever kind of patriot we are, we have every reason to try to find a basis for dialogue with the competitor, the Spartan, or the Andromedan, for it supplements the possibility of winning by force or trickery with the possibility of winning (or cutting losses) by reasoning and persuasion. But it also adds the possibility of being obliged to lose. This is a way of saying that it is to my advantage that the beings I must confront be members of one of my moral communities, for that means that we share a noninstrumental good, which in turn opens the possibility of persuading them that they ought not to eat me or enslave me.

An impartial patriot is someone who maintains that *only* such considerations count. In defending his country's policy in a war or international confrontation he appeals only to truly international principles of political morality, for example, that his country is democratic, or is on the side of "the people," or was intolerably provoked. His position is that he ought to support whichever country has features *a . . . n*; and, as luck would have it, that happens to be his own country. Impartial patriotism is not loyalty in the sense defined in section I because the reasons such "patriots" give do not contain uneliminable singular terms. An impartial patriot says that he supports his country just because it has features *a . . . n*, and therefore he is committed to the position that if his country and its adversary exchanged features *a . . . n*, he should support the adversary. If it is true that he supports his country solely because he thinks it is in the right, it follows that the fact that one of the countries is his does not enter at all into his decision. Such "patriots" believe themselves to be objective, like ideal observers, and simply lucky that their own country is right, whereas I think that most of us believe that their underlying motives usually are pure loyalty and their reasons rationalizations.

Perhaps we should recognize a second type of impartial patriot, namely, anyone who has actually convinced himself that his country is always the best, and does not merely believe that he should support it *if* it is the best. This condition rules out having to support adversaries in consequence of the kind of role reversal described above. I think, however, that we are willing to acknowledge either type as patriotism only because we believe that the reasons impartial patriots give are rationalizations: we call impartial patriots "patriots" because we think that, deep down, they are loyalty patriots and not because we think that impartial patriotism, in itself, is a form of patriotism,

A loyalty patriot concedes that his judgment of what he should do is partly determined by the fact that the good of *his* country is at stake. But he need not affirm that it is *wholly* determined by this. He thinks that the fact that *P* is his country can outweigh some (but not necessarily all) reasons of the sort that a disinterested international observer would consider. The fact that a party to the dispute is his own country is a relevant consideration in his thinking about which country he should support. To a loyalist, the thought, "*P* is my country," though it counts for something, need not outweigh moral arguments against reprisal or military intervention, whereas, to an impartial patriot, the thought, "*P* is my country," is not conceded to count for anything. A distinction should be noted between what a patriot thinks he is personally obliged to do and what he thinks his country should do, although I do not think this distinction is crucial to the inquiry. Many patriotic normative judgments can be expressed only by public affirmation or the ballot, unless a citizen happens to be president or secretary of state. A patriot may say, "America ought to take reprisal if hostages held in a foreign country are killed," although this is not something he personally can do, nor even something he necessarily should assist, since his assistance (in military service or otherwise) depends on his personal circumstances; for example, a pregnant woman with five other children to care for may have no personal obligation in the matter.

It might be thought that loyalty can be based on a special obligation that a citizen has and a disinterested international observer lacks, which derives from the education, protection, and freedoms a country provides its citizens. Obligations based on loyalty would then be universalizable, owed out of gratitude to any country that provided one with certain benefits and protections. However, though gratitude might justify ceremonial patriotism such as celebrations and flag-tending, it is questionable whether gratitude can ever override moral reasons for or against anything. Suppose that George and Harry are deadly rivals in the heroin trade, and I owe George a debt of gratitude. If I help George kill Harry, the wrongness of my act is not diminished in the slightest by the fact that I owe gratitude to George. In general, it seems that, if I owe George something out of fairness or because of a contract, these considerations can compete with other moral considerations; but if I owe him out of gratitude, the gratitude does not compete at all with contrary moral considerations. So too, it appears, if America is in conflict with P, whatever moral reasons there are against supporting the American cause are not countered by any amount of gratitude owed to America. But this assumes that we always can sharply distinguish gratitude from loyalty. Certainly, the services for which one owes gratitude, such as education and protection, can also be causes of loyalty.

The patriot's dilemma is that he seems forced to choose between the death of loyalty and mindless confrontations of pure tribalism. On the one hand, patriotism is a mere bigotry if it is true that national interests must be completely subordinated to impartial adjudication in terms of more general principles. The impartial patriot grasps this horn of the dilemma, but still chooses to call himself a patriot. On the other hand, a patriot who says he should help P defeat Q because P is his country seems required to admit that Q's patriots have a corresponding duty to help defeat P. That is, he seems required to maintain that this is what they really ought to do, not just that it is what *they* think they ought to do. The question of what other nations' patriots ought to do arises as surely as the egoist's familiar problem regarding what he thinks other egoists ought to do. If an egoist is either formally or "pragmatically" inconsistent when he universalizes, as when an egoist in a lifeboat with another egoist says that *each* ought to throw the other to the sharks, a patriot who says that competing foreign patriots have obligations like his own will be inconsistent for the same reason.

The sports patriot grasps this horn of the dilemma and attempts to cope with universalized patriotic obligations by modeling them after loyalties to sports teams. Suppose that a loyal fan of the Ohio State football team is asked by a philosopher, "But which team ought to win?" The fan is loathe to claim either that his team ought to win just because it is his, or that he should abandon his loyalty and support the team that most deserves to win in the light of impartial criteria. He therefore says that each team ought to *try* to win, and, if pressed about which of them ought to succeed, he may say that the "best" team should win. A patriot who takes this line claims that each nation's citizens ought to try to further their respective national interests and, in the case of war, try to defeat the other. In doing so the sports patriot, like the impartial patriot, masks his loyalty by affirming more universal values which have nothing to do with national loyalty. His values are "trying" and, at his final level of defense, such qualities as toughness and competence. He is worse off than the impartial patriot, who at least rationalizes that his country is the best. The reasons that impartial patriots offer have nothing to do with what really motivates them, and, even if they do, they have nothing to do with patriotism. The position of the sports patriot is scarcely intelligible: committed to univer-salizing, he claims that when it comes to war Q ought to try to do in his country and his ought to try to do in Q; but he cannot explain why someone who calls himself a patriot should affirm *both* of these propositions.

This leaves us with loyalty patriotism. How is it to be defended? Since it is fashionable in some quarters to have contempt for patriotism, I shall defend the easier case of family loyalty, and assume that I have shown that whatever we can conclude about the one case we can conclude in principle about the other. For I wish to defend the *idea* of loyalty patriotism, not some particular instance of it.

A felt obligation to assist one's family is a case of taking care of one's own. Yet the obligation is not just one of self-interest or prudence. The judgments we are inclined to make about someone who is unwilling to save his own child first are very unlike our response to imprudence.

Suppose that we witness the following scene. A family is vacationing at the beach; as the father walks up on the pier he sees his daughter and her acquaintance fall out of their canoe, swim for a minute in different directions, and then both begin to drown. Being sure he can save only one, he lets his daughter drown and saves the other girl. Asked why, he says either (a) he was ever so slightly surer of being able to reach the acquaintance in time, or (b) the acquaintance was well on her way to being a brilliant scientist, bound to con-tribute more to the general happiness than his daughter, and, given that he could not save both, the choice he made produced more positive value. What do we think of this father? Would we want to shake his hand, or tell the story in the local paper as a moral lesson? Is he not a great fool, an object of pity and contempt? Indeed, this is the kind of incident we are embarrassed even to talk about, unlike cases of moral heroism or gross selfishness.

If he had been in the canoe with the acquaintance and had sacrificed his own life instead of his daughter's, in order to save the acquaintance, we might feel awe, but not contempt or pity. Therefore the bad emotion we feel in the first case cannot be explained in terms of the father's sacrifice of self-interest, for there is a greater sacrifice of self-interest in the second case and we do not feel that emotion in the second case. A natural explanation is that the father owes something to his daughter that he does not owe to an acquaintance or a stranger. It is easy to say, "Yes, of course, we have special obligations to our children: utility is maximized if each takes care of his own." But I do not think that such a belief can begin to explain the contempt and embarrassment; besides, the case in which the father lets his daughter drown is one that *does* maximize expected utility.

It is not just that people are as a matter of fact blindly loyal or biased toward various social units, this being a fact of human nature that we lament; rather, loyalty behavior elicits approbation and opposite behavior typically elicits guilt in the agent and disapproval in observers. The contempt we feel toward traitors is not unlike what we feel toward the father who lets his daughter drown. Our loyalties are values that contribute to what we think we should do, all things considered. Therefore they can compete with what are called "considerations of social morality." This is even more plausible if, as was suggested earlier, every group loyalty creates and grounds a domain of social morality. When these loyalties themselves are challenged in the name of "social morality," the wider obligations determined by a wider loyalty are being asserted to have greater moral authority. As in any case of conflicting normative considerations, sometimes a person will judge his family or national obligations to take precedence over wider societal obligation and sometimes he will not. It depends, among other things, on how much is at stake in each domain, on the possibility of a given action satisfying both loyalties to differing degrees, and on the "strengths" of the loyalties themselves.

This line of argument, if it applies to any loyalty, applies to all loyalties including national loyalty. The implication is that patriotic considerations are, for people who have a basis for patriotism, genuinely normative considerations, partly determinative of what they should do, all things considered.

V. ALIENATION

Marxists define alienation as occurring when the conditions and products of labor have become independent of the laborers in the sense of being determined by market forces that have, as it were, a life of their own. I wish to suggest a broader use for the term which has the advantage of being free of political ideology. Let us say provisionally that someone is alienated from C when, given his situation, he would normally be expected to have a sense of loyalty toward C but in fact does not. He can normally be expected to have community loyalty if he has lived in a community for a long time, it has at least roughly identifiable boundaries and a name, and if he works there and knows its people and byways. If he is alienated he does not view his community as his own and consequently does not much care what happens to it or what it looks like; he is loathe to support it financially; and if its deterioration threatens his safety or the value of his property his inclination is to move rather than work for improvement.

Anything to which a person can be loyal he can also, in principle, be alienated from, and conversely. Feeling shame about something is as much a sign of loyalty as is pride, and their absence can be evidence of alienation; I cannot be proud or ashamed, or loyal or alienated, unless I somehow view the thing as mine. I can be neither proud nor ashamed of an iceberg unless I am able to discover or create some connection between myself and the iceberg which enables me to think of it as *my* iceberg. However, failing to view a community as one's own plainly is not sufficient for alienation. I felt alien living in Moscow but not alienated, because there never was anything for me to be alienated from. Moscovites and New Yorkers, however, can be and often are alienated from their cities, institutions, or jobs. But neither will it do to say that someone must first be loyal to C before he can become alienated from it, else we could never truly say that he *always* was alienated from C or that he grew up alienated.

We are forced instead to speak of causal conditions that "normally" create loyalty and lead us to expect it, and of alienation as an undesirable state that can exist in spite of the presence of these normal conditions. When can we "expect" group loyalty? What conditions "normally" lead to it? The difficulty lies in distinguishing a causal environment that contributes to alienation from a causal environment in which we would never expect loyalty in the first place and which therefore rules out alienation. If I visit Chicago for a few weeks civic loyalty toward Chicago is not expected of me; it is expected of a reasonably successful person whose home and work have been there all his life. So we want to say that the latter person is alienated if he doesn't care at all about the good, safety, beauty, or reputation of his city.

But what if the lifelong resident is on welfare, uneducated, and unemployable, or mentally retarded, or so totally engrossed in his work or in drugs or drinking, that he cares for nothing else? If we knew certain causes we would not expect civic loyalty; but this is as true of successful people as it is of the retarded or the casual visitor: if civic loyalty is caused, disappointed expectation of it is just a function of our ignorance. I have assumed that loyalty is caused. Yet, for all that, loyalty and alienation plainly are normative notions. I mean that when we call someone alienated we are saying that something has gone wrong with the causal machinery that we think it both desirable and possible should operate in our society, *and also* that he is subject to criticism for lacking civic loyalty. It is neither essential nor feasible that casual visitors, infants, or mental defectives should view Chicago as their city. But we are disappointed and disapproving if slum dwellers and busy business people do not. The idea of alienation falls between the disloyal and the alien: we are outraged by disloyalty and we expect nothing from aliens; there is nothing we can do about either. But alienated people are still part of our moral community, however marginally, and we "expect" their civic loyalty in the sense that we demand it, which we do not do in the case of aliens. And, unlike traitors, they have not betrayed us but have somehow "gone wrong." Alienated people are bad citizens and, like the coward in Aristotle's ethics, even though alterable social arrangements largely made them so, we disapprove of them nonetheless.

I can be alienated from what I legally own, belong to, or have membership in, and I can come to view as mine things to which I have no legal ties or rights. To be alienated from one's job is to lack any sense of possession regarding its activities, products, fellow workers, or the concern or institution of which it is part. It is to feel, "I just work here." Conditions under which someone is alienated in the Marxist sense can be causes of alienation in the sense I explain. If exactly how a thing gets made and how the work routines are organized are determined externally and are none of the worker's business, it may be more difficult for him to identify with his work than if things were organized in a way that involves his consultation. But these are only *some* of the factors relevant to loyalty and alienation. The inferiority of the Marxist concept lies in its abstractness: someone is alienated if certain theoretical conditions are satisfied, quite regardless of how he actually feels and behaves toward his work. He can be well paid, happy, loyal, interested in his work, and alienated. The sense of alienation I explain is phenomenological in the sense that lacking a sense of possession implies empirical claims about attitudes and behavior. When people are alienated in my sense, something has gone wrong and quite observably so. This sense of alienation is applicable to any kind of social unit and within either socialist or free-market contexts.

There are many people who seem not to care at all about their neighborhoods, their cities, or various larger or other wholes. The effects of this attitude can range through indifference, automatic negative votes on tax and bond levies, cynical exploitation of the social services systems, vandalism, and crime. If it is true, as I think it is, that alienation in the sense of absence of group loyalties is a major contributing cause of this, it will be socially useful to investigate and cultivate the conditions under which people are likely to come to view various social units as their own. For the main problem American society currently faces is not so much the competition of group loyalties as their absence. The absence of a sense of possession toward one's job or the enterprise of which it is part, and hence not being proud or ashamed of how one performs, is a form of alienation that transcends the social and political differences between American and Soviet society. The notorious alienation of many American industrial workers is matched if not surpassed by the sullen indifference of many Moscow service workers.

Three basic kinds of motives are candidates for grounding the societal concern that can diminish hooliganism, neglect, and crime. These are rational self-interest, social morality, and group loyalties. My suggestion is that an empirical procedure for actually augmenting the societal concern we require is more readily available if we make pivotal the concept of group loyalty. This is because the question of what makes people come to perceive, or fail to perceive, their communities or cities as their own is a causal question and therefore amenable to a search for correlations between community commitment and the physical, institutional, and economic features of different communities. Among many possibilities, one would want to look at aesthetic, symbolic, or interest- and attention-generating features of the physical environment which may engender sense of ownership and pride; at the diversity, uniqueness, or complexity of a community; and at ways to reduce transience, sterile construction projects, the flight of local stores, and other things that threaten residents' sense of community.

If, however, we construe the problem of urban alienation either in terms of stimulating rational self-interest or in terms of impersonal morality, it becomes much more difficult to imagine what one might actually *do* in addition to making arguments. There are obvious reasons why one wants to be able to appeal to rational self-interest as the basis for good citizenship. But it is just not true that general good citizenship brings personal reward to someone who lacks a sense of community, civic, or national loyalty in the first place. If we try to tell a person in an affluent neighborhood that he will personally gain by paying higher taxes for better schools and municipal services in a slum that is ten miles away, we simply will not be believed.

The appeal to moral principles fares no better. If we tell the person in the affluent neighborhood that he morally ought to pay higher taxes for the benefit of the slum, or that he owes the people in the slum, the most likely response will be indignation. Similarly, arguing with potential delinquents about fairness and respect for property does not have a good track record, however sound the arguments might be. As a matter of historical and sociological fact, moral motives for good citizenship are marginally effective and harder to produce in the first place; it is primarily group loyalties—group egoism and tribal morality—that have produced the caring and commitment that keep our social worlds going.

VI. GROUP LOYALTY, INDIVIDUATION, AND THE SELF

A defense of group loyalty as essential to a moral community constitutes a criticism of individualistic conceptions of a person's relation to society. It invites us to reexamine some elements of the organic theory of society. The very idea that a society, whether a nation or a neighborhood, is a moral community whose members are bound together by the possession of a common, noninstrumental good, clashes with classic individualism and its "commercial" conception of the individual's relation to society. Unfortunately, most American thinkers cannot even read the expression 'organic theory of the state' without hearing the crash of jack boots in the backs of their minds. However, there is another side to the notion of group loyalty which is more congenial to individualism. If the common good of one's moral community is taken absolutely for granted and not explicitly taught or even discussed, it does not have to be defended or justified. Historically, this has been true of homogeneous or isolated societies: nobody, except a Socrates, asks why what their gods command them to do is right. And when an alien, technological culture enters the scene and is heedless of these basic cultural values, alienation and cultural dissolution are common consequences. Modern Man who, unlike his simpler ancestor, belongs to many different tribes at the same time, is subject to an analogous form of lost innocence. Our family, neighborhood, or city cannot help but be perceived as just one among a great many, all of which are pretty much alike from the point of view of the wider national and human societies that we also recognize as ours. So we are threatened with having to wear these narrower loyalties on our sleeves, in all their nakedness, or else abandon them, which creates for parts of our social lives a problem not unlike that which islanders or native American tribesmen faced when they met modern Western civilization. How can a person maintain community and civic loyalties if he is led to conclude that his community and his city are no better, and deserve no more, than a thousand others?

Suppose that a person lives in a gigantic, uniform housing project, devoid of artistic embellishment, and that beyond it are ever more such projects which, so far as he can tell, are qualitatively exactly similar. If you "cloned" a person—suddenly produced ten exact replicas of him—his concept of self and self-interest would be thrown into confusion; if you "clone" his environment his group egoism is thrown into confusion. If you felt you should stand by your old friend, but I put him in my thirty-fifth-century machine and replicated ten of him, complete with identical memories, personalities, etc., you would want to know *which* of these particulars was your friend. You would try to track him through space/time; when you lost the track you would seek criteria of individuation, and when that failed, eventually you would cease to care which was which and your loyalty to your friend would die. What would replace it, if anything, would be the logically very different judgment that each of the ten was valuable because of the kind of being it was.

The object of community loyalty is a particular, and this means that our special concern for it does not depend on our thinking that its differentiating features make it *better* than others; our concern depends on our thinking it is *ours*. Nevertheless there must *be* important differentiating features or we will not be able to individuate it in a way that allows it to retain significance. Just as in the case of loyalty to the friend who was replicated ten times, community loyalty dies if we see that our community is exactly like all the others. If I pick up a pebble from the beach I can individuate it as "the pebble in *my* hand," but I would feel foolish calling it "*my* pebble" unless there were something distinctive about it, which made it different from the millions of others on the beach. Someone who set out to show a visitor what he was proud of, but became confused and couldn't tell his neighborhood or street from adjoining ones, would be humiliated. And insofar as one's sense of oneself as an individual and object of self-interest and esteem is bound up with the institutions, places, and social units one comes to view as one's own, individuality is threatened and confused by the "cloning" of one's environment.

Certain collectivistic and individualistic aspects of how a person relates to society are inextricably bound together. People do not belong to moral communities and possess meaningful noninstrumental values unless they join with others in adopting certain institutions and social units as their own. But at the same time, we cannot escape alienation unless we are able to individuate the social entities that are ours in public ways which render them unique and easily distinguishable from social units that are not ours. Merely saying "my community is the one *I* live in" will not do, any more than will "my pebble is the one I hold in *my* hand." The differentiating features on which community pride and loyalty focus must be understood as criteria of social individuation and not merely as the "good-making properties" with which moral philosophers have been traditionally concerned.

One conclusion we can draw is that there is a fairly direct connection between the concept of self-identity and urban planning. Diversity is as much an essential social good as is a sense of common possession, and therefore it should be a serious principle of urban planning, beginning with the smallest units of a society, such as individual apartments and buildings. Original public art, because original art is always unique, can play an important role in individuating communities and subcommunities in concrete, visible ways, thus turning them into more viable objects of local loyalty. It is one of the great merits of pride and loyalty that the objects of them need not be scarce things or necessities, the possession of which by my community or city diminishes your community or city or subtracts from its fair share. They need only be different from what other communities possess, not obviously harmful, and well cared for, so that the particularity of what one loves is associated with features that other people acknowledge and do not find silly. It is impossible to love a bare particular and equally impossible to love something that is not a particular. This is the ultimate basis of individualism, as well as that aspect of collectivism which is constituted by our group loyalties.

Chapter Two
ALASDAIR MacINTYRE

IS PATRIOTISM A VIRTUE?

I

*O*ne of the central tasks of the moral philosopher is to articulate the convictions of the society in which he or she lives so that these convictions
may become available for rational scrutiny. This task is all the more urgent
when a variety of conflicting and incompatible beliefs are held within one and
the same community, either by rival groups who differ on key moral questions
or by one and the same set of individuals who find within themselves competing moral allegiances. In either of these types of case the first task of the
moral philosopher is to render explicit what is at issue in the various disagreements and it is a task of this kind that I have set myself in this lecture.

For it is quite clear that there are large disagreements about patriotism in
our society. And although it would be a mistake to suppose that there are only
two clear, simple, and mutually opposed sets of beliefs about patriotism, it is at
least plausible to suggest that the range of conflicting views can be placed on
a spectrum with two poles. At one end is the view, taken for granted by almost
everyone in the nineteenth century, a commonplace in the literary culture of
the McGuffey readers, that 'patriotism' names a virtue. At the other end is the
contrasting view, expressed with sometimes shocking clarity in the nineteen
sixties, that 'patriotism' names a vice. It would be misleading for me to suggest
that I am going to be able to offer good reasons for taking one of these views
rather than the other. What I do hope to achieve is a clarification of the issues
that divide them.

A necessary first step in the direction of any such clarification is to distinguish patriotism properly so-called from two other sets of attitudes that are all

This essay was first presented as an E. H. Lindley Lecture, University of Kansas, 1984.
Copyright © 1984 Department of Philosophy, University of Kansas. Reprinted by permission.

too easily assimilated to it. The first is that exhibited by those who are protagonists of their own nation's causes because and only because, so they assert, it
is their nation which is *the* champion of some great moral ideal. In the Great
War of 1914–18 Max Weber claimed that Imperial Germany should be supported because its was the cause of *Kultur*, while Emile Durkheim claimed
with equal vehemence that France should be supported because its was the
cause of *civilization*. And here and now there are those American politicians
who claim that the United States deserves our allegiance because it champions
the goods of freedom against the evils of communism. What distinguishes their
attitude from patriotism is twofold: first it is the ideal and not the nation which
is the primary object of their regard; and secondly insofar as their regard for
the ideal provides good reasons for allegiance to their country, it provides good
reasons for anyone at all to uphold their country's cause, irrespective of their
nationality or citizenship.

Patriotism by contrast is defined in terms of a kind of loyalty to a particular nation which only those possessing that particular nationality can exhibit.
Only Frenchmen can be patriotic about France, while anyone can make the
cause of *civilization* their own. But it would be all too easy in noticing this to fail
to make a second equally important distinction. Patriotism is not to be confused with a mindless loyalty to one's own particular nation which has no
regard at all for the characteristics of that particular nation. Patriotism does
generally and characteristically involve a peculiar regard not just for one's own
nation, but for the particular characteristics and merits and achievements of
one's own nation. These latter are indeed valued *as* merits and achievements
and their character as merits and achievements provides reasons supportive of
the patriot's attitudes. But the patriot does not value in the same way precisely
similar merits and achievements when they are the merits and achievements of
some nation other than his or hers. For he or she—at least in the role of
patriot—values them not just as merits and achievements, but as the merits
and achievements of this particular nation.

To say this is to draw attention to the fact that patriotism is one of a class
of loyalty-exhibiting virtues (that is, if it *is* a virtue at all), other members of
which are marital fidelity, the love of one's own family and kin, friendship, and
loyalty to such institutions, as schools and cricket or baseball clubs. All these
attitudes exhibit a peculiar action-generating regard for particular persons,
institutions, or groups, a regard founded upon a particular historical relationship of association between the person exhibiting the regard and the relevant
person, institution, or group. It is often, although not always, the case that
associated with this regard will be a felt gratitude for the benefits which the
individual takes him or herself to have received from the person, institution, or
group. But it would be one more mistake to suppose patriotism or other such
attitudes of loyalty to be at their core or primarily responses of gratitude. For
there are many persons, institutions, and groups to which each of us have good

reason to feel grateful without this kind of loyalty being involved. What patriotism and other such attitudes involve is not just gratitude, but a particular kind of gratitude; and what those who treat patriotism and other such loyalties as virtues are committed to believing is not that what they owe their nation or whomever or whatever it is is simply a requital for benefits received, based on some relationship of reciprocity of benefits.

So although one may as a patriot love one's country, or as a husband or wife exhibit marital fidelity, and cite as partially supporting reasons one's country's or one's spouse's merits and one's own gratitude to them for benefits received these can be no more than *partially* supporting reasons, just because what is valued is valued precisely as the merits of *my* country or spouse or as the benefits received by *me* from *my* country or spouse. The particularity of the relationship is essential and ineliminable, and in identifying it as such we have already specified one central problem. What *is* the relationship between patriotism as such, the regard for this particular nation, and the regard which the patriot has for the merits and achievements of his or her nation and for the benefits which he or she has received? The answer to this question must be delayed for it will turn out to depend upon the answer to an apparently even more fundamental question, one that can best be framed in terms of the thesis that, if patriotism is understood as I have understood it, then 'patriotism' is not merely not the name of a virtue, but must be the name of a vice, since patriotism thus understood and morality are incompatible.

II

The presupposition of this thesis is an account of morality which has enjoyed high prestige in our culture. According to that account to judge from a moral standpoint is to judge impersonally. It is to judge as any rational person would judge, independently of his or her interests, affections, and social position. And to act morally is to act in accordance with such impersonal judgments. Thus to think and to act morally involve the moral agent in abstracting him or herself from all social particularity and partiality. The potential conflict between morality so understood and patriotism is at once clear. For patriotism requires me to exhibit peculiar devotion to my nation and you to yours. It requires me to regard such contingent social facts as where I was born and what government ruled over that place at that time, who my parents were, who my great-great-grandparents were, and so on, as deciding for me the question of what virtuous action is—at least insofar as it is the virtue of patriotism which is in question. Hence the moral standpoint and the patriotic standpoint are systematically incompatible.

Yet although this is so, it might be argued that the two standpoints need not be in conflict. For patriotism and all other such particular loyalties can be restricted in their scope so that their exercise is always within the confines imposed by morality. Patriotism need be regarded as nothing more than a perfectly proper devotion to one's own nation which must never be allowed to violate the constraints set by the impersonal moral standpoint. This is indeed the kind of patriotism professed by certain liberal moralists who are often indignant when it is suggested by their critics that they are not patriotic. To those critics however patriotism thus limited in its scope appears to be emasculated, and it does so because in some of the most important situations of actual social life either the patriotic standpoint comes into serious conflict with the standpoint of a genuinely impersonal morality or it amounts to no more than a set of practically empty slogans. What kinds of circumstances are these? They are at least twofold.

The first kind arises from scarcity of essential resources, often historically from the scarcity of land suitable for cultivation and pasture, and perhaps in our own time from that of fossil fuels. What your community requires as the material prerequisites for your survival as a distinctive community and your growth into a distinctive nation may be exclusive use of the same or some of the same natural resources as my community requires for its survival and growth into a distinctive nation. When such a conflict arises, the standpoint of impersonal morality requires an allocation of goods such that each individual person counts for one and no more than one, while the patriotic standpoint requires that I strive to further the interests of my community and you strive to further those of yours, and certainly where the survival of one community is at stake, and sometimes perhaps even when only large interests of one community are at stake, patriotism entails a willingness to go to war on one's community's behalf.

The second type of conflict-engendering circumstance arises from differences between communities about the right way for each to live. Not only competition for scarce natural resources, but incompatibilities arising from such conflict-engendering beliefs may lead to situations in which once again the liberal moral standpoint and the patriotic standpoint are radically at odds. The administration of the *pax Romana* from time to time required the Roman *imperium* to set its frontiers at the point at which they could be most easily secured, so that the burden of supporting the legions would be reconcilable with the administration of Roman law. And the British empire was no different in its time. But this required infringing upon the territory and the independence of barbarian border peoples. A variety of such peoples—Scottish Gaels, Iroquois Indians, Bedouin—have regarded raiding the territory of their traditional enemies living within the confines of such large empires as an essential constituent of the good life; whereas the settled urban or agricultural communities which provided the target for their depredations have regarded the subjugation of such peoples and their reeducation into peaceful pursuits as one of their central responsibilities. And on such issues once again the impersonal moral standpoint and that of patriotism cannot be reconciled.

For the impersonal moral standpoint, understood as the philosophical protagonists of modern liberalism have understood it, requires neutrality not only between rival and competing interests, but also between rival and competing sets of beliefs about the best way for human beings to live. Each individual is to be left free to pursue in his or her own way that way of life which he or she judges to be best; while morality by contrast consists of rules which, just because they are such that any rational person, independently of his or her interests or point of view on the best way for human beings to live, would assent to them, are equally binding on all persons. Hence in conflicts between nations or other communities over ways of life, the standpoint of morality will once again be that of an impersonal arbiter, adjudicating in ways that give equal weight to each individual person's needs, desires, beliefs about the good and the like, while the patriot is once again required to be partisan.

Notice that in speaking of the standpoint of liberal impersonal morality in the way in which I have done I have been describing a standpoint whose truth is both presupposed by the political actions and utterances of a great many people in our society and explicitly articulated and defended by most modern moral philosophers; and that it has at the level of moral philosophy a number of distinct versions—some with a Kantian flavor, some utilitarian, some contractarian. I do not mean to suggest that the disagreements between these positions are unimportant. Nonetheless the five central positions that I have ascribed to that standpoint appear in all these various philosophical guises: first, that morality is constituted by rules to which any rational person would under certain ideal conditions give assent; secondly, that those rules impose constraints upon and are neutral between rival and competing interests— morality itself is not the expression of any particular interest; thirdly, that those rules are also neutral between rival and competing sets of beliefs about what the best way for human beings to live is; fourthly, that the units which provide the subject-matter of morality as well as its agents are individual human beings and that in moral evaluations each individual is to count for one and nobody for more than one; and fifthly, that the standpoint of the moral agent constituted by allegiance to these rules is one and the same for all moral agents and as such is independent of all social particularity. What morality provides are standards by which all actual social structures may be brought to judgment from a standpoint independent of all of them. It is morality so understood allegiance to which is not only incompatible with treating patriotism as a virtue, but which requires that patriotism—at least in any substantial version—be treated as a vice.

But is this the only possible way to understand morality? As a matter of history, the answer is clearly "No." This understanding of morality invaded post-Renascence Western culture at a particular point in time as the moral counterpart to political liberalism and social individualism and its polemical stances reflect its history of emergence from the conflicts which those movements engendered and themselves presuppose alternatives against which those polemical stances were and are directed. Let me therefore turn to considering one of those alternative accounts of morality, whose peculiar interest lies in the place that it has to assign to patriotism.

III

According to the liberal account of morality *where* and *from whom* I learn the principles and precepts of morality are and must be irrelevant both to the question of what the content of morality is and to that of the nature of my commitment to it, as irrelevant as *where* and *from whom* I learn the principles and precepts of mathematics are to the content of mathematics and the nature of my commitment to mathematical truths. By contrast on the alternative account of morality which I am going to sketch, the questions of *where* and *from whom* I learn my morality turn out to be crucial for both the content and the nature of moral commitment.

On this view it is an essential characteristic of the morality which each of us acquires that it is learned from, in and through the way of life of some particular community. Of course the moral rules elaborated in one particular historical community will often resemble and sometimes be identical with the rules to which allegiance is given in other particular communities, especially in communities with a shared history or which appeal to the same canonical texts. But there will characteristically be *some* distinctive features of the set of rules considered as a whole, and those distinctive features will often arise from the way in which members of that particular community responded to some earlier situation or series of situations in which particular features of difficult cases led to one or more rules being put in question and reformulated or understood in some new way. Moreover the form of the rules of morality as taught and apprehended will be intimately connected with specific institutional arrangements. The moralities of different societies may agree in having a precept enjoining that a child should honor his or her parents, but what it is so to honor and indeed what a father is and what a mother is will vary greatly between different social orders. So that what I learn as a guide to my actions and as a standard for evaluating them is never morality as such, but always the highly specific morality of some highly specific social order.

To this the reply by the protagonists of modern liberal morality might well be: doubtless this is how a comprehension of the rules of morality is first acquired. But what allows such specific rules, framed in terms of particular social institutions, to be accounted moral rules at all is the fact they are nothing other than applications of universal and general moral rules and individuals acquire genuine morality only because and insofar as they progress from particularized socially specific applications of universal and general moral rules to comprehending them as universal and general. To learn to understand oneself as a moral agent just is to learn to free oneself from social particularity and to adopt a standpoint independent of any particular set of social institutions and the fact that everyone or almost everyone has to learn to do this by starting out from a standpoint deeply infected by social particularity and partiality goes no way towards providing an alternative account of morality. But to this reply a threefold rejoinder can be made.

First, it is not just that I first apprehend the rules of morality in some socially specific and particularized form. It is also and correlatively that the goods by reference to which and for the sake of which any set of rules must be justified are also going to be goods that are socially specific and particular. For central to those goods is the enjoyment of one particular kind of social life, lived out through a particular set of social relationships and thus what I enjoy is the good of *this* particular social life inhabited by me and I enjoy *it* as what *it* is. It may well be that it follows that I would enjoy and benefit equally from similar forms of social life in other communities; but this hypothetical truth in no way diminishes the importance of the contention that my goods are as a matter of fact found *here*, among *these* particular people, in *these* particular relationships. Goods are never encountered except as thus particularized. Hence the abstract general claim, that rules of a certain kind are justified by being productive of and constitutive of goods of a certain kind, is true only if these and these and these particular sets of rules incarnated in the practices of these and these and these particular communities are productive of or constitutive of these and these and these particular goods enjoyed at certain particular times and places by certain specifiable individuals.

It follows that *I* find *my* justification for allegiance to these rules of morality in *my* particular community; deprived of the life of that community, *I* would have no reason to be moral. But this is not all. To obey the rules of morality is characteristically and generally a hard task for human beings. Indeed were it not so, our need for morality would not be what it is. It is because we are continually liable to be blinded by immediate desire, to be distracted from our responsibilities, to lapse into backsliding and because even the best of us may at times encounter quite unusual temptations that it is important to morality that *I* can only be a moral agent because *we* are moral agents, that I need those around me to reinforce my moral strengths and assist in remedying my moral weaknesses. It is in general only within a community that individuals become capable of morality, are sustained in their morality and are constituted as moral agents by the way in which other people regard them and what is owed to and by them as well as by the way in which they regard themselves. In requiring much from me morally the other members of my community express a kind of respect for me that has nothing to do with expectations of benefit; and those of whom nothing or little is required in respect of morality are treated with a lack of respect which is, if repeated often enough, damaging to the moral capacities of those individuals. Of course, lonely moral heroism is sometimes required and sometimes achieved. But we must not treat this exceptional type of case as though it were typical. And once we recognize that typically moral agency and continuing moral capacity are engendered and sustained in essential ways by particular institutionalized social ties in particular social groups, it will be difficult to counterpose allegiance to a particular society and allegiance to morality in the way in which the protagonists of liberal morality do.

Indeed the case for treating patriotism as a virtue is now clear. *If* first of all it is the case that I can only apprehend the rules of morality in the version in which they are incarnated in some specific community; and *if* secondly it is the case that the justification of morality must be in terms of particular goods enjoyed within the life of particular communities; and *if* thirdly it is the case that I am characteristically brought into being and maintained as a moral agent only through the particular kinds of moral sustenance afforded by my community, *then* it is clear that deprived of this community, I am unlikely to flourish as a moral agent. Hence my allegiance to the community and what it requires of me—even to the point of requiring me to die to sustain its life— could not meaningfully be contrasted with or counterposed to what morality required of me. Detached from my community, I will be apt to lose my hold upon all genuine standards of judgment. Loyalty to that community, to the hierarchy of particular kinship, particular local community, and particular natural community, is on this view a prerequisite for morality. So patriotism and those loyalties cognate to it are not just virtues but central virtues. Everything however turns on the truth or falsity of the claims advanced in the three preceding if-clauses. And the argument so far affords us no resources for delivering a verdict upon that truth or falsity. Nonetheless some progress has been achieved, and not only because the terms of the debate have become clearer. For it has also become clear that this dispute is not adequately characterized if it is understood simply as a disagreement between two rival accounts of morality, as if there were some independently identifiable phenomenon situated somehow or other in the social world waiting to be described more or less accurately by the contending parties. What we have here are two rival and incompatible moralities, each of which is viewed from within by its adherents as morality-as-such, each of which makes its exclusive claim to our allegiance. How are we to evaluate such claims?

One way to begin is to be learned from Aristotle. Since we possess no stock of clear and distinct first principles or any other such epistemological resource which would provide us with a neutral and independent standard for judging between them, we shall do well to proceed dialectically. And one useful dialectical strategy is to focus attention on those accusations which the adherents of each bring against the rival position which the adherents of that rival position treat as of central importance to rebut. For this will afford at least one indication of the issues about the importance of which both sides agree and about the characterization of which their very recognition of disagreement suggests that there must also be some shared beliefs. In what areas do such issues arise?

IV

One such area is defined by a charge which it seems reasonable at least prima facie for the protagonists of patriotism to bring against morality. The morality for which patriotism is a virtue offers a form of rational justification for moral rules and precepts whose structure is clear and rationally defensible. The rules of morality are justifiable if and only if they are productive of and partially constitutive of a form of shared social life whose goods are directly enjoyed by those inhabiting the particular communities whose social life is of that kind. Hence qua member of this or that particular community I can appreciate the justification for what morality requires of me from within the social roles that I live out in my community. By contrast, it may be argued, liberal morality requires of me to assume an abstract and artificial—perhaps even an impossible—stance, that of a rational being as such, responding to the requirements of morality not qua parent or farmer or quarterback, but qua rational agent who has abstracted him or herself from all social particularity, who has become not merely Adam Smith's impartial spectator, but a correspondingly impartial actor, and one who in his impartiality is doomed to rootlessness, to be a citizen of nowhere. How can I justify to myself performing this act of abstraction and detachment?

The liberal answer is clear: such abstraction and detachment is defensible, because it is a necessary condition of moral freedom, of emancipation from the bondage of the social, political, and economic status quo. For unless I can stand back from every and any feature of that status quo, including the roles within it which I myself presently inhabit, I will be unable to view it critically and to decide for myself what stance it is rational and right for me to adopt towards it. This does not preclude that the outcome of such a critical evaluation may not be an endorsement of all or some of the existing social order; but even such an endorsement will only be free and rational if I have made it for myself in this way. (Making just such an endorsement of much of the economic status quo is the distinguishing mark of the contemporary conservative liberal, such as Milton Friedman, who is as much a liberal as the liberal liberal who finds much of the status quo wanting—such as J. K. Galbraith or Edward Kennedy—or the radical liberal.) Thus liberal morality does after all appeal to an overriding good, the good of this particular kind of emancipating freedom. And in the name of this good it is able not only to respond to the question about how the rules of morality are to be justified, but also to frame a plausible and potentially damaging objection to the morality of patriotism.

It is of the essence of the morality of liberalism that no limitations are or can be set upon the criticism of the social status quo. No institution, no practice, no loyalty can be immune from being put in question and perhaps rejected. Conversely the morality of patriotism is one which precisely because it is framed in terms of the membership of some particular social community with some particular social, political, and economic structure, must exempt at least some fundamental structures of that community's life from criticism. Because patriotism has to be a loyalty that is in some respects unconditional, so in just those respects rational criticism is ruled out. But if so the adherents of the morality of patriotism have condemned themselves to a fundamentally irrational attitude—since to refuse to examine some of one's fundamental beliefs and attitudes is to insist on accepting them, whether they are rationally justifiable or not, which is irrational—and have imprisoned themselves within that irrationality. What answer can the adherents of the morality of patriotism make to this kind of accusation? The reply must be threefold.

When the liberal moralist claims that the patriot is bound to treat his or her nation's projects and practices in some measure uncritically, the claim is not only that at any one time certain of these projects and practices will be being treated uncritically; it is that some at least must be permanently exempted from criticism. The patriot is in no position to deny this; but what is crucial to the patriot's case is to identify clearly precisely what it is that is thus exempted. And at this point it becomes extremely important that in outlining the case for the morality of patriotism—as indeed in outlining the case for liberal morality—we should not be dealing with strawmen. Liberalism and patriotism are not positions invented by me or by other external commentators; they have their own distinctive spokesmen and their own distinctive voices. And although I hope that it has been clear throughout that I have only been trying to articulate what those voices would say, it is peculiarly important to the case for patriotic morality at this point that its actual historical protagonists be identified. So what I say next is an attempt to identify the common attitudes on this point of Charles Péguy and Charles de Gaulle, of Bismarck and of Adam von Trott. You will notice that in these pairs one member is someone who was at least for a time a member of his nation's political establishment, the other someone who was always in a radical way outside that establishment and hostile to it, but that even those who were for a time identified with the status quo of power, were also at times alienated from it. And this makes it clear that whatever is exempted from the patriot's criticism the status quo of power and government and the policies pursued by those exercising power and government never need be so exempted. What then is exempted? The answer is: the nation conceived *as a project*, a project somehow or other brought to birth in the past and carried on so that a morally distinctive community was brought into being which embodied a claim to political autonomy in its various organized and institutionalized expressions. Thus one can be patriotic towards a nation whose political independence is yet to come—as Garibaldi was; or towards a nation which once was and perhaps might be again—like the Polish patriots of the 1860s. What the patriot is committed to is a particular way of linking a past which has conferred a distinctive moral and political identity upon him or her with a future for the project which is his or her nation which it is his or her responsibility to bring into being. Only this allegiance is unconditional and allegiance to particular governments or forms of government or particular leaders will be entirely conditional upon their being devoted to furthering that project rather than frustrating or destroying it. Hence there is nothing inconsistent in a patriot's being deeply opposed to his country's contemporary rulers, as Péguy was, or plotting their overthrow as Adam von Trott did.

Yet although this may go part of the way towards answering the charge of the liberal moralist that the patriot must in certain areas be completely uncritical and therefore irrationalist, it certainly does not go all the way. For everything that I have said on behalf of the morality of patriotism is compatible with it being the case that on occasion patriotism might require me to support and work for the success of some enterprise of my nation as crucial to its overall project, crucial perhaps to its survival, when the success of that enterprise would not be in the best interests of mankind, evaluated from an impartial and an impersonal standpoint. The case of Adam von Trott is very much to the point.

Adam von Trott was a German patriot who was executed after the unsuccessful assassination attempt against Hitler's life in 1944. Trott deliberately chose to work inside Germany with the minuscule, but highly placed, conservative opposition to the Nazis with the aim of replacing Hitler from within, rather than to work for an overthrow of Nazi Germany which would result in the destruction of the Germany brought to birth in 1871. But to do this he had to appear to be identified with the cause of Nazi Germany and so strengthened not only his country's cause, as was his intention, but also as an unavoidable consequence the cause of the Nazis. This kind of example is a particularly telling one, because the claim that such and such a course of action is "to the best interests of mankind" is usually at best disputable, at worst cloudy rhetoric. But there are a very few causes in which so much was at stake—and that this is generally much clearer in retrospect than it was at the time does not alter that fact—that the phrase has clear application: the overthrow of Nazi Germany was one of them.

How ought the patriot then to respond? Perhaps in two ways. The first begins by reemphasizing that from the fact that the particularist morality of the patriot is rooted in a particular community and inextricably bound up with the social life of that community, it does not follow that it cannot provide rational grounds for repudiating many features of that country's present organized social life. The conception of justice engendered by the notion of citizenship within a particular community may provide standards by which particular political institutions are found wanting: when Nazi anti-Semitism encountered the phenomena of German Jewish ex-soldiers who had won the Iron Cross, it had to repudiate German particularist standards of excellence (for the award of the Iron Cross symbolized a recognition of devotion to Germany). Moreover the conception of one's own nation having a special mission does not necessitate that this mission may not involve the extension of a justice originally at home only in the particular institutions of the homeland. And clearly particular governments or agencies of government may defect and may be understood to have defected from this mission so radically that the patriot may find that a point comes when he or she has to choose between the claims of the project which constitutes his or her nation and the claims of the morality that he or she has learnt as a member of the community whose life is informed by that project. Yes, the liberal critic of patriotism will respond, this indeed *may* happen; but it may not and it often will not. Patriotism turns out to be a permanent source of moral danger. And this claim, I take it, cannot in fact be successfully rebutted.

A second possible, but very different type of answer on behalf of the patriot would run as follows. I argued earlier that the kind of regard for one's own country which would be compatible with a liberal morality of impersonality and impartiality would be too insubstantial, would be under too many constraints, to be regarded as a version of patriotism in the traditional sense. But it does not follow that some version of traditional patriotism may not be compatible with some other morality of universal moral law, which sets limits to and provides both sanction for and correction of the particularist morality of the patriot. Whether this is so or not is too large and too distinct a question to pursue in this present paper. But we ought to note that even if it is so—and all those who have been both patriots and Christians *or* patriots and believers in Thomistic natural law *or* patriots and believers in the Rights of Man have been committed to claiming that it is so—this would not diminish in any way the force of the liberal claim that patriotism is a morally dangerous phenomenon.

That the rational protagonist of the morality of patriotism is compelled, if my argument is correct, to concede this does not mean that there is not more to be said in the debate. And what needs to be said is that the liberal morality of impartiality and impersonality turns out also to be a morally dangerous phenomenon in an interestingly corresponding way. For suppose the bonds of patriotism to be dissolved: would liberal morality be able to provide anything adequately substantial in its place? What the morality of patriotism at its best provides is a clear account of and justification for the particular bonds and loyalties which form so much of the substance of the moral life. It does so by underlining the moral importance of the different members of a group acknowledging a shared history. Each one of us to some degree or other understands his or her life as an enacted narrative; and because of our relationships with others we have to understand ourselves as characters in the enacted narratives of other people's lives. Moreover the story of each of our lives is characteristically embedded in the story of one or more larger units. I understand the story of my life in such a way that it is part of the history of my family or of this farm or of this university or of this countryside; and I understand the story of the lives of other individuals around me as embedded in the same larger stories, so that I and they share a common stake in the outcome of that story and in what sort of story it both is and is to be: tragic, heroic, comic.

A central contention of the morality of patriotism is that I will obliterate and lose a central dimension of the moral life if I do not understand the enacted narrative of my own individual life as embedded in the history of my country. For if I do not so understand it I will not understand what I owe to others or what others owe to me, for what crimes of my nation I am bound to make reparation, for what benefits to my nation I am bound to feel gratitude. Understanding what is owed to and by me and understanding the history of the communities of which I am a part is on this view one and the same thing.

It is worth stressing that one consequence of this is that patriotism, in the sense in which I am understanding it in this paper, is only possible in certain types of national community under certain conditions. A national community, for example, which systematically disowned its own true history or substituted a largely fictitious history for it or a national community in which the bonds deriving from history were in no way the real bonds of the community (having been replaced for example by the bonds of reciprocal self-interest) would be one towards which patriotism would be—from any point of view—an irrational attitude. For precisely the same reasons that a family whose members all came to regard membership in that family as governed only by reciprocal self-interest would no longer be a family in the traditional sense, so a nation whose members took up a similar attitude would no longer be a nation and this would provide adequate grounds for holding that the project which constituted that nation had simply collapsed. Since all modern bureaucratic states tend towards reducing national communities to this condition, all such states tend towards a condition in which any genuine morality of patriotism would have no place and what paraded itself as patriotism would be an unjustifiable simulacrum.

Why would this matter? In modern communities in which membership is understood only or primarily in terms of reciprocal self-interest, only two resources are generally available when destructive conflicts of interest threaten such reciprocity. One is the arbitrary imposition of some solution by force; the other is appeal to the neutral, impartial, and impersonal standards of liberal morality. The importance of this resource is scarcely to be underrated; but how much of a resource is it? The problem is that some motivation has to be provided for allegiance to the standards of impartiality and impersonality which both has rational justification and can outweigh the considerations provided by interest. Since any large need for such allegiance arises precisely and only when and insofar as the possibility of appeals to reciprocity in interests has broken down, such reciprocity can no longer provide the relevant kind of motivation. And it is difficult to identify anything that can take its place. The appeal to moral agents qua rational beings to place their allegiance to impersonal rationality above that to their interests has, just because it is an appeal to rationality, to furnish an adequate reason for so doing. And this is a point at which liberal accounts of morality are notoriously vulnerable. This vulnerability becomes a manifest practical liability at one key point in the social order.

Every political community except in the most exceptional conditions requires standing armed forces for its minimal security. Of the members of these armed forces it must require both that they be prepared to sacrifice their own lives for the sake of the community's security and that their willingness to do so be not contingent upon their own individual evaluation of the rightness or wrongness of their country's cause on some specific issue, measured by some standard that is neutral and impartial relative to the interests of their own community and the interests of other communities. And, that is to say, good soldiers may not be liberals and must indeed embody in their actions a good deal at least of the morality of patriotism. So the political survival of any policy in which liberal morality had secured large-scale allegiance would depend upon there still being enough young men and women who rejected that liberal morality. And in this sense liberal morality tends towards the dissolution of social bonds.

Hence the charge that the morality of patriotism can successfully bring against liberal morality is the mirror-image of that which liberal morality can successfully urge against the morality of patriotism. For while the liberal moralist was able to conclude that patriotism is a permanent source of moral danger because of the way it places our ties to our nation beyond rational criticism, the moralist who defends patriotism is able to conclude that liberal morality is a permanent source of moral danger because of the way it renders our social and moral ties too open to dissolution by rational criticism. And each party is in fact in the right against the other.

V

The fundamental task which confronts any moral philosopher who finds this conclusion compelling is clear. It is to enquire whether, although the central claims made on behalf of these two rival modern moralities cannot both be true, we ought perhaps not to move towards the conclusion that both sets of claims are in fact false. And this is an enquiry in which substantial progress has already been made. But history in its impatience does not wait for moral philosophers to complete their tasks, let alone to convince their fellow-citizens. The *polis* ceased to be the key institution in Greek politics even while Aristotle was still restating its rationale and any contemporary philosopher who discusses the key conceptions that have informed modern political life since the eighteenth century is in danger of reliving Aristotle's fate, even if in a rather less impressive way. The owl of Minerva really does seem to fly at dusk.

Does this mean that my argument is therefore devoid of any immediate practical significance? That would be true only if the conclusion that a morality of liberal impersonality and a morality of patriotism must be deeply incompatible itself had no practical significance for our understanding of our everyday politics. But perhaps a systematic recognition of this incompatibility will enable us to diagnose one central flaw in the political life characteristic of modern Western states, or at least of all those modern Western states which look back for their legitimation to the American and the French revolutions. For polities so established have tended to contrast themselves with the older regimes that they displaced by asserting that, while all previous polities had expressed in their lives the partiality and one-sidedness of local customs, institutions, and traditions, they have for the first time given expression in their constitutional and institutional forms to the impersonal and impartial rules of morality as such, common to all rational beings. So Robespierre proclaimed that it was an effect of the French Revolution that the cause of France and the cause of the Rights of Man were one and the same cause. And in the nineteenth century the United States produced its own version of this claim, one which at the level of rhetoric provided the content for many Fourth of July orations and at the level of education set the standards for the Americanization of the late-nineteenth-century and early-twentieth-century immigrants, especially those from Europe.

Hegel employs a useful distinction which he marks by his use of words *Sittlichkeit* and *Moralität*. *Sittlichkeit* is the customary morality of each particular society, pretending to be no more than this. *Moralität* reigns in the realm of rational universal, impersonal morality, of liberal morality, as I have defined it. What those immigrants were taught in effect was that they had left behind countries and cultures where *Sittlichkeit* and *Moralität* were certainly distinct and often opposed and arrived in a country and a culture whose *Sittlichkeit* just is *Moralität*. And thus for many Americans the cause of America, understood as the object of patriotic regard, and the cause of morality, understood as the liberal moralist understands it, came to be identified. The history of this identification could not be other than a history of confusion and incoherence, if the argument which I have constructed in this lecture is correct. For a morality of particularist ties and solidarities has been conflated with a morality of universal, impersonal, and impartial principles in a way that can never be carried through without incoherence.

One test therefore of whether the argument that I have constructed has or has not empirical application and practical significance would be to discover whether it is or is not genuinely illuminating to write the political and social history of modern America as in key part the living out of a central conceptual confusion, a confusion perhaps required for the survival of a large-scale

modern polity which has to exhibit itself as liberal in many institutional set-
tings, but which also has to be able to engage the patriotic regard of enough of
its citizens, if it is to continue functioning effectively. To determine whether
that is or is not true would be to risk discovering that we inhabit a kind of
polity whose moral order requires systematic incoherence in the form of public
allegiance to mutually inconsistent sets of principles. But that is a task which—
happily—lies beyond the scope of this lecture.

Chapter Three
MARCIA BARON

PATRIOTISM AND "LIBERAL" MORALITY

*M*y paper takes up a challenge put forward by Alasdair MacIntyre in his 1984 Lindley lecture, "Is Patriotism a Virtue?"[1] MacIntyre argues that if we accept the following view of morality, we cannot recognize patriotism to be a virtue, and indeed must hold it to be a vice. The view in question holds that "to judge from a moral standpoint is to judge impersonally . . . as any rational person would judge, independently of his or her interests, affections and social position"; and that "to act morally is to act in accordance with such impersonal judgments" (p. 5). MacIntyre dubs this view alternatively "the morality of liberalism," "impersonal morality," and "liberal impersonal morality." *Is* it inconsistent to accept impersonal morality while believing patriotism to be virtuous? I will argue that it is not.

I

The claim that those of us who accept the morality of liberalism cannot regard patriotism as a virtue will strike many as worthy of a yawn, not a paper. "So what?" some readers may say. "Suppose MacIntyre is right. What self-respecting liberal would be troubled by his claim?" This response supposes that MacIntyre means by 'liberals' only political liberals, and that political liberals have no reason to be concerned if they cannot, without inconsistency, regard patriotism as a virtue. Both suppositions need to be challenged.

The first is just a mistake about terminology. MacIntyre does not mean by 'liberals' only political liberals. While his use of 'liberal' is probably deliberately

The original version of this essay appeared as "Patriotism and 'Liberal' Morality," by Marcia Baron, in *Mind, Value, and Culture: Essays in Honor of E. M. Adams*, edited by D. Weissbord (Copyright © 1989 by Ridgeview Publishing Co., Atascadero, Calif.). Reprinted by permission of Ridgeview Publishing Company.

ambiguous, his primary meaning is the broader one, according to which not only Franklin Delano Roosevelt, the Kennedys, and George McGovern count as liberals, but also right-wing libertarians and indeed virtually everyone who is a "modern" and not a communitarian of any stripe (socialist, MacIntyrean, Jerry Falwellian, etc.). His claim that the liberal account of morality emerged with the Enlightenment supports the broader reading.

But while those other than the people who, in contemporary U.S. political debate, are called "liberals" count as "modern liberals," there is a connection between the liberal account of morality that MacIntyre believes cannot treat patriotism as a virtue, and liberalism, as the term is understood in contemporary U.S. politics.[2] Liberalism in the latter sense finds support in the account of morality developed as part of modern liberalism. For this reason conservatives may, if there really is a deep conflict between patriotism and the liberal account of morality, be more able to ignore the dictates of modern liberalism and wave the flag than are liberals. Still, if MacIntyre is right, the problem he poses should worry conservatives as well as liberals, and prompt them to reconsider whether they really do—or should—accept the morality of liberalism.

This is only the first part of the reply. I need to address the suspicion that patriotism just isn't something to value at all. There is no dearth of reasons for being suspicious. In her essay "Patriotism: A Menace to Liberty," Emma Goldman writes:

> What, then, is patriotism? "Patriotism, sir, is the last resort of scoundrels," said Dr. Johnson. Leo Tolstoy, the greatest anti-patriot of our times, defines patriotism as the principle that will justify the training of wholesale murderers; a trade that requires better equipment for the exercise of man-killing than the making of such necessities of life as shoes, clothing and houses; a trade that guarantees better returns and greater glory than that of the average workingman. Gustave Hervé, another great anti-patriot, justly calls patriotism a superstition—one far more injurious, brutal, and inhumane than religion.[3]

When one reflects on typical appeals to patriotism it is hardly surprising that patriotism is often thought of more as a vice than a virtue. Who is branded as unpatriotic? Those who do not hate enough; those who are courageously critical of government or social policies that badly need to be subjected to scrutiny. Patriotism, wrote Horatio Smith, is "too often the hatred of other countries disguised as the love of one's own."[4] Sometimes the disguise isn't even bothered with: patriotism takes the form of hatred toward a nation or community with a different form of government, one which threatens certain interests of the elite in one's own nation (called "the national interest"). Appeals to patriotism are often inseparable from hate campaigns: those who show insufficient hatred are branded unpatriotic. In addition, those lauded as patriots—people like Oliver North—are typically public figures most of us find less than admirable, especially in the respects in which they are held to be patriotic. It's bad enough that patriotism is the last refuge of a scoundrel; it makes matters still worse when those who most vigorously wave the flag join the scoundrel in proclaiming him a great patriot.

Nonetheless, that patriotism is often appealed to for nefarious purposes should not sour us on patriotism itself. Patriotism may be a virtue without patriotism as it is typically thought of in our country (or indeed in a great many countries, even all countries) being a virtue. Since the epithets 'patriotic' and 'unpatriotic' are so frequently used for questionable political purposes, typically to extol those who support the particular government in power at that time and disparage those who are critical of it (especially when the critics oppose their government's engagement in, or creation of, a war), we should be less concerned than we might in discussing other (possible) virtues to capture ordinary usage. If we do look toward ordinary language for guidance, patriotism is likely to turn out to be a vice, the vice of mindlessly upholding whatever one's government favors (and of being ready, depending on one's age and station, to fight for one's country no matter what the cause and what the wisdom or folly of the country's military engagement). But if we do not, patriotism may well be worth taking seriously.[5] Let us turn now to MacIntyre's challenge, and see what he takes patriotism to be and why he thinks it is in conflict with the morality of liberalism.

II

Patriotism, he writes, is "one of a class of loyalty-exhibiting virtues (that is, if it is a virtue at all), other members of which are marital fidelity, the love of one's own family and kin, friendship, and loyalty to such institutions as schools and cricket or baseball clubs" (p. 4). It is "defined in terms of a kind of loyalty to a particular nation which only those possessing that particular nationality can exhibit" (p. 4). Importantly, the attitude of "those American politicians who claim that the United States deserves our allegiance because it champions the goods of freedom against the evils of communism" (p. 3) is not that of patriotism. This is so for two reasons.

> [F]irst it is the ideal and not the nation which is the primary object of their regard; and secondly insofar as their regard for the ideal provides good reasons for allegiance to their country, it provides good reasons for anyone at all to uphold their country's cause, irrespective of their nationality or citizenship. (p. 4)

The essence of patriotism is not commitment to some ideal, but allegiance to one's country or community. The foundation of this allegiance is not (a) that the country stands for some ideal (*Kultur*, *civilisation*, anticommunism) (pp. 3–4); nor (b) that one owes a debt of gratitude to one's country (pp. 4–5); nor (c) that it just is one's country, one's country "right or wrong" (as the bumper stickers popular in the United States in the late 1960s suggested). MacIntyre does not say explicitly what its foundation is, but it seems to be this. The country to which one is loyal is one's own, and it is *partly* in virtue of this particularity—that it is my country—that I am loyal to it. But this isn't all; patriotism is "not to be confused with a mindless loyalty to one's own particular nation which has no regard at all for the characteristics of that particular nation" (p. 4). The patriot has some notion of what the "particular characteristics and merits and achievements of her nation" are, and can cite these characteristics as reasons supportive of her attitude of patriotism (p. 4).

The foundation of patriotism thus has two aspects. First of all, the patriot has to be able to cite particular merits and achievements of her nation as reasons supportive of her attitude. But, and this is the second aspect, they are reasons supportive of her attitude only if it is *her country*; they are not reasons for anyone, no matter where born, where raised, where a citizen, to have the same stance toward that country. Thus MacIntyre asserts that the "particularity of the relationship" between her and her country is "essential and ineliminable." If some of the achievements of her country are surpassed by achievements of a similar sort on the part of another country, this fact in no way militates in favor of saying that she should be as loyal (or more loyal) to that other country. The primary object of patriotism is one's country, not a moral ideal, just as the primary object of love and friendship is a particular person, not certain qualities which, as it happens, that person has. Crucial to patriotism is *particularity*: one is loyal to one's country *as one's own country*. One values its achievements as its achievements. Like other loyalty-exhibiting virtues, patriotism exhibits a "peculiar action-generating regard . . . , a regard founded upon a particular historical relationship of association between the person exhibiting the regard" (p. 4) and the relevant object. It is worth noting that in MacIntyre's view, patriotism is not, and does not require, blind obedience to one's government. Patriotism in no way bars one from criticizing one's government. The only thing exempt from the patriot's criticism is the nation "conceived *as a project*" (p. 13).

> What the patriot is committed to is a particular way of linking a past which has conferred a distinctive moral and political identity upon him or her with a future for the project which is his or her nation which it is his or her responsibility to bring into being. Only this allegiance is unconditional and allegiance to particular governments or forms of government or particular leaders will be entirely conditional upon their being devoted to furthering that project rather than frustrating or destroying it.[6] (p. 14)

Characterized primarily by a sense of being from, and part of, one's country, and cleansed of its most objectionable features, patriotism as

MacIntyre understands it is considerably more attractive than it is on Emma Goldman's report. Yet if we accept liberal morality, MacIntyre says, we have to regard patriotism as a vice. What is this liberal morality?

The morality of liberalism, as MacIntyre presents it, includes some positions which I will bracket.[7] Distilling from the "five central positions" which he ascribes to "the standpoint of liberal impersonal morality" what seems to be the crux of the conflict between the morality of liberalism and that of patriotism, I will focus on impartiality and impersonality. According to the legacy of the Enlightenment, morality—not social mores, not positive social morality, but morality in the sense of whatever *really* is right, whatever *really* is wrong— is (a) *universal* (i.e., valid for all persons; not just for the elite, or for all but the elite, or for members of this culture but not that one) and therefore its judgments are (b) *impartial* (neutral between rival and competing interests, and of course to be complied with accordingly; no blaming other parties for violating a principle to which one does not hold oneself and one's compatriots). In addition, the moral stance is, on this view (c) *impersonal*. In adopting a moral stance I try to view the matter at hand, whatever it is, from the standpoint of a generic person rather than from my particular perspective.

III

We are now in a position to locate the conflict between patriotism and the morality of liberalism. The clash is between the particularity essential to patriotism and the impartiality and impersonality central to the morality of liberalism. As MacIntyre puts it, "patriotism requires me to exhibit peculiar devotion to my nation and you to yours."[8] In this sense it does not allow me to be *impersonal*: I am to judge not as I think anyone should in those circumstances, regardless of his or her nationality; I am not to judge as a generic person, or as if I were an ideal observer, stripped of knowledge of particular facts about me that differentiate me from others and could "distort" or "slant" my judgment. None of this; I am to judge as an American. Moreover, I am to judge as an American not simply in the sense that as an American I prize certain ideals; in this sense I might judge as an American, but for everyone equally. But patriotism, according to MacIntyre, requires that I judge *partially* (i.e., not impartially): I am to put U.S. interests before others.[9]

Patriotism asks that I put my own group's interest first, and judge as a member of that group. The morality of liberalism does not permit this, for it requires that I judge impersonally and impartially. But is the conflict inevitable? Just how deep is it? On closer inspection it looks to be fairly superficial. One clue that it may well be superficial is the unclarity that taints the explanation: what sort of judging is spoken of each time the word "judge" appears in the previous paragraph?

This unclarity could be the conflict's undoing. Surely it is plausible to think that impartiality and impersonality are required for some judgments but not for others. Is there any reason why the morality of liberalism could not recognize the value of special attachments, including (but not restricted to) a special attachment to one's own country, and allow that with respect to certain matters and within limits, it is *good* for an American to judge as an American, and to put American interests first? If so, patriotism and liberalism could be compatible after all. They'd be compatible if some suitable version of the morality of liberalism recognized the value of special ties to one's country and accordingly permitted partiality—constrained, however, by a requirement of impartiality. That is, from the impartial standpoint, partiality is recognized as good; but it is, to quote MacIntyre without suggesting that he holds this view, "restricted in its scope so that its exercise is always within the confines imposed by morality"(p. 6).[10] To see the point more clearly, distinguish two levels. At level one I think, "It's my country! Of course I'll go to war to defend it against the mercenaries trying to overthrow our government." At this level my thoughts are not impersonal, and do not reflect an impartial stance. From level two I reflect on the sort of thoughts I and others have at level one. My thoughts are more abstract, on the order of "Special ties to one's own country are morally justifiable, but only insofar as. . . ." These thoughts issue from (what at least aims to be) an impartial stance. While itself "partial" and "personal," patriotism could, it would seem, be recognized as a virtue by a moral theory which emphasizes impartiality and impersonality, as long as that theory doesn't require impartiality and impersonality at level one.

MacIntyre considers this attempt to resolve the conflict but deems it a failure. Harmony is achieved, he holds, only at the cost of disfiguring patriotism. The patriotism that is consistent with liberalism is "emasculated" (p. 6).[11] "Real" patriotism requires that in certain circumstances (indeed "in some of the most important situations of actual social life") we must act contrary to the dictates of a "genuinely impersonal morality" (p. 6). How so?

MacIntyre illustrates by citing two types of conflict between communities, conflicts which are such that the patriot and the liberal will have sharply opposing views as to how the conflict should be resolved. The first is a conflict over the use of essential resources, where two communities each require as "the material prerequisite" for their "survival as a distinctive community" and their "growth as a distinctive nation," exclusive use of the same natural resources.

The second type of conflict "arises from differences between communities about the right way for each to live" (p. 6). How will the patriot and the liberal approach such conflicts, if they approach them morally? Speaking of the first type of conflict, MacIntyre says that the patriotic standpoint requires that

> I strive to further the interests of my community and you strive to further those
> of yours, and certainly where the survival of one community is at stake, and some-

times perhaps even when only large interests of one community are at stake, patriotism entails a willingness to go to war on one's community's behalf (6).

In contrast, impersonal morality requires that we think in terms of fairness. The same disagreement arises between the patriot and the liberal concerning the second type of conflict. The "impersonal moral standpoint, understood as the philosophical protagonists of modern liberalism have understood it, requires neutrality . . . between rival and competing sets of beliefs about the best way for human beings to live." In "conflicts between nations or other communities over ways of life, the standpoint of morality will once again be that of an impersonal arbiter." The patriot, by contrast, "is once again required to be partisan" (p. 7).[12]

IV

Thus understood, the clash between impartial morality and patriotism does indeed appear unresolvable. But thus understood, patriotism hardly seems worth recognizing as a virtue.

To see this, let us look more closely at what MacIntyre's "real" patriotism amounts to. The indented quote (two paragraphs above) says that patriotism requires that I strive to further the interests of my community, apparently without any regard to how my doing so affects the interests of your community (except where I need to consider how that effect will bear on my community). This is disturbing. Despite MacIntyre's statement that patriotism is not mind- less loyalty (p. 4), the patriotism that he describes does indeed seem to be just that. More precisely, it seems to be mindless in one respect but not in another.[13] It is not mindless loyalty in that it *is* based on an appreciation of the merits and achievements of that particular nation. When MacIntyre states that "patriotism is not to be confused with a mindless loyalty to one's own particular nation which has no regard for the characteristics of that particular nation," perhaps he is only concerned to deny that it is mindless in *that* respect. In another respect it is mindless. On any matters which concern her country, the question for MacIntyre's patriot will be, "What is best for my country?" Considerations about the effects on other countries, or on individuals, are ignored. They are irrelevant to the patriot, or to the proponents of the morality of patriotism.

To see the difficulty more vividly, consider what his remarks about what patriotism requires would seem to entail. Suppose that what is distinctive about my community is that we are conspicuous consumers, a town that prides itself on its spanking new, large, sleek, and clean automobiles. We also pride ourselves on our bright green lawns, and the fact that every home has a swimming pool. These are the things we care about. The opulent life is the good life, we think, and the more conspicuous, the better.

A large part of our culture as a community is our pool parties. Alas, we have a water shortage and require exclusive use of a body of water nearby; if we have to share the water with the impoverished and overpopulated town across the border, we will be forced to ration water, and this will mean dirty cars, shabby lawns, and during some months of the year, many swimming pools left sadly empty. If I subscribe to the morality of patriotism, as MacIntyre here describes it, my position is clear: I strive to further the interests of my community. The survival of my community as a distinctive community is, after all, at stake. Never mind that the other community has rather more compelling reasons to use the water, viz., that without it they will be entirely without running water and that a considerable portion of the residents will be without safe drinking water; never mind that it is for them a matter of life or death for thousands in their community, while for us it is a question of survival, all right, but only survival of our "culture."

This example might seem unfair. Perhaps MacIntyre could by spelling out just what he means by "survival as a distinctive community" rule out such examples. But since his own examples are only slightly less disturbing, this seems unlikely. In connection with the second type of conflict, a conflict over what constitutes the good life, he writes the following.

> The administration of the *pax Romana* from time to time required the Roman *imperium* to set its frontiers at the point at which they could be most easily secured, so that the burden of supporting the legions would be reconcilable with the administration of Roman law. And the British empire was no different in its time. But this required infringing upon the territory and the independence of barbarian border peoples. . . . [O]n such issues . . . the impersonal moral standpoint and that of patriotism cannot be reconciled. (pp. 6–7)

His examples support my reading: the patriot is to uphold the interests of his community, even if its interests are its interests only because it is expansionist and imperialist. "Survival" is not intended in a reasonably minimal sense; it is not simply that as a patriot I am to put the survival (i.e., nonannihilation) of the members of my community above that of the members of another community. Rather, I am to put the survival of my community as the particular community that it is before the interests of other communities, even if that means massacring neighboring peoples (or enslaving them?) so as to maintain our integrity as a burgeoning empire, to better establish ourselves as what we distinctively are—e.g., the most powerful military presence in the world—or to grow as a distinctive nation (p. 6).

If this is what patriotism is, there is little reason for worrying about its incompatibility with impartial morality, for there is little reason to accord it any moral value. It hardly seems a weighty challenge to impartial morality to point out that it cannot recognize patriotism, thus understood, as a virtue, for surely it is not a virtue. But rather than leave the matter here, we should consider whether some other conception of patriotism — perhaps the emasculated sort, perhaps some other type — might be more worthy of consideration, and consistent with impartial morality.

V

One revision we might consider could be construed either as a charitable interpretation or as a reconstruction of MacIntyre's patriotism (though the latter construal is more plausible). While his examples as well as his characterization of patriotism suggest that the patriot thinks strictly in terms of what is good for her community, he does not stipulate that the patriot *cannot* pay any attention to other considerations, and someone might suggest that his neglect to mention other considerations was only an oversight. He might not oppose an amendment which would build in a sense of measure, an appreciation that very severe needs on the part of other communities should override comparatively minor needs of his community, as should some other moral considerations.

In a paper similar in spirit to MacIntyre's Lindley lecture, Andrew Oldenquist suggests that a patriot need not take into account *only* considerations having to do with his country's welfare: "the thought, '*p* is my country,' though it counts for something, need not outweigh moral arguments against reprisal or military intervention."[14] Patriotism, like any other loyalty, Oldenquist says, "determines obligations only prima facie."[15]

> Even if someone admits that, say, family loyalty is his strongest loyalty, it should not be forgotten that the good and harm at stake come in degrees. Such a person has no reason to deny that a small family sacrifice still can be outweighed when it is balanced against some great harm to be avoided (or good to be achieved) by his community or his country.[16]

Is this picture of patriotism one which MacIntyre would find attractive or at least tolerable? Or does it count as what he calls "emasculated patriotism"? As Oldenquist conceives it, it decidedly does not count as emasculated patriotism. This is clear from the distinction he draws (and is at pains to emphasize) between his view and a view that holds there to be general principles or values which justify the loyalty of any patriot similarly situated toward her respective community. Patriotism as he conceives it cannot be reconciled with impartial morality, for his patriot does not accept the position that a patriot in another country is as justified in supporting her country because it is hers as he is justified in supporting his because it is his. Oldenquist and his patriot do not recognize "universalized patriotic obligations."[17]

His view might thus be acceptable to MacIntyre, since his patriotism is not the type that MacIntyre dismissed as emasculated. The revision it suggests for MacIntyre's conception of patriotism might seem to address the most worrisome problem we found with that conception without rendering it compatible with the morality of liberalism. Insofar as patriotism, thus revised, is a virtue, the suggestion that it is a flaw of impartial morality that it cannot regard patriotism as a virtue has been buttressed. It has been buttressed, that is, if patriotism really *can* be revised in the way suggested without rendering it compatible with impartial morality—and if there isn't an equally good or better conception of patriotism which is consistent with impartial morality.

But in fact there is good reason for doubting that patriotism can be revised in the way suggested without "emasculating" it. The problem is this. By denying that patriotism is compatible with impartial morality, Oldenquist has deprived himself and his patriot of any way to make sense of the idea of balancing one good against another. The "good and harm at stake" do indeed "come in degrees," but to have a sense of measure we have to be able to step back from them, to adopt a standpoint other than that of our own group's interest. If the patriot is not to look at the action he thinks of as patriotic from an "external" standpoint, and see if it is defensible from that standpoint, what are we to make of the suggestion that he can compare the magnitude of the expected benefit or harm to his community with that expected to acrue to the wider community, or to the general good? Or again, how is the patriot supposed to take into account "moral arguments against reprisal or military intervention" as arguments that weigh *against* doing what is best for his community, if he is not to take a detached perspective and weigh the conflicting considerations from that standpoint? The dilemma is clear: *either* the patriot is going to lack a sense of measure which takes into account considerations other than those of the good of his community *or* he is going to have to take an external perspective and try to judge impartially, rather than as someone from Community A who is concerned only with the good of Community A.

It looks, in short, as if there is no avoiding emasculated patriotism unless we want to give up on the idea that patriotism is a virtue rather than a vice. Either patriotism is not a virtue, because it doesn't allow the patriot to take into account (in deciding whether to support a particular social policy, etc.) considerations other than those of his community's interests, or it allows this and in so allowing recognizes it to be right to adopt an "external" standpoint, and to try to judge impersonally and impartially. But on the latter disjunct patriotism is "emasculated," by MacIntyre's standards (and consistent with impartial morality).

Another set of considerations also leads us to the conclusion that there is no avoiding emasculated patriotism. Let us take as our point of departure an exchange that MacIntyre imagines between a proponent of the morality of liberalism and a defender of the morality of patriotism. The latter, MacIntyre suggests, might challenge the former in the following manner:

[L]iberal morality requires of me to assume an abstract and artificial—perhaps even an impossible—stance, that of a rational being as such, responding to the requirements of morality not qua parent or farmer or quarterback, but qua rational agent who has abstracted him or herself from all social particularity, who has become not merely Adam Smith's impartial spectator, but a correspondingly impartial actor, and one who in his impartiality is doomed to rootlessness, to be a citizen of nowhere. How can I justify to myself performing this act of abstraction and detachment?

MacIntyre envisions the following as the liberal's reply: "such abstraction and detachment is . . . a necessary condition of moral freedom, of emancipation from the bondage of the social, political and economic *status quo*" (p. 12). Commenting on the reply, he observes: "Thus liberal morality does after all appeal to an overriding good, the good of this particular kind of emancipating freedom" (p. 12).

A more likely liberal reply would be that although we need to be able to take up the standpoint of the impartial spectator, we need not—and ought not—*live* in it. Why do we need to be able to take up that standpoint at all? Because the willingness, on the part of those who disagree, to take it up is our only hope of finding a way of living together in harmony, living together in a way that involves respect—and not a condescending respect which hardly deserves the label 'respect,' but equal respect. In a tiny harmonious community, such detachment may not be necessary. (It might, however. Otherwise dissent or nonstandard lifestyles may be impossible, requiring those whose sexual orientation or religious practices do not conform to the traditions of the community either to leave the community or to conceal their differences.) But in a larger community or in a world with many communities, it is critical that people be able and willing to view themselves and others as *persons*, not exclusively as particular persons who are either "us" or "others."

Like the reply that MacIntyre envisions, this reply could also be said to appeal to an overriding good (though it is perhaps more accurately thought of as an ideal); but this time it is the possibility of cohabiting the earth harmoniously with people different from us. Nor is this all; for there are many ways to achieve harmony. It is part of this ideal that harmony is not won by conquering and subduing, enslaving or pacifying. To the extent that it is attained, harmony is rooted in a stance of impartiality, a stance which is based on the ideals of respect and equality. This overriding good will, I think, strike many as more meaningful and more pressing than the rather vague good of "emancipating freedom."

VI

Patriotism, I have been arguing, deserves to be regarded as a virtue only if it is what MacIntyre calls "emasculated"—that is, defensible from an impartial stance and thus consistent with impartiality. Why is this position, which seems so sensible as to border on boring, found so repugnant? Why is it resisted? Four reasons come to mind, some of them suggested by MacIntyre's discussion.

First, emasculated patriotism may be thought not to leave room for particularity. Second, the "detachment" required if patriotism has to be defensible from an impartial stance may seem drastic. Third, there are times, it may be said, when patriotism requires one to support one's country, notably at a time of war; yet the requirement of impartiality seems to be at odds with this. Finally, it may seem that given all the "restrictions" on patriotism, it is left without any content. With respect to what is a patriot whose patriotism is defensible from an impartial stance to be patriotic? If, contrary to MacIntyre's assertion, patriotism does not entail "a willingness to go to war on one's community's behalf" (p. 6), what does it entail?

Let us take these objections one at a time. The first asks whether patriotism can leave room for particularity if it is required to be consistent with impartiality—that is, defensible from an impartial stance. Oldenquist expresses the worry when he derisively characterizes what he labels "impartial patriotism" as follows. The "impartial patriot" holds "that he ought to support whichever country has features *a* . . . *n*; and as luck would have it, that happens to be his own country."[18] This view, Oldenquist asserts and MacIntyre agrees, should not even count as patriotism. It involves no essential particularity, no ineliminable possessive pronouns or proper names.[19]

Must patriotism, to be impartial, be what Oldenquist calls "impartial patriotism"? No. Recall our distinction between two levels at which impartiality might be required. There is no reason to think that patriotism has to be impartial at level one just because it has to be impartial at level two. To see this, consider familial love, friendship, and other special ties: they involve an essential particularity, yet at the same time are consistent with impartiality. Impartiality does not require that I love everyone equally; it just requires that whatever I do in the name of love (or love for my sister) be equally permissible for anyone to do in the name of love (or love for her or his sister). There is an essential particularity to special ties: I have a special fondness for my friend. It is not a fondness for humanity which, because she was there, a convenient subject on which to focus my love for humans as such, happened to "land" on her. Similarly with my love for my child: it is not love for all children (or all people) which I choose to bestow on my child, judging that it is best if people direct their love for children to a particular object, and if they have a child, make that child their object. However, if I defend a course of action based on that love — e.g., finagling a job for my daughter in the agency where I work — my defense will be general. It will not involve an essential particularity. Even if I said "It's my daughter!" by way of defense, what I said (if it purports to be a justification) is shorthand for something like "It's my daughter, and I think it quite all right for anyone to do that for his or her child." My justification would indicate that the partiality involved (doing something for my child because she's my child; or putting my child before other children) is fine for anyone: the action taken is something that I think is okay for anyone to take. Patriotism works the same way: it is consistent with impartiality, i.e., with the requirement that for one's actions to be permissible, they must be permissible for anyone in relevantly similar circumstances.

These points provide an answer to the second objection as well as the first. One might grant that there is some wisp of particularity that can be a part of "emasculated" patriotism (and likewise of "emasculated" friendship and familial love), but maintain that the particularity is not robust enough. The problem, it might be said, is that one must be *detached*. In a passage quoted above MacIntyre complains of that "abstract and artificial . . . stance, that of a rational being as such, responding to the requirements of morality . . . *qua* rational agent . . . who has become not merely Adam Smith's impartial spectator, but a correspondingly impartial actor, and one who in his impartiality is doomed to rootlessness, to be a citizen of nowhere." Once we have distinguished two levels at which impartiality might be required, it is clear that nothing as dramatic as the detachment that MacIntyre describes is involved. The requirement that one take an abstract, general perspective and ask whether it is permissible from that perspective to support, for example, one's country's immigration policy, does not condemn one to "rootlessness." It does not ask us to pretend, throughout our lives, in our every activity, that we are not from any particular country or to treat the fact that we *are* as no more important than, say, the time of day at which we were born. This would be a ludicrous requirement. But impartiality at level two does not require this at all; it requires only that we be able to justify our actions and our views, including those that are based on the claims of patriotism, by general principles. The justification need not be direct: my immediate justification may be "This is my country," but that cannot be the final justification.

Impartiality at level two requires that we adopt a detached perspective at the relevant times, i.e., that we take up a particular perspective for certain purposes. That MacIntyre thinks this a preposterous expectation is hinted at in much of his writing but made explicit in a review of Bernard Williams's *Moral Luck*. Commenting on a retort that Thomas Nagel makes to Williams ("Why can't there be, as different defenders of impartial morality have thought, a form of insight about our non-unique place in the world which leads us to acknowledge that we should live in a way we can endorse from outside, and for everyone similarly situated, as well as from within?"), MacIntyre says, "If the argument is posed in these terms, Williams is surely going to win. The transformation of *me* with purely personal motivations that are distinctively *mine* into a moral agent of pure impersonality who is *anyone* legislating for *everyone* seems a project for moral alchemists rather than for philosophers."[20] We need not linger over this claim; a famous passage from Hume's *Treatise* supplies all the reply that is needed.

> Our situation, with regard both to persons and things, is in continual fluctuation; and a man, that lies at a distance from us, may, in a little time, become a familiar acquaintance. Besides, every particular man has a peculiar position with regard to others; and 'tis impossible we cou'd ever converse together on any reasonable terms, were each of us to consider characters and persons, only as they appear from his peculiar point of view. In order, therefore, to prevent those continual *contradictions*, and arrive at a more *stable* judgment of things, we fix on some *steady* and *general* points of view; and always, in our thoughts, place ourselves in them, whatever may be our present situation. In like manner, external beauty is determin'd merely by pleasure; and 'tis evident, a beautiful countenance cannot give so much pleasure, when seen at the distance of twenty paces, as when it is brought nearer us. We say not, however, that it appears to us less beautiful: Because we know what effect it will have in such a position; and by that reflexion we correct its momentary appearance.[21]

No "alchemy" is needed; we quite routinely alter our perspectives, recognizing that ours is not the only one, and indeed simple conversation—conversation at a degree of sophistication beyond that of, roughly, a four-year-old—leads us to speak and judge from perspectives other than our own. We can retain our "particularity" while learning to think from other perspectives, perspectives of varying degrees of "generality." And so it works with special ties, such as friendship and patriotism.

VII

This addresses the first two objections to "emasculated" patriotism. I turn now to the third, which concerns the patriot's readiness to take his country's side at a time of war, and moreover to go to war. This was the centerpiece of MacIntyre's rejection of "emasculated" patriotism. Patriotism, he said, "entails a willingness to go to war on one's community's behalf" certainly where the survival of the community is at stake and "sometimes perhaps even when only large interests" of the community are at stake (p. 6). Yet if patriotism is required to be consistent with impartiality, the patriot will take her country's side only if she judges that it would be permissible for a citizen of another country in relevantly similar circumstances to take her country's side.

MacIntyre does not explicitly reject this requirement, and portrays the "liberal moralist's" view of the situation somewhat differently. He says that when a conflict between communities arises over, for instance, scarce resources, "the standpoint of impersonal morality requires an allocation of goods such that each individual person counts for one and no more than one" (p. 6). This introduces an extraneous issue: whether we are to think in terms of the needs of individuals or in terms of the needs of communities. The standpoint of "impersonal morality" need not differ from that of MacIntyre's patriot with respect to this issue.[22] But I take it that he would reject the impartiality requirement, which obviously qualifies the patriot's readiness to support her country at a time of war and to take up arms against those proclaimed "the enemy." Such qualification is a mark against the morality of liberalism, and unqualified willingness to come to one's country's "defense" tells, he thinks, strongly in favor of the morality of patriotism.[23]

To someone convinced that MacIntyre is correct and that patriotism, understood to require what he says it requires, is a virtue, I have no argument. What I can do is display more fully what MacIntyre's position entails and what seems to be left out (or rather, ruled out of court), and in that way leave the reader better able to decide what to think on this matter.

First, it is worth noting that his position entails that a pacifist cannot be a patriot. This seems to me a most unfortunate implication, but I shall say no more about it, and to simplify matters (but not to acquiesce in the assumption that pacifists cannot be patriots) will limit my discussion of potential patriots to nonpacifists.

Turning now to nonpacifists, I take it that the virtuous person would see her country's interest to be *one* consideration that bears on a decision as to whether to go to war (or to support her government's plan or threat to go to war), but not the sole consideration.[24] Imagine someone who loves her country and sees its demise (as the community it is) to be a terrible thing, yet also takes very seriously the effects of a war, especially a protracted one. If she believes that her community can be saved with fairly little bloodshed—suppose she thinks that the "enemy" community will quit fighting once it emerges how effectively her side fights—then she may well judge that they should go to war. Not necessarily, however, for there are other considerations to take into account. Surely if she is virtuous she will ask herself just what the death of their community will mean for her and for her compatriots: will it reemerge as a very different sort of community, yet still linked by common bonds, still constituted by roughly the same people, and their offspring? Or will they be, rather, vigorously oppressed, and thus unable (except at enormous cost) to remain a community? In addition, she will, if she is virtuous, take into account what claims each party has to whatever is contested (land, autonomy, etc.). And of course she will take into account death other than death of communities: if her community dies because all the people in it are massacred, that is considerably worse than death by transformation into a very different sort of community, or even death through emigration.

I see no oddity in the idea that a patriotic person would take into account the likely costs of going to war and those of not going to war. The wise patriotic person would ask both whether her community is, in the latter scenario, likely to undergo a transformation but still survive, and if so, in what form it is likely to reemerge, and what the effects on the individuals will be if their community is either thus transformed or completely destroyed (because its members choose to flee, or because the mores, laws, or even physical arrangement of the society into which it is incorporated weaken the communal bond).[25] Even if she judges that the effects on her community will be very bad, the patriot should consider whether these are the sorts of changes that often come anyway, and may take place even if a war is "successfully" fought. Is it futile to expect to preserve her community as it is? And is war, in addition to taking a large toll on human life, likely to change the community, even if it is successful?[26]

These are the kinds of considerations that a virtuous person would take into account. If it is unpatriotic to do so, then patriotism is not a virtue or if a virtue, a virtue very much in need of tempering. But I see no reason why we have to understand patriotism as precluding that one take into account such considerations.

One might reply that MacIntyre is not barred from saying that the patriot should be mindful of at least some of these considerations — at least those that do not call upon the patriot to adopt a "nonpartisan" perspective. (The patriot, he said, is "required to be partisan" [p. 7].) I do not think it is enough to grant this — if indeed MacIntyre would grant it. Think of the matter in the following way:

Imagine that two countries, despite their lack of ill will, have a border dispute. Imagine that some citizens of one of the countries consider two options (having decided that they really need to have the dispute resolved, and really want the land that is contested). One option is to take the matter to the World Court, if the two countries can agree to make a joint request. The other is to go to war. Suppose that the discussants (all of nation A) agree that (a) their country is more powerful militarily than the other, and therefore likely to win the war and (b) the determination of the World Court will probably be a compromise for each nation and thus less favorable to nation A than the agreement that the two nations would sign after a war.

Now, if the discussants considering these two options disagree — to simplify, there are just two, and one favors going to war, while the other favors taking the matter to the World Court — must we regard the latter as less patriotic? He is giving a lower priority to the interests of his country than is his interlocutor because (we imagine) he is taking the toll on human life — on both sides — and war's other disastrous effects into account. Of course one might argue that it is in fact in his country's interest to remain on good terms with the neighboring country, and this certainly is better achieved by jointly requesting a determination by the World Court than by waging war. And in this way his patriotism might be vindicated. But must he defend his stance in terms of his country's interests? Must he, to be virtuous? No. There is nothing wrong at all—nothing that betokens a flaw in character or conduct—in taking into account the loss of life (or arable land) to the other country, taking it into account as such, not in terms of what effects this will have on one's own country. But must he defend his stance in terms of his country's interests if he is patriotic? I see no reason why patriotism should require this. It is not the case that to be a friend, one must base any decisions that affect one's friend on what is in one's friend's interests—e.g., decisions whether to vote for the friend in an election in which she is a candidate, whether to lie for her on the witness stand, whether to cancel one's vacation so as to help her to move across town. The same is true of being a good parent, a good son or daughter, a good sibling, and a good club member. (If it were not, one couldn't both be a good friend and a good club member or good son, and couldn't be a good friend to more than one person.) Why should patriotism be any different?[27]

VIII

The fourth objection I want to consider is that patriotism thus fettered by the requirement that it be consistent with impartiality is rendered empty, insubstantial. The challenge is to indicate what sort of content patriotism, thus constrained, could have, and what its expression would be. In this last section I will sketch one such form of patriotism with the aim that it meet four conditions. It should be consistent with the requirement of impartiality, suitably replete with particularity, and a plausible candidate for being a virtue, and it should also bear some resemblance, however little, to what we think of as patriotism.[28] I am more hopeful of showing that patriotism can be conceived in a way that meets these conditions than I am of figuring out the best way to construe patriotism, and hope that my sketch will prompt readers to propose other ways of construing patriotism which they think better meet these conditions.

Put very generally, the characteristic expression of patriotism, as I envision it, would be a *greater (and qualitatively different) concern for the flourishing of one's own country than for that of any other.* 'Flourishing' here includes moral excellence, as well as, or (depending on how broadly we understand 'moral') including, cultural excellence. Patriotism is a love of one's country, but the form of expression that this love takes is remote from jingoism, and no more based on a correlative disdain for other countries than your love for your parents is based on a disdain for other people's parents.

The patriot's concern for the flourishing of her country will have a different character than her concern for the flourishing of other countries, because it is her country, and she sees herself as part of it. The more specific expression that this takes will of course vary from person to person; an example might be a greater concern to preserve historic buildings or a wilderness area in one's own country than in another country (where the preference can't be explained by a difference in proximity). This patriotism thus preserves a feature that MacIntyre emphasizes: the patriot's tie to her country is based on its being *her* country, not on its being, in her view, the country most deserving of support. But it differs in two crucial respects from the way we, at least in the United States, typically think of patriotism, and because of these differences it will strike some as not having much to do with patriotism.

First, it is not based on an adversarial or Us-against-Them attitude. Patriotism, if it is a virtue, has none of the hatefulness that Emma Goldman correctly identifies in the sort of patriotism that is appealed to in defense of military expansion. If an adversarial attitude is not the basis of patriotism, then a desire to gain or retain military superiority over other nations (or in other ways to be, as standard jingoistic jargon puts it, "the most powerful nation on earth") is no inherent part of patriotism. That is not to say that a desire for military superiority has nothing to do with this reconstructed patriotism. In circumstances where one believes with good reason that another country with a comparable or superior military force is plotting to overthrow the government of her own country, a nonpacifist patriot will (especially if there is good reason to believe that the government that emerges after the coup will be far worse than the present one) favor military escalation to thwart the aggressor's attempts, and if possible to discourage it from making the attempt in the first place.

While support for military escalations in circumstances such as those I have described is certainly to be expected of patriots (excluding pacifist patriots), as is a willingness to make sacrifices on behalf of one's country when so much is at stake, standard conceptions of patriotism in the United States put far greater emphasis on these sorts of expressions of patriotism than is in order. Moreover, in putting emphasis on these expressions, common views of patriotism portray the person who is most ready to fight, most enthusiastic about military escalation, least trusting of those who at times appear to be a threat to our country, and most ready to take "preemptive" measures, as the most patriotic. The more virulently anti-Communist, the more patriotic.[29]

Patriotism as I envision it would place far less emphasis on militaristic expressions of patriotism and far more on expressions which tend to be ignored: a sense of culture, an interest in the history of one's community (not to be confused with a stubborn pride which refuses to recognize terrible mistakes), a concern to improve one's community. But before saying more about this, let me explain the second respect in which this reconstructed patriotism differs sharply from the way that we usually understand patriotism.

The second difference is located in the nature of the patriot's concern with the moral excellence of his or her community. On the standard picture, the patriot believes firmly in his country's moral superiority, indeed, so firmly that he is reluctant to consider the possibility that his country's history contains shameful chapters (or if he admits that it does, he prefers that these chapters be ignored, especially by schoolteachers). He tends to be even less willing to subject his government and society as it currently is to moral scrutiny than he is to question past practices, though of course there are eras where the mood is one of dissent or revolution, and at that time he will be quick to condemn the upstarts—and if his government consists of upstarts, he will criticize it, too. In contrast, the concern of the patriot, in the idealized sense of 'patriotism,' is not to adhere to the view that his community is morally flawless, but to recognize injustices and strive to overcome them. The latter's concern with the moral excellence of his community takes the form of a commitment to improve his community, not to defend it against every criticism or to argue that it is the morally best community. It spurs him to take action, to join in civic projects, at times to protest government policies that he believes to be immoral; it does not tempt him toward complacency or (collective) self-deception.

Although this way of thinking about patriotism certainly does not accord with the usual ways of thinking about it in our culture, I think that it does accord with the intuitions, or more precisely the experiences, of a lot of us. My horror at my country's bombing of Libya or attack on Grenada is of a different character than my horror at France's bombing of the Greenpeace ship, the *Rainbow Warrior.* By the same token, my glee, my sense of a community accomplishment when President Reagan's nomination of Robert Bork to the Supreme Court was defeated has a special character which is absent from my pleasure at a comparable event abroad. This is not just because I realize that the constitution of the Supreme Court will affect my life and the lives of those to whom I am close. My delight is not based only on these pragmatic thoughts, but also reflects a sense of pride in us as a society for caring this much about individual rights and social justice, and devoting the time and energy needed to thwart this threat to (among other things) progress toward racial and sexual equality.

I emphasize this sense of pride, because it is often easier to pinpoint as an expression of patriotism that is familiar to many of us the shame we feel over our government's actions—and over our compatriots, for supporting a leader we believe to be morally abominable. While this shame *does* reflect a concern for our country's flourishing, and thus really does, I think, express a patriotic attitude, the claim that it expresses patriotism might understandably raise suspicions if it were the only form we could cite in which our alleged patriotism is expressed. But there is pride as well as shame, and there is commitment, too— commitment to trying to improve our community, rather than giving up on it.

A special tie to one's particular community is important for some of the reasons that MacIntyre brings out in his Lindley lecture and his other work: it helps to provide one with a sense of identity, of belonging, and of a culture, and to protect one against rootlessness and isolation. Yet since the special tie is not based on an assumption of superiority to other communities, or a mission of converting them to one's own society's ways or, if that fails, destroying them, or on bettering the lot of one's own community at the expense—no matter how great—of other communities, patriotism as I have described it is not encumbered by the morally dubious aspects that infect both traditional patriotism and (to a lesser extent) MacIntyre's patriotism. The special tie is not based on, or conducive to, hostility toward outsiders or disdain for other ways of organizing a community. This point needs further development. ? ??

The expressions that patriotism (as reconstructed) takes are not typically at odds with those of members of other communities. Canadians' efforts to sharpen their sense of Canadian culture are not at odds with the efforts of citizens of other countries to define and appreciate their culture. A sense of Canadian pride is not in conflict with a sense of U.S. pride (unless the pride takes the corrupt form of arrogance, or of a silly competitiveness ["Our poetry is better than yours!"]). More generally, patriotism need not set countries or communities against one another; the tie that A feels to A's community need not be in tension (except in times of war) with B's tie to B's community.

If the standard expression of patriotism is a concern to promote the moral flourishing of one's community—if it is this, rather than a concern to promote the interest of one's community, that best characterizes patriotism—then in general, none of us is worse off for the existence of patriots in other countries. There is a basic harmony in everyone's being patriotic, as there is not in everybody's being patriotic either in the way that patriotism is generally thought of or as MacIntyre understands patriotism. Indeed, we will often be better off for the existence of patriots in other countries. Patriots everywhere will— depending on how virtuous they are, and how much time and opportunity they have for such activities—strive to make their communities morally better.

In *After Virtue* MacIntyre criticizes the turn away from Aristotelianism toward thinking of morality as "offering a solution to the problems posed by human egoism." On the Aristotelian view,

> what education in the virtues teaches me is that my good as a man is one and the same as the good of those others with whom I am bound up in human community. There is no way of my pursuing my good which is necessarily antagonistic to you pursuing yours because *the* good is neither mine peculiarly nor yours peculiarly—goods are not private property. Hence Aristotle's definition of friendship, the fundamental form of human relationship, is in terms of shared goods. The egoist is thus, in the ancient and medieval world, always someone who has made a fundamental mistake about where his own good lies and someone who has thus and to that extent excluded himself from human relationships.[30]

An analogous point could be made about MacIntyre's patriot. The patriot is too individualistic, where the unit is not individual persons, but individual cultures. *Our flourishing as a culture need not be at odds with another culture's flourishing.*

MacIntyre's emphasis on the patriot's commitment to the nation as a "morally distinctive community" (more fully: "the nation conceived as a project, a project . . . brought to birth in the past and carried on so that a morally distinctive community was brought into being . . . [p. 13]") bears the imprint of that individualism that he deplores. Why suppose that each nation *has* a distinctive project? If the assumption is rejected, it becomes easier for patriots to care about the flourishing of their particular nations without being unreasonable about it, since flourishing need not be defined in terms of a particular project and thus can be flexible, more reconcilable with the claims of impartial morality.

One might object that I am overlooking a problem. While my proposed understanding of patriotism facilitates greater harmony between patriots on an international level, it might threaten to increase conflict between patriotic compatriots. What if they have sharply opposing views of what constitutes the moral flourishing of their community? In this scenario patriotism would hardly be a desirable character trait! The existence of a lot of people striving to make their community morally better is a blessing only insofar as their conception of moral excellence is tolerably plausible, and their notions of what means it is permissible to use to forward their aims tolerably acceptable.

This is a complex problem, and I cannot hope to deal with it adequately here. One solution, suggested by recent work by Rawls and Nagel, would be to circumscribe the moral considerations that are appropriately the concern of a patriot, so as to rule out of court considerations which, while appropriate for individuals or perhaps a small group of people trying to improve their characters and lives, should not be appealed to in proposing how to improve the larger community. Appeal to such a division would work best if the patriots were in fact citizens of what Rawls calls "the well-ordered society," since in such a society there is a public conception of justice, against which social institutions are to be evaluated and in light of which reforms are proposed.[31] There it would be clear that striving for the moral excellence of one's community should not take the form of, say, struggling to convert as many people as possible to one's religion. But even without the public consensus provided by a conception of justice supported in a community by an overlapping consensus, one could appeal to the underlying idea of distinguishing between a public standpoint, and methods of justification acceptable from the public standpoint, and on the other hand the various conceptions of morality that we have as individuals or as members of particular political or religious organizations, and modes of debating or reasoning about moral issues that we use within these contexts. This approach would be tantamount to clarifying and expanding the impartiality requirement, so as to indicate at what level of generality, or how described, my "acts" are to meet the requirement.[32]

Assuming that this problem can be adequately addressed, I think that the conception of patriotism I have outlined meets the four conditions listed above: it is suitably replete with particularity, in keeping with the requirement of

impartiality, not entirely disconnected from what we usually think of as patriotism, and a plausible candidate for being a virtue—all the more plausible
because it recognizes the responsibilities we have, especially as citizens in a
democracy, for our country's policies.[33]

POSTSCRIPT (NOVEMBER 2001)

I wrote this essay in the Reagan years. At that time, the main patriotic sentiment that I could identify in myself was shame over appalling actions taken by
my government. I saw that sentiment (and still do) as a reflection of patriotism,
understood as a greater concern for the flourishing, including the moral flourishing, of one's nation than for the flourishing of any other nation. For examples of other patriotic sentiments that I thought of as at least not vicious, I usually looked to other countries—imagining, for instance, the patriotic sentiments of a Nicaraguan in the face of the attempt by the United States to
topple, by various strategies, the Sandinista government.

Now there are more "local" sentiments for me to draw upon. The sentiments aroused from being under attack, where the attack (at least the one on
the World Trade Center) seems to have been aimed specifically at killing as
many civilians as possible, merit philosophical scrutiny, more than I can provide in this brief postscript. Instead, I'll consider the following question (with
a few side comments on patriotism today in the United States): if I were
writing the essay now, would only the examples be different, or would the
position I took on patriotism also be different?

I have no doubts about the following: there is no incompatibility between
treating patriotism as a virtue and accepting "liberal morality." Although one
hears such expressions as "If I were commander in chief, we'd have nuked
them in hours, turned Afghanistan into a sand puddle,"[34] few thinking people
would regard it as unpatriotic to dissent from that view of how the United
States should have proceeded. Of course even the person who endorses Mac-
Intyre's idea that the patriot must put his own country's interests first would
dissent, since such a response to the September 11 attack would hardly be in
the interest of the United States. But quite apart from that, it seems clear that
it is *not* unpatriotic to take into account the welfare of the Afghan people. It
has been encouraging to see very little suggestion that it is unpatriotic for U.S.
citizens to express concern for the plight of the Afghan people, or to suggest
that we should halt the bombing at least long enough to address the humanitarian crisis. That my compatriots (from what I can tell) share this view—that
they apparently endorse what MacIntyre regards as an emasculated patriotism—contributes to a sense of solidarity.

What about my claim that patriotism is best understood as a greater concern for the flourishing, including the moral flourishing, of one's own nation,

than that of any other nation? That, too, I see no reason to give up, but I would add now that this sentiment is closely related to a sense of solidarity with one's compatriots. The solidarity arises not only from the sense of being under attack as a group, and from experiencing in common what for most of us is an unfamiliar sense of insecurity.[35] It also arises (speaking for myself) from pride in such facts as that we are debating openly (at least in such publications as the *Nation*), and that though there are social pressures to wave the flag, mindless (or even thoughtful!) support for our country's military actions is not socially required—at least where I live in the U.S. It has been interesting, given my view that a concern with the moral flourishing of one's nation is part of patri-otism, to observe that moral self-scrutiny has itself been an issue in the debate since September 11, with some bravely saying that we need to think about why we are hated, and consider how we should perhaps conduct ourselves, as a nation, differently, and others taking this amiss, as if it entailed that we deserved to have airplanes flown into the World Trade Center. There seems, at least, not to be a consensus that to morally evaluate the role our nation plays in the world is unpatriotic, and I find that somewhat encouraging.

What about that flag-waving? Why is it that some of us, while not thinking that patriotism is a vice, choose not to wave our flags? The difficulty is that in the United States, anyway, flag-waving is often interpreted as a call to go to war (or as approval, even enthusiasm, for our military activities). Indeed there was a public sentiment, expressed by those in the Bush adminis-tration and those in the media, that the flag-waving in the weeks just after Sep-tember 11 *was* a demand that we take military action. The public was told to "Be patient," as if there was great eagerness to wage war, and to do so as soon as possible. It is unfortunate that we don't have a way to display patriotic feel-ings at such a time that is not interpreted as a call for war.

There is another matter I want to mention here, realizing that I said too little about it in my essay. I argued that patriotism, properly understood, is not incompatible with impartial morality—and more generally, that it is permis-sible; but is it a virtue? Is it more virtuous to have a special, and greater, con-cern for the flourishing of one's own nation than to feel just as much concern for the flourishing of other nations as for the flourishing of one's own nation? Is it more virtuous to feel particularly badly for the New Yorkers than to feel no greater anguish for them than for those in another country afflicted by roughly comparable suffering, and to feel greater anguish for those, such as the Afghan civilians, whose suffering is on the whole far greater than that of most New Yorkers? I am reluctant to say that it is more virtuous. It is easier to see the virtue of patriotism if we focus on a part of it that I emphasized in my essay: a greater concern for the moral flourishing of one's own country than for the moral flourishing of any other country. It is only appropriate to be more concerned to right the wrongs of one's own nation, and to feel shame for its failure to sign on to international accords or to stand by the Kyoto Accord, and its periodic unnecessary waging of war, than to be concerned to right the wrongs of another nation. Whether it is more virtuous to be concerned especially with the flourishing of one's own nation than the flourishing of others—apart from the moral flourishing—is, however, less clear to me. It has been noted in the press that reactions among Americans to the attacks divide into those who view it as an attack on America (or perhaps, Americans) and those who view it as an attack on people (or perhaps, civilians).[36] I certainly do not see the first as more virtuous than the second; nor do I see any greater virtue in a focus on how the attacks affect the well-being of America and Americans than on how they affect people (or the world) in general.[37]

NOTES

1. Alasdair MacIntyre, "Is Patriotism a Virtue?" (Lawrence: University of Kansas, 1984). Page numbers to this essay will be given parenthetically in the text of the paper.

2. For insight into how they are connected, see Ronald Dworkin's "Liberalism" and especially Thomas Nagel's "Moral Conflict and Political Legitimacy." "Liberalism" first appeared in *Public and Private Morality*, ed. Stuart Hampshire (New York: Cambridge University Press, 1978), pp. 113–43 and is reprinted, slightly revised, as chap. 8 of Dworkin's *A Matter of Principle* (Cambridge: Harvard University Press, 1985). "Moral Conflict and Political Legitimacy" is in *Philosophy and Public Affairs* 16, no. 3 (summer 1987): 215–40.

3. Emma Goldman, "Patriotism: A Menace to Liberty," in her *Anarchism and Other Essays* (1910; reprint, Port Washington, N.Y.: Kennikat Press, 1969), pp. 134–45.

4. In *The Tin Trumpet* (1836). Quoted in the *Oxford English Dictionary*.

5. We should note that although we usually think of patriotism as loyalty to one's nation, there is also what the *Oxford English Dictionary* calls "local patriotism," and one possible position is that patriotism is a virtue only if sufficiently "local." Objections to nationalism thus need not be objections to seeing patriotism (in all forms) as a virtue. If patriotism is understood as devotion to the well-being of one's nation, someone who advocates aiming to form an international commonwealth, in which individual nations, if they remain as separate nations, shape our identities and loyalties far less than they now do, would have reason to regard patriotism as a vice. If, however, patriotism can take the form of loyalty to one's town or province, moral qualms about nationalism provide less reason to reject the view that patriotism (in certain forms) is a virtue. (Of course if the towns or provinces had standing armies or became militarized, the same worries about nationalism might emerge in connection with local patriotism. If nations withered away and towns and cities came to function militarily as small nations, the "internationalist" would have as much reason to find local patriotism objectionable as she now has with respect to national patriotism.)

6. I will follow MacIntyre in understanding patriotism to be roughly the same as loyalty to one's country and in regarding the elements of hierarchy and obedience to authority suggested by 'patr' (and affirmed in common parlance as well as some classical writings) to be nonessential to patriotism.

7. The five positions he lists are as follows: (1) "morality is constituted by rules to which any rational person would under certain ideal conditions give assent"; (2) "those rules impose constraints upon and are neutral between rival and competing interests — morality itself is not the expression of any particular interest"; (3) "those rules are also neutral between rival and competing sets of beliefs about what the best way for human beings to live is"; (4) "the units which provide the subject-matter of morality as well as its agents are individual human beings and . . . in moral evaluations each individual is to count for one and nobody for more than one"; and (5) "the standpoint of the moral agent constituted by allegiances to these rules is one and the same for all moral agents and as such is independent of all social particularity" (pp. 7–8).

8. What it takes for a country to be mine I will not address here, but it is worth noting that MacIntyre's examples are of patriots who are "from" the country to which they are patriotic. Its past is their past, and so on. (See his *After Virtue*, 2d ed. [Notre Dame: University of Notre Dame, 1987], chap. 15.) His account might not accommodate the patriotism of a naturalized citizen who prior to adulthood had never been in the country to which she now is loyal.

Questions of MacIntyre's account aside, it is, interestingly, not clear what *should* determine whether a country is mine. (1) Is there anything wrong with feeling patriotic both toward one's country of origin and toward the country of which I am a citizen? I would think not; though the expressions of patriotism toward each country, like the bases of the patriotism, would probably differ. (2) A question Henry Sidgwick brings up: Can one "by voluntary expatriation . . . rightfully relieve himself of all moral obligations to the community in which he was born?" In a footnote Sidgwick comments, "In 1868 it was affirmed, in an Act passed by the Congress of the United States, that 'the right of expatriation is a natural and inherent right of all people.' I do not know how far this would be taken to imply that a man has a moral right to leave his country whenever he finds it convenient—provided no claims except those of Patriotism retain him there. But if it was intended to imply this, I think the statement would not be accepted in Europe without important limitations: though I cannot state any generally accepted principle from which such limitations could be clearly deduced." *The Methods of Ethics*, 7th ed. (New York: Dover Publications, 1966), p. 252.

9. Although I will not emphasize the distinction between impartiality and impersonality, a clarification may be helpful. Impartiality is in conflict with the requirement that I put American interests first. Impersonality clashes with the requirement that I judge as an American, i.e., allow my American attitudes, ideals, ways of thinking, etc. to affect my judgment. The requirements of impartiality and impersonality are, of course, related: a reason why it is supposed to be so important to judge impersonally — as a generic person—is that insofar as I succeed in doing so I avoid slanting my judgment in favor of my interest, or my group's interest. For a helpful discussion of the distinction between impersonality and impartiality, see Adrian Piper, "Moral Theory and Moral Alienation," *Journal of Philosophy* 84, no. 2 (February 1987): 102–18.

10. For simplicity, I am focussing on impartiality; but similar points could be made concerning impersonality.

11. More cautiously he says that to critics of the morality of liberalism it "appears to be emasculated." But it is clear that he counts himself among those critics and is asserting that such a patriotism is emasculated.

12. It is not clear why it would be unpatriotic to adopt a position of tolerance. I suppose MacIntyre would say that a position of tolerance is open to the patriot only insofar as that position is part of (or would it suffice if it were consistent with?) her community's conception of virtue (assuming it has a collective conception).

13. Perhaps we should distinguish two respects in which it is not mindless. A second respect in which it is not mindless is that the patriot, seeking to promote her country's interests, need not be (and if virtuous is not) mindless in seeking to determine what is in her country's interest. She need not, for example, confuse supporting the current government with promoting her country's interest.

14. Andrew Oldenquist, "Loyalties," *Journal of Philosophy* 79, no. 4 (April 1982): 173–93. The quote is from p. 184.

15. Ibid., p. 182.

16. Ibid.

17. Ibid., p. 185. Oldenquist invents the label "sports patriot" to distinguish his patriot from the sports patriot who believes that "each nation's citizens ought to try to further their respective national interests" and thus accepts universalized patriotic obligations (p. 185). I should note that the view I propose in sections VI–VIII is different from that of the sports patriot, though it is closer to it than to any other conception of patriotism that Oldenquist describes.

18. Oldenquist, "Loyalties," p. 183.

19. We think of the impartial patriot as a patriot, Oldenquist believes, only insofar as we think his impartiality is a sham (p. 183).

20. MacIntyre, "The Magic in the Pronoun 'My,'" *Ethics* 94, no. 1 (October 1983): 113–25.

21. David Hume, *A Treatise of Human Nature*, ed. Selby-Bigge (1888; reprint, 1965), pp. 581–82.

22. MacIntyre thinks it does because he takes one of the points of disagreement between the morality of liberalism and that of the patriot to be position #4, quoted above in note 7.

23. MacIntyre's final objection to the morality of liberalism is this: "Every political community except in the most exceptional conditions requires standing armed forces for its minimal security. Of the members of these armed forces it must require both that they be prepared to sacrifice their own lives for the sake of the community's security and that their willingness to do so be not contingent upon their own individual evaluation of the rightness or wrongness of their country's cause on some specific issue, measured by some standard that is neutral and impartial relative to the interests of their own community and the interests of other communities. And, that is to say, good soldiers may not be liberals and must indeed embody in their actions a good deal at least of the morality of patriotism" (pp. 17–18).

24. One might reply, "This would be virtuous; but would it be patriotic?" We need to keep in mind, though, that we are interested not simply in what patriotism is, but in what it is if it is a virtue. Of course one could argue that there may be particular virtues which are such that being virtuous does not coincide with acting as that virtue directs or pulls one, and patriotism may be among those virtues. If so, we need not hold that because it is virtuous to do x, the patriotic person will, if patriotism is a virtue, do x. It is certainly true that the latter doesn't follow from the former; we could hold that

patriotism is a virtue and that the patriot would do x, but that patriotism needs to be tempered, and that the fully virtuous person would do not-x. This is a possibility to keep in mind. Nonetheless, if much tempering is needed, we have reason to question whether the alleged virtue really is a virtue at all. And if it is always the same type of tempering that is needed, it is plausible to suggest that perhaps it isn't V, but V-when-tempered that is the virtue.

25. As an example of how a physical arrangement of the larger society might transform or destroy a community, take the building of a university campus in the midst of a large ethnic community in a major U.S. city (e.g., the University of Illinois at Chicago). Or again, consider an Amish community, once at a safe distance from mainstream America, which gradually finds itself bumping up against the ever-expanding suburbs of a city in the vicinity, and begins to lose some of its youth to the dominant culture.

26. Cf. Sidney Axinn's "Honor, Patriotism and Ultimate Loyalty" in *Nuclear Weapons and the Future of Humanity*, ed. Avner Cohen (Totowa, N.J.: Rowman and Allenheld, 1986), pp. 273–88. Axinn observes, "If one looks at a nation twenty or thirty years after a war, it is not always easy to understand whether it won or lost that war. The point is that whatever the characteristics of a nation, perhaps characteristics so morally sublime that they are worth making the nation an ultimate loyalty, time and war itself will make changes in that nation" (p. 283).

27. Actually, it is different from a parent's special bond to his or her child, but in a way which strengthens the case for my view. Because of the dependency of children on adults, it is important for a parent to show a child unconditional love. This will limit the extent to which other interests can supercede the child's. In particular, while a friend has no obligation to continue to be a good friend to someone who drains all his energy, treats him badly, and so on, a parent does have an obligation to the child which is not conditional on the child being good to the parent. There is no analogous need for unconditional devotion or love on the part of the citizen to her country.

28. That it is a virtue I will not try to show, partly because that would require something I don't have, namely, a general theory (or at least a set of criteria for deciding whether or not something is a virtue). The other reason is that my aim is not the lofty one of showing that properly understood, patriotism is a virtue, but only that there is, for someone who accepts the "morality of liberalism," at least one conception of patriotism which it is plausible for her to hold to be a virtue.

29. No wonder that the many people who testified before Congress in 1987 about their role in the illegal channeling of money to the Contras (seeking to topple the Sandanista government in Nicaragua) were frequently treated by their questioners as heroes—even if heroes who erred.

30. MacIntyre, *After Virtue*, p. 229.

31. The conception of justice includes both "certain principles of justice for the basic structure to specify its content" and "certain guidelines of enquiry and publicly recognized rules of assessing evidence to govern its application." John Rawls, "The Idea of an Overlapping Consensus," *Oxford Journal of Legal Studies* 1, no. 1 (1987).

A different way of constructing my paper would have been to respond to MacIntyre's challenge as follows: "Liberals can value patriotism and be patriotic—read Rawls, and think about the standpoint of a citizen in a well-ordered society." Part of what it means for a society to be well-ordered is that it be stable, where "the stability of a well-ordered society is not founded merely on a perceived balance of social forces the upshot of which all accept since none can do better for themselves. On the contrary," Rawls explains in the Dewey Lectures ("Kantian Constructivism in Moral Theory," *Journal of Philosophy* 77, no. 9 [1980]: 515–72), "citizens affirm their existing institutions in part because they reasonably believe them to satisfy their public and effective conception of justice." The robust affirmation of their institutions insofar as they are just, and their active concern to see to it that their institutions are and remain just, constitute an admirable patriotism.

32. See Thomas Nagel, "Moral Conflict and Political Legitimacy," for a fascinating discussion of this distinction, and an attempt to defend the higher-order notion of impartiality on which liberalism as a political doctrine rests.

33. I would like to thank James Hart for stimulating discussion which helped to shape the paper, and members of the philosophy department at the University of Wisconsin who discussed the paper when I presented it there in November 1987.

34. I'm paraphrasing a quote from a *New York Times* article by Jane Gross, "A Difference of Generations: Reactions to a World Gone Awry" (November 14, 2001), p. A22. The part beginning "we'd have nuked" is a direct quote from someone interviewed in the article.

35. It is not new for everyone. As was noted on National Public Radio, older African Americans who lived through eras of periodic lynchings are not unfamiliar with the sense that there will be more attacks, without having any clue of where and when. And of course many Americans are refugees from countries where sporadic killings of civilians (sometimes by armies supported by the United States) were common.

36. The point here isn't that many people killed in the attacks were not, in fact, Americans, but rather a difference in the terms used to decry the attacks, and the attendant sentiments.

37. The reflections in the last paragraph are prompted in part by the discussions of the attacks, but also by Igor Primoratz's "Patriotism: Morally Allowed, Required, or Valuable?" in *Nationalism and Ethnic Conflict: Philosophical Perspectives*, ed. Nenad Miscevic (Chicago: Open Court, 2000): 101–13. Primoratz points out that in the previously published version of this essay, I do not make it clear whether I am saying only that patriotism is morally permissible, or whether I mean to claim that it really is a virtue. My response is that in one manifestation it is a virtue: a particular concern with the moral flourishing of one's country is a virtue. But beyond that, I am undecided: I am not convinced that in its other manifestations patriotism is a virtue.

Chapter Four
STEPHEN NATHANSON

IN DEFENSE OF "MODERATE PATRIOTISM"

*P*atriotism is an ideal that makes many thoughtful people uncomfortable. They find it difficult to label themselves as "patriots" because they are uncomfortable with the rituals and symbols of national loyalty and because they worry that national loyalty implies indifference or hostility to people of other nations. Since they condemn national chauvinism and are disturbed by the associations between patriotism, militarism, and blind allegiance, they shun the word "patriot."

At the same time, such people do not want to be considered disloyal. They may attach great value to many of their country's political practices and traditions, and they may even carry out the duties of citizenship conscientiously. They do not see themselves as unpatriotic and certainly do not want to be seen as traitors.

Yet, the language of patriotism and loyalty seems to force them into a difficult choice. To say that one is not patriotic suggests that one lacks the loyalty that is appropriate to citizens. It is not surprising, then, that the ideas of nonpatriotic citizens are often viewed with suspicion, for their lack of patriotism seems to imply that they possess neither loyalty nor a basic concern for the well-being of the nation. Hence, their views on national conduct and policy are suspect.

It appears, then, that one must either accept patriotism in spite of its undesirable features, or place oneself in the role of an outsider, whose claims about the national welfare have an uncertain status. The result for many is a chronic form of discomfort and a hope that the subject of patriotism can be kept out of political discussions.

In this paper, I want to defend a conception of patriotism that thoughtful, morally conscientious people can be comfortable with. Like Alasdair MacIntyre, I will be trying to provide an affirmative answer to the question "Is Patriotism a Virtue?"[1] Unlike MacIntyre, however, I have great sympathy with

From *Ethics* 99, no. 3 (1988/89): 535–52. Copyright © 1989 The University of Chicago. Reprinted by permission of The University of Chicago Press.

those who think (or fear) that patriotism is a vice, and I shall begin by considering some antipatriotic arguments that were forcefully stated by the great Russian novelist and thinker, Leo Tolstoy.[2] In response to Tolstoy, I will describe a conception of patriotism that does not possess the evil features that he thinks are a necessary part of patriotism. I call the conception I defend "moderate patriotism." After showing that this form of patriotism escapes Tolstoy's attack, I will turn to MacIntyre's vigorous criticisms of this view and will try to show that his objections do not succeed in discrediting it.

IS PATRIOTISM A VIRTUE?

It is no surprise that the established authorities of all nations encourage patriotism and support the view that it is a virtue. Spokesmen for a nation want to encourage devotion to it so that they can appeal to patriotic motives in bringing about compliance with the law and encouraging citizen support for government policies. In making this point, I do not mean to encourage cynicism or suggest that patriotism is not a virtue. Even for those not accustomed to seeing themselves as patriotic, the idea that patriotism is a vice is somewhat shocking. Since for most of us, our "country" includes not just its politics but its language, culture, familiar history, natural beauties, customs, literature, folk heroes, and personal histories, it is not surprising that most people feel some degree of love for their country. In this sense, even politically alienated people may have patriotic sentiments.[3]

Patriotism, however, is not just love for one's country and its traditions. MacIntyre rightly stresses that patriotism involves loyalty and a preference for the well-being of one's own country over others. The problem is not whether it is a virtue to have warm feelings toward some aspects of one's country. Rather, the question is, Can it be a virtue to feel loyalty toward one's country and to be willing to promote its well-being, even if that can only be done at the cost of diminishing the well-being of other countries?

In two essays, entitled "Patriotism" and "Patriotism, or Peace?" Tolstoy answered this question with a vehement no. One of Tolstoy's primary reasons for rejecting patriotism is that it is linked to war. As he writes, "The root of war . . . [is] the exclusive desire for the well-being of one's own people; it is patriotism. Therefore, to destroy war, destroy patriotism" (pp. 106–107). Earlier, he describes war as "the inevitable consequence of patriotism" (p. 104).

Now, one might think that Tolstoy is overstating his point here, claiming that patriotism inevitably leads to war. While acknowledging that there is an association between patriotic fervor and warfare, one might think that this does not show the connection to be inevitable. But if one grants his definition of patriotism as exclusive concern for the well-being of one's own nation, then I think that Tolstoy is only minimally guilty of overstatement. If one cares only for one's own nation and if—as seems plausible—one's nation could profit from things of value possessed by other nations, then if possible, one's nation should engage in any activities necessary to obtain the desired goods. Since we can suppose that other nations will not voluntarily give up their valued possessions, then warfare becomes the inevitable policy choice for those who can expect victory.

I assume, as Tolstoy does, that war is an undesirable state, involving, as it does, large-scale killing and injury to soldiers and frequently civilians as well. If war is an evil and if patriotism is the root cause of war, then patriotism is an evil. As Tolstoy asks rhetorically, "How can this patriotism, whence come human sufferings incalculable both physical and moral, be necessary, and be a virtue?" (p. 109).

In a second argument, Tolstoy condemns patriotism as both "stupid and immoral." It is stupid, he writes, "because if every country were to consider itself superior to others, it is evident that all but one would be in error; and [it is] immoral because it leads all who possess it to aim at benefiting their own country or nation at the expense of every other" (p. 75).

Tolstoy's point about the stupidity of patriotism is on target. Self-proclaimed patriots frequently talk about the superiority of their nation to all other nations. Myths of being "number one," "divinely chosen," "a special people" are the common fare of patriotic remarks. Yet, the mere multiplicity of nations implies that most patriots must be wrong when they make such remarks.

The immorality of patriotism resides in its according special status to the well-being of some people. This, Tolstoy thinks, flies in the face of both the Golden Rule and the principle of moral equality. Again, he asks rhetorically, "how can patriotism be a virtue . . . when it requires . . . an ideal exactly opposite to that of our religion and morality—an admission, not of the equality and fraternity of all men, but of the dominance of one country or nation over all others?" (p. 75). Morality, as Tolstoy suggests, requires that we take seriously the interests of all people, not simply those of our own nation's citizens. Yet patriotism, he says, involves an exclusive interest in members of one national group. It gives no moral weight to the interests of others. Hence, from his point of view, patriotism is totally opposed to the fundamental ideals of morality.

PATRIOTISM WITHIN THE LIMITS OF MORALITY

In spite of the power of Tolstoy's arguments, there is an obvious reply to them. While it would be unfair to suggest that his description of patriotism is his own creation or that it is a caricature, one could object that the extreme conception he describes is not the only form of patriotism. Indeed, all his arguments hinge on a single word—"exclusive." The extreme patriots that Tolstoy describes have an exclusive concern for their country. They care only about its well-being and not at all about the well-being of other peoples. They perceive only the virtues of their own country and not those of other countries. They think that morality applies only within their country, that only their own fellow citizens are persons with moral standing, that citizens of other countries fall outside the moral umbrella.

This exclusive concern for one's own country, however, is not a necessary part of patriotism. Even Tolstoy, in a different passage, describes patriotism as "the preference for one's own country or nation above the country or nation of anyone else." This definition permits (as the earlier one did not permit) patriots to feel some concern for those who are not their fellow countrymen. One can have a preference for one's own country, a greater love for it, and a greater concern for its well-being without going so far as to think that morality ceases to apply at the border. If patriotism involves this sort of preference and leads people to do good things on behalf of their country but always within the limits of what is morally permissible, then patriotism would have none of the dreadful implications that Tolstoy attributes to it.

There seems, therefore, to be an easy way out of the dilemmas we face in evaluating patriotism. We need not say categorically either that patriotism is a virtue or that it is a vice. Rather, we can hold that patriotism is a virtue so long as the actions it encourages are not themselves immoral. So long as devotion and loyalty to one's country do not lead to immoral actions, then patriotism can be quite laudable. When concern for their own country blinds people to the legitimate needs and interests of other nations, then patriotism becomes a vice.

That a morally acceptable form of patriotism is possible can be seen by comparing patriotism to love or family loyalty. People may (and, one hopes, typically do) have a special interest and concern for their parents, spouses, and children. They really do care more about those "near and dear" than about strangers. Yet, so long as this concern is not an exclusive concern, there is nothing the matter with it. That is, so long as family loyalty does not violate the rights of nonmembers of one's family, then actions inspired by family loyalty or love are perfectly permissible and may reveal important virtues in a person.

Tolstoy is correct to criticize that kind of patriotic loyalty that puts the nation before all else. Patriotism is exactly like other forms of loyalty. My loyalty to my family may lead me to strive for its well-being in many laudable ways and so may be counted as a virtue. Nonetheless, I may not do *anything* on behalf of my family's well-being. I may not legitimately kill my child's competitor for a school prize or threaten a neighbor whose house we would like to own. When one engages in immoral actions in order to promote one's own family's well-being, then family devotion is excessive and is no virtue. It remains a virtue so long as it is constrained by other moral principles.

Tolstoy is mistaken, then, in his total condemnation of patriotism. The proper answer to the question, Is patriotism a virtue? is that the moral value of patriotism depends on the circumstances in which patriotism is exhibited and the actions that it motivates. When patriotism is in the service of valuable ends and is limited to morally legitimate means of attaining them, then it is a virtue. When patriotism leads to support of immoral ends or immoral means to achieve otherwise legitimate ends, then it is a vice.

The moderate patriotic view appears to provide both a reply to Tolstoy and a simple solution to our original questions about the status of patriotism. Moreover, it accords with moral common sense. Most people who think of themselves as patriots want to distinguish their attitude from jingoism and chauvinism. They shy away from adopting the attitude of "My country, right or wrong." They sense that patriotism can be carried too far and that moral constraints do apply to actions taken on behalf of one's country.

MACINTYRE'S ATTACK ON MODERATE PATRIOTISM

In spite of the appeal of this conception of patriotism, MacIntyre rejects it and devotes most of "Is Patriotism a Virtue?" to criticizing it. Unlike Tolstoy, however, he rejects it because it is too weak a form of patriotism and too subservient to the demands of universal morality. MacIntyre appears to defend the extreme form of patriotism that Tolstoy and the moderate patriot both reject.

Like Tolstoy, MacIntyre begins by noting the tension between morality and patriotism, although he describes it as a conflict between two different conceptions of morality rather than a conflict between patriotism and morality as such. While a universalist conception of morality requires a certain detachment from one's own position, patriotism is a version of a particularist morality. It emphasizes personal bonds and the moral significance of membership in a particular group. From the point of view of the patriot, universalists (including moderate patriots who support impersonal constraints on loyalty) are insufficiently attentive to the importance of personal bonds and loyalties. From the universalist perspective, patriots are too restrictive in their application of moral principles and ideals, too concerned about persons and groups to whom they are directly related.

The conflict could be resolved, MacIntyre notes, if patriotism were regarded as "nothing more than a perfectly proper devotion to one's own nation which must never be allowed to violate the constraints set by the impersonal moral standpoint." He goes on to say that it is this form of patriotism that is "professed by certain liberal moralists who are often indignant when it is suggested by their critics that they are not patriotic" (p. 6).

Since I have argued that the moderate patriotism that MacIntyre attributes to "liberal moralists" is the correct view, I want to look at the specific criticisms he raises in order to show that none of them succeeds in damaging the moderate patriotic view. Since my discussion is entirely critical, I would like to preface it by crediting MacIntyre with having written a rich and challenging treatment of an important, somewhat neglected subject.

MACINTYRE'S ARGUMENTS

MacIntyre begins his criticism by expressing sympathy with the charge that moderate patriots are not genuinely patriotic. He writes, "Patriotism thus limited in its scope appears to be emasculated, and it does so because in some of the most important situations of actual social life either the patriotic standpoint comes into serious conflict with the standpoint of a genuinely impersonal morality or it amounts to no more than a set of practically empty slogans" (p. 6).

The point here seems to be that if moderate patriotism always makes loyalty subservient to universal morality, then it is empty. Whether expressions of patriotism are genuine or merely slogans is revealed only in situations of conflict. Genuine patriotism, according to MacIntyre, requires loyalty to one's country in just those conflict situations in which universal morality (and thus moderate patriotism) would counsel backing away from devotion to one's country. To illustrate his point, MacIntyre gives examples of two types of conflict.

CONFLICT OVER RESOURCES

The first type of conflict arises from the scarcity of resources that might be necessary for the life of a national community. At its most extreme, the very survival of a nation might be at stake. In such conflict situations, MacIntyre writes, "the standpoint of impersonal morality requires an allocation of goods such that each individual person counts for one and no more than one, while the patriotic standpoint requires that I strive to further the interests of my community and you strive to further those of yours." He goes on to say that when survival or other "large interests" are at stake, "patriotism entails a willingness to go to war on one's community's behalf" (p. 6).

The force of MacIntyre's argument derives from the sense he conveys of the unavoidability of conflict. Only one national community can survive, while the other will perish. Moderate patriots would be precluded by their universalist morality from standing by their own country because they cannot count their own country more than the other. Extreme patriots, on the other hand, would make an unequivocal choice for their own country in this setting, showing that they and they alone are genuinely loyal. According to MacIntyre, the moderate position shows itself to be mere words, an empty expression of patriotism that evaporates in the heat of the tragic conflicts that occur in the real world.

There is a certain power to MacIntyre's argument, but I think that it dissipates when we consider his example more carefully. How would extreme and moderate patriots behave in this situation? Extreme patriots would see that there was a serious conflict between the interests of their own country and those of another. In thinking about what actions to take, they would consider only the interests of their own country as having value and would unhesitatingly pursue them by any means. Since their morality requires loyalty only to their own community, they would not count the destruction of the other community and its members as serious losses.

Moderate patriots would act quite differently. Because they do consider the value of persons in the opposing community, they would examine the conflict to see if there is any way of accommodating the needs of both communities. They would evaluate the legitimacy of the claims made by both sides, and if the moral weight of the opposing side's claims is greater, they might well urge a sacrifice by their own community. Because they count the well-being of both sides, they would strive to discover or devise a just accommodation.

Suppose that no just accommodation of both sides' legitimate interests is possible. What if the choice is between the death of one community or the other? What would moderate patriots do? Would their commitment to universal morality mean that they would be indifferent to which community survives? Would it lead them to urge collective suicide by their own community? Would they be willing to fight for their community, though it had no greater moral claim than the opposition?

In this extreme situation, many actions are possible, but universal morality would not require moderate patriots to abandon or betray their own communities. Morality does not require that people be indifferent to which community survives, since their deepest emotional ties are to one group. This would be like expecting a person to be indifferent to whether it is his own family that is killed in an auto accident or some family of strangers.

Likewise, morality would not require group suicide in such a case. That degree of sacrifice and altruism goes beyond what we think is required by morality. So, if indifference and altruism are unreasonable to require in this setting, then a regretful entry into the struggle for survival could not be criticized, and it is hard to see why moderate patriots would be forced to reject or condemn this option. The fact that the defense of their own community would be undertaken with deep regret points to the moral superiority of their position. In contrast, extreme patriots, as MacIntyre describes their view, need not care in the least about the well-being of members of the opposing community. The choice to fight for survival would be made with ease and need not be preceded by any search for alternatives.

In response to MacIntyre's argument, then, we can note two things. First, in the heat of struggle, the moderate patriot is not forced to renounce his community or sacrifice its existence. He can defend it as well as the extreme patriot. Second, in dealing with serious conflict, the extreme patriot betrays a high level of callousness and disregard for the legitimate rights and interests of those in the competing group. The moderate position leads to the appropriate responses: a search for compromise and reconciliation, a sense of regret when conflict is unavoidable and either/or choices must be made. Nothing in this case serves to discredit the moderate patriotic view.

Before leaving this argument, it is worth noting that MacIntyre's sense that loyalty and universal morality are incompatible appears to rest on an over-simplified view of the kind of impartiality required by universal morality. While it is true that some advocates of universal morality (like Tolstoy) seem to think that universal morality rules out special ties to any particular individuals, this is not a necessary feature of universal morality. Commonsense morality certainly permits and encourages local loyalties and even frowns on extreme detachment or total impartiality.

While there are deep problems to be worked out, it would appear that the impartiality of universal morality can consistently allow for special obligations and various forms of particularist commitments.[4] Thus, to take a simple example, while the Ten Commandments may be understood as being impartially addressed to everyone (to every "Thou"), they nonetheless contain the rule "Honor thy mother and father." This rule clearly commands that each person accord special treatment to specific individuals. Hence, as a model of a moral code, the Ten Commandments contains a mix of partiality and impartiality.[5] The requirement that we be "partial" to our parents applies impartially to all persons.

In a similar way, a universal morality may well contain special duties that people have to advance the interests of their own countries, duties that could be expressed in a commandment to "honor thy country." Hence, there is no inconsistency in being committed to universal moral principles that both sanction special obligations to one's country and impose constraints on the actions one may take in pursuit of one's country's well-being. This mixture of universalism and particularism is both coherent and appears to be embodied in ordinary moral thought.[6]

COMPETING CONCEPTIONS OF THE GOOD LIFE

The second type of conflict MacIntyre describes involves competing conceptions of the good life. He raises the problem in the context of a problem faced by empires in their dealings with "barbarian border peoples." He writes:

> A variety of such peoples—Scottish Gaels, Iroquois Indians, Bedouin—have regarded raiding the territory of their traditional enemies . . . as an essential constituent of the good life; whereas the settled urban or agricultural communities which provided the target for their depredations have regarded the subjugation of such peoples and their reeducation into peaceful pursuits as one of their central responsibilities. And on such issues once again the impersonal moral standpoint and that of patriotism cannot be reconciled. For the impersonal moral standpoint, understood as the philosophical protagonists of modern liberalism have understood it, requires neutrality not only between rival and competing interests, but also between rival and competing sets of beliefs about the best way for human beings to live. (p. 71)

This passage suggests two different criticisms. The first argues again that moderate patriotism is empty, since it requires sacrificing one's own community's way of life if objective moral assessment shows it to be in the wrong. The second would show that the ideal of liberal neutrality associated with moderate patriotism precludes it from yielding any opinion at all about conflicts between ways of life.[7]

According to the first argument, moderate patriots are again shown to lack genuine loyalty because they are committed to sacrifice an "essential constituent of the good life" of their community if pursuit of that good conflicts with impersonal moral standards. This willingness to sacrifice the good of the community betrays an indifference that is incompatible with genuine patriotism.

This is a misleading description, however. Moderate patriots would see that the practice of "raiding the territory" of traditional enemies is incompatible with respect for the humanity of members of the enemy communities. If these enemies are themselves engaged in such raiding, then counterraids may be justified by self-defense. But if other communities do not seek out conflict, then the necessity of raiding is called into question. Raiding as an exercise of community virtues is not legitimate. One's community may feel that the personal valor shown in such raids or the martial skills exhibited are the highest achievements, but these goods must not be purchased at the cost of innocent lives. Moderate patriots would see this and would favor ending the raids. This need not show indifference to their community, however. Unlike outsiders, moderate patriots would realize the genuine value of the martial skills and virtues, and they would regret the loss of the goods associated with that way of life. Unlike outsiders, they might work to foster the development of other practices that preserve some of the community's traditional values. They would not be indifferent to the community's losses, even though they think it necessary that the community pay this price.

The crucial point here is that being an "essential constituent" of some conception of the good life does not exempt a practice or activity from moral evaluation and criticism. If it did, we would be unable to condemn the actions of religious zealots who devote their lives to wiping out heathens. We would be unable to condemn slavery because the niceties of Southern plantation life required it. We would be unable to condemn Nazism because its conception of the good life required genocide and conquest to bring about "racial" dominance.

MacIntyre's argument seems to imply an extreme form of ethical permissiveness.[8] While moderate patriotism applies the constraints of morality to the pursuit of a community's well-being, MacIntyre's view exempts community practices from moral judgment.

NEUTRALITY AND MORAL SKEPTICISM

This brings me to the second interpretation of MacIntyre's argument. He might be arguing that moderate patriots are themselves unable to judge practices like territorial raids. The reason is that moderate patriotism is linked to a larger theory of liberal universalism and that this form of liberalism is committed to "neutrality . . . between rival and competing sets of beliefs about the best way for human beings to live" (p. 7). Liberal universalism, on this view, claims to be able to judge community practices from the standpoint of impersonal morality. In fact, however, it provides no basis for condemning the territorial raiders and their way of life because it is committed to neutrality about ideals. Liberals, on this argument, are reduced to skepticism and indecision about the value of the raiders' form of life, while MacIntyre's (extreme) patriot will have no difficulty making a choice about whom to support.

If this is MacIntyre's point, it misrepresents the position of the moderate patriot by failing to distinguish various senses of "neutrality." On the face of it, it is clear that liberalism is a normative political philosophy, so it cannot be committed to complete value neutrality. We need to ask what forms of "neutrality" liberal universalism is (or is not) committed to.

First, moderate patriots are committed to neutrality in the sense that they are committed to making impartial judgments of the issues over which communities are in conflict. Likewise, they are committed to applying universal moral principles to the actions of their own country as well as to others. As I have already argued, these forms of neutrality do not imply indifference to one's own country. Nor do they rule out the possibility of people having special obligations to their own country. Second, liberals have often claimed that their view is neutral in that it neither implies nor presupposes substantive ideals about the best way to live. As a political philosophy, this translates into defenses of free speech, even speech that is known or thought to be false, and freedom of religion, even of religions that are thought to be false. Liberals oppose using the state to determine which of competing ideals of life is best.[9] Moreover, they think that people committed to very different ideals could come to see that this sort of neutral state is the best form of political arrangement.

This neutrality, however, must not be confused with ethical skepticism, relativism, or indifference.[10] It is not total neutrality, and thus it permits liberals to condemn the territorial raiders' activities, not on the ground that martial virtues are bad but because the exercise of them in this situation conflicts with the rights of other persons. If killing members of other communities is the only way for the raiders to live the good life as they see it, then their way of life will be condemned by the liberal.

A central tenet of liberal political thought is that the protection of certain "civil" or "primary" goods is the central function of the state. Thus, as Locke argued in his *Letter concerning Toleration*, although religious ideals may be the highest ones within a person's life, protection of people's "life, liberty, health, and . . . possession[s]" takes priority in the political realm.[11] Similarly, in *A Theory of Justice*, Rawls argues that primary goods like liberty and wealth should be protected and that specific personal ideals should not be given special preference by social institutions.[12]

The justification for the priority of primary goods over ideals is admittedly a central and a difficult problem for liberal political theory.[13] Nonetheless, there is no doubt that liberal thought involves this priority. At this level, liberal morality is far from neutral in its evaluation of various conceptions of the good life. Neutrality with respect to ideals does not imply neutrality with respect to evaluations of particular actions or practices.[14]

Much of the liberal view developed in connection with religious conflict and church-state separation remains a paradigm of liberal politics.[15] What is crucial to our purposes is to see that, while liberalism is committed to governmental neutrality about which religion is best, this does not preclude liberals either from personally believing that one particular religion is best or from working to advance a particular religion through nonpolitical means. Nor, finally, does it preclude one from condemning the use of violence to promote religious ideals. Violent promotion of religious ideals is forbidden because it involves severe deprivations of primary goods, those goods whose protection is one of the central functions of government.

This last case is, of course, exactly parallel to the problem of the territorial raiders, whose ideals, according to MacIntyre, can only thrive at the cost of unprovoked assault on the lives and well-being of persons who are not members of the tribe. Liberals can favor the prohibition of this practice without judging the tribe's ideals to be without value, though they must, of course, judge that the "cost" of following these ideals is too high.

In thinking about liberalism, it is important to distinguish the liberal political perspective from the variety of theoretical elaborations and defenses of liberalism. Liberals have defended their views in a variety of ways, some of which claim to be based on neutral, value-free principles of rationality, some on "thin" theories of value that make only minimal value assumptions, and others of which derive from substantive conceptions about the good life.[16] While MacIntyre's comments point to the need for articulating and defending the liberal perspective, it is not clear that he reveals any fundamental deficiencies in it. Liberal universalism does provide a plausible basis, rooted in both history and theory, for limiting the ways in which people pursue their conception of the good life.

In short, whichever interpretation we make of MacIntyre's point about conflict over ideals, his argument fails. He does not establish either the disloyalty of moderate patriots or their inability to make judgments and decisions. Moderate patriots need not be either indifferent to their own community's way of life or incapable of evaluating conflicts between ways of life. Finally, while I have defended liberalism from MacIntyre's attacks, the moderate patriotic attitude need not be derived from a liberal political philosophy. It could be based on substantive moral or religious ideals or on historically based beliefs about the nature of governments and nations.

LIBERAL DETACHMENT VERSUS COMMUNITY IMMERSION

Moderate patriots distinguish between patriotism and morality and seek to subject patriotism to moral constraints. MacIntyre, however, rejects the view that morality and patriotism can be distinguished in this way. As he writes, "What we have here are two rival and incompatible moralities, each of which is viewed from within by its adherents as morality-as-such" (p. 11). Proponents of universal morality assume that we can detach ourselves from our particular community and evaluate its practices, just as we evaluate the practices of any community. MacIntyre denies that this is possible. He believes that our understanding of morality is itself so deeply entwined with our relationship to a particular community that no such detachment can be achieved.

MacIntyre does not claim to prove this view, but he finds it attractive and presents it sympathetically. While not denying the existence of what he calls "lonely moral heroism," he asserts that "it is in general only within a community that individuals become capable of morality, are sustained in their morality, and are constituted as moral agents. . . . And once we recognize that typically moral agency and continuing moral capacity are engendered and sustained in essential ways by particular institutionalized social ties in particular social groups, it will be difficult to counterpoise allegiance to a particular society and allegiance to morality in the way in which the protagonists of liberal morality do" (p. 10).

Drawing on this communitarian conception of morality, MacIntyre develops his argument for the impossibility of detachment and the necessity of patriotism's being a virtue. He writes,

> *If* first . . . I can only apprehend the rules of morality in the version in which they are incarnated in some specific community; and *if* secondly . . . the justification of morality must be in terms of particular goods enjoyed within the life of particular communities; and *if* thirdly . . . I am characteristically brought into being and maintained as a moral agent only through the . . . moral sustenance afforded by my community, *then* it is clear that . . . my allegiance to the community and what it requires of me—even to the point of requiring me to die to sustain its life—could not meaningfully be contrasted with . . . what morality required of me.[17] (pp. 10–11)

If this argument is correct, then the kind of moral reflection moderate patriots appeal to is either totally impossible or exists only as an atypical and aberrant version of normal moral reflection.

But how plausible is this argument?

I will limit my comments to the first premise, which says that we can only understand the rules of morality "in the version" in which they are "incarnated in some specific community." This is a crucial premise, since it identifies a person's understanding of morality with his understanding of the morality of his community. It is this identification that makes the contrast between community morality and morality as such impossible.

There is clearly some truth in what MacIntyre says. Typically, people do derive their understanding of what is worthwhile and what is right from the culture of the communities in which they grow up. In this sense, individual moral understanding derives from and is dependent on community values.[18] If we think of a community's morality as a set of highly specific judgments and take moral development to be the internalization of precisely those judgments, then MacIntyre's conclusion follows. Morality just is what the community says, and no detached moral judgment of the community's values is possible.

Typically, however, the morality of a community is not simply a collection of particular judgments. Rather, in addition to specific judgments, it contains an open-ended set of general values, principles, ideals, and paradigms of proper behavior. The morality that a person acquires from his community will, therefore, contain large elements of vagueness, ambiguity, and indeterminacy. There will be no rigid set of judgments which simply is the community morality. Hence, different notions of morality and of the requirements of loyalty may grow out of the same social soil and may make possible the sort of flexibility of moral thought that permits individuals to contrast their community's acts and policies with the requirements of morality as such.

This point emerges most clearly, perhaps, when we see that community moralities are themselves likely to contain inconsistent and competing elements that generate conflict. Virtually every community, for example, encourages some degree of loyalty to the group as a whole. Yet, loyalty to one's own family is also likely to be encouraged, as is loyalty to one's friends.[19] In most circumstances, people do not find it difficult to be loyal to all these groups, but sometimes the claims of one group will conflict with those of the other, and the community morality may not provide any way of resolving the conflict.

The idea of "morality as such" may emerge from just such situations, since individuals would feel the pull of these competing claims but would be unable to identify any one of them with what morality requires. The more abstract notion of morality as such would be generated by the inability of the community morality to issue a verdict, combined with the individual's sense that there is a right answer to his moral quandary. The idea of morality as such could emerge as a distinct (even if idealized version of) the community morality. Once this degree of independence and abstraction is reached, there is nothing to prevent the sort of reflection MacIntyre seeks to call into question.

This leads me to a final point about MacIntyre's argument. Even if his communitarian conception of morality were correct and even if the process of moral development insured that group loyalty would emerge as a central virtue, no conclusion would follow about the importance of patriotism. The group to which our primary loyalty would be owed would be the group from which we had obtained our moral understanding. This need not be the community as a whole or any political unit, however. It could be one's family, one's town, one's religion. The nation need not be the source of morality or the primary beneficiary of our loyalty.

Indeed, if we think about patriotism historically and reflect on the relative novelty of national loyalties, it is clear that the forging of nations has involved a huge effort to overcome the pull of diverse local attachments. Patriotism has had to compete with familial, tribal, racial, religious, and regional identities. Moreover, in its efforts to overcome these narrower forms of attachment, proponents of national loyalty have laid the basis for supranational attachments by drawing attention to the arbitrariness and parochialism of various forms of localism. The arguments for national patriotism have themselves often contained the seeds of internationalism and universal morality.[20]

THE WILLINGNESS TO DIE FOR ONE'S COUNTRY

In his final argument against moderate patriotism, MacIntyre concedes that liberal critics are correct in thinking that "patriotism is a morally dangerous phenomenon" (p. 15). It is morally dangerous because it leads to placing the good of one's nation above the good of human beings in general.

Nonetheless, he says, liberalism and moderate patriotism are subject to an equal and opposite sort of danger. Political liberalism portrays the relation of citizens within a state as deriving from relations of reciprocal self-interest and impersonal morality. Yet, in situations of conflict within a country and in situations of wartime, it is impossible to base allegiance on this combination of motivations. Reciprocal self-interest and universal morality may be too weak to sustain the state and its policies, leading MacIntyre to suggest that a state might not be able to survive if "the bonds of patriotism" were dissolved. MacIntyre writes:

> Every political community . . . requires standing armed forces for its minimal security. Of the members of these armed forces it must require both that they be prepared to sacrifice their lives for the sake of the community's security and that their willingness to do so be not contingent upon their own individual evaluation of the rightness or wrongness of their country's cause on some specific issue, measured by some standard that is neutral and impartial. . . . [T]hat is to say, good soldiers may not be liberals. . . . So the political survival of any polity in which liberal morality had secured large-scale allegiance

would depend upon there still being enough young men and women who
rejected that liberal morality. And in this sense liberal morality tends toward
the dissolution of social bonds. (pp. 17–18)

There are a number of powerful and disturbing points suggested by this
argument. First, there is the suggestion that moderate patriotism may be self-
defeating. If it is widely believed by the citizens of a country, that country is
less likely to survive. Second, if survival requires large numbers of unquestioning patriots, then moderate patriots are in fact social parasites, unwilling to
support their country unquestioningly, but accepting the benefits of unquestioning obedience by others. Indeed, the moderate patriot may well be in the
unenviable position that Sidgwick described in connection with utilitarianism—believing that his own view was true but also believing that it would
be better if most people did not accept it.[21]

Is moderate patriotism dangerous and unattractive for these reasons? I
think not. First, an important assumption of MacIntyre's is that willingness to
defend one's country cannot be motivated by moral reasons. Unquestioning
obedience to one's own country is, he thinks, necessary. There is an air of
realism about MacIntyre's psychological claim that morality is a weak moti-
vator that must be supplemented by blind patriotism. Yet it is doubtful that his
view is shared by national leaders, who always go to great lengths to show that
their country's cause is morally just. They do not rely solely on appeals to blind
patriotism. Instead, they always describe themselves as being on the side of
good, while opponents are always portrayed as evil. Perhaps it is not so realistic to minimize the power of moral motivation.

Beyond this factual question, however, is the key question of the desirability of encouraging blind patriotic loyalty of the sort MacIntyre describes.
In deciding this, perhaps we need to assess the consequences of promoting
extreme versus moderate patriotism. Are we more threatened by the possibility that too many moderate patriots will weaken the social fabric, that a
good society will be defeated because too few of its members are willing to give
it uncritical support? Or are we more threatened by the possibility that evil
deeds will be done because of excessive allegiance to particular national communities?

While there is no definitive way to answer these questions, there is reason
to believe that some of the more dreadful policies of recent wars have been
motivated by too much patriotism and too little morality. I have in mind the
bombing of cities in Britain, Germany, and Japan; the use of atomic weapons
at Hiroshima and Nagasaki; the extreme communitarian, pseudo-biological
nationalism of Nazism; and the indiscriminate killings promoted by various ter-
rorist groups who care only about their own members. Many commentators
have also noted the difficulty of controlling nuclear weapons in a context in
which national sovereignty is given such primacy. These are among the dangers

associated with unconstrained patriotism, and they provide reasons for wanting to subject patriotic impulses to the constrains of universal morality.

Moderate patriots would be willing to risk the dissolution that worries MacIntyre because they are more worried about excessive patriotism. Moreover, they are committed to the value of moral agents reflecting on the causes for which they are willing not only to risk their own lives but also to take the lives of others. As long as moderate patriots are open about their views and do not exploit the unquestioning obedience of others, they cannot be charged with deceit or parasitism.

Moderate patriots in fact look forward to a time when governments will have to work even harder to justify their desire to risk the lives of their countrymen and take the lives of citizens of other countries. National survival may require military service by some, and military service may require relatively automatic assent in battle. Neither of these, however, requires citizens to abstain from independent moral thought or to commit themselves uncritically to the goals and policies of their country.

CONCLUSION

Both Tolstoy and MacIntyre argue as if extreme patriotism were the only possible form of patriotism. In spite of the vast differences between them, they both reinforce the idea that one must choose between chauvinism and disloyalty. I have argued that this is a mistake, and I have defended the moderate patriotic attitude as one that makes compatible the demands of national loyalty and the requirements of universal morality. In this sense, I have defended the view that it is possible for patriotism to be a virtue.

Nothing I have said, however, implies that citizens of all nations ought to be patriots. Whether people ought to be patriotic depends on the qualities of their particular nations and governments. If nations lack the qualities that make them merit loyalty and devotion, then patriotism with respect to them is an inappropriate attitude. A morally constrained version of patriotism is both limited in the range of actions that it requires citizens to support and conditional on the nature of the nation to which loyalty is directed. In this paper, I have dealt only with the limits of patriotic demands. A full treatment of patriotism would have to describe the conditions that nations must meet to be suitable objects of patriotic loyalty.

Some may think that a patriotism that is so bounded by limits and conditions cannot count as genuine loyalty. The alternative, however, is a form of patriotism that is so free of moral limits and conditions that it requires automatic assent to even the vilest evils, so long as they are done in the name of the nation. To insist that patriotism must take this extreme form in order to be genuine is to undermine the claim that patriotism is a worthwhile ideal for morally conscientious people to adopt.

NOTES

I would like to thank Larry Blum, Bill DeAngelis, Marvin Kohl, Nelson Lande, and the editors of *Ethics* for discussions and suggestions that helped me in writing this paper.

1. "Is Patriotism a Virtue?" is the title of Alasdair MacIntyre's Lindley Lecture, University of Kansas, Philosophy Department, 1984.

2. Leo Tolstoy's arguments appear in "Patriotism," and "Patriotism, or Peace?" both of which are reprinted in *Tolstoy's Writings on Civil Disobedience and Non-Violence* (New York: New American Library, 1968; New York: Bergman, 1967); page references in the text are to the New American Library edition.

3. Leonard Doob describes the psychological associations between one's country and positive features of one's environment in *Patriotism and Nationalism* (New Haven, Conn.: Yale University Press, 1964), chap. 2.

4. For an excellent discussion of the interrelations between various forms of impartialism and particularism, see Lawrence Blum, "Gilligan and Kohlberg: Implications for Moral Philosophy," *Ethics* 98 (1988): 472–91. The problem of special obligations is also treated in an enlightening way by Robert Goodin in *Protecting the Vulnerable* (Chicago: University of Chicago Press, 1985).

5. For a similar point, see Marcia Baron, *The Moral Status of Loyalty* (Dubuque, Iowa: Kendall/Hunt, 1984), p. 26.

6. For a defense of the thesis that universalist morality sanctions particularist duties, see Alan Gewirth, "Ethical Universalism and Particularism," *Journal of Philosophy* 85 (1988): 283–303.

7. MacIntyre's identification of moral impartiality with liberalism is somewhat misleading. In Tolstoy's case, e.g., his moral universalism is grounded in Christianity. He condemns patriotism for its "incompatibility . . . with the very lowest demands of morality in a Christian society" (Tolstoy, p. 108).

8. One might describe MacIntyre's view as relativistic, since it resists the imposition of external standards on the practices of particular communities. On the other hand, it could be argued that his view makes sense only on the supposition that there is an absolute value involved in a community's pursuing its own conception of the good life.

9. Compare Ronald Dworkin: "Government must be neutral on what might be called the question of the good life" (quoted from "Liberalism," in *Public and Private Morality*, ed. S. Hampshire [Cambridge: Cambridge University Press, 1978], p. 127).

10. For an example of an antiliberal critique that seems to rest on such confusions, see Allan Bloom, *The Closing of the American Mind* (New York: Simon & Schuster, 1987). Bloom draws no distinctions between relativism, pluralism, skepticism, and nihilism. Nor does he distinguish personal judgments from political ones.

11. John Locke, *A Letter concerning Toleration* (Indianapolis: Bobbs-Merrill, 1955), p. 17.

12. John Rawls, *A Theory of Justice* (Cambridge, Mass.: Harvard University Press, 1971), p. 206. See, too, Rawls's more recent discussion of neutrality in "Justice as Fairness: Political not Metaphysical," in *Philosophy and Public Affairs* 14 (1985): 245 ff.

13. In *A Theory of Justice*, Rawls appears to argue that a concern for the primary goods follows simply from a person's being a rational agent. For a criticism of this view, see my *The Ideal of Rationality* (Atlantic Highlands, N.J.: Humanities Press International, 1985), pp. 101–107.

14. For two recent discussions of these issues, see Charles Larmore, *Patterns of Moral Complexity* (Cambridge: Cambridge University Press, 1987), chaps. 2–5; and Thomas Nagel, "Moral Conflict and Political Legitimacy," *Philosophy and Public Affairs* 16 (1987): 215–40.

15. Compare Rawls, "Justice as Fairness: Political not Metaphysical," p. 249.

16. Mill exemplifies the third approach, while aspects of the first and second can be found in Rawls. Locke seems to appeal to a "thin" theory of the good, as well as to special premises about the nature of religion and government.

17. For another attempt to develop this line of thought, see Michael Sandel, *Liberalism and the Limits of Justice* (Cambridge: Cambridge University Press, 1982). Both Sandel and MacIntyre are criticized in Amy Gutmann, "Communitarian Critics of Liberalism," *Philosophy and Public Affairs* 14 (1985): 308–22.

18. For a nice description by a novelist of a moral insight that seems to come from outside a person's community, see John Barth, *The Tidewater Tales* (New York: Putnam's, 1987), pp. 231–32.

19. As Michael Walzer has written, "the processes through which men incur obligations are unavoidably pluralistic"; see his essay, "The Obligation to Disobey," in *Obligations: Essays on Disobedience, War, and Citizenship* (New York: Simon & Schuster, 1971), p. 15.

20. For a brief historical survey that usefully distinguishes various forms of nationalism and their relations with internationalist ideas, see Hans Kohn, "Nationalism," in *Dictionary of the History of Ideas* (New York: Scribner's, 1973), vol. 3, pp. 324–39.

21. In Henry Sidgwick's words, "a Utilitarian may reasonably desire . . . that some of his conclusions should be rejected by mankind generally; or even that the vulgar should keep aloof from his system as a whole, in so far as . . . it [is] likely to lead to bad results in their hands" (*The Methods of Ethics*, 7th ed. [New York: Dover, 1966], p. 490, bk. 4, chap. 5, sec. 3): original edition, 1907.

Chapter Five

PAUL GOMBERG

PATRIOTISM IS LIKE RACISM

*S*tephen Nathanson's "In Defense of 'Moderate Patriotism'" tries to show
that there is a moderate patriotism that does not collapse into an unpatriotic universal morality or become an immoderate patriotism that no universalist
could endorse.[1] It fails. I will argue this much in the first part of this note. In the
second I will draw some more constructive lessons, arguing that, on the most
plausible assumptions about our world, patriotism is no better than racism.

NATHANSON'S MODERATE PATRIOTISM
AND ITS PROBLEMS

Nathanson defines moderate patriotism as preference (presumably, in action)
for one's nation, its traditions and institutions, and one's fellow nationals, but
within the limits of morality, that is, provided one does not violate the "legitimate needs and interests of other nations" and their nationals (p. 538). He
argues that there is a moderate patriotism that is compatible both with the
imperatives of commonsense morality and with moral universalism. I will not
dispute compatibility with commonsense morality. Since I will question compatibility with moral universalism, it is important to characterize it. Let us say
that moral universalism implies that actions are to be governed by principles
that give equal consideration to all people who might be affected by an action.

   Moral universalism is often thought to be uncontroversial and coextensive
with commonsense morality, but I believe it is neither. Christian universalism is
often based on an interpretation of the parable of the good Samaritan: Jesus is
explicating the principle, "Love thy neighbor as thyself," by answering the
question, "Who is my neighbor?" The point of the parable is that the Samaritan

From *Ethics* 101, no. 1 (1990/91): 144–50. Copyright © 1990 The University of
Chicago. Reprinted by permission of The University of Chicago Press.

helped a Jew, thus transcending the narrow loyalty of nationality. Jesus concludes his discussion by saying, "Go, and do thou likewise." His purpose is to take what is already an exacting morality—love your neighbor as yourself—and to make it more exacting by adding that nationality is irrelevant to this commandment. This is one kind of moral universalism, and it is pretty clear that this is not identical with commonsense morality, either of that time or ours.

Of course, a moral universalism that commands us to love our neighbor as ourselves is not the only possible one, but part of moral universalism is that moral regard is universal—all count equally and positively in deciding what to do. And, at first glance, this does seem incompatible with a preference for one's fellow nationals or for one's own traditions and institutions over those of others. Nathanson tries to show that universalism and national preference are compatible in his discussion of examples of two sorts [of] conflict, examples that are raised by Alasdair MacIntyre.[2] MacIntyre's argument is that in conflicts between nationalities the moral universalist will not be patriotic. Nathanson's reply is that in conflicts between nationalities the moderate patriot will act differently from both the unpatriotic moral universalist and the nonuniversalist patriot.

The first example is of conflict between nations over resources, typically land and its products and often population. In the extreme case, the way of life of a national community might be at stake (although claims that this is so are often hyperbole—does the U.S. national way of life depend on imported oil?). MacIntyre claims that the patriot will fight for the national community while the moral universalist will not. Nathanson replies that moderate patriots will follow a third course, seeking a just compromise between nations, but supporting their nations when and only when such compromise is impossible or conflict is unavoidable (he puts his condition in both ways) (pp. 541–42). The two formulations are significantly different, and in the difference lies the problem of establishing that there is a genuine third alternative between chauvinistic patriotism and unpatriotic universalism.

On the first formulation of the condition—that compromise is impossible—the moderate patriot must be reasonably assured that there is no possible just compromise. This is a huge burden that moderate patriots may be unable to fulfill, and it may, in practice, lead to a neutrality that precludes patriotism. Are the conflicts between Jews and Arabs on the West Bank impossible to compromise in a just way? the conflict between the United States and Japan over trade? In considering real cases, whether contemporary or historical, it seems hard to find a clear case of conflicts of national interest where just accommodation is or was impossible. If so, then Nathanson has not shown that the moderate patriot will be different from the unpatriotic moral universalist.

But Nathanson's other condition—that conflict is unavoidable—seems to imply that the moderate patriot will support the national community once conflict has started, when "either/or choices must be made." Would the moderate patriot have supported the U.S. war effort against Mexico in 1846? the war effort in Southeast Asia? The second condition fails to distinguish the moderate patriot from the chauvinist patriot.

The second sort of conflict is over competing conceptions of the good life—MacIntyre gives the example of peoples for whom the good life involves raids on their neighbors. Here Nathanson strongly endorses the moral universalist conclusion that such a conception of the good must be abandoned because it fails to respect the humanity of others. Then his task is to show how the moderate patriot is different from the moral universalist—what the moderate patriot would do that the moral universalist would not. His answer is that "moderate patriots would realize the genuine value of . . . the goods associated with that way of life. Unlike outsiders, they might work to foster the development of other practices that preserve some of the community's traditional values. They would not be indifferent to the community's losses" (pp. 543–44). But this fails to distinguish the moderate patriot from the moral universalist. The moral universalist can hardly be "indifferent to the community's losses." And, like anthropologists and others who know of and cherish the traditional way of life that was practiced by Khoisan (bushmen) of the northwest Kalahari Desert, the moral universalist might well "work to foster the development of other practices that preserve some of the community's traditional values."

Would the moderate patriot be more committed to the preservation of the institutions and traditions of his or her own nationality than to those of other nationalities? If the answer is yes, this can be construed in two ways. On the one hand, it might be a division of moral labor, where universal duties must be divided among us and where the equally valuable traditions of all nationalities are best preserved if members of each nationality take care of their own traditions. In that case, the devotion to the traditions of one's own nation is contingent and dependent on this claim about ends and means. It is a consequence of this view that if, for some reason, some national traditions cannot be preserved by their own peoples, we are equally duty bound to uphold those. On the other hand, this greater commitment to our own nation might not be contingent in this way and might represent assigning greater value to one's own national traditions than to those of other nationalities. But this looks a lot like racism, at least in the broad sense in which I will use that word here, where it includes ethnic and national chauvinism.

PATRIOTISM AND MORAL THEORY

Consider two ways to define the relationship between universal morality and moderate patriotism. Moderate patriotism might be allowed by universal morality, but not required by it. Alternatively, the duty to be moderately patriotic might be a consequence of a universal morality and facts about an individual's particular situation.

In the first case, where moderate patriotism is allowed but not required by universal morality, it would have to be the case that universal morality does not render judgments about all acts. For if it did, it would either command or forbid patriotic acts. Universal morality would have to contain a significant zone of discretion, where acts are neither required nor forbidden. This zone may be occupied either by acts that are indifferent or supererogatory or by acts that are required by special moralities, such as patriotism or moralities of kinship.

It is not hard to imagine moralities that meet this condition, and common-sense morality may indeed have this logical structure. Suppose universal morality requires only respect for minimal rights of all others, for example, the right not to be killed without cause, these rights specified by an objective list of injunctions and prohibitions. Special moralities may specify duties to others with special relations to the agent, such as kin or fellow nationals. While universal morality would prohibit killing, deceiving, and exploiting others, it would leave a large area where one may (or must, by the injunctions of a special morality) pursue one's own interests or those of one's family, community, or nation with relative indifference to others.

Surely, a moderate patriotism, including preference for fellow nationals, is consistent with universal morality so conceived. In this sense, one might also speak of a "moderate racism" that would be compatible with universal morality, for surely someone could discriminate against black or Hispanic people or against immigrants or noncitizens in hiring and promotion without violating their fundamental rights—unless we say that their fundamental rights include being treated impartially without regard to race, nationality, or citizenship. But if we say this is a fundamental right, then doesn't this preclude favoring others of one's own nationality?

In order to appreciate the difficulty of finding a significant distinction between racism and patriotism, we must consider an example in some detail. In our society money earned is considered our own, so that it is permissible and even obligatory to spend a significant portion of our earnings in providing for our families.[3] Whatever is required by universal morality, most think that this practice does not violate those requirements. And if one owns a small business, a travel agency, let us say, there is nothing wrong with hiring a teenage daughter part-time to do paperwork for pay. (In contrast, a public employee who hires a family member violates a public trust because the money spent is not her own.) As long as the business is your own, you may hire your family if you wish.

Now suppose you need more employees, more than your family can provide. Is it morally permissible to hire old school chums and people from the neighborhood? Given the degree of residential and school segregation in most big cities in the United States, it would not be surprising if these were of a single ethnic group, and it would be quite likely that if they were either white or Hispanic, they would not include any or many black people, and if black, not many white or Hispanic. Now, in these circumstances is it morally permissible to hire employees from one's "natural" circle of friends and acquaintances, which happens to be severely limited in ethnic composition? Or suppose that one has benefited by being raised in an ethnic community and trained in one's vocation by one's co-nationals. Is it now permissible to show gratitude by favoring one's nationality in hiring and promotion?

I imagine that seventy or eighty years ago most people saw nothing wrong with these practices. How was it argued that they were wrong? I think the crucial argument is that, given residential and school segregation and given the greater initial disadvantage of most black people in access to capital and business opportunities generally, the practice will tend to maintain or exacerbate poverty in intensely impoverished inner-city black ghettos.[4]

In a society where all ethnic groups had roughly equal economic resources, a practice of favoring one's own nationality or ethnic group might not be unjust. We—or at least I—believe it is racism, undermining human equality. The belief that favoring one's own nationality is wrong is based on the estimation that the practice contributes to segregation and subordination of black people.

It is at least plausible that considerations parallel to these apply in the case of favoring compatriots (citizens of the same state). Consider the practice of a U.S. citizen's favoring compatriots in employment. The considerations that were convincing regarding racism against black people can be applied internationally. People from other countries immigrate to the United States because of international inequality. International income gaps are vastly greater than domestic racial inequality. So favoritism toward a more prosperous nationality or discrimination against nationals from poor nations contributes to a morally objectionable inequality.

Large percentages of the populations of many countries, particularly in the southern parts of the world, fail to get enough calories to lead a normal, active life, making for short life expectancy. Moral universalism must regard this as very bad. If, as seems plausible, favoritism by nationals of more prosperous countries for hungry compatriots over others who are hungry would contribute to this situation, then such favoritism is, from a universalist viewpoint, no better than racism. The question, "How are patriotism and moral universalism related?" is primarily a question about the effects of patriotism. There seem to be plausible, but not conclusive, arguments that the effects are bad and that favoritism toward one's compatriots is as objectionable as ethnic favoritism.[5]

A different argument can be made against patriotism that is not directed against oppressed nationalities. Consider the imperative, "Buy American!" which is certainly presented as a patriotic duty. Now, if directed against Philippine, Brazilian, or Chinese imports, the earlier argument applies. But suppose it is directed against Japanese imports. Here the Japanese are regarded as both privileged and unfair (although the main consideration offered in favor of this imperative is common national interest). This imperative, however, may contribute toward a climate of war, as did similar movements toward national autarky in the 1930s. Anti-Japanese sentiment in the United States has already been reciprocated in Japan. The effect of the imperative, "Buy American!" is likely to be increased national antagonism. Once again, this is not a conclusive argument against the imperative but a substantive question which would strongly affect whether a moderate patriotism can be distinguished from a harmful national chauvinism.

We have been investigating the possibility of a moderate patriotism within the framework of a limited universal morality of basic rights specified by an objective list. If we try to allow patriotism and forbid racism on the basis of a universal morality that makes racial discrimination a violation of a fundamental right but makes discrimination based on national citizenship permissible, the universal morality with this structure looks implausible and arbitrary. We want to know by what criterion we decide what is on the list and what is not.

Philosophical moral theory, in either a Kantian or a utilitarian vein, has attempted to provide a single principle or a closely related set of principles from which a morality might be derived. Can either a universalist utilitarianism or a universalist Kantianism show why (some) patriotism is good and racism is bad? The task for the universalist utilitarian is easy to describe: it must be shown that we achieve the overall best results, everyone's interests counting equally, if we (or some of us) are patriotic, but that we do not achieve the best results if people practice racism. Such an argument requires an estimate of the effects of patriotism and racism in human societies. Some of the arguments endorsing patriotism are familiar enough. It was common in the nineteenth century for British intellectuals to argue that the spread of British imperialism had a civilizing and uplifting effect on non-European peoples. We are familiar with U.S. politicians who identify U.S. interests with the interests of all the world's peoples in human rights and democracy. Or one might argue, as Sidgwick does with respect to devotion to family and associates, that limitations on power, knowledge, and affection make it best overall that people concentrate other-regarding concerns on members of their community.[6]

These arguments are about the effect of patriotism or a particular patriotism; needless to say, there is much room for argument. In the eighteenth and nineteenth centuries many believed that particular nationalisms, especially U.S. and French, represented universal human interests and progress.[7] We are now more skeptical about the effects of nationalism. Earlier in the century communists believed that national liberation struggles were part of universal human progress. But the outcomes in Algeria, Vietnam, and elsewhere leave much room for doubt. So it is hard to accept utilitarian arguments that some limited patriotism will lead to the best results universally.

The most plausible strategy for defending patriotism is to argue for an indirect universalism, either utilitarian or Kantian: in order to realize universal principles (promoting well-being and respect for human rights) we need social norms that bind people together, and those norms create special relationships, with corresponding special duties. Hence universal principles can be realized only through relationships that require preferential treatment.[8] I have no quarrel with this general conclusion. But are nation-states and patriotic culture—a culture of preference for one's compatriots and country—among the institutions that in fact realize universal principles? I have argued that there are substantial reasons to doubt this.

The problematic relationship between patriotism and moral universalism derives from our history. Universalism arose fairly recently in human societies, perhaps first in the philosophies and religions of hellenistic society.[9] The parable of the good Samaritan is a typical expression of the rejection of nationalism that characterized Christian universalism. This remained the dominant ethical ideal in Europe until the rise of the nation-state and, later, of conscious nationalism in the eighteenth century. There were various efforts to reconcile nationalism and patriotism with the tradition of universalism. Efforts at reconciliation are essentially conceptions of human history that say that patriotism helps to realize universal well-being or human rights. This positive estimate of patriotism can be derived either from an optimistic view that patriotism is a stage in our progress toward a more universal moral regard or from a pessimistic view that widespread patriotism is the closest most of us can get to consciously practicing universal moral ideals. I am suggesting that neither the pessimism nor that particular optimism is warranted: a genuine universalism is possible, but only as a result of a struggle against patriotism and nationalism.

NOTES

1. Stephen Nathanson, "In Defense of 'Moderate Patriotism,'" *Ethics* 99 (1989): 535–52. Page references to Nathanson are in the text.

2. Alasdair MacIntyre, "Is Patriotism a Virtue?" Lindley Lecture (University of Kansas Philosophy Department, Lawrence, 1984).

3. The reader should not assume that the author believes that family-centered morality, the money economy, and the wage system are compatible with promoting a better world for all. For a communist critique of these, see "Road to Revolution IV—A Communist Manifesto (1982)," *PL: A Journal of Communist Theory and Practice* (1989): 9–14.

4. William Julius Wilson, *The Truly Disadvantaged* (Chicago: University of Chicago Press, 1987), p. 60, cites the absence of social networks linking a jobless individual to others who have jobs to explain joblessness, especially in inner-city black ghettos. On widening black-white disparities, see U.S. Bureau of the Census, *Statistical Abstract of the United States: 1988*, 108th ed. (Washington, D.C.: Government Printing Office, 1987), p. 427.

5. It has been common in left-wing circles to distinguish between the nationalism of more prosperous nations and that of oppressed nations or oppressed nationalities in

multiethnic nations and to regard the nationalism of the oppressed as good. The above argument should not be understood as endorsing that position. The experience of black nationalism in the United States seems to indicate that the nationalism of oppressed peoples does little or nothing to alleviate oppression. But that is another argument.

6. Henry Sidgwick, *The Methods of Ethics*, 7th ed. (Indianapolis: Hackett, 1984), pp. 433–34.

7. Hans Kohn made this point in different places. See, e.g., *The Age of Nationalism* (New York: Harper, 1962), pp. 3–4.

8. This argument is made convincingly, from a human rights perspective, by Alan Gewirth, "Ethical Universalism and Particularism," *Journal of Philosophy* 85 (1988): 283–302.

9. See, e.g., Hans Kohn, *The Idea of Nationalism: A Study in Its Origins and Background* (New York: Macmillan, 1944), chap. 2.

Chapter Six

STEPHEN NATHANSON

IS PATRIOTISM LIKE RACISM?

*I*n his provocative essay, "Patriotism Is Like Racism," Paul Gomberg argues that there is no morally defensible form of patriotism.[1] In his view, attempts to avoid extreme patriotism and to develop a moderate form of patriotism that is compatible with universal moral values must fail.[2] It is no more possible to develop a moral form of patriotism than it is to develop a moral form of racism.

In this paper, I want to defend the possibility of a morally legitimate form of patriotism by showing that Gomberg's arguments are not sound. As part of my argument, I will attempt to show that just as we need to distinguish different forms of patriotic loyalty and evaluate them separately, so we must distinguish different forms of racial loyalty and evaluate them differently.

Gomberg uses two general types of arguments to discredit patriotism. He argues both that patriotism is inherently immoral and that it is immoral because of its bad effects.

Let me begin with arguments for the inherent immorality of patriotism. Here again, there are two possible kinds, and Gomberg seems to use both. First, one may argue that patriotism is wrong because it involves an illegitimate degree of special concern for some people and fails to accord equal consideration to all human beings.[3] The trouble with this radical universalist argument is that it forces us to condemn all forms of special concern and special duties. If accepted, this argument would then force us to reject not only patriotism but also love, friendship, family ties, connections to neighbors, colleagues, and any other relationships that generate special concerns and duties to restricted groups.

While I do not think that radical universalism is foolish, there is much that

From the *APA Newsletter on Philosophy and the Black Experience* 91, no. 2 (1992): 9–12. Copyright © 1992 American Philosophical Association. Reprinted by permission of the American Philosophical Association.

is frightening and unattractive about it.[4] At the least, there is a strong burden of proof on the universalist to show that this radical restructuring of our lives is necessary. I myself doubt that a convincing argument can be made that all special ties are inherently immoral. If, however, some special ties (family, friendship, etc.) are acknowledged to be morally permissible, then in principle, a special tie to one's country could be morally permissible as well.

A second argument for the inherent immorality of patriotism grants that special ties to some people or groups are permissible but claims that a special claim to one's *country* is not. It is here that Gomberg's analogy with racism plays a role. If racism is an inherently evil special tie, then there can be no good form of racism, and if patriotism is like racism, it too must be rejected.

In order to evaluate this argument, we need to have clearer ideas about the nature of both patriotism and racism. In its primary sense, "patriotism" names a complex set of attitudes that includes:

1. A special affection for one's own country;
2. A sense of personal identification with one's country;
3. A special concern for the well-being of one's country;
4. A willingness to make sacrifices to aid or protect one's country.

If this definition is correct, then all patriotic people must possess these features. Nonetheless, patriots may differ among themselves in important ways. In particular, those whom I call *extreme patriots* believe in the superiority of their own country and wish it to dominate over others. They have little to no concern for persons outside their own country and recognize few if any constraints on what their country may do to promote its own good. Those that I call *moderate patriots*, however, have a special affection for their country but do not believe in its superiority or seek dominance over others. In addition, moderate patriots do have concern for others besides their fellow citizens and want their country to pursue its good within the limits of various moral constraints. For example, moderate patriots would condemn going to war against another country because they want its land or wealth, while extreme patriots would not object to this.

I believe that moderate patriotism is morally permissible while extreme patriotism is not. Extreme patriotism is a form of fanaticism that countenances wanton cruelty and disregard of the rights of others. Moderate patriotism encourages support of one's own country but does not have these immoral implications. That is why it is a morally permissible form of attachment.

With these distinctions in mind, one might try to present a similar perspective on racism. If we substitute the word "race" for the word "country" in the list of features above, we get a description of an attitude that involves a sense of special connectedness between people and their racial group. A person who feels this special connection would have the following attributes:

1. A special affection for one's own race;
2. A sense of personal identification with one's race;

3. A special concern for the well-being of one's race;

4. A willingness to make sacrifices to aid or protect one's race.

This definition seems to capture something important and gives some support to Gomberg's claim that patriotism and racism have something in common. The question, however, is whether we should call this set of attitudes "racism." As a definition, it departs sharply from ordinary usage. When speaking of racism, we tend to mean not just a positive attitude toward one's own race but a negative attitude toward other races.[5] While our language permits us to distinguish patriotism from chauvinism and xenophobia, we have no such vocabulary with respect to racism. Racism, as we ordinarily speak of it, is the analog of *extreme* patriotism, for it implies not just special regard for one's own group but a special disregard for other groups. Hence, there is a sense in which racism is necessarily immoral, while patriotism is not similarly immoral by definition because it can take extreme or nonextreme forms.

If racism in its ordinary sense means "extreme racism" (the analogue of extreme patriotism), then one might think it possible, as Gomberg ironically suggests, to construct a morally legitimate form of racism which we can call "moderate racism." Gomberg's suggestion is ironic because he thinks that any form of racism is morally tainted.

Gomberg's claim raises two separate questions. First, is there a morally acceptable form of racial loyalty that is comparable to moderate patriotism? Second, should this attitude be thought of as a form of racism?

My answer is that there is a form of racial loyalty that is analogous to moderate patriotism, and this moderate form of racial loyalty is not inherently immoral. It is a mistake, however, to call this attitude a form of racism because racism involves not just a sense of positive connection with one's own group but also a negative attitude toward members of other races. Racism necessarily involves a belief in the superiority and inferiority of various groups. Hence, we can no more speak of "moderate racism" than we can speak of "moderate chauvinism" or "moderate xenophobia."[6]

While racists believe in the superiority of their own race and seek its dominance over others, moderate racial loyalists have special affection for their own racial group and may devote special efforts to achieving its well-being. Nonetheless, unlike racists, they would recognize and respect the rights of members of other races and would honor moral constraints that limit the actions that may be done to advance their own group's well-being.[7]

One might still wonder, however, whether any form of attachment to others based on race could be morally legitimate. Don't people who seek racial equality and an end to discrimination want to do away with race-based discrimination entirely, whether it is negative or positive? How can any form of racial loyalty be morally acceptable?

In addressing these questions, it is helpful to consider the case of reformers like Martin Luther King Jr. King's central mission was to promote the rights and the well-being of African Americans. In part, no doubt, he was motivated by universal moral ideals. Nonetheless, it is hard to believe that his special affection for, concern for, and identification with black people played no role in his activities. If this is the case, then he would qualify as a moderate racial loyalist, and anyone who condemns this form of attachment to a particular group would have to judge King's motivation and activities negatively.[8]

One might object, however, that King championed the rights of African Americans not because he and they were black but because they were oppressed. Surely, that is correct. Nonetheless, if racial identification had nothing to do with his activities, then prior to his engaging in acts to improve the status of blacks, King would have had to judge which of the various groups in the world was the most oppressed and which he was in the best position to support. Only if this group turned out to be the American blacks would he be justified in supporting their cause rather than that of other oppressed people. It is doubtful that King engaged in such a universalistic form of deliberation. Likewise, it is doubtful that we think such deliberation would be necessary in order to make his actions morally acceptable. Hence, if what King did was right and if it was motivated by his sense of connection and loyalty to other black Americans, then the type of racial loyalty he exhibited is not inherently wrong.[9]

Once we distinguish between racist and nonracist forms of racial loyalty, then, we can see that there is a form of racial loyalty that is comparable to moderate patriotism. Because this form is morally legitimate, however, its existence does nothing to discredit moderate patriotism. Moderate patriotism is analogous to moderate racial loyalty. It is not analogous to *racism* because racism is by definition a nonmoderate point of view. For these reasons, Gomberg's attempt to discredit patriotism by likening it to racism fails.

Let me now turn to Gomberg's second type of argument against patriotism. If patriotism is not inherently evil, perhaps it is contingently evil because of its effects.

Gomberg makes the plausible claim that the special preferences that operate among families, friends, and ethnic groups have led in the past to a system in which some groups—blacks, immigrants, and others—are excluded from jobs and other important social goods. Even innocuous-looking practices like having one's children work in one's own business when they are common within a society end up conferring important advantages and disadvantages on particular groups. Likewise, the preference for citizens of one's own country may lead to the continuation of great poverty in other countries. Hence, even if special, morally constrained preferences are not inherently evil, they may be contingently evil because they create and support systems that cause discrimination, oppression, and misery for many people.

This utilitarian argument against special preferences is difficult to evaluate because we do not know what would happen if we were to loosen or undermine special connections. We might move from patriotism to absolute egoism rather than to universalism. Certainly, a lack of concern for our own cities, states, and nation seems to have led to a situation in which people are unwilling to pay taxes or otherwise contribute to the public good.[10] Globalism is not the only alternative to patriotism, and the alternatives we actually get may be worse than those Gomberg condemns.

Nonetheless, Gomberg raises a serious point. We may discover that preferences that look innocuous and that even appear to be laudatory may need to be reassessed if we see that they operate in a systematic way that creates avoidable hardship and misery.

I do not see this as refuting the moderate patriotic position, however. Instead, it draws attention to the constraints that morality imposes on all special duties and preferences. If preferring our own country leads to widespread poverty and starvation in other countries, then we need to revise our practices. In general, special preferences need to be constrained when the preferred groups are especially privileged and other groups are oppressed or in dire need. Unlike Gomberg, however, I interpret this to be a part of the moderate patriotic perspective. Hence, I do not take his examples to be arguments against moderate patriotism. Part of the point of moderate patriotism is that one is to have a critical attitude toward duties to one's country and that one have some concern for people in other countries. If one's own country is already well-served, then the needs of others may outweigh the needs of those to whom one has special ties. Likewise, if our identification with our country leads us to want it to behave morally, then we will not favor policies that perpetuate our unfair advantages while others remain in dreadful conditions.

In this respect, patriotism is like parenthood. Parents may wish for their children's well-being, but this is not the same as wanting their children to have unfair advantages over others or thinking that all that matters is that one's own children do well. A good parent need not be indifferent to the fate of the children of other parents. Nor need patriots be indifferent to the fate of people beyond one's national borders.

With this point in mind, let me consider an objection to my defense of moderate racial loyalty. I defended racial partiality on the part of Martin Luther King and other black advocates of equality for African Americans. One might object, however, that this requires me to defend "moderate" white loyalists as well and that this seems to be a mistaken position.

Recall that my key point was that a racial preference might not be inherently wrong or evil. American blacks have been an oppressed group that has needed special attention. Whites are not similarly oppressed as a group. Thus, a person with a special affection and concern for whites might not be equally justified in promoting their interests if their interests are already well served and those of other racial groups are not. This is precisely like the case of the patriot whose country is already much better off than other countries. In general, special efforts on behalf of a group might be redundant and might simply be wrong if they require neglect of the much more pressing needs of others.

My main concern has been to show that patriotism and other special preferences are not inherently immoral. I do not want to claim, however, that acting on these special preferences is always morally right. Whether it is right depends on both the historical context and on the nature of the moral constraints that limit our special duties and preferences.

Just what these moral constraints are and how much persons and groups are required to sacrifice for the well-being of others is, of course, a difficult and controversial matter. Until these issues are resolved, the exact nature of the limitations on pursuing the good of those to whom we have special ties will remain indeterminate. My central point here is that moderate patriots will be appropriately responsive to these moral demands.

Gomberg has one other argument that needs to be considered. My defense of patriotism rests on the claim that there is a moderate form of patriotism that is a middle position between pure universalism and extreme chauvinism. Gomberg doubts that this middle position is sustainable, and he offers historical cases to show that in practice, moderate patriotism will collapse either into universalism or chauvinism.[11]

While I cannot discuss his cases here, I think I can prove that moderate patriotism is a distinct position. My confidence that it is a genuine alternative to both extreme universalism and extreme chauvinism rests on the fact that these are structurally similar sorts of views. We understand what an extreme egoist would be (a person who only acts for his or her own good) and what an extreme altruist would be (a person who genuinely counts his own good as having no more weight than others).[12] Most of us fall in between. We believe that morality permits a preference for ourselves and those we care about, but we acknowledge restrictions on what we may do in pursuit of our own good and of those we care about. We have personal preferences but recognize impersonal constraints on action. Since it is obvious that these middle views — which we could call either "moderate egoism" or "moderate altruism" — exist and do not collapse into either extreme, there is no reason why moderate patriotism must collapse into either universalism or chauvinism.

In defending patriotism, I have argued first that extreme universalism is unattractive because it forbids all special connections and not just patriotism. Second, Gomberg's analogy between patriotism and racism does not discredit patriotism because (a) it fails to distinguish racism from racial loyalty, and (b) it does not recognize the existence of a morally legitimate form of moderate "racial loyalty." Finally, moderate patriots agree that where special preferences lead to or support systems of injustice, then their special attachment to their own country should give way to more universalistic concerns. There is all the difference in the world between racism and this form of acceptable patriotism.[13]

NOTES

1. *Ethics* 101 (1990): 144–50.

2. Gomberg's essay is a criticism of my paper "In Defense of 'Moderate Patriotism,'" *Ethics* 99 (1989): 535–52.

3. For this type of argument, see Tolstoy's powerful essay "Patriotism, or Peace?" in *Tolstoy's Writings on Civil Disobedience and Nonviolence* (New York: New American Library, 1968).

4. Thomas Nagel provides a forceful statement on the basis of moral universalism in *Equality and Partiality* (New York: Oxford University Press, 1991).

5. Andrew Oldenquist makes this point about the negative aspect of racism and concludes (wrongly, I think) that racism is not a genuine form of loyalty. See his "Loyalties," *Journal of Philosophy* 79 (1982): 176–77.

6. In earlier versions of this paper, I did use the term "moderate racism" in this way. I appreciate the comments of those who convinced me that it was an error to do so.

7. For a valuable discussion of related issues, see Lawrence Blum, "Antiracism, Multiculturalism, and Interracial Community: Three Educational Values for a Multicultural Society" (Boston: University of Massachusetts, 1992). Kwame Anthony Appiah describes various racial doctrines and does allow for a morally permissible form of "racism" in his "Racisms," in David Theo Goldberg, ed., *Anatomy of Racism* (Minneapolis: University of Minnesota Press, 1990). In the same volume, see Lucius Outlaw, "Toward a Critical Theory of Race" for a valuable general discussion of race and racism. For a historical survey, see Robert Miles, *Racism* (London: Routledge, 1989), chap. 2.

8. King's moral and political views are cogently and eloquently expressed in *Where Do We Go From Here?—Chaos or Community* (Boston: Beacon Press, 1968). I discuss King's views on civil disobedience in *Should We Consent to Be Governed? A Short Introduction to Political Philosophy* (Belmont, Calif.: Wadsworth, 1992).

9. For arguments that lend support to this position, see Bernard Gert, *Morality: A New Justification of the Moral Rules* (Oxford University Press, 1988), pp. 163–64, 239–40.

10. This point is stressed in Oldenquist in "Loyalties," as well as in such recent books as Robert Bellah et al., *Habits of the Heart* (Harper and Row, 1986) and Morris Janowitz, *The Reconstruction of Patriotism* (University of Chicago Press, 1983).

11. A similar argument is raised by Alasdair MacIntyre in "Is Patriotism a Virtue?" Lindley Lecture (Lawrence, Kan.: University of Kansas Press, 1984), pp. 6–7.

12. Peter Singer appears to advocate this ideal in parts of "Famine, Affluence, and Morality," *Philosophy & Public Affairs* 1 (1972): 229–44.

13. I am indebted to Norman Fischer, Paul Gomberg, Judith Green, Leonard Harris, and Nelson Lande for helpful reactions to earlier versions of this paper.

Chapter Seven
DAVID McCABE

PATRIOTIC GORE, AGAIN

*T*he antinomy between liberal morality and patriotism has long been taken for granted. Liberal morality emphasizes impartiality, universality, and showing all individuals equal concern. Patriotism—by which I mean the doctrine that co-nationality is a morally significant relationship that may impose special duties and sanction special treatment—stresses partiality, particularity, and showing special concern for one's co-nationals. While moral philosophers for some time have tended to believe that the persuasiveness of liberal morality demonstrates the moral inadequacy of patriotism, recent years have seen several notable efforts to revise this appraisal and to defend the legitimacy of the moral partiality sanctioned by patriotism. While the forces behind these revisionary arguments are manifold, three factors have played especially important roles: the development of communitarianism and its critique of atomized selves and impartial principles of liberal morality; the importance that moral philosophers such as Bernard Williams and Thomas Nagel have accorded to the connection between moral agency and issues like particular relations and life projects; and the increased prominence around the globe of movements championing the importance of special moral relationships between co-nationals.

The question of the origins of the revisionists, however, is secondary. What is most important for normative ethics, of course, is assessing their arguments that the claims of patriotism have genuine normative force which liberal moralists have been wrong to deny. A survey of recent revisionist writing reveals two general strategies at work, which I shall call hard and soft patriotism, for restoring legitimacy to patriotism. Hard patriots allow that the partiality implicit in patriotism is often incompatible with liberal morality, but

From the *Southern Journal of Philosophy* 35, no. 2 (1997): 203–23. Copyright © 1997 The University of Memphis. Reprinted by permission of the *Southern Journal of Philosophy*.

they argue that the former is nonetheless morally significant and may sometimes legitimately override the demands of the latter. Advocates of this
approach thus see the legitimacy of patriotism as revealing serious limitations
to liberal morality. Soft patriots, on the other hand, argue that patriotism and
universalism are not fundamentally incompatible and that liberal morality can
recognize and incorporate many of the central claims of patriotism. Advocates
of this view, then, suggest that the conflict between liberal morality and patriotism has been overstated and that a reasonable moral scheme can be outlined
incorporating central elements from each.

In this paper I argue that neither of these ways of defending patriotism is
satisfactory and that the skeptical view remains the right view: liberal morality
and patriotism are fundamentally at odds, and this should lead to a general suspicion of any defense of patriotism, insofar as the latter may help tempt people
away from the appropriate claims of equal moral treatment and towards something resembling group egoism. I shall defend this thesis through an indirect
argument: since there are broadly three options in the debate between liberal
morality and patriotism (one can defend liberal morality over patriotism,
defend patriotism over liberal morality, or argue that the two can be reconciled), I will consider the last two and, in giving reasons to reject them both,
will thereby endorse the third. So while my argument is largely critical, it aims
at establishing the positive theses that liberal morality cannot be reconciled
with patriotism and that it constitutes an approach to morality superior to that
of patriotism. To forestall one criticism, I should say straight away that my critique of patriotism is in no way intended as a general rejection of the importance of partialities and particular relationships in approaching morality.
Though this broader question has some points of contact with my argument,
in ways I shall discuss, it is distinct from the one being investigated here. In
this paper my focus is solely on the legitimacy of co-nationality as a morally
significant feature, and my negative assessment is confined to this particular
form of partiality.

I

I begin by considering two influential arguments in favor of what I am calling
hard patriotism, those put forth by Andrew Oldenquist in his article "Loyalties"[1] and by Alasdair MacIntyre in his Lindley Lecture, "Is Patriotism a
Virtue?"[2] Both Oldenquist and MacIntyre allow that a morality grounded in
special concern for one's co-nationals is incompatible with liberal morality's
emphasis on universalism, but both offer strong arguments suggesting that this
incompatibility is no reason to reject the partiality implicit in patriotism. Oldenquist, in fact, goes farther than this. He argues that even apparently universalist moral systems like utilitarianism and Kantianism implicitly defend loyal-

ties of some sort (to human beings in both cases, he claims) which cannot themselves be defended by invoking impartial criteria consistent with universal moral concern. According to Oldenquist, loyalties specify the domains within which agents are willing impartially to apply moral principles, but loyalties are not themselves justified by principles of universal concern. Since they are the necessary condition for the application of impartial principles, loyalties are thus in an important sense prior to moral universalism and so cannot be rejected from the standpoint of universal morality. Liberal morality therefore cannot be understood as superior to a morality centered around group loyalties, says Oldenquist, because there simply is no morality that is not ultimately rooted in group loyalties. On these grounds Oldenquist criticizes liberal morality's rejection of patriotism and defends what he calls loyalty patriotism, which sanctions showing special concern to one's co-nationals simply because they are one's own and denying equal consideration to others simply because they are not.

In making his argument, Oldenquist relies on three crucial moves. If any one of these is weak, his overall argument will suffer. But in fact all three are problematic, and the collective weaknesses seriously undermine his account.[3] First, he argues against the general presumption that wider loyalties are better than narrower ones. As his treatment of utilitarianism and Kantianism shows, Oldenquist recognizes that the ideals of impartial morality and equal concern could be understood in terms of his own model of loyalty, i.e., as commanding simply a wider loyalty (to the human race) than that which patriotism demands—and that he must therefore refute the claim that wider loyalties should always take precedence over narrower ones. This he does on two fronts: first, he argues that, for most persons, expanding one's loyalty tends to dilute one's moral concern, rendering it "weak and pallid";[4] second, as we have seen, he suggests that even apparently impartial moral systems like utilitarianism and Kantianism are at root loyalty-based and not universalist in the way they claim. Thus, Oldenquist concludes that there is no good reason to demand that a person's loyalty extend to all human beings rather than to his co-nationals. But this is too quick, for intuitively there seems a very good moral reason to encourage people to adopt wider over narrower loyalties— namely, that the chief moral danger for most people is that they will fail to give appropriate attention to the needs not of those closest to them, but of those more distant. The very idea of moral development as moral psychologists since the Stoics have pointed out, involves the expansion of our circle of moral concern: the egoism of the child gets expanded to include the family, then friends, then the community, and so on. Neither of the two reasons Oldenquist gives for rejecting this account of moral growth is persuasive enough to alter our commitment to this ideal. No doubt many persons do find it difficult to expand their circle of moral concern so as to give due weight to those they may not know very well or care very much for. But this fact just demonstrates more dramatically the importance of embracing wider loyalties over narrower ones—as a corrective to our natural multiplying glasses, to use Hobbes's term, which ensure that our own interests consistently loom disproportionately large in our field of moral vision. There may even be, as Oldenquist claims, a psychological limit to the circle of loyalty to whom human beings can show concern, but this in itself does nothing to show that we should not strive to approach that ideal as much as possible. Nor does the fact (if it is one) that allegedly impartial moralities incorporate undefended claims of partiality show that partiality is therefore legitimate: the proper response, if indeed Oldenquist's claim is true, is instead to demand that such theories either justify the partiality they tacitly invoke or expand their circle of moral concern.

Oldenquist's second questionable move is to argue from the specific case of family loyalty to the general proposition that partiality towards those in one's loyalty group is acceptable. Declaring that his strategy is to "defend the easier case of family loyalty, and assume that whatever we can conclude about the one case we can conclude in principle about [loyalty patriotism]," Oldenquist invokes our shared agreement that parents act quite rightly in showing partiality to their own drowning child over a stranger and goes on to suggest that "this line of argument, if it applies to any loyalty, applies to all loyalties including national loyalty."[5] But this form of argument by analogy is inadequate on at least two grounds. First, even if we grant the analogy, all the argument shows is that patriots do nothing wrong in defending their own country rather than another when both are under attack. The argument does not establish the broader point that attending to the needs of those in one's loyalty circle generally overrides the duties one has to those outside one's group. While many may agree that parents act appropriately in providing goods for their children even when the same good could benefit another child slightly more, as this differential grows one reaches a point at which it is wrong to confer trivial benefits on one's family at the expense of others' serious needs. By analogy, then, there are limits to what one may do to aid one's co-nationals when the needs of others are urgent, and Oldenquist's argument does not sufficiently address this important point.

The second, more serious weakness in the argument by analogy is that Oldenquist has chosen an archetypically legitimate relation of justified partiality, but he has not looked closely enough at the nature of the relationship involved to distill a general principle indicating which loyalties sanction partiality and which do not. Consider, for example, a situation where someone had a chance to save one of two drowning people, one of whom was of her race and one of whom was not. Most of us would feel that a decision to act based solely on a sense of racial loyalty would not be justified. Indeed, acting on this sort of loyalty tends to make such a decision appear morally abominable. What this shows, then, is that loyalties differ in the extent to which they sanction partial treatment. So from the fact that some loyalties justify partial treatment we cannot conclude *tout court* that all loyalties justify partial treatment. What is needed is an argument explaining what it is about a particular type of loyalty that makes it a legitimate grounding for partial treatment; once that has been spelled out, we can then go on to determine whether loyalty patriotism satisfies the relevant criteria. This sort of argument would allow us to distinguish good instances of loyalty from bad ones and thus to gain the critical moral distance towards loyalties that Oldenquist fails to account for.[6] Absent such an argument, Oldenquist's account does little more than sanction bare preference.

The distinction between good and bad loyalties brings us to Oldenquist's third crucial move: his claim that the good loyalty of patriotism can be clearly distinguished from bad loyalties like racism. Oldenquist attempts to distinguish patriotism from racism on two fronts. First, he claims that racism, unlike patriotism, often depends on ignorance of the facts and false claims about other races. Second, he suggests that racism is negative, whereas patriotism and community loyalty are positive. But neither of these distinctions is as firm as Oldenquist's argument requires. First, as scholars of nationality have pointed out,[7] nations are held together largely by joint subscription to national myths that are often quite at variance with their actual history. As Renan put it, "to get one's history wrong [is an] essential factor in the making of a nation."[8] So if racism is to be ruled out because it relies on mistaken beliefs, patriotism may have to be ruled out for the same reason.[9] Nor does the distinction between patriotism being positive and racism negative withstand close scrutiny. Oldenquist acknowledges that loyalty to one's community cannot be sustained if one believes "that his community and his city are no better, and deserve no more, than a thousand others."[10] Patriotism requires, then, that one believe one's nation is better, and for this reason deserves more. But how can a patriot believe this without also believing that other nations are not as good, and for this reason deserve less? This seems a decidedly negative judgment about other nations (and one about which most patriots must be in error if there do exist objective criteria for the merits of a nation). Thus, loyalty patriotism as Oldenquist describes it will inevitably involve a negative judgment about other nations. In this respect again, as is the case with the other two crucial moves in Oldenquist's argument, serious problems plague Oldenquist's argument. The cumulative effect of these weaknesses renders his defense of hard patriotism unconvincing.

II

Alasdair MacIntyre has offered an alternative account of patriotism that, while not as hostile to liberal morality as Oldenquist's, also constitutes an example of what I am calling hard patriotism. Unlike Oldenquist, MacIntyre does not argue that all moralities ultimately rely on group loyalties. Instead, he claims

that liberal morality and the morality of patriotism constitute two rival moralities, each with distinctive strengths and weaknesses. Liberal morality offers the
attractive vision of a rational agent free to critically reflect on the ideals and
standards of her community and who can thus attain a level of free agency that
the morality of patriotism cannot offer. But the morality of patriotism, MacIntyre suggests, builds from an alternative and equally compelling account of
moral agency. The morality of patriotism begins from the assumption that moral
rules can sensibly make a claim on us only if we see them as protecting human
goods; without this connection, there is no reason to act morally. But since
human goods are always grounded in one's own nation and institutions, which
constitute what MacIntyre calls the "particular kind of social life" in which
goods are possible,[11] it follows that there is no good reason to follow morality's
constraints when confronted by members of societies outside our own, for in
such cases morality will appear cut off from the goods by reference to which it
is justified. One's conception of what morality requires will therefore extend
only to members of one's nation who share one's distinctive ways of life and
goods. MacIntyre's defense of the morality of patriotism depends, he acknowledges, on the truth of three crucial premises: (1) that we learn rules of morality
from within particular societies, (2) that our community is needed to sustain us
as moral agents, and (3) that the justification of morality must be in terms of
particular goods enjoyed within particular communities.[12] "I If these premises
are true (and though he declares himself agnostic, MacIntyre appears strongly
disposed to accept them), then the morality of patriotism is right to see loyalty
to the community as the central moral ideal and to believe that the universal
concern endorsed by liberal morality cannot meaningfully be contrasted with
what loyalty to one's community requires of one.[13] Patriotism would then constitute a morality that is at least as compelling and defensible as liberal morality.

The two critical questions are thus: Are these premises true? And if they
are, can liberal morality accommodate them without conceding the legitimacy
of patriotism? Certainly liberals will not deny that we learn moral rules within
particular societies, and since even a full-blown liberal like John Rawls has in
A Theory of Justice provided a sustained account of how this process works,
there seems no inconsistency between this premise and liberal morality. Nor
need liberals deny the second premise, that our community helps sustain us as
moral agents. Again, though, it is not clear how this fact tells against liberal
morality. Surely MacIntyre is not denying that situations may arise where
patriots are torn between what they believe morality requires and what their
nation requires, for this is precisely the situation he describes when he writes,
"the patriot may find that a point comes when he or she has to choose between
the claims of the project which constitutes his or her nation and the claims of
the morality that he or she has learnt as a member of the community whose life
is informed by that project."[14] These cases may well be tragic, for in them individuals may have to choose between doing what they take to be wrong and

preserving their nation, or doing what they take to be right and thereby damaging, and perhaps cutting themselves off from, their nation. But it is not clear how the second premise shows that the only reasonable decision in such cases is to act on behalf of one's nation. After all, there is something rather self-defeating in the suggestion that one should act immorally in order to preserve the community necessary to sustain oneself as a moral agent. And even if one rejects this argument and holds with MacIntyre that liberal morality cannot accommodate the second premise, its relevance extends only to those cases where the survival of one's community is at stake, but not to other, less dire conflicts of the sort nations frequently find themselves in.

The third premise, then, must be the one that distinguishes and legitimates the morality of patriotism. But even if we grant this premise, i.e., grant that moral systems depend on the recognition of there being particular goods within particular communities that morality protects, this premise would sanction the morality of patriotism only if we assume that there is a radical incommensurability of human goods between nations and that human beings are for the most part unable to extrapolate from their own pursuits of the good to understand those of others. For there are two ways in which we can understand what MacIntyre means in the third premise when he talks about the need for citizens to see morality as protective of certain socially contextual goods. He might mean that an individual has to see how *her own* good is furthered by her abiding by moral rules, or he might mean that an individual has to see how *some human being's* good is furthered by her abiding by moral rules. If he means the first of these, then he is right that patriots might have no reason to consider the welfare of citizens outside their nation, for the welfare of such people might well not be connected to their own good. But this is too high a demand to put on morality, for what morality sometimes requires (if it is at all different from self-interest) is precisely that on occasion an individual sacrifice her own good where the interests of others are more important.

To be plausible, then, MacIntyre's third premise must take the other interpretation—that an individual has a reason to act morally only if some human being's good is thereby furthered. But unless we assume a radical incommensurability between the sorts of goods that various communities make possible, liberal morality can accommodate MacIntyre's third premise, understood this way, without it being a problem. For if the citizens of one nation are able to recognize the goods that another offers as genuine goods, then it is consistent with MacIntyre's third premise that they will feel the force of morality's constraints. We should not make the mistake of thinking that one can recognize another's pursuit of the good only if one embraces that conception; instead, what one needs to be able to do is adopt a sufficiently charitable perspective that will allow one to recognize the parallels (if any exist) between the conceptions of the good to which one is committed and those that others pursue. For example, though I may worship as a Catholic, I can nonetheless recognize that my Islamic counterpart is engaged in a comparable quest for a human good through his particular form of worship, and I can understand that for both of us religious worship is a human good.

My claim, then, is that MacIntyre's third premise fails to legitimate the morality of patriotism as long as there are sufficient similarities between the types of goods that various nations make possible for their citizens. One could argue for the existence of such similarities by claiming somewhat controversially that virtually all civilizations have consistently recognized certain pursuits as human goods (e.g., religious worship, ceremonies of public remembrance, family structures, activities of play). But a more compelling argument for these similarities is found, ironically, in MacIntyre's own writings, which have repeatedly stressed the ideas that human goods are always localized within and dependent upon distinct human communities and that the good of any person is vitally connected to the flourishing of her social institutions.[15] If we admit this, then we must acknowledge that any nation's way of life makes possible certain human goods that could not be achieved in its absence, and this acknowledgment provides a reason (assuming, again, that morality is not simply coextensive with self-interest) to take into account how our actions will affect the fortunes of other nations and their citizens. So even if we allow with MacIntyre that moral rules, to appear compelling, must be shown to protect particular goods, this does not mean that they must be shown to protect any one particular good. To assume this is to commit the fallacy of which some have thought Aristotle guilty in his pursuit of the good at which all things aim: while all moral rules must be justified by their connection to some good, this does not mean that there is one good by connection to which all moral rules must be justified. I am claiming, then, that the morality of patriotism is defensible only in cases where one nation confronts another whose distinctive way of life make possible certain activities that the former cannot in any way envision as connected to human good. Perhaps such confrontations may occur. But in the far greater number of cases where this radical incommensurability does not obtain, the morality of patriotism is unwarranted.

III

Perhaps in response to the appearance of powerful arguments defending the partiality of patriotism against liberal morality, a number of scholars have recently sought a middle ground and argued for the compatibility of these two ideals. Two prominent examples of this line of argument are found in Yael Tamir's *Liberal Nationalism*,[16] and Stephen Nathanson's *Patriotism, Morality and Peace*.[17] The compatibility both are defending is, I think, deeply attractive: if it could be shown that the special concern many of us feel towards our co-nationals is consistent with the idea that all human beings should count equally in our moral deliberations, this would suggest a satisfying harmony in our eth- ical composition and would go some way towards taming the threat that many liberals fear in patriotism. And both Tamir and Nathanson have offered pow- erful arguments that merit and repay close attention. Nonetheless, I think serious problems remain with the arguments for reconciliation that each offers, and I want, by indicating where these problems lie, to suggest some reasons to be deeply skeptical that liberal morality can in any substantial sense accom- modate the claims of patriotism.

The central move in Tamir's argument consists in her exposing what she sees as the false dichotomy between the patriot's notion that we are simply born into our national identity and the liberal idea that we create our identity through our unconstrained choices. To embrace this dichotomy, she suggests, is to repeat the two central failings that characterize the patriot and the liberal: while patriots overlook the extent to which national allegiances are not con- ferred on human beings but are instead the products of choice, liberals gener- ally fail to acknowledge the importance of being rooted within a nation and the constitutive role that such rootedness has for any individual's identity. According to Tamir, the simplified approaches of the extreme forms of patrio- tism and liberalism obscure the fact that our identities are formed through a constant back and forth between the context provided by the national culture we inhabit and the free choices we make, as individuals situated within those contexts, either to affirm or reject membership in them. Thus she insists that while our national identities may be to an important degree optional and the result of our choices, such choices are made not by radically free agents of the kind that atomistic liberals posit, but by individuals who are always already influenced by and situated within a particular national context. Keeping this complementarity in clear view is the chief advantage that Tamir believes her vision of liberal patriotism[18] possesses over either chauvinistic patriotism or atomistic liberalism. A second, related virtue of her position, she claims, is its ability to explain how liberal societies can defend their tendency to focus on justice as it involves primarily members of their society and not persons in other countries, a position that some have seen as a betrayal of liberalism's avowed commitment to universal moral concern.[19]

On both of these points, though, Tamir's argument runs into trouble. Let me deal with the second one first. As a psychological observation, Tamir is cor- rect: the perceived moral significance of our shared nationality no doubt explains why many think partiality towards co-nationals is warranted. The important question here, however, is not a psychological one but a normative one. For it might be quite true that citizens of liberal states *feel* they have spe- cial obligations to their fellow citizens without it being true that they *really have* such special obligations; the latter does not follow from the former. Further, given Tamir's commitment to the liberal ideal of the equal moral standing of human beings and her recognition of the importance both of having one's national culture preserved and of having a sufficient number of national options to choose from, it follows from her argument that as long as one's own national culture is preserved to some minimally effective degree, one ought to take steps to ensure that as many other people as possible are positioned to preserve their own national cultures and to have a variety of national options from which to choose.[20] For this reason the legitimacy of showing partiality to one's co-nationals will depend on a prior assessment of how well nonnationals are situated to pursue their own national aspirations, and this suggests that expressions of partiality are distinctly subordinate to moral universalism.

Even if Tamir could resolve this problem, her defense of soft patriotism faces a deeper, more serious problem that strikes at the foundation of her argument. In her effort to show that patriotism is compatible with liberalism, Tamir stresses repeatedly the element of free choice in one's national allegiances, thereby laying the foundation for her reconciliation of the patriot's need for rootedness with the liberal ideal of autonomy. But there is good reason to doubt that these values can easily be reconciled, without significantly weakening one or the other, in the way Tamir suggests. After all, it is not simply a historical accident that patriots and nationalists have tended to stress that one's national identity is something one is born into rather than something one chooses. Instead, the prevalence of this theme reflects the fact that a sense of connection to the nation will more effectively satisfy one's need for roots if one feels that one's nation has in some sense chosen one, rather than the other way around. But this raises a severe problem for Tamir's argument, because it suggests that in order for my sense of nationality to satisfy my longing for rootedness, two conditions must be met which her account works to undermine. First, I will have to see my connection to my nation not as the product of human choices that could have been otherwise, but instead as a given about the world into which I find myself born. For how can I feel deeply, one might almost say onto-logically, rooted in a nation if I know that my bond to it is constituted by my act of free choice, which I can always revoke at some point in the future should I choose to? The inadequacy of this model of voluntary connection to the nation is the reason that, as Clifford Geertz has noted, nations are characterized by "primordial attachments" that have "an ineffable, and at times overpowering, coerciveness in and of themselves. One is bound to one's kinsman, one's neighbor, one's fellow believer, ipso facto; as the result not merely of personal affection, practical necessity, common interest, or incurred obligation, but at least in part by virtue of some unaccountable absolute import attributed to the very tie itself."[21] To persons drawn to a nation for these reasons, the idea that all individuals may freely choose from a menu of national identities is bound to seem incompatible with the sort of patriotism they want to preserve. Indeed, to understand their national allegiance in this way would threaten to rob it of the very qualities that enable it to satisfy their need to be rooted. So while Tamir's argument relies on a conception of national allegiance as the product of conscious and free choices, this understanding is both alien to, and likely to be resisted by, those individuals who most strongly feel the need to be rooted.[22]

The second condition that must be met if my nationality is to provide me with a satisfactory feeling of rootedness is that I see the nation of which I am a part as constituting a moral community of distinctive value. On this point the hard patriots are right: patriots do not see national allegiance per se as something valuable; they see allegiance to their own nation as especially valuable because of what their nation uniquely stands for.[23] Thus Tamir's argument, which tries to build on the features common to patriots of various nations, faces an insuperable problem arising from the fact that patriotism, to fulfill the psychological function Tamir allows, must be understood on inherently particularist grounds. A universalist theory that builds from the shared elements involved in such particularisms is likely in the end to offer only a pale simulacrum of patriotism, and not the real thing. If one begins as Tamir does from the assumption that nations are intrinsically valuable because they provide the cultural contexts for meaningful choices, one will inevitably misdescribe what motivates the patriot: the patriot does not value his nation just because it provides a context for choice (were this so, he should value all nations equally). Instead, he values his nation because it provides a particularly valuable context of choice, one that distinguishes his own nation from others.

The importance of the two conditions I am stressing, and the inadequacy of Tamir's account in meeting them, can be seen if we adopt a point that Charles Taylor has made in *The Ethics of Authenticity*. Taylor argues persuasively that my act of making a choice cannot by itself confer value and that in order for my choices to appear valuable to me, I must understand them within a horizon of significance that I see as binding on me independent of my choice. But if this is so, then the nation's ability to constitute a meaningful horizon of significance will be diminished to the extent that I come to see my connection to it as simply the result of a choice that might have been different. Nor does the fact that a nation's existence reflects choices that many individuals have made change the central problem here. For if my individual choice does not by itself confer significance, and the nation in which I root myself owes its existence to several such choices, why should I regard this act of collective choosing as providing significance? The more that citizens are taught to see their nation as a product of conscious choices originated by their forebears and propagated by their conscious choices, the more their nation is likely to lose its capacity to provide the ballast that roots them and gives meaning to their choices and, in some instances, their lives and deaths. Of course, this problem is avoided if one understands one's nation as distinctly valuable compared with other nations, but if this admission is made then there is no longer good reason to see the plurality of cultures as having intrinsic value in the way Tamir's argument requires.

I am suggesting, then, that Tamir's argument is caught in a dilemma. The three premises central to it—(1) that a feeling of rootedness in a nation, and

with it a willingness to show partiality to co-nationals, is an essential component in human well-being, (2) that one's nationality is properly the result of
one's free choice, and (3) that nations themselves are chiefly the results of collective acts of imagining—are at odds with one another, for recognition of the
second and third will work to undercut the feeling of rootedness the first mentions. Given this dilemma, two responses are possible. One is to deny the first
premise and embrace the sort of cosmopolitanism endorsed famously by Kant,
which seeks to downplay the moral implications of co-nationality and to
encourage a sense of connectedness to humanity at large. Whether human
sympathies can consistently be extended to such a wide number of people,
many of whom are radically alien to one another, remains unknown, though
there is nothing in principle against the suggestion, and certain figures in
human history have exemplified this sort of concern. The other possible
response is to deny the second and third premises and claim that people do not
choose their nationality and that nations are not simply imagined communities
but instead correspond to divisions that are somehow ontologically given in
the world. It is not hard to see how this second response would be supported
by such factors as quasi-racist ideologies, mythologies of divine provenance,
and a carefully cultivated aversion to all that is alien. For this reason, the oft-
noted connection between patriotic fervor and a strain of fierce irrationalism
should be seen not simply as an accident in the history of patriotism, but rather
as a vital element in the propagation of this form of partiality. For this reason
as well liberals have good reason to be skeptical about the sort of reconciliation Tamir proposes.

IV

Stephen Nathanson's attempt to reconcile patriotism and liberal morality
through what he calls "moderate patriotism" is less philosophically ambitious
than Tamir's, but its comparatively modest aim renders it in some ways more
persuasive. Nathanson acknowledges that to be worthy of the name, patriotism must involve "loyalty and a preference for the well-being of one's own
country over others," and that it may require one to promote its well-being
"even if that can only [sic] be done at the cost of diminishing the well-being of
other countries."[24] Like Tamir, Nathanson aims to show that this sort of patriotism is compatible with the premise that all persons' lives are of equal worth
and that universalist morality can therefore accommodate patriotism. In
arguing his case Nathanson distinguishes two kinds of universalism. The first
requires "absolutely equal treatment of everyone,"[25] by which he means taking
into concern equally the needs of all people affected by one's decision.
Nathanson allows that this sort of universalism (which I shall call universalism
of concern) is obviously inconsistent with patriotism, but he declares that this

gives no reason to reject patriotism because our deepest moral intuitions suggest that certain types of special concern (e.g., that which a parent has for a child, or a doctor for a patient) are often not only morally acceptable but requisite. The second sort of universalism requires, more modestly, only that one act on principles that one would be willing to universalize. This sort of universalism (which I shall call universalism of principle) is, Nathanson points out, compatible with showing partiality to some. As an example Nathanson offers the commandment "Thou shalt honor thy father and mother." Though this imposes special obligations regarding how one treats one's parents, in showing them special concern one is still abiding by a universalism of principle as long as one allows that all other children have similar special obligations to their parents. For this reason Nathanson claims that patriotism, i.e., the idea that one ought to show partiality towards one's nation and co-nationals, is compatible with moral universalism because it universalizes the principle that all people may show partiality to their own nation and co-nationals.[26]

At this point we must note an important qualification to the universalism of principle that Nathanson fails to develop but which has critical consequences for his argument: the mere fact that one would be willing to allow a principle to be universalized does not by itself show that acting on the principle is morally acceptable. Were this so, certain kinds of racists would be morally acceptable as long as they were willing to have everyone universalize the commandment "Thou shalt show special concern for members of thy race." If we ask ourselves what precisely is wrong with a universalist who adopts such a principle and look more closely into the distinction between racism and patriotism, we can begin to see the inadequacy of relying solely on a universalism of principle and the consequent limits on the sort of moderate patriotism Nathanson defends. Such an examination reveals, I shall argue, that the extent of partiality sanctioned by moderate patriotism may be quite small indeed, and that in many respects the attitudes of moral concern demanded by moderate patriotism overlap significantly with those demanded by a morality of universal concern.

One popular way of distinguishing racism from patriotism is to say that racism relies on a mistaken belief that objective differences exist between races, whereas patriotism makes reference to differences between nationalities that objectively exist. This response, however, faces several problems. First, it is open to the counterobjection that the same kind of generalizing that supports the belief in objective differences between nations may also support some beliefs in objective differences between races, at least within nations. If the moderate patriot then tries to distinguish the two cases by noting that racists are irrational because they believe in particular kinds of differences that do not meet objective criteria, one can charge that patriots are also guilty of irrationality, for they tend to feel that their nation's way of doing things is better than that of others, and this, as Nathanson himself points out, is a belief that in most cases must be false. Thus patriotism, like racism, also appears to rest on false beliefs. And if the moderate patriot denies that patriotism must involve feelings of superiority, and suggests instead, as Nathanson on occasion implies,[27] that the patriot might be especially devoted to his country just because he feels at home there and is familiar with it, we can imagine a racist especially devoted to members of his race for the same reasons. In this case, the charge that racism relies on false beliefs will not be warranted, for it may be quite true that the racist feels more at home and more familiar with those of his own race.

If we ask ourselves what it is about racism that so obviously strikes us as wrong, we see fairly quickly that our worries are rooted largely in the fact that racism has helped prop up centuries of oppression that have had seriously harmful consequences for large numbers of human beings. But this suggests, crucially, that the universalism of principle is subordinate to the universalism of concern in the following way: for a universalism of principle to be acceptable, it must be the case that universalizing the principle will not seriously violate universal moral concern. For this reason, it is not enough to show patriotism's compatibility with a universalism of principle. Nathanson must also show that the effects of patriotism are not likely to constitute a serious departure from the universalism of concern. This is why Nathanson says that "our loyalties must be fulfilled within the limits that morality imposes on us," and that our partiality is limited by our "duty to help others when they are in dire conditions and when our own community is sufficiently well off that it will not be seriously harmed by the diversion of resources to others."[28] What this means, of course, is that moderate patriots need to ask themselves about the sorts of effects their patriotism can be expected to have on people throughout the world.[29]

While Nathanson's argument for moderate patriotism is strengthened by his acknowledgment that it must fall within the limits morality imposes, the force of this concession for moderate patriots is far more severe than he allows. For the key question facing Nathanson's account has thus become, as he recognizes, something of an empirical one: namely, are the inequities that characterize the levels of wealth among countries around the world of such a magnitude, and do they involve such severe threats to human well-being, threats to what we might call a minimally decent life, that the acceptable degree of partiality that patriots may show co-nationals threatens to disappear? Once one recognizes the existence of severe disparities between nations and realizes that the partial treatment one shows one's co-nationals will come at the cost of helping nonnationals who may more urgently need it, one may be forced to conclude that very little partiality towards one's co-nationals is justified within the limits of morality. There is no doubt that we may all feel greater affection for our fellow nationals and may feel justified in giving priority to their welfare. But the crucial question, as I have said before, is not whether we feel that we have special obligations, but whether we in fact have them. In allowing that this question can be answered only after taking into account the need of nonnationals for the various goods that will enable them to lead a minimally decent life, Nathanson's moderate patriotism risks forfeiting its defense of partiality and collapsing into a morality of universal concern: for if many nonnationals are lacking such goods, and if they have, as Nathanson allows, positive rights to aid from others who are better off, then any substantial degree of partiality towards co-nationals will be difficult to defend.[30]

Nathanson does try to meet this objection by suggesting that wealthy countries of the West could substantially increase aid to other countries by redirecting government money away from unnecessarily high expenses like defense spending, but this response leaves two important questions unresolved. First, should citizens of wealthy nations refrain from embracing patriotism until their countries do much more to aid poorer nations? If yes, this means that many of those to whom Nathanson's argument is directed should not embrace the moderate patriotism he outlines. If no, then he is endorsing patriotism towards a nation that allows a great moral evil to go unaddressed, and this seems inconsistent with his insistence that the value of patriotism is conditional on the moral qualities of the nation. Second, if nations ought to help those in dire circumstances, why not those in slightly less difficult circumstances, or those facing only some serious hardships? Though Nathanson's argument assumes a duty to help only those in "dire conditions" (and thus endorses only what he calls an "ultra-minimal kind of sacrifice"), he shows some sympathy for the position that morality might in fact require more stringent sacrifices.[31] But the latter position (which seems at least as intuitively appealing as the ultra-minimal assumption he relies on) suggests that our duties extend not just to redressing dire poverty, but more broadly to improving the lives of citizens of other nations in substantial ways. If this be granted, the realm of partiality to co-nationals that moderate patriotism allows narrows even more, and the difference between moderate patriotism and a morality of universal concern becomes even harder to make out.

Moderate patriotism thus seems to sanction partiality to co-nationals in only two sorts of cases: if one is a citizen of a country that does not enjoy sufficient prosperity to help less fortunate citizens in other countries, or if one lives in a world that is not characterized by vast differences in the quality of life available to people. But as long as severe poverty continues to affect millions throughout the world, the extent of the partiality that Nathanson's account allows, at least for citizens of relatively prosperous nations, will be rather small indeed. And while one might be tempted to think that patriotism would remain an option for citizens of poorer states, strictly speaking this is not so. The central claim of patriotism is that the fact of co-nationality is intrinsically morally significant; but since the legitimacy of citizens in poorer nations showing special concern for their co-nationals is grounded in the fact that, from an impartial perspective, they are so much worse off than citizens of other nations, the partiality in this case is legitimated by universal moral concern. In this case co-nationality does not possess intrinsic moral significance, but instead functions as a useful way of indicating which human beings, impartially considered, stand in greatest need of aid. This helps explain, incidentally, why partiality between members of groups who have suffered or continue to suffer oppression (for example, blacks in the United States) does not offend against the principles of liberal morality in the same way that partiality by whites towards whites does. In the former case the legitimacy of partiality derives not from the intrinsic significance of racial similarity but from a commonality of shared oppression within a system that used racial classification as a means of oppression.[32] Liberal moralists can allow such partiality without suggesting that racial kinship is in itself a morally significant feature, just as they can allow partiality between citizens of poor nations without seeing co-nationality as a morally significant feature.

V

Given the apparent antinomy between patriotism and liberal morality, three broad responses are possible: one can argue in favor of liberal morality over patriotism, in favor of patriotism over liberal morality (hard patriotism), or for a reconciliation between the two (soft patriotism). Since these three positions exhaust our possibilities and since both hard and soft patriotism have weaknesses that make them unacceptable, my argument endorses the traditional liberal skepticism towards the partiality implicit in patriotism. It is worth repeating that nothing in my argument rules out the possibility that, in certain instances, showing partiality to one's co-nationals may be warranted. What I have argued, however, is that in such instances the justification for partiality is to be found not in the intrinsic moral significance of co-nationality, as patriots would have it, but rather in the way in which co-nationality helps identify features of a situation that are morally relevant from the standpoint of universal moral concern.

To some extent, the generally negative judgment about soft patriotism that I am defending may seem especially disappointing, for it suggests a deep obstacle to attaining the attractive ethical harmony between universal morality and our feelings of special obligations to co-nationals that soft patriotism promises. But there are two important reasons that we should not see this conclusion as indicating any deep incoherence in our moral frameworks. First, it is naive to expect that moral reflection will validate all the moral judgments one has uncritically formed over time. Instead, the process of reflecting on our moral judgments should be expected, on occasion, to reveal their inadequacies, and this is one of those times. Second, my argument does not show that liberal morality always trumps all claims of partiality. I have argued here only against the claims of partiality grounded in co-nationality. The partialities inherent in family relationships, loving relationships, and friendships, for example, may well stand up better against liberal morality than does the partiality in patriotism.[33] This difference may be easily lost sight of, for allowing intrinsic moral significance to any partiality is inherently incompatible with liberal morality's emphasis on universal moral concern. Some patriots may be tempted to argue that this incompatibility just points to a deep incommensurability and that there are thus no good reasons to endorse liberal morality over patriotism. Such an argument would, however, be weak, for the fact of incompatibility does not by itself imply incommensurability, and in weighing the merits of patriotism against those of liberal morality, the balance remains firmly on the side of liberal morality.

NOTES

1. Andrew Oldenquist, "Loyalties," *Journal of Philosophy* 79 (1982): 173–94.

2. Alasdair MacIntyre, "Is Patriotism a Virtue?" in *Communitarianism: A New Public Ethics*, ed. Markate Daly (Belmont: Wadsworth, 1994), pp. 307–18.

3. Though I will criticize much in Oldenquist's argument, it is a great virtue of his essay that he turns his attention to problems plaguing American urban life and suggests that many of these have their sources in a general pathology of alienation from the city as a meaningful focus of loyalty and community.

4. Oldenquist, "Loyalties," p. 181.

5. Ibid., pp. 186, 187.

6. John Cottingham, for example, has offered all argument defending some partialities on the grounds that they are essential components of the good life ("Partiality, Favoritism and Morality," *Philosophical Quarterly* 36 [1986], 357–73). This is one way Oldenquist might try to repair his argument, though the claim that strong national loyalty is central to the good life seems prima facie far more difficult to substantiate than claims about the importance of, say, loving or family relationships. An alternative strategy would be to claim first that shared commonalities of value ground partial treatment and then go on to claim that co-nationals overwhelmingly share such commonalities. Aside from the dubious nature of the claim about shared commonalities sanctioning partial treatment, the argument's particular relevance to co-nationality faces serious objections, as Jeff McMahan has pointed out in "The Limits of National Partiality," in *The Morality of Nationalism*, ed. Robert McKim and Jeff McMahan (New York: Oxford University Press, 1997).

7. The seminal work of this kind remains Benedict Anderson's *Imagined Communities* (London: Verso, 1983). Anthony Smith's *The Ethnic Origin of Nations* (Oxford: Blackwell, 1986) argues a similar point.

8. Ernest Renan, "What Is a Nation?" quoted in David Miller's *On Nationality* (New York: Oxford University Press, 1995), p. 34.

9. Some might think that at this point Oldenquist could defend his position by referring to the distinction between constitutive and background beliefs that David Miller sets forth in "The Ethical Significance of Nationality" (*Ethics* 98 [1988]: 647–62). According to Miller, constitutive beliefs are those which if mutually agreed to are sufficient, regardless of their truth or falsity, to constitute the relationship; what is central is that all people in the relationship share agreement on a belief, not that the agreed upon belief be true. While background beliefs are believed by members in the

relationship to be true, public revelation of their objective falsity would destroy the relationship. So some might argue that as long as co-nationals believe the national myth, and its objective falsity has not come to light, the conditions for partiality are satisfied. But this move would not get Oldenquist out of the problem raised by the parallel with racism, for if co-nationality justifies partiality among co-nationals because it is grounded in a shared commitment to a belief that is probably false, then racism justifies partiality among racists for the same reason.

10. Oldenquist, "Loyalties," p. 191.

11. MacIntyre, "Is Patriotism a Virtue?" p. 311.

12. Ibid., p. 312.

13. Ibid.

14. Ibid., p. 314.

15. One could also point out, as Charles Larmore has done in *Patterns of Moral Complexity* (Cambridge: Cambridge University Press, 1987), that there is one sense in which MacIntyre does believe that there is a universal human good, as evidenced by his "provisional conclusion" in *After Virtue* that "the good life for man is the life spent in seeking for the good life for man" (Notre Dame: University of Notre Dame Press, 1984), p. 219.

16. Yael Tamir, *Liberal Nationalism* (Princeton: Princeton University Press, 1993).

17. Stephen Nathanson, *Patriotism, Morality and Peace* (Boston: Rowman & Littlefield, 1993).

18. Tamir talks about liberal nationalism rather than liberal patriotism, but the position she describes shares the central element that I am focusing on in my examination of patriotism, i.e., the view that co-nationality is an intrinsically morally significant relationship that sanctions partiality.

19. For instance, Thomas Pogge sees this as a serious omission in Rawls's *A Theory of Justice* and tries to remedy it on what he claims are Rawlsian lines. See his *Realizing Rawls* (Ithaca: Cornell University Press, 1989).

20. Cf. Tamir's conclusion that "the plurality of cultures thus acquires an intrinsic value" (Tamir, *Liberal Nationalism*, p. 30).

21. "The Integrative Revolution: Primordial Sentiments and Civil Politics in the New States," quoted in *Nationalism*, ed. Anthony Smith and John Hutchinson (New York: Oxford University Press, 1994), p. 31. Tamir on occasion indicates an awareness of the importance of the idea Geertz is stressing, referring at one point to the tendency for nationalists to see the nation as a "collective destiny" (Tamir, *Liberal Nationalism*, p. 65). She does not, however, make clear how this view is compatible with national identity as the product of choice.

22. A similar problem plagues two other thoughtful attempts to marry autonomy and rootedness. See Jeff Spinner, *The Boundaries of Citizenship* (Baltimore: Johns Hopkins University Press, 1994) and David Hollinger, *Postethnic America* (New York: Basic Books, 1995).

23. "Patriotism does generally and characteristically involve a peculiar regard not just for one's own nation, but for the particular characteristics and merits and achievements of one's own nation. These latter are indeed valued *as* merits and achievements and their character as merits and achievements provides reasons supportive of the patriot's attitudes" (MacIntyre, "Is Patriotism a Virtue?" p. 308).

24. Stephen Nathanson, "In Defense of Moderate Patriotism," *Ethics* 99 (1989): 536. Nathanson's book expands on the themes of this essay.

25. Nathanson, *Patriotism, Morality and Peace*, p. 70.

26. I say "may show partiality" because Nathanson allows that some countries may be committed to a national project so unjust that its members may have a moral obligation to stand in its way.

27. Nathanson, *Patriotism, Morality and Peace*, p. 30.

28. Ibid., pp. 191, 174.

29. This important point was first brought to my attention by Paul Gomberg's critique of Nathanson, "Patriotism Is Like Racism," *Ethics* 101 (1990): 144–50. The argument of this paragraph owes much to Gomberg's analysis there.

30. At this point one might think that if one embraces a libertarian moral theory that sees rights as imposing only side constraints but not any positive duties of assistance, then one will have an easier time reconciling moderate patriotism with liberal morality. This attempt to resolve the incompatibility does not work, however, for the same libertarian arguments that discount positive duties to nonnationals also discount positive duties to co-nationals, and thus a libertarian theory forfeits the special obligation to aid one's fellow citizens that is central to patriotism.

31. Nathanson, *Patriotism, Morality and Peace*, pp. 180 ff.

32. McMahan has pressed the same point in "The Limits of National Partiality," forthcoming.

33. It is possible, however, that arguments defending these partialities may logically lead to conclusions not all that different from those that universal morality requires. Marilyn Friedman has offered such an argument with respect to Cottingham's defense of partiality (see "The Practice of Partiality," *Ethics* 101 [1991]: 818–35).

Chapter Eight

ROBERT E. GOODIN

WHAT IS SO SPECIAL ABOUT OUR FELLOW COUNTRYMEN?

*T*here are some "general duties" that we have toward other people, merely because they are people. Over and above those, there are also some "special duties" that we have toward particular individuals because they stand in some special relation to us. Among those are standardly supposed to be special duties toward our families, our friends, our pupils, our patients. Also among them are standardly supposed to be special duties toward our fellow countrymen.

Where those special duties come from and how they fit with the rest of morality is a moot point. I shall say little about such foundational issues, at least at the outset. In my view, the best way of exploring foundations is by examining carefully the edifice built upon them.

The bit of the edifice that I find particularly revealing is this: When reflecting upon what "special treatment" is due to those who stand in any of these special relations to us, ordinarily we imagine that to be especially *good* treatment. Close inspection of the case of compatriots reveals that that is not completely true, however. At least in some respects, we are obliged to be more scrupulous—not less—in our treatment of nonnationals than we are in our treatment of our own compatriots.[1]

This in itself is a politically important result. It shows that at least some of our general duties to those beyond our borders are at least sometimes more compelling, morally speaking, than at least some of our special duties to our fellow citizens.

This finding has the further effect of forcing us to reconsider the bases of our special duties to compatriots, with yet further political consequences. Morally, what ultimately matters is not nationality per se. It is instead some further feature that is only contingently and imperfectly associated with shared nationality. This further feature may sometimes be found among

From *Ethics* 98, no. 4 (1988): 663–86. Copyright © 1988 by The University of Chicago. Reprinted by permission of The University of Chicago Press.

foreigners as well. When it is, we would have duties toward those foreigners that are similar in their form, their basis, and perhaps even their strength to the duties that we ordinarily acknowledge toward our fellow countrymen.

I. THE PARTICULARIST'S CHALLENGE

A

Modern moral philosophy has long been insistently universalistic. That is not to say that it enjoins identical performances, regardless of divergent circumstances. Of course universal laws play themselves out in different ways in different venues and demand different things from differently placed agents. But while their particular applications might vary, the ultimate moral principles, their form and content, has long been regarded as essentially invariant across people. The same basic precepts apply to everyone, everywhere, the same.

A corollary of this universality is impartiality.[2] It has long been supposed that moral principles—and therefore moral agents—must, at root, treat everyone the same. Of course, here again, basic principles that are perfectly impartial can (indeed, usually will) play themselves out in particular applications in such a way as to allow (or even to require) us to treat different people differently. But the ultimate principles of morality must not themselves play favorites.

On this much, at least utilitarians and Kantians—the great contending tribes of modern moral philosophy—can agree. Everyone counts for one, no one for more than one, in the Benthamite calculus. While as an upshot of those calculations some people might gain and others lose, the calculations themselves are perfectly impartial. So too with Kant's Categorical Imperative. Treating people as ends in themselves, and respecting the rationality embodied in others, may require us to do different things to, for, or with different people. But that is not a manifestation of any partiality between different people or their various projects. It is, instead, a manifestation of our impartial respect for each and every one of them.

Furthermore, this respect for universality and impartiality is no mere quirk of currently fashionable moral doctrines. Arguably, at least, those are defining features of morality itself. That is to say, they arguably must be embodied in any moral code in order for it to count as a moral code at all.

B

Despite this strong attachment to canons of universality and impartiality, we all nonetheless ordinarily acknowledge various special duties. These are different in content and form from the general duties that universalistic, impartial moralities would most obviously generate for us. Whereas our general duties tell us how we should treat anyone, and are hence the same toward everyone, special duties vary from person to person. In contrast to the universality of the general moral law, some people have special duties that other people do not. In contrast to the impartiality of the general moral law, we all have special duties to some people that we do not have to others.[3]

Special duties, in short, bind particular people to particular other people. How this particularism of special duties fits with the universality and impartiality of the general moral law is problematical. Some say that it points to a whole other branch of the moral law, not captured by any of the standard canons. Others, Kantians and utilitarians among them, say that it is derivative in some way or another from more general moral laws. Yet others say that this particularism marks the limits of our psychological capacities for living up to the harsh standards that the general moral law sets for us.[4]

Be all these foundational questions as they may, it is not hard to find intuitively compelling examples of special duties that we would all acknowledge. At the level of preposterous examples so favored among philosophers, consider this case. Suppose your house is on fire. Suppose two people are trapped in the fire, and you will clearly have time to rescue only one before the roof collapses killing the other. One of those trapped is a great public benefactor who was visiting you. The other is your own mother. Which should you rescue?

This is a story told originally by an impartialist, William Godwin. Being a particularly blunt proto-utilitarian, he had no trouble plunking for the impartialist position: "What magic is there in the pronoun 'my' that should justify us in overturning the decisions of impartial truth?"[5] Nowadays, however, it is a story told more often against impartialists. Few, then or now, have found themselves able to accept the impartialist conclusion with quite such equanimity as Godwin. Many regard the example as a reductio ad absurdum of the impartialist position. And even those who want to stick up for the impartialist side are obliged to concede that impartialists have a case to answer here.[6]

But the debate is not confined to crazy cases like that one. In real life, just as surely as in moral fantasies, we find ourselves involved in special relations of all sorts with other people. And just as we intuitively feel that we should save our own mothers rather than Archbishop Fenelon in Godwin's example, so too do we intuitively feel we should show favoritism of some sort to all those other people likewise. The "mere enumeration" of people linked to us in this way is relatively uncontentious and has changed little from Sidgwick's day to Parfit's. Included in both their lists are family, friends, benefactors, clients, and coworkers, and—especially important, in the present context—compatriots.[7]

Intuitively, we suppose that, on account of those special relations between us, we owe all of those people special treatment of some sort or another: special "kindnesses," "services," or "sacrifices"; "we believe that we ought to try to give them certain kinds of benefit."[8] According to Parfit, "Common-Sense Morality largely consists in such obligations"; and, within commonsense morality, those obligations are particularly strong ones, capable of overriding (at least at the margins) our general duties to aid strangers.[9]

C

Here, I do not propose to focus (initially, at least) upon the precise strength of those duties. Rather, I want to direct attention to their general tendency. Notice that there is a presumption, running through all those standard discussions of special duties, that the special treatment due to those who are linked to us by some special relation is especially *good* treatment. We are said to be obliged to do more for those people than for unrelated others in an effort to spare them harm or to bring them benefits. To those who stand in some special relation to us, we are said to owe special "kindnesses," "services," or "sacrifices."

That assumption seems to me unwarranted. Agreed, special relations do sometimes permit (and sometimes even require) us to treat those specially related to us better than we need to, absent such a link. Other times, however, special relations permit (and perhaps even sometimes require) us to treat those thus linked to us worse than we would be obliged to treat them, absent such a link.[10] Exploring how that is so, and why, sheds light upon the true nature and strength of special duties. It also, not incidentally, limits the claims for exclusive special treatment that can be entertained under that heading.

II. THE CASE OF COMPATRIOTS

When discussing what special claims compatriots, in particular, have against us, it is ordinarily assumed that we owe more to our fellow countrymen and less to foreigners. The standard presumption is that "compatriots take priority" over foreigners, "at least in the case of duties to aid"; "the state in determining what use shall be made of its own moneys, may legitimately consult the welfare of its own citizens rather than that of aliens."[11] Thus, it makes a salutory start to my analysis to recall that, at least with respect to certain sorts of duties, we must be more scrupulous—not less—in our treatment of foreigners.

In the discussion that follows, "we" will be understood to mean "our community, through its sovereign representatives." In discussing what "we" may and may not do to people, I shall require some rough-and-ready guide to what our settled moral principles actually are. For these purposes, I shall have recourse to established principles of our legal codes: though the correspondence is obviously less than perfect, presumably the latter at least constitute a rough approximation to the former. Public international law will be taken as indicative of what we may do to foreigners, domestic public law as indicative of what we may do to our compatriots. In both cases, the emphasis will be upon customary higher law rather than upon merely stipulative codes (treaties, statutes, etc.).[12]

Consider, then, all these ways in which we must treat foreigners in general better than we need to treat our compatriots:[13]

Example a. —We, through our public officials, may quite properly take the property of our fellow citizens for public purposes, provided they are duly compensated for their losses; this is especially true if the property is within our national boundaries but is even true if it is outside them. We cannot, however, thus commandeer an identical piece of property from a foreigner for an identical purpose in return for identical compensation. This is especially true if the property is beyond our borders;[14] but it is even true if the property is actually in our country, in transit.[15]

Example b. —We can conscript fellow citizens for service in our armed forces, even if they are resident abroad.[16] We cannot so conscript foreign nationals, even if they are resident within our own country.[17]

Example c. —We can tax fellow citizens, even if they are resident abroad.[18] We cannot so tax foreigners residing abroad on income earned abroad.[19]

Example d. —We can dam or divert the flow of a river lying wholly within our national territory to the disadvantage of fellow citizens living downstream. We may not so dam or divert rivers flowing across international boundaries to the disadvantage of foreigners downstream.[20]

Example e. —We can allow the emission of noxious factory fumes that damage the persons or property of fellow citizens. We may not do so if those fumes cross international frontiers, causing similar damage to the persons or property of foreigners there.[21]

Example f. —We may set arbitrarily low limits on the legal liability of manufacturers for damages done by their production processes or products domestically to our fellow citizens. We may not so limit the damage recoverable from them for harm done across international boundaries to foreigners.[22]

Example g. —According to international law, we may treat our fellow citizens "arbitrarily according to [our own] discretion." To aliens within our national territory, however, we must afford their persons and property protection "in accordance with certain rules and principles of international law," that is, "in accordance with ordinary standards of civilization."[23] Commentators on international law pointedly add, "It is no excuse that [a] State does not provide any protection whatever for its own subjects" in those respects.[24]

These are all examples of ways in which we must treat foreigners better than compatriots. In a great many other respects, of course, the conventional wisdom is perfectly right that we owe better treatment to our compatriots than we do to foreigners. For example, we have a duty to protect the persons and property of compatriots against attack, even when they are abroad.[25] Absent treaty obligations, we have no such duty to protect noncitizens beyond our borders. We have a duty—morally, and perhaps even legally—to provide a minimum level of basic necessities for compatriots. Absent treaty obligations, we have no such duty—legally, anyway—to assist needy noncitizens beyond our borders.

Even within our borders, we may treat citizens better in all sorts of ways than we treat noncitizens, just so long as some "reasonable" grounds for those discriminations can be produced and just so long as the protection we provide aliens' persons and property comes up to minimal internationally acceptable standards.[26] Not only are aliens standardly denied political rights, like voting and office-holding, but they are also standardly excluded from "public service." This has, in the past, been interpreted very broadly indeed: in the United States, an alien could have been debarred from being an "optometrist, dentist, doctor, nurse, architect, teacher, lawyer, policeman, engineer, corporate officer, real estate broker, public accountant, mortician, physiotherapist, pharmacist, pedlar, pool or gambling-hall operator";[27] in the United Kingdom the range of prohibited occupations has included harbor pilots, masters of merchant ships, and skippers of fishing vessels.[28] Besides all those quasi-public functions from which aliens are excluded, they also suffer other disadvantages of a purely material sort. Perhaps the most significant among them are the rules found in some states denying aliens the right to own land.[29] All of this can be perfectly permissible, both under international law and under higher domestic law.

Thus, the situation is very much a mixed one. Sometimes we are indeed permitted (sometimes even required) to treat our fellow citizens better than we treat those who do not share that status with us. Other times, however, we are required to treat noncitizens better than we need to treat our own fellow citizens.

I pass no judgment on which pattern, on balance, predominates. The point I want to make here is merely that the situation is much more mixed than ordinary philosophical thinking on special duties leads us to expect. That in itself is significant, as I shall now proceed to show.

III. SPECIAL DUTIES AS MAGNIFIERS AND MULTIPLIERS

In attempting to construe the effect that special relationships have on our moral duties, commonsense morality tends to employ either of two basic models (or both of them: they are nowise incompatible). On the face of things, these two models can only offer reinforcing interpretations for the same one-half of the phenomenon observed in section II above. Digging deeper to see how such models might account for that other half of the phenomenon drives us toward a model that is even more deeply and familiarly flawed.

A

One standard way of construing the effect of special relationships on our moral duties is to say that special relationships "merely magnify" preexisting moral duties. That is to say, they merely make more stringent duties which we have, in weaker form, vis-à-vis everyone at large; or, "imperfect duties" are transformed by special relationships into "perfect" ones. Thus, perhaps it is wrong to let anyone starve, but it is especially wrong to let kin or compatriots starve. And so on.

That kind of account fits only half the facts, as sketched in section II above, though. If special relationships were merely magnifiers of preexisting duties, then the magnification should be symmetrical in both positive and negative directions. Positive duties (i.e., duties to provide positive assistance to others) should become more strongly positive vis-à-vis those linked to us by some special relationship. Negative duties (i.e., duties not to harm others) should become more strongly negative vis-à-vis those linked to us by some special relationship. When it comes to our duties in relation to compatriots, however, the former is broadly speaking true, while the latter is not.

It is perfectly true that there is a variety of goods that we may or must provide to compatriots that we may at the same time legitimately deny to nonnationals (especially nonresident nonnationals). Rights to vote, to hold property, and to the protection of their persons and property abroad are among them. In the positive dimension, then, the "magnifier" model is broadly appropriate.[30]

In the negative dimension, it is not. All the examples *a* through *f* in section II above point to ways in which we may legitimately impose burdens upon compatriots that may not properly be imposed upon nonnationals (especially nonresident nonnationals). We may poison our compatriots' air, stop their flow of water, deprive them of liberty by conscription, deny them legal remedies for damage to their persons and their property — all in a way that we cannot do to nonresident nonnationals. If anything, it is our negative duties toward nonnationals, not our negative duties toward compatriots, that are here magnified.

B

A second way of construing the effect of special relationships on our moral duties is to say that special relationships "multiply" as well as magnify preexisting duties. That is to say, special relationships do not just make our ordinary general duties particularly stringent in relation to those bound to us by some special relationship; they also create new special duties, over and above the more general ones that we ordinarily owe to anyone and everyone in the world at large. Thus, contracts, for example, create duties de novo. I am under no general duty, strong or weak, to let Dick Merelman inhabit a room in my house; that duty arises only when, and only because, we sign a lease. The special (here, contractual) relationship has created a new duty from scratch.

The "multiplier" model bolsters the "mere magnifier" model's already broadly adequate account of why we have especially strong positive duties toward those linked to us by some special relationship. Sometimes those special relationships strengthen positive duties we owe, less strongly, to everyone at large. Other times, special relationships create new positive duties that we owe peculiarly to those thus linked to us. Either way, we have more and stronger positive duties toward those who stand in special relationships to us than we do the world at large. And that broadly fits the pattern of our special duties vis-à-vis compatriots, as revealed in section II above.

On the face of it, though, it is hard to see how this multiplier model can account for the weakening of negative duties toward compatriots observed there. If special relationships multiply duties, then we would ordinarily expect that that multiplication would produce more new duties in each direction. Consider the paradigm case of contracts. Sometimes contracts create new special duties enjoining us to help others in ways that we would not otherwise be bound to do. Other times, contracts create new special duties enjoining us not to harm others (e.g., by withdrawing trade, labor, or raw materials) in ways that we would otherwise be at liberty to do. It is hard, on the face of it, at least, to see what the attraction of special duties would be—either for agents who are anxious to incur them or for philosophers who are anxious to impose them— if they make people worse off, opening them up to new harms from which they would otherwise be protected.

Yet, judging from examples *a* through *f* in section II above, that is precisely what happens in the special relationship between compatriots. Far from simply creating new negative duties among compatriots, that special relationship seems sometimes to have the effect of canceling (or at least weakening or mitigating) some of the negative duties that people owe to others in general. That hardly looks like the result of an act of multiplication. Ordinarily, we would expect that multiplication should produce more—not fewer—duties.

C

Digging deeper, we find that there may be a way to explain why special relationships have this curious tendency to strengthen positive duties while weakening negative ones. This model quickly collapses into another, more familiar one—and ultimately falls prey to the same objections standardly lodged against it, as section IV will show. Still, it is worth noting how quickly all the standard theories about special duties, when confronted with certain elementary facts about the case of compatriots, collapse into that familiar and flawed model that ordinarily we might have regarded as only one among many possible ways of filling out those theories.

The crucial move in reconciling standard theories about special duties with the elementary facts about compatriots laid out in section II is just this: whether special relationships multiply duties or merely magnify them, the point remains that a relationship is inherently a two-way affair. The same special relation that binds me to you also binds you to me. Special duties for each of us will usually follow from that fact.[31]

Each of us will ordinarily benefit from others' being bound by those extra (or extra strong) duties to do for us things that they are not obliged (or not so powerfully obliged) to do for the world at large. Hence the apparent "strengthening" of positive duties in consequence of special relationships.

Each of us will also ordinarily suffer from those extra (or extra strong) duties imposing an extra burden on us. Hence the apparent "weakening" of negative duties in consequence of the special relationship. We may legitimately impose burdens upon those standing in special relationships to us that we may not impose upon those in no special relation to us, merely because we have special rights against them, and they have special duties toward us. Those extra burdens upon them are no more, and no less, than the fair price of our being under special duties to provide them with valued assistance.

Many of the findings of section II above lend themselves quite naturally to some such interpretation. When we say that compatriots may have their incomes taxed, their trucks commandeered, or other liberties curtailed by conscription, that is surely to say little more than that people may be required to do what is required in order to meet their special duties toward their fellow citizens—duties born of their fellow citizens' similar sacrifices to benefit them.[32] When we say that nonnationals (especially nonresident nonnationals) may not be treated in such ways, that is merely to say that we have no such special claims against them nor they any such special duties toward us.

Others of the examples in section II above (especially examples *d* through *g*) do not lend themselves quite so obviously to this sort of analysis. But perhaps, with a sufficiently long story that is sufficiently rich in lurid details, we might be persuaded that polluting the air, damming rivers, limiting liability for damages, and denying people due process of law really is to the good of all; and suffering occasional misfortunes of those sorts really is just the fair price that compatriots should be required to pay for the benefits that they derive from those broader practices.

Notice that, given this account, the motivational quandary in section III*B* disappears. People welcome special relationships—along with the attendant special rights and special duties (i.e., along with the strengthening of positive duties and the weakening of negative ones)—because the two come as part of an inseparable package, and people are on net better off as a result of it. That is just to say, their gains from having others' positive duties toward them strengthened exceeds their costs from having others' negative duties toward them weakened, and it is impossible for them to realize the gains without incurring the costs.

Notice, however, how quickly these standard theories of how special relationships work on our moral duties—the magnifier and the multiplier models—have been reduced to a very particular theory about "mutual-benefit societies." Initially, the magnifier and multiplier theories seemed to be much broader than that, open to a much wider variety of interpretations and not committing us to any particular theory about why or how the "magnification" or "multiplication" of duties occurred. Yet if those models are to fit the elementary facts about duties toward compatriots in section II at all, they must fall back on a sort of mutual-benefit logic that provides a very particular answer to the question of how and why the magnification or multiplication of duties occurred. As section IV will show, that is not an altogether happy result.

IV. THE MUTUAL-BENEFIT-SOCIETY MODEL

According to the conventional wisdom about international relations, we have a peculiarly strong obligation to leave foreigners as we found them. "Nonintervention" has long bid fair to constitute the master norm of international law.[33] That is not to say that it is actually wrong to help foreigners, of course. It is, however, to say that it is much, much more important not to harm them than it is to help them. Where compatriots are concerned, almost the opposite is true. According to the flip side of that conventional wisdom, it is deeply wrong to be utterly indifferent toward your fellow countrymen; yet it is perfectly permissible for fellow countrymen to impose hardships on themselves and on one another to promote the well-being of their shared community.

Perhaps the best way to make sense of all this is to say that, within the conventional wisdom about international relations, nation-states are conceptualized as ongoing mutual-benefit societies. Within mutual-benefit-society logic, it would be perfectly permissible to impose sacrifices on some people now so that they themselves might benefit in the future; it may even be permissible to impose sacrifices on some now so that others will benefit, either now or in the future.

Precisely what sorts of contractarian or utilitarian theories are required to underpin this logic can be safely left to one side here. It is the broad outline, rather than the finer detail, that matters for present purposes. The bottom line is always that, in a mutual-benefit society, imposing harms is always permissible—but only on condition that some positive good comes of it, and only on condition that those suffering the harm are in some sense party to the society in question.

Suppose, now, that national boundaries are thought to circumscribe mutual-benefit societies of this sort.[34] Then the broad pattern of duties toward compatriots and foreigners, respectively, as described in section II above, becomes perfectly comprehensible. In dealing with other people in general (i.e., those who are not party to the society), the prime directive is "avoid harm": those outside our mutual-benefit society ought not be made to bear any of our burdens; but neither, of course, have they any claim on any of the benefits which we have produced for ourselves, through our own sacrifices. In dealing with others in the club (i.e., compatriots), positive duties wax while negative ones wane: it is perfectly permissible to impose hardships, so long as some positive good somehow comes of doing so; but the point of a mutual-benefit society, in the final analysis, must always be to produce positive benefits for those who are party to it.

There are many familiar problems involved in modeling political communities as mutual-benefit societies.[35] The one to which I wish to draw particular attention here is the problem of determining who is inside the club and who is outside it. Analysis of this problem, in turn, forces us back to the foundational questions skirted at the outset of the article. These will be readdressed in section V below, where I construct an alternative model of special duties as not very special, after all.

From the legalist perspective that dominates discussion of such duties, formal status is what matters. Who is a citizen? Who is not? That, almost exclusively, determines what we may or must do to people, qua members of the club.

Yet formal status is only imperfectly and contingently related to who is actually generating and receiving the benefits of the mutual-benefit society. The mismatch is most glaring as regards resident aliens: they are often net contributors to the society, yet they are equally often denied its full benefits.[36] The mismatch also appears only slightly less glaringly, as regards natural-born citizens who retain that status although they are and will inevitably (because, e.g., severely handicapped) continue to be net drains on the mutual-benefit society.[37]

In its starkest form, mutual-benefit-society logic should require that people's benefits from the society be strictly proportional to the contributions they have made toward the production of those benefits. Or, minimally, it should require that no one draw out more than he has paid in: the allocation of any surplus created by people's joint efforts may be left open. On that logic, we have special duties toward those whose cooperation benefits us, and to them alone. That they share the same color passport—or, indeed, the same parentage—is related only contingently, at best, to that crucial consideration.

It may well be that mutual-benefit logic, in so stark a form, is utterly inoperable. Constantly changing circumstances mean that everything from social insurance to speculative business ventures might benefit us all in the long run, even if at any given moment some of them constitute net drains on the system. And lines on the map, though inherently arbitrary at the margins, may be as good a way as any of identifying cheaply the members of a beneficially interacting community. So we may end up embracing the formalistic devices for identifying members of the mutual-benefit society, knowing that they are imperfect second-bests but also knowing that doing better is impossible or prohibitively expensive.

The point remains, however, that there are some clear, straightforward adjustments that ought to be made to such "first stab" definitions of membership, if mutual-benefit logic underlay membership. That they are not made—and that we think at least one of them ought not be made—clearly indicates that it is not mutual-benefit logic that underlies membership, after all.

Reflect, again, upon the case of resident aliens who are performing socially useful functions over a long period of time. Many societies egregiously exploit "guest workers," denying them many of the rights and privileges accorded to citizens despite the fact that they make major and continuing contributions to the society. Politically and economically, it is no mystery why they are deprived of the full fruits of their labors in this way.[38] But if the moral justification of society is to be traced to mutual-benefit logic, that is transparently wrong. The entry ticket to a mutual-benefit society should, logically, just be conferring net benefits on the society.[39] That membership is nonetheless denied to those who confer benefits on the society demonstrates that the society is not acting consistently on that moral premise. Either it is acting on some other moral premise or else it is acting on none at all (or none consistently, which morally amounts to the same).

Or consider, again, the case of the congenitally handicapped. Though born of native parents in the homeland, and by formalistic criteria therefore clearly qualified for citizenship, such persons will never be net contributors to the mutual-benefit society. If it were merely the logic of mutual-benefit that determined membership such persons would clearly be excluded from the benefits of society.[40] (If their parents cared about them, they could give them some of *their* well-earned benefits.) Yet that does not happen, no matter how sure we are that handicapped persons will be net drains on the society for the duration of their lives. And most of us intuitively imagine that it is a good thing, morally, that it does not happen. Thus, society here again seems to be operating on something other than mutual-benefit logic; and here, at least, we are glad that it is.

V. THE ASSIGNED RESPONSIBILITY MODEL

The magnifier, multiplier, and mutual-benefit-society models all take the specialness of special duties particularly seriously. They treat such duties as if they were, at least in (large) part, possessed of an independent existence or of an independent moral force. I want to deny both of those propositions.

My preferred approach to special duties is to regard them as being merely "distributed general duties." That is to say, special duties are in my view merely devices whereby the moral community's general duties get assigned to particular agents. For this reason, I call mine an "assigned responsibility" model.[41]

This approach treats special duties as much more nearly derivative from general duties than any of the other approaches so far considered. Certainly it is true that, on this account, special duties derive the whole of their moral force from the moral force of those general duties. It may not quite be the case that, existentially, they are wholly derivative from general duties: we cannot always deduce from considerations of general duties alone who in particular should take it upon themselves to discharge them; where the general principle leaves that question open, some further (independent, often largely arbitrary) "responsibility principle" is required to specify it. Still, on this account, special duties are *largely* if not wholly derivative from considerations of general duty.

The practical consequences of this finding are substantial. If special duties can be shown to derive the whole of their moral force from their connections to general duties, then they are susceptible to being overridden (at least at the margins, or in exceptional circumstances) by those more general considerations. In this way, it turns out that "our fellow countrymen" are not so very special after all. The same thing that makes us worry mainly about them should also make us worry, at least a little, about the rest of the world, too.

These arguments draw upon larger themes developed elsewhere.[42] Here I shall concentrate narrowly upon their specific application to the problem of our special duties toward compatriots. The strategy I shall pursue here is to start from the presumption that there are, at root, no distinct special duties but only general ones. I then proceed to show how implementing those general duties gives rise to special duties much like those we observe in the practice of international relations. And finally I shall show how those special duties arising from general duties are much more tightly circumscribed in their extended implications than are the special duties deriving from any of the other models.[43]

A

Let us start, then, from the assumption that we all have certain general duties, of both a positive and negative sort, toward one another. Those general injunctions get applied to specific people in a variety of ways. Some are quasi-naturalistic. Others are frankly social in character.

For an example of the former, suppose we operate under some general injunction to save someone who is drowning, if you and you alone can do so. Suppose, further, that you happen to find yourself in such a position one day. Then that general injunction becomes a compelling commandment addressed specifically to you.

The same example is easily adapted to provide an instance of the second mode as well. Suppose, now, that there are hundreds of people on the beach watching the drowning swimmer flounder. None is conspicuously closer or conspicuously the stronger swimmer; none is related to the swimmer. In short, none is in any way "naturalistically" picked out as the appropriate person to help. If all of them tried to help simultaneously, however, they would merely get in each other's way; the probable result of such a melee would be multiple drownings rather than the single one now in prospect. Let us suppose, finally, that there is one person who is not naturalistically but, rather, "socially" picked out as the person who should effect the rescue: the duly-appointed lifeguard.[44] In such a case, it is clearly that person upon whom the general duty of rescue devolves as a special duty.

Notice that it is not a matter of indifference whom we choose to vest with special responsibility for discharging our general moral duties. Obviously, some people would, for purely naturalistic reasons, make better lifeguards than others. It is for these naturalistic reasons that we appoint them to the position rather than appointing someone else. But their special responsibility in the matter derives wholly from the fact that they *were* appointed, and not at all from any facts about why they were appointed.

Should the appointed individuals prove incompetent, then of course it is perfectly proper for us to retract their commissions and appoint others in their places. If responsibility is allocated merely upon the bases here suggested, then its reallocation is always a live issue. But it is an issue to be taken up at another level, and in another forum.[45] Absent such a thoroughgoing reconsideration of the allocation of responsibilities, it will almost always be better to let those who have been assigned responsibility get on with the job. In all but the most exceptional cases of clear and gross incompetence on the part of the appointed individual, it will clearly be better to get out of the way and let the duly appointed lifeguard have an unimpeded chance at pulling the drowning swimmer out of the water.

That seems to provide a good model for many of our so-called special duties. A great many general duties point to tasks that, for one reason or another, are pursued more effectively if they are subdivided and particular people are assigned special responsibility for particular portions of the task. Sometimes the reason this is so has to do with the advantage of specialization and division of labor. Other times, it has to do with lumpiness in the information required to do a good job, and the limits on people's capacity for processing requisite quantities of information about a great many cases at once. And still other times it is because there is some process at work (the adversarial system in law, or the psychological processes at work in child development, e.g.) that presuppose that each person will have some particular advocate and champion.[46] Whatever the reason, however, it is simply the case that our general duties toward people are sometimes more effectively discharged by assigning special responsibility for that matter to some particular agents. When that is the case, then that clearly is what should be done.[47]

Thus, hospital patients are better cared for by being assigned to particular doctors rather than having all the hospital's doctors devote one nth of their time to each of the hospital's n patients. Someone accused of a crime is better served, legally, by being assigned some particular advocate, rather than having a different attorney appear from the common pool of attorneys to represent him at each different court date.[48] Of course, some doctors are better than others, and some lawyers are better than others; so it is not a matter of indifference which one is handling your case. But any one is better than all at once.

B

National boundaries, I suggest, perform much the same function. The duties that states (or, more precisely, their officials) have vis-à-vis their own citizens are not in any deep sense special. At root, they are merely the general duties that everyone has toward everyone else worldwide. National boundaries simply visit upon those particular state agents special responsibility for discharging those general obligations vis-à-vis those individuals who happen to be their own citizens.[49]

Nothing in this argument claims that one's nationality is a matter of indifference. There are all sorts of reasons for wishing national boundaries to be drawn in such a way that you are lumped together with others "of your own kind"; these range from mundane considerations of the ease and efficiency of administration to deep psychological attachments and a sense of self that may thereby be promoted.[50] My only point is that those are all considerations that bear on the drawing and redrawing of boundaries; they are not, in and of themselves, the source of special responsibilities toward people with those shared characteristics.[51]

The elementary facts about international responsibilities set out in section II above can all be regarded as fair "first approximations" to the implications of this assigned responsibility model. States are assigned special responsibility for protecting and promoting the interests of those who are their citizens. Other states do them a prima facie wrong when they inflict injuries on their citizens; it is the prima facie duty of a state, acting on behalf of injured citizens, to demand redress. But ordinarily no state has any claim against other states for positive assistance in promoting its own citizens' interests: that is its own responsibility. Among its own citizens, however, it is perfectly proper that in discharging that responsibility the state should compel its citizens to comply with various schemes that require occasional sacrifices so that all may prosper.[52]

C

So far, the story is strictly analogous in its practical implications to that told about mutual-benefit societies in section IV above. Here, as there, we have special duties for promoting the well-being of compatriots. Here, as there, we are basically obliged to leave foreigners as we found them. The rationale is different: here, it is that we have been assigned responsibility for compatriots, in a way that we have not been assigned any responsibility for foreigners. But the end result is much the same—so far, at least.

There are, however, two important points of distinction between these stories. The first concerns the proper treatment of the useless and the helpless. So far as a mutual-benefit society is concerned, useless members would be superfluous members. Not only may they be cast out, they ought to be cast out. If the raison d'être of the society is mutual benefit, and those people are not benefiting anyone, then it is actually wrong, on mutual-benefit logic, for them to be included. (That is true, at least insofar as their inclusion is in any way costly to the rest of the society—ergo, it is clearly wrong, in those terms, for the severely handicapped to draw any benefits from a mutual-benefit society.) The same is true with the helpless, that is, refugees and stateless persons. If they are going to benefit society, then a mutual-benefit society ought to take them in. But if they are only going to be a net drain on society (as most of the "boat people" presumably appeared to be, e.g.), then a mutual-benefit society not only may but *must*, on its own principles, deny them entry. The fact that they are without any other protector in the international system is, for mutual-benefit logic, neither here nor there.

My model, wherein states' special responsibilities are derived from general ones of everyone to everyone, cancels both those implications. States are stuck with the charges assigned to them, whether those people are a net benefit to the rest of society or not. Casting off useless members of society would simply amount to shirking their assigned responsibility.

The "helpless" constitute the converse case. They have been (or, anyway, they are now) assigned to no one particular state for protection. That does not mean that all states may therefore ignore or abuse them, however. Quite the contrary. What justifies states in pressing the particular claims of their own citizens is, on my account, the presumption that everyone has been assigned an advocate/protector.[53] Then, and only then, will a system of universal special pleading lead to maximal fulfillment of everyone's general duties toward everyone else worldwide.

Suppose, however, that someone has been left without a protector. Either he has never been assigned one, or else the one he was assigned has proven unwilling or unable to provide the sort of protection it was his job to provide. Then, far from being at the mercy of everyone, the person becomes the "residual responsibility" of all.[54] The situation here is akin to that of a hospital patient who, through some clerical error, was admitted with some acute illness without being assigned to any particular physician's list: he then becomes the residual responsibility of all staff physicians of that hospital.

To be sure, that responsibility is an "imperfect" one as against any particular state. It is the responsibility of the set of states, taken as a whole, to give the refugee a home; but it is not the duty of any one of them in particular.[55] At the very least, though, we can say this much: it would be wrong for any state to press the claims of its own citizens strongly, to the disadvantage of those who have no advocate in the system;[56] and it would not be wrong (as, perversely, it would be on the mutual-benefit-society model) for any state to agree to give refugees a home. Both these things follow from the fact that the state's special responsibility to its own citizens is, at root, derived from the same considerations that underlie its general duty to the refugee.

The second important difference between my model and mutual-benefit logic concerns the critique of international boundaries and the obligation to share resources between nations. On mutual-benefit logic, boundaries should circumscribe groups of people who produce benefits for one another. Expanding those boundaries is permissible only if by so doing we can incorporate yet more mutually beneficial collaborators into our society; contracting those boundaries is proper if by so doing we can expel some people who are nothing but liabilities to our cooperative unit. On mutual-benefit logic, furthermore, transfers across international boundaries are permissible only if they constitute mutually beneficial exchanges. The practical consequence of all this is, characteristically, that the rich get richer and the poor get poorer.[57]

On the model I have proposed, none of this would follow. Special responsibilities are, on my account, assigned merely as an administrative device for discharging our general duties more efficiently. If that is the aim, then they should be assigned to agents capable of discharging them effectively; and that, in turn, means that sufficient resources ought to have been given to every such state agent to allow for the effective discharge of those responsibilities. If there has been a misallocation of some sort, so that some states have been assigned care of many more people than they have been assigned resources to care for them, then a reallocation is called for.[58] This follows not from any special theory of justice but, rather, merely from the basis of special duties in general ones.[59]

If some states prove incapable of discharging their responsibilities effectively, then they should either be reconstituted or assisted.[60] Whereas on mutual-benefit logic it would actually be wrong for nations to take on burdens that would in no way benefit their citizens, on my model it would certainly not be wrong for them to do so; and it would in some diffuse way be right for them to do so, in discharge of the general duties that all of them share and that underwrite their own grant of special responsibility for their own citizens in the first place.[61]

VI. CONCLUSION

Boundaries matter, I conclude. But it is the boundaries around people, not the boundaries around territories, that really matter morally. Territorial boundaries are merely useful devices for "matching" one person to one protector. Citizenship is merely a device for fixing special responsibility in some agent for discharging our general duties vis-à-vis each particular person. At root, however, it is the person and the general duty that we all have toward him that matters morally.

If all has gone well with the assignment of responsibilities, then respecting special responsibilities and the priority of compatriots to which they give rise would be the best way of discharging those general duties. But the assignment of responsibility will never work perfectly, and there is much to make us suppose that the assignment embodied in the present world system is very imperfect indeed. In such cases, the derivative special responsibilities cannot bar the way to our discharging the more general duties from which they are derived.

In the present world system, it is often—perhaps ordinarily—wrong to give priority to the claims of our compatriots.

NOTES

Earlier versions of this article were presented to the European Consortium for Political Research (ECPR) Workshop on "Duties beyond Borders" in Amsterdam and to seminars at the universities of Essex and Stockholm. I am grateful to those audiences, and to Hillel Steiner, for comments.

    1. Unlike David Miller, "The Moral Significance of Nationality," in this issue, I shall here make no distinction between "state" and "nation," or between "citizenship" and "nationality." In this article, they will be used interchangeably.

    2. Or so it is standardly supposed. Actually, there could be a "rule of universal partiality" (e.g., "everyone ought to pursue his own interests," or "everyone ought to take care of his own children"). A variant of this figures largely in my argument in section V below.

    3. The terms "special" and "general" duties—and to a large extent the analysis of them as well—are borrowed from H. L. A. Hart, "Are There Any Natural Rights?" *Philosophical Review* 64 (1955): 175–91.

    4. See Robert E. Goodin, *Protecting the Vulnerable* (Chicago: University of Chicago Press, 1985), chap. 1 and the references therein. The strongest arguments for such partiality have to do with the need to center one's sense of self, through personal attachments to particular people and projects; see, e.g., Bernard Williams, *Moral Luck* (Cambridge: Cambridge University Press, 1981), chap. 1. But surely those arguments apply most strongly to more personal links, and only very weakly, if at all, to impersonal links through shared race or nationality. John Cottingham pursues such points in "Partiality, Favouritism and Morality," *Philosophical Quarterly* 36 (1986): 357–73, pp. 370–71.

    5. William Godwin, *Enquiry Concerning Political Justice* (1793; reprint, Oxford: Clarendon, 1971), bk. 2, chap. 2.

    6. See, e.g., Williams, *Moral Luck*, pp. 17–18, for the former position; and R. M. Hare, *Moral Thinking* (Oxford: Clarendon, 1981), p. 138, for the latter.

    7. Henry Sidgwick, *The Methods of Ethics*, 7th ed. (London: Macmillan, 1907), bk. 3, chap. 4, sec. 3; Derek Parfit, *Reasons and Persons* (Oxford: Clarendon, 1984), pp. 95, 485.

    8. Sidgwick, *The Methods of Ethics*, bk. 3, chap. 4, sec. 3; Parfit, *Reasons and Persons*, pp. 95, 485.

    9. Parfit, *Reasons and Persons*, p. 95.

    10. Sometimes special duties specifically require the opposite. Parents, teachers, and prison wardens are all, from time to time, required by special duties to inflict punishment upon those under their care. But at least some—and arguably all—of these are pains inflicted for the recipient's own greater, long-term good. See Herbert Morris, "A Paternalistic Theory of Punishment," *American Philosophical Quarterly* 18 (1981): 263–71; cf. John Deigh, "On the Right to Be Punished: Some Doubts," *Ethics* 94 (1984): 191–211.

    11. Henry Shue, *Basic Rights* (Princeton, N.J.: Princeton University Press, 1980),

p. 132; Benjamin Cardozo, *People* v. *Crane*, 214 N.Y. 154, 164, 108 N.E. 427, 437. This report of what constitutes the conventional wisdom is echoed by: Thomas Nagel, "Ruthlessness in Public Life," in *Public and Private Morality*, ed. Stuart Hampshire (Cambridge: Cambridge University Press, 1978), pp. 75–93, p. 81; Charles R. Beitz, *Political Theory and International Relations* (Princeton, N.J.: Princeton University Press, 1979), p. 163; and Goodin, *Protecting the Vulnerable*, chaps. 1 and 2. Among them, only Cardozo could be said to accept that conventional wisdom uncritically.

12. Unlike stipulative law, which might be made by a small body of people on the spur of the moment, customary law represents the settled judgments of a great many people over some long period. Thus, it is better qualified for use in a quasi-Rawlsian "reflective equilibrium." For other uses of legal principles in such a role, see Robert E. Goodin, *The Politics of Rational Man* (London: Wiley, 1976), chap. 7, and *Protecting the Vulnerable*, chap. 5.

13. These all refer to ways that we must treat foreigners in general, absent specific contractual or treaty commitments. The latter may require better treatment, or permit worse, or both in different respects. The principles set out in the text, however, constitute the normative background against which such contracts or treaties are negotiated.

14. This is true even if it is a piece of movable property, so there is no question of expropriating a piece of another nation's territory. Suppose, e.g., that the British government needs to requisition a privately owned ship to provision troops in the South Atlantic: it may so requisition a ship of British registry, even if it is lying in Dutch waters; it may not so requisition a ship of Dutch registry, even if lying in British waters (except in a case of extreme emergency).

15. Adrian S. Fisher, chief reporter, *Restatement (Second) of the Foreign Relations Law of the United States* (St. Paul, Minn.: American Law Institute, 1965), sec. 185c. The "right of safe passage" for people and goods in transit, for purposes of commerce or study, was firmly established even in early modern international law; see Hugo Grotius, *On the Law of War and Peace*, trans. F. W. Kelsey (1625; reprint, Oxford: Clarendon Press, 1925), bk. 2, chap. 2, secs. 13–15; Christian Wolff, *The Law of Nations Treated according to a Scientific Method*, trans. Joseph H. Drake (1749; reprint, Oxford: Clarendon, 1934), sec. 346; and Emerich de Vattel, *The Law of Nations, or the Principles of Natural Law*, trans. Joseph Chitty (1758; reprint, Philadelphia: T. and J. W. Johnson, 1863), bk. 2, chap. 10, sec. 132. This rule, too, is subject to an "extreme emergency" exception.

16. L. Oppenheim, *International Law: A Treatise*, ed. H. Lauterpact (London: Longman, 1955), 1:288. This, and the similar result in example *c* below, follows from the fact that a state enjoys continuing "personal" sovereignty over its own citizens but possesses merely those powers derived from its "territorial" sovereignty over aliens within its borders. This distinction, emphasized in modern international law (e.g., throughout the first volume of Oppenheim's treatise, *International Law*), appears in a particularly clear early formulation in Francisco Suárez's 1612 *Treatise on Laws and God the Lawgiver*, in *Selections from Three Works*, trans. and ed. Gwladys L. Williams, Ammi Brown, John Waldron, and Henry Davis (Oxford: Clarendon, 1944), chap. 30, sec. 12.

17. Oppenheim, *International Law*, 1:288. The practice in the United States, of course, is to conscript alien nationals who are permanently resident in the country into its armed forces; see Alexander M. Bickel, *The Morality of Consent* (New Haven, Conn.: Yale University Press, 1975), p. 49. But the long-standing rule in international law is

that, while we may require resident aliens to help with police, fire, and flood protection, foreigners are exempt from serving in the militia; see Vattel, *The Law of Nations*, bk. 2, chap. 8, secs. 105–106 for one early statement of the rule.

18. Oppenheim, *International Law*, 1:288. Bickel, *The Morality of Consent*, p. 48. Again, this is a long-standing rule of international law; see Wolff, *The Law of Nations Treated*, sec. 324; and Vattel, *The Law of Nations*, bk. 2, chap. 8, sec. 106. Of course, having the right to tax nationals abroad, states may waive that right (as, e.g., through double-taxation agreements).

19. A partial exception to this rule might be that an alien with permanent residency in one state but temporarily resident in another might be taxable in the first country for earnings in the second; the United States, at least, would try to collect. Some authors maintain that even resident aliens should be exempt from certain sorts of taxes. One example Wolff offers (*The Law of Nations Treated*, sec. 324) is a poll tax: since aliens are precluded by reason of noncitizenship from voting, they ought for that reason to be exempt from a poll tax, too. Another example, offered by Vattel (*The Law of Nations*, bk. 2, chap. 8, sec. 106), is that foreigners should be "exempt from taxes . . . destined for the support of the rights of the nation"; since resident aliens are under no obligation to fight in defense of the nation, they should be under no obligation to pay taxes earmarked for the defense of the nation either.

20. Oppenheim, *International Law*, 1:290–91, 348, 475.

21. Ibid., 1:291.

22. Thus, e.g., the Price-Anderson Act sets the limit for liability of operators of civilian nuclear reactors within the United States at $560 million. But had the Fermi reactor in Detroit experienced a partial meltdown similar to that at Chernobyl, spreading pollution to Canada, international law would not have recognized the legitimacy of that limit in fixing damages due to Canadians. "It is," according to Oppenheim's *International Law*, 1:350, "a well-established principle that a State cannot invoke its municipal legislation as a reason for avoiding its international obligations."

23. Oppenheim, *International Law*, 1:686–87. Indeed, "black letter" international law— as codified in the American Law Institute's *Restatement (Second) of the Foreign Relations Law of the United States*, sec. 165(l)(a)—holds that "conduct attributable to a state and causing injury to an alien is wrongful under international law . . . if it departs from the international standard of justice." For elaboration, see Oppenheim, *International Law*, 1:290, 350, 641; and J. L. Brierly, *The Law of Nations*, 2d ed. (Oxford: Clarendon, 1936), pp. 172 ff.

24. Oppenheim, *International Law*, 1:687–88. Elsewhere Oppenheim explicitly draws attention to the "paradoxical result" that "individuals, when residing as aliens in a foreign state, enjoy a measure of protection . . . denied to nationals of a State within its own territory" (1:641, n. 1). In the past, this has been the subject of some controversy. Premodern international lawyers tended to hold that there was some external (god-given) standard of "just suitable" laws that must be adhered to in prescribing differential treatment for aliens; see Suárez, *Treatise on Laws and God the Lawgiver*, chap. 33, sec. 7. But early modern writers like Wolff, *The Law of Nations Treated* (sec. 302); and Vattel, *The Law of Nations* (bk. 2, chap. 8, sec. 100)—right down to Henry Sidgwick, *The Elements of Politics* (London: Macmillan, 1891), pp. 235–36—seemed to suppose that, since the state could refuse admission to aliens altogether, it could impose any conditions it liked upon their remaining in the country, however discriminatory and however

short that treatment may fall from any international standards of civilized conduct. At the very least, aliens are not wronged if they are treated no worse than nationals—or so it was thought by many (predominantly European and Latin American) international lawyers prior to 1940 (Ian Brownlie, *Principles of Public International Law* [Oxford: Clarendon, 1966], p. 425). By now, it is decidedly the "prevailing rule" of international law that "there is an international standard of justice that a state must observe in the treatment of aliens, even if the state does not observe it in the treatment of its own nationals, and even if the standard is inconsistent with its own law" (*Restatement [Second] of the Foreign Relations of the United States*, sec. 165, comment *a*; and Louis B. Sohn and R. R. Baxter, "Responsibility of States for Injuries to the Economic Interests of Aliens [Harvard Law School Draft Convention]," *American Journal of International Law* 55 [1961]: 545–84, pp. 547–48). There is no longer any doubt that "national treatment" is not enough; the only persisting question is whether the international standard demanded should vary with, e.g., the wealth or educational attainments of the people to whom it is being applied—as, e.g., standards of "due diligence" and "reasonable care" perhaps should (Brownlie, *Principles of Public International Law*, p. 427).

25. States are under obligations arising from customary and higher domestic law to do so, even if those obligations are unenforceable under international law, as they seem to be (see Oppenheim, *International Law*, 1:686–87).

26. Suárez, *Treatise on Laws and God the Lawgiver*, chap. 33, sec. 7; Wolff, *The Law of Nations Treated*, sec. 303; Sidgwick, *Elements of Politics*, p. 235; Brierly, *The Law of Nations*, pp. 172–73; Oppenheim, *International Law*, 1:689–91; Brownlie, *Principles of Public International Law*, pp. 424–48; Gerald M. Rosberg, "The Protection of Aliens from Discriminatory Treatment by the National Government," *Supreme Court Review* (1977), pp. 275–339; Edward S. Corwin, *The Constitution, and What It Means Today*, ed. H. W. Chase and C. R. Ducat (Princeton, N.J.: Princeton University Press, 1978), pp. 90–92, and *1980 Supplement*, pp. 159–61; "Developments in the Law: Immigration Policy and the Rights of Aliens," *Harvard Law Review* 96 (1983): 1286–1465.

27. Bickel, *The Morality of Consent*, pp. 45–46. Also, see Corwin, *The Constitution*, pp. 90–92, and *1980 Supplement*, pp. 159–61; and "Developments in the Law."

28. Brierly, *The Law of Nations*, p. 173; Oppenheim, *International Law*, 1:690.

29. Brierly, *The Law of Nations*, p. 173; Bickel, *The Morality of Consent*, p. 46; "Developments in the Law," pp. 1300–1301.

30. "Broadly" because example *g* above arguably does not fit this pattern. It all depends upon whether we construe this as a positive duty to provide aliens with something good ("due process of law") or as a negative duty not to do something bad to them ("deny them due process of law"). This, in turn, depends upon where we set the baseline of how well off they would have been absent our intervention in the first place.

31. I say "usually" because there are some unilateral power relations (like that of doctor and patient or parent and child) that might imply special duties for one but not the other party to the relationship; see Goodin, *Protecting the Vulnerable*.

32. The sacrifices might be actual or merely hypothetical (i.e., should the occasion arise, they would make the sacrifice).

33. Standard prescriptions along these lines of medieval churchmen were strengthened by each of the early modern international lawyers in turn—Grotius, Wolff, and Vattel—so that by the time of Sidgwick's *Elements of Politics*, the "principle

of mutual non-interference" (p. 231) could be said to be "the fundamental principle" of international morality with no equivocation. It remains so to this day, in the view of most lawyers and of many philosophers; see, e.g., Michael Walzer, *Just and Unjust Wars* (New York: Basic, 1977), and "The Moral Standing of States," *Philosophy and Public Affairs* 9 (1980): 209–30.

34. This thought finds its fullest contemporary expression in the notion of the "circumstances of justice" that John Rawls, *A Theory of Justice* (Cambridge, Mass.: Harvard University Press, 1971), pp. 126–30, borrows from David Hume, *A Treatise of Human Nature* (London: John Noon, 1739), bk. 3, pt. 2, sec. 2, and *An Enquiry Concerning the Principles of Morals* (London: Cadell, 1777), sec. 3, pt. 1. Some international relations theorists defend this analysis at length; see e.g., Wolff's *Law of Nations*, and Beitz's *Political Theory and International Relations*, pp. 143–53 (cf. his "Cosmopolitan Ideals and National Sentiment," *Journal of Philosophy* 80 [1983]: 591–600, p. 595). Other commentators seem almost to fall into this way of talking without thinking (see Nagel, "Ruthlessness in Public Life," p. 81; and Tony Honoré, "The Human Community and the Principle of Majority Rule," in *Community as a Social Ideal*, ed. Eugene Kamenka [London: Edward Arnold, 1982], pp. 147–60, p. 154).

35. These are addressed, in their particular applications to the mutual-benefit model of international obligations, in Brian Barry, "Humanity and Justice in Global Perspective," in *NOMOS XXIV: Ethics, Economics and the Law*, ed. J. R. Pennock and J. W. Chapman (New York: New York University Press, 1982), pp. 219–52, pp. 225–43; and in Goodin, *Protecting the Vulnerable*, pp. 154–60.

36. Both domestic and international law go some way toward recognizing that in many respects resident aliens are much more like citizens than they are like nonresident aliens. But by and large those acknowledgments come not in the form of awarding them the same benefits as are enjoyed by citizens but, rather, in the form of imposing many of the same burdens on resident aliens as on citizens. A state may, e.g., compel resident aliens to pay taxes and rates and to serve in local police forces and fire brigades "for the purpose of maintaining public order and safety" in a way it may not require of nonresident aliens; Oppenheim, *International Law*, 1:680–81.

37. Brian Barry, "Justice as Reciprocity," in *Justice*, ed. Eugene Kamenka and Alice E.-S. Tay (London: Edward Arnold, 1979), pp. 50–78, pp. 68–69; Robert E. Goodin, *Political Theory and Public Policy* (Chicago: University of Chicago Press, 1982), pp. 77–79.

38. The argument here would perfectly parallel that for supposing that, if a workers' cooperative needed more labor, it would hire workers rather than selling more people shares in the cooperative. Demonstrations of this have been developed independently by J. E. Meade, "The Theory of Labour-Managed Firms and of Profit Sharing," *Economic Journal* 82 (1972): 402–28; and David Miller, "Market Neutrality and the Failure of Cooperatives," *British Journal of Political Science* 11 (1981): 309–21.

39. The "participation" model of citizenship is a close cousin to this mutual-benefit-society model. Participating in a society is usually (if not quite always) a precondition for producing benefits for others in that society; and usually (if not quite always) the reason we think participants in society deserve to enjoy the fruits of formal membership is that that is seen as fair return for the benefits they have produced for the society. See "Developments in the Law," pp. 1303–11; and Peter H. Schuck, "The Transformation of Immigration Law," *Columbia Law Review* 84 (1984): 1–90.

40. Since they are, ex hypothesi, congenital handicaps, there is no motive for those who have safely been born without suffering the handicap to set up a mutual insurance scheme to protect themselves against those risks.

41. "Nationality" and the duties to compatriots to which such notions give rise are just the sorts of "institutions" that Henry Shue ("Mediating Duties," this issue) shows to be so crucial in implementing any duties of a positive sort. How, precisely, the "assignment" of responsibility is accomplished can safely be left open: sometimes, people and peoples get assigned to some national community by some specific agency (the UN Trusteeship Council, e.g.); more often, assignments are the products of historical accidents and conventions. However they are accomplished, these "assignments" must specify both who is responsible for you and what they are responsible for doing for you. Even so-called perfect duties, which specify the former precisely, are characteristically vague on the latter matter (specifying, e.g., a duty to provide a "healthful diet" for your children), and require further inputs of a vaguely "institutional" sort to flesh out their content.

42. Goodin, *Protecting the Vulnerable*; Philip Pettit and Robert E. Goodin, "The Possibility of Special Duties," *Canadian Journal of Philosophy* 16 (1986): 651–76.

43. Broadly the same strategy is pursued by Shue in "Mediating Duties," this issue.

44. This, incidentally, provides an alternative explanation for why we should appoint lifeguards for crowded but not uncrowded beaches. The standard logic—true, too, in its way—is that it is a more efficient allocation of scarce resources since it is more likely that more people will need rescuing on crowded beaches. Over and above all that, however, it is also true that an "obvious" lifesaver will be needed more on crowded than uncrowded beaches to keep uncoordinated helpers from doing each other harm.

45. That is to say that the ascription of "role responsibilities" takes on the same two-tier structure familiar to us from discussions of "indirect consequentialism"; see Hare, *Moral Thinking*, pp. 135–40, 201–205; and Bernard Williams, "Professional Morality and Its Dispositions," in *The Good Lawyer*, ed. David Luban (Totowa, N.J.: Rowman & Allanheld, 1983), pp. 259–69.

46. Nagel, "Ruthlessness in Public Life," p. 81; Williams, *Moral Luck*, chap. 1.

47. Assigning responsibility to some might have the effect of letting others off the hook too easily. It is the job of the police to stop murders, so none of the onlookers watching Kitty Genovese's murder thought it their place to get involved; it is the lifeguard's job to rescue drowning swimmers, so onlookers might stand idly by watching her botch the job rather than stepping in to help themselves; and so on. This emphasizes the importance of back-up responsibilities, to be discussed below, specifying whose responsibility it is when the first person assigned the responsibility fails to discharge it.

48. This is the "division of labor model" of the adversary system discussed by Richard Wasserstrom, "Lawyers as Professionals: Some Moral Issues," *Human Rights* 5 (1975): 1–24, p. 9, and "Roles and Morality," in Luban, *The Good Lawyer*, pp. 25–37, p. 30.

49. This is, I believe, broadly in line with Christian Wolff's early analysis. Certainly he believes that we have special duties toward our own nations: "Every nation ought to care for its own self, and every person in a nation ought to care for his nation" (sec. 135). But it is clear from Wolff's preface (*The Law of Nations Treated*, secs. 9–15) that those special rights and duties are set in the context of, and derived from, a scheme

to promote the greater common good of all nations as a whole. Among contemporary writers, this argument is canvassed, not altogether approvingly, by Shue, *Basic Rights*, pp. 139–44; and William K. Frankena, "Moral Philosophy and World Hunger," in *World Hunger and Moral Obligation*, ed. William Aiken and Hugh La Follette (Englewood Cliffs, N.J.: Prentice-Hall, 1977), pp. 66–84, p. 81. Hare, *Moral Thinking*, pp. 201–202, is more bullish on the proposal.

50. Sidgwick, *Elements of Politics*, chap. 14; Brian Barry, "Self-government Revisited," in *The Nature of Political Theory*, ed. David Miller and Larry Siedentop (Oxford: Clarendon, 1983), pp. 121–54; Alasdair MacIntyre, "Is Patriotism a Virtue?" (Lawrence: University of Kansas, Lindley Lecture, March 26, 1984). Compare Cottingham, "Partiality, Favouritism and Morality," pp. 370–74. Notice that the principle urged by David Miller in arguing for "The Moral Significance of Nationality" (this issue) is very much in line with my own in its practical implications: *if* people have national sentiments, then social institutions should be arranged so as to respect them; but Miller gives no reason for believing that people should or must have such sentiments, nor does he pose any objection to people's extending such sentiments to embrace the world at large if they so choose.

51. That is to say, if general duties would be better discharged by assigning special responsibilities to a group of people who enjoy helping one another, then we should so assign responsibilities—not because there is anything intrinsically good about enjoying helping one another, but merely because that is the best means to the intrinsically good discharging of general duties.

52. If example *g* in section II is construed as a special positive duty toward aliens, as n. 30 above suggests it might be, then it poses something of a problem for all three other models of special responsibilities. All three, for diverse reasons, would expect *positive* duties to be stronger vis-à-vis compatriots, not toward aliens. The assigned responsibility model alone is capable of explaining the phenomenon, as a manifestation of our general duty toward everyone at large which persists even after special responsibilities have been allocated. More will be said of that residual general duty below.

53. Thus, in international law aliens typically have no right themselves to protest directly to host states if they have been mistreated by it; instead, they are expected to petition their home governments, who make representations to the host state in turn (Oppenheim, *International Law*, vol. 1, chap. 3). Similarly, the reason aliens may be denied political rights in their host states is presumably that they have access to the political process in their home states. It is an implication of my argument here that, if states want to press the special claims of their own citizens to the exclusion of all others, then they have a duty to make sure that everyone has a competent protector—just as if everyone at the seashore wants to bathe undisturbed by any duty to rescue drowning swimmers, then they have a duty to appoint a lifeguard.

54. See Goodin, *Protecting the Vulnerable*, chap. 5; and Pettit and Goodin, "The Possibility of Special Duties," pp. 673–76.

55. Vattel, *The Law of Nations*, bk. 1, chap. 19, sec. 230; see, similarly, Wolff, *The Law of Nations Treated*, secs. 147–49; and Grotius, *On the Law of War and Peace*, bk. 2, chap. 2, sec. 16. Vattel and Wolff specifically assert the right of the exile to dwell anywhere in the world, subject to the permission of the host state—permission which the host may properly refuse only for "good" and "special reasons" (having to do, in Vattel's formulation at

least, with the strict scarcity of resources in the nation for satisfying the needs of its pre-existing members). The duty of the international community (i.e., the "set of states, as a whole") to care for refugees derives from the fact that refugees "have no remaining recourse other than to seek international restitution of their need," as the point has been put by Andrew E. Shacknove, "Who Is a Refugee?" *Ethics* 95 (1985): 274–84.

56. Similarly, in the "advocacy model" in the law, it is morally proper for attorneys to press their clients' cases as hard as they can if and only if everyone has legal represen-tation; if institutions fail to guarantee that, it is wrong for attorneys to do so. See Wasser-strom, "Lawyers as Professionals," pp. 12–13, and "Roles and Morality," pp. 36–37.

57. Ideally, of course, this model would have both the rich getting richer and the poor getting richer. Even in this ideal world, however, it is almost inevitable that the rich would get richer at a faster rate than the poor. Assuming that the needs of the poor grow more quickly than those of the rich, then in some real sense it may well be inevitable, even in this ideal world, that the poor will actually get (relatively) poorer.

58. Or, as Miller puts it, it is wrong to put the poorly-off in charge of the poorly-off and the well-off in charge of the well-off ("The Moral Significance of Nationality," this issue). That is not a critique of my model but, instead, a critique of existing inter-national boundaries from within my model.

59. Compare Barry, "Self-government Revisited," pp. 234–39.

60. Some have offered, as a reductio of my argument, the observation that one way of "reconstituting" state boundaries as I suggest might be for a particularly poor state to volunteer to become a colony of another richer country. But that would be a true implication of my argument only if (a) citizens of the would-be colony have no very strong interests in their national autonomy and (b) the colonial power truly discharges its duties to protect and promote the interests of the colony, rather than exploiting it. The sense that this example constitutes a reductio of my argument derives, I submit, from a sense that one or the other of those propositions is false. But in that case, it would not be an implication of my argument, either.

61. This duty to render assistance across poorly constituted boundaries might be regarded as a "secondary, back-up responsibility" that comes into play when those assigned primary responsibility prove unwilling or unable to discharge it. In *Protecting the Vulnerable*, chap. 5, I argue that such responsibilities come into play whatever the reason for the default on the part of the agent with primary responsibility. There, I also argue that one of our more important duties is to organize political action to press for our community as a whole to discharge these duties, rather than necessarily trying to do it all by ourselves. That saves my model from the counterintuitive consequence that well-off Swedes, knowing that the welfare state will feed their own children if they do not, should send all their own food to starving Africans who would not otherwise be fed rather than giving any of it to their own children.

Chapter Nine

RICHARD W. MILLER

COSMOPOLITAN RESPECT AND PATRIOTIC CONCERN

*E*ven in countries where average income and wealth are much greater than in the world at large, most people take themselves to have a duty to show much more concern for the needs of compatriots than for the needs of foreigners in their political choices concerning tax-financed aid. For example, in the United States, most reflective, generally humane people who take the alleviation of poverty to be an important task of government think they have a duty to support laws that are much more responsive to neediness in the South Bronx than to neediness in the slums of Dacca. This patriotic bias has come to play a central role in the debate over universalist moralities, moralities whose fundamental principles prescribe equal concern or respect for all individuals everywhere and lay down no independent, fundamental duty toward people in a special relation to the agent. Particularists, i.e., those who locate an independent principle of group loyalty in the foundations of morality, challenge universalists to justify the pervasive patriotic bias in tax-supported aid that is a deep-seated commitment of most of those who are, in general, attracted to universalism.[1]

So far, universalist justifications of patriotic bias in aid have not risen to the particularist challenge. Granted (as Goodin noted in an important contribution to this debate), if someone has equal concern for all humanity everywhere, she will take certain considerations of efficiency to favor a worldwide system of institutional responsibilities including special responsibilities toward compatriots, as opposed to similarly needy foreigners. People's tendency to be more sensitive to compatriots' deprivation than foreigners' concentrates the collective attention of an effective social group and facilitates the deliberative coordination of giving; on the whole, people have a better understanding of compatriots' needs, and can more easily provide aid to the needy within the nation's borders. However, the grim facts of international inequality override

From *Philosophy and Public Affairs* 27, no. 3 (1998): 202–24. Copyright © 1998 by Princeton University Press. Reprinted by permission of Princeton University Press.

these considerations, when one assesses bias toward compatriots in a per-capita rich country as compared with the poor of the world at large from a perspective of equal concern for all. The neediness of people in countries such as Bangladesh is desperate enough, their local resources meager enough, their numbers great enough, and current transportation, information, and transnational institutions are effective enough, to put responsibility for the needy of per-capita poor foreign countries on a par with responsibility for needy compatriots in per-capita rich ones, when responsibilities are allocated in ways that most efficiently provide for worldwide needs.[2]

The other main universalist strategy for justifying special concern for compatriots has appealed to mutual benefit as the appropriate basis for unchosen terms of cooperation.[3] Tax-financed giving to compatriots is more apt than tax-financed giving to foreigners to be part of an arrangement in which, over the long run, the contribution of each is compensated by proportionate benefits. For example, domestic giving often contributes to an insurance scheme that is in the long-run self-interest of current benefactors, or serves as a means by which the better-off compensate worse-off compatriots for otherwise unrewarded benefits of their participation in shared institutions. However, a rationale for aid that is solely based on long-term mutual benefit will hardly satisfy the vast majority of universalists, who think that those who contribute more to social output can have a duty to make sacrifices over the long run to help those who contribute less when the lesser contribution is due to unchosen disadvantages. Yet once the moral relevance of neediness is acknowledged, it is hard to see why it loses force across borders.

The particularist challenge has begun to seem so powerful that it forces a choice between abandoning universalism and abandoning the patriotic bias in tax-financed aid that is a deep commitment of the vast majority of reflective people who are otherwise strongly attracted to universalism. I will describe a way of avoiding this hard choice, a way of basing a special duty expressing this bias on a universalist morality. For reasons I sketched in connection with Goodin's proposal, I do not think this reconciling project can succeed on the basis of a universalist morality of equal concern for all. Instead, I will derive the patriotic bias from a morality of equal respect for all. A plausible comprehensive morality of universal respect produces a strongly biased duty of special concern for compatriots in matters of tax-financed aid, largely because it dictates a special interest in leading a social life based on mutual respect and trust and a special commitment to provide adequate incentives for compatriots to conform to the shared institutions that one helps to impose on them. (The required incentives are not proportionate to contribution.) In a moral discussion, guided by this perspective, between Kevin, a corporate lawyer living in a rich suburb of New York, and Khalid, who collects scrap metal in a slum of Dacca, Kevin could say, "In my political choices, I must give priority to helping my needy compatriots if my most important relations of interdependence are to be based on respect and trust, and if those compatriots are to have an incentive that their self-respect requires if they are to uphold political measures I help to force upon them." Khalid could accept this rationale even though he suffers from the worldwide consequences of Kevin's sort of patriotic bias, because his own moral responsibility leads him to accord a special importance to the kind of social and political relations Kevin seeks, an importance that entails allowing others to treat the pursuit of such relations in their own lives as a basis for choice among rules for giving.

According to this argument, special concern for those in certain unchosen relations to oneself, including relations of specially intense interdependence and mutual subordination, *is* part of the foundations of morality, but it is not an independent part. Such special concern is entailed by a comprehensive universalist morality of equal respect for all.

THE BIAS

The attempt to meet the particularist challenge requires a more detailed description of its terms, i.e., the terms of a bias toward compatriots in tax-supported aid that is plausibly ascribed to most reflective people who are otherwise strongly attracted to universalism. In defining this bias, I will construe "compatriot" broadly, as including all long-term, law-abiding fellow-residents of a country. Particularists are in no position to claim that there is a pervasive attachment to a substantial bias of narrower scope: as recent American controversies over denials of benefits to resident aliens imply, there is no broad consensus that mere law-abiding, long-term residents deserve much less concern than those with such further accoutrements as fellow-citizenship or fellow-membership in a cultural or ethnic community that predominates within the country's borders. Still, it is probably common coin that fellow-citizenship strengthens duties of public aid to some degree and that cultural or ethnic ties can justify some special aid (for example, the special support that the Federal Republic of Germany has given ethnically German immigrants from eastern Europe). My arguments for the larger bias will also suggest how these smaller ones might be justified.

In addition, the proper appreciation of the particularist challenge depends on assessing the strength and depth of the pervasive patriotic bias. The broad consensus to which particularists appeal does not just dictate patriotic bias in most countries or in circumstances of approximate international equality. It entails a patriotic bias in tax-supported aid, despite the grim facts of international inequality, in all or virtually all of the most technologically advanced and materially productive countries, the ones that are, per-capita, relatively rich, as well as in all other countries. The "virtually all" is meant to allow for the possibility of a few countries in which deprivation is so rare that the project of government aid to the needy is, properly, concentrated on foreign aid. On a sufficiently rosy view of Liechtenstein, Liechtensteinian concentration on foreign aid would offend no widespread view of patriotic duty.

In addition to this strength, the prevalent bias is deep in the sense of being insensitive to the outcome of certain empirical controversies. In particular, the bias toward compatriots in per-capita rich countries does not depend on pessimism about the efficacy of helping foreigners in poor countries through foreign aid. Even if optimism on the Oxfam model is right, and, dollar for dollar, feasible varieties of foreign aid would be especially economical means of relieving suffering, the primary concern should be aid to compatriots. (This is not to deny that the pervasive patriotic bias is conditional on other empirical assumptions, which might reasonably be questioned. Rather than seeking to describe these presuppositions at the outset, I will use a morality of equal respect to reveal them, as the factual assumptions in a case for favoring compatriots which rests on this moral foundation.)

Finally, it will be useful to distinguish two kinds of bias that are both prevalent and both fall under the heading "patriotic bias in tax-supported aid." The first is priority of attention to compatriots' needs, i.e., a commitment to oppose policies seriously detracting from provision for relevant needs of compatriots. The second is budgetary bias toward compatriots, i.e., support for a total aid bill in which tax-supported aid to foreigners is a small proportion of tax-supported aid to compatriots. Both biases are prevalent, but they are not the same. If Americans were to satisfy the first priority, removing all relevant burdens from compatriots, they would live in a world in which many foreigners in per-capita poor countries still struggled with similar burdens. In principle, these needs could generate further moral duties so demanding that they require support for an aid budget mostly devoted to foreigners' needs, violating the second, budgetary bias. ("Charity begins at home" does not exclude the possibility that discharging all duties to give will mostly require giving to strangers in the end.)

Given the facts of international inequality, an argument for budgetary bias in rich countries must be based on a prior case for some form of biased attention to compatriots' needs. Observing this order, I shall begin by arguing that full and equal respect for all dictates priority of attention, and then I shall describe the additional considerations sustaining budgetary bias.

Although I have committed myself to defending a strong, deep form of patriotic bias in tax-supported aid, I have said nothing about bias in private, voluntary contributions. And it is a striking fact (which ought to make particularists nervous) that there is no broad, deep-seated consensus that cosmopolitanism in individual charity is wrong. Americans who respond to appeals of the Save the Children program can check a box that indicates their desire to help a child who lives in the United States. Those who check the "Where the need is greatest" box instead (or the "Africa" or "Asia" box) are not widely held to have violated a duty. My argument from equal respect to patriotic bias in political choice will not, in fact, support the corresponding private duty. This helps to account for their different roles in the pervasive consensus, and so, helps to confirm the argument itself.

COSMOPOLITAN RESPECT

Any universalist morality worthy of the name will ground moral obligations on some fundamental standpoint in which everyone's life is regarded as equally valuable. Because of the facts of international inequality, it seems impossible to ground duties of patriotic bias in tax-financed aid on a standpoint of equal concern for all. But, on the face of it, according equal value to different people's lives does not entail equal concern for them. I certainly regard the life of the girl who lives across the street as no less valuable than the life of my own daughter. But I am not equally concerned for her. For example, I am not willing to do as much for her. The existence of obstacles to her enjoying the pursuit of her goals is a prima facie reason for me to help remove the obstacles, but my special concern for my own goals, including my wishes for my daughter, can provide a legitimate excuse for neglecting to help, without any of the disrespect involved in treating her life as less valuable than others'.

Three broad, interrelated themes in Kantian moral theory, which are well-connected with moral common sense, define one highly attractive approach to questions of right and wrong in the space that I have just created for universalisms not grounded on equal concern for all. First of all, rather than grounding obligation on equal concern, this approach makes equal respect fundamental. One avoids moral wrongness just in case one conforms to some set of rules for living by which one could express equal respect for all, as distinguished from equal concern for all.

Of course, there are a variety of ways of specifying the demands of equal respect. A second common feature of the universalisms from which I will derive a patriotic bias is some version of Kant's view that the rules expressing equal respect for all are the rules that could be the joint, self-imposed, fully autonomous legislation of all. Kant's emphasis on full autonomy is not essential, here. Within this tradition, Scanlon, for example, describes the relevantly unanimous legislation as any total system of shared rules that no one could reasonably reject, while Rawls, in his most Kantian phase, took the principles of justice to be shared premises for political discourse through which each could express her highest-order interests in fair terms of cooperation and the rational revision of final ends. Despite these differences, the various more specific Kantianisms can each be seen as specifying and defending, in its own way, a vaguer, more colloquial standard deploying the ordinary notion of self-respect whose rich moral implications Hill has explored.[4] At least to a first approximation, broadly Kantian universalism affirms that a choice is wrong just in case it violates every set of shared rules of conduct to which everyone could be freely and rationally committed without anyone's violating his or her own self-respect.

As Scanlon has emphasized, some such principle is a natural development of the extremely attractive thought that avoiding moral wrongness is a matter of avoiding actions that are not permitted by rules that are relevantly justifiable, as a shared code of conduct, to those burdened by the action.[5] In this moral context, the irrelevant justifications are those depending on the burdened one's fear or ignorance or her lack of self-respect. It may have been rational for the native peoples of nineteenth-century Rhodesia to accept the rule, "If black, give up your land when whites demand it," since otherwise they would have been subjected to fierce repression, but this hardly shows that Cecil Rhodes and his henchmen did no wrong. Obviously, one does not justify rules in a morally relevant way by getting a victim to accept them out of misinformation or muddle. Finally, justifications that lead to acceptance because of the victim's lack of self-respect (alternatively: her taking her life to be less valuable than others') do not make the permitted conduct all right. If all slaves in the antebellum South had shown a lack of self-respect by freely accepting the rules that made them property of whites, support for slavery would still have been wrong.

A final common feature of broadly Kantian moralities is the distinction they draw between negative and positive duties. These universalisms condemn those who lie or initiate the use of force in pursuit of mere personal advantage, but they do not impose a duty to make every sacrifice that would improve the world on balance. It is enough to adopt policies through which one takes on one's fair share of world improvement. One must adopt policies toward giving that impose some significant lifelong sacrifice. Otherwise, one could not claim to regard the lives of the needy as just as valuable as one's own. But grave self-sacrifice is not required, even if it is productive of great good.

Suppose I see a full-size adult fall, headfirst, out of a tenth-story window. No one else is nearby. Because of my deep knowledge of ballistics and anatomy, I know that if I rush to catch him, I will save his life, by cushioning his fall and keeping his head from striking the sidewalk. But if I cushion his fall, I am very likely to break some bones, which will heal, perhaps painfully and incompletely, in the course of several months. Even if there is no question that the cost of helping to me would be much less than the cost of not helping to the man hurtling toward the sidewalk, I can do my fair share in making the world a better place while turning down this chance for world improvement.

The limits to burdensome giving derive from the fundamental view of moral impartiality. I do not show disrespect for the person falling out the window, do not express the attitude that his life is less valuable than my own, in saving my bones from breakage. Even if specially needy, one shows no lack of self-respect in letting others withhold aid when the cost to them is severe injury. (Thomson's violinist will be quite disturbed if you unplug him, but given the cost of continued connection, he will not take this as an expression of disrespect and will not display a lack of self-respect in permitting the unplugging.[6])

No doubt, my brief, relatively colloquial statements of the demands of equal respect have to be elaborated—for example, to cope with special problems of noncompliance posed by those who do not share in the fundamental moral attitude. No doubt, much more has to be said to justify this approach to morality. Still, I hope I have evoked a familiar strand of universalist thinking, which has been developed and defended for decades, indeed centuries. If, as I hope to show, the broadly shared features of this sort of universalism entail the routine patriotic biases, this will, at least, rebut the particularist claim that no currently viable version of universalism has room for the duties of patriotic bias that express a strong conviction of most people who are otherwise attracted to universalism.

PATRIOTIC PRIORITY

The morality of equal respect for everyone that I have described creates a duty to give priority, in providing tax-financed aid, to the serious deprivations of compatriots. In particular, one must give priority to relieving serious burdens due to inferior life-prospects among compatriots, i.e., inferior chances of success in pursuing life-goals given equal willingness to make sacrifices. This priority does not totally exclude support for foreign aid in the presence of relevant domestic burdens. Still, until domestic political arrangements have done as much as they can (under the rule of law and while respecting civil and political liberty) to eliminate serious burdens of domestic inequality of life-prospects, there should be no significant sacrifice of this goal in order to help disadvantaged foreigners. Here, significant sacrifice consists of foreseeable costs to a disadvantaged compatriot so severe that she need not willingly accept them, even though she equally values everyone's life and realizes that these costs to her are part of an arrangement helping even more disadvantaged others. For example, poor people in virtually all per-capita rich countries confront low prospects of interesting, valued work; effective political participation; and intellectually liberating education, and are at special risk of long-term ill health, in the absence of extensive aid. These are the sorts of grave burdens that one can be unwilling to take on, as part of an arrangement that relieves even more serious burdens of others, even though one respects them and regards their lives as no less valuable than one's own.

There are two main arguments for this duty of prior attention to compatriots. Both involve special concerns, specially attentive to domestic life-prospects, that are entailed by commitment to the outlook of equal respect that I have described. The first is an argument from excessive costs in lost social trust, the second an argument from the need to provide compatriots with adequate incentives to obey the laws one helps to create.

First of all, consider the cost in disrupted social trust of the failure to provide tax-financed aid sufficient to relieve serious burdens of inferior life-
prospects among compatriots, when this shortfall is due to provision for neediness abroad. As a consequence of this shortfall, disadvantaged compatriots
would suffer from inferior life-prospects that better-off compatriots do not try
to alleviate because their concern for the needy is diffused worldwide.
Inevitably, this will reduce the extent to which the disadvantaged can be relied
on to cooperate with advantaged compatriots on the basis of their rationally
pursuing shared goals, as opposed to their merely acquiescing in the superior
coercive power of the state, or deferring out of self-abnegation, or cooperating
because they lack awareness of what is going on. For example, if this global
evenhandedness is well-entrenched, needy compatriots cannot be expected to
take part in a trusting and respectful political practice of using principled persuasion to seek common ground. The avoidable burdens of seeking self-
advancement under the nation's laws and policies make it psychologically
insupportable to engage respectfully in the political process that ultimately
enforces these rules. So, in response to a settled commitment to the worldwide
diffusion of concern, the domestic disadvantaged will, inevitably, withdraw
from politics or treat politics as a means of exerting pressure on others, with
no special role for principled persuasion.[7] For similar reasons, the worldwide
diffusion of concern would be accompanied by less friendliness in the routine
interactions with nonintimates that determine the overall tone of life. Rather
than being based on mutual respect and trust, people's relations of interdependence with compatriots would often be based on resentful fear or servility,
the horror from which Huck Finn and Jim made their lonely escape.[8]

Admittedly, someone committed to the morality of equal respect will not
be interested in receiving trust that depends on attitudes of disrespect for
others. (Huck would have been a much worse person if he had not been reluctant to purchase social trust on this basis from his fellow whites.) However, the
limits to trust on the part of the domestic disadvantaged do not reflect their
lack of full and equal respect for disadvantaged foreigners. For patriotic priority of attention is violated only when they suffer losses sufficiently serious
that they do not have to take them on, as part of provision for neediness elsewhere, in order to express full and equal respect for all.

Like the risk to one's bones of cushioning the man hurtling toward the
sidewalk, this cost in distrust of foreign aid violating patriotic priority is a legitimate excuse for not helping, an excuse that could be part of the code endorsed
by someone who has full and equal respect for all. This assessment (which is,
I hope, plausible at the outset) gains credibility when one reflects on the role
of the interest in basing dependence on trust and respect in rationalizing the
morality that I have described. The unconditional commitment to live by some
code that all could freely, rationally, and self-respectfully share can require for-
swearing indefinitely great advantages, because they depend on exploitation or

domination that such codes prohibit. Yet doing the right thing is always one rational option for a normal human being. What normal human interest could rationalize the life-practice of someone who forswears advantages violating those bases for general agreement, while otherwise pursuing the projects to which she is personally attached?

The answer would seem to be: an interest in having one's relationships of dependence be relationships of mutual respect and trust. All of us have reason to want to be able to rely on others to act in ways that we expect to benefit us, acting in these ways despite tempting opportunities to benefit themselves by noncompliance. The morally responsible people among us, those who seek to avoid wrongdoing, do not want others' dependability to be due to their fear, irrationality, or lack of self-respect, even if these sources of compliance are reliable. Their overriding preference, when they depend on others, is for dependability based on common concerns that each can willingly embrace even if everyone regards her life as no less valuable than anyone else's. Such a person, if a middle-income U.S. citizen, would not really prefer to be Louis XIV, even after the Fronde has been suppressed and putting to one side the inferiority of seventeenth-century medicine. Using coercion and superstition to frustrate peasants' interests in relaxed enjoyment, creative reflection, and meaningful work is, in the end, too disgusting a prospect.

Because this overriding preference that one's relationships of dependence be based on mutual respect and trust is what rationalizes an overriding commitment to self-regulation by rules expressing equal respect for all, one can express this commitment in choices giving special weight to the promotion of those trusting relationships in one's own life. (In much the same way, when a concern for another's well-being is motivated by love, one expresses that concern in choices giving special weight to continued loving interaction with the other. "I wish her well, and I don't care whether I ever see her again" is not an expression of loving parental concern.) So, in a morality based on rules expressing equal respect, the fact that aid to disadvantaged compatriots is specially important for one's engagement in trusting, respectful forms of interdependence provides a legitimate excuse for patriotic bias.

It might seem that the argument from social trust to patriotic bias underrates the bearing of foreign needs on respect and trust, in two different ways. First of all, this argument might seem to ignore the existence of international economic interdependence. But the argument is only meant to justify a bias, and only relies on the fact that interdependence among compatriots is specially intense and specially vulnerable to distrust and disrespect. This special vulnerability is, in part, a consequence of the political vulnerability implicit in the compatriot relation: politically active people support the coercive imposition of laws on their compatriots. (It is largely because of my location in a distinct network of political vulnerabilities that social distrust in Quebec does not taint my social life, even though I live much closer to Quebec than to most of the United States.)

In the second place, the argument so far might seem to ignore the socially disruptive effects of the poverty in poor countries that foreign aid could relieve. The violation of primary attention to compatriots' needs by people like Kevin would reduce social trust on the part of people like Carla, who lives in the South Bronx and makes a meager living cleaning other people's apartments. Nonetheless, the increased foreign aid might lead to strengthened bonds linking Khalid and his compatriots, as Khalid's situation becomes less desperate. Perhaps, because of the special desperation of the worst-off in the poorest countries and the cheapness of the measures that would relieve it, violation of patriotic priority in per-capita rich countries would be part of the most efficient means of promoting social trust worldwide. If so, wouldn't the special interest in social trust that is implicit in equal respect for all exclude, rather than support, patriotic bias, making consequent costs to oneself as irrelevant as costs of foregoing feasible theft or exploitation?

Since I am trying to justify a bias deep enough to be compatible with optimistic views of the efficacy of foreign aid, the supposition about the special effectiveness of foreign aid in the worldwide enhancement of social trust is certainly fair. But taking this efficacy to cancel the excuse for neglecting foreign needs would involve a misunderstanding of a morally responsible person's special valuing of relationships of mutual respect and trust. It would be like the mistake of supposing that someone who specially values the relationship of parental nurturing must be willing to neglect his daughter if this is needed to save two other people's daughters from parental neglect. Granted, if the special valuing of a relationship is a dictate of moral responsibility, then all instances of it, everywhere, are specially valuable. However, as Scheffler has recently emphasized, the special valuing of a relationship entails, not just a high appreciation of the value of its instances, but taking participation in this relationship with another to be a specially demanding reason for appropriate forms of concern for the other.[9] I don't specially value the relationship of parental nurturance if I willingly neglect my child just because this is part of a more effective way to promote nurturance in the world at large. Kevin does not specially value social trust if he jeopardizes his relationship with compatriots such as Carla so that foreigners such as Khalid may enjoy more trust on balance. By the same token, Khalid, as a morally responsible person, will take relations of respect and trust to be specially important and will all the more regret the social strains of Bangladeshi poverty. But, taking such relations to be specially valuable, he will take their maintenance to be a specially powerful reason for action. This is why Khalid, despite his plight, can allow Kevin to favor needy compatriots, without showing a lack of self-respect.

So far, I have argued that a certain bias is all right, not that it is morally obligatory: the better-off in per-capita rich countries have a legitimate excuse for giving priority to compatriots' needs in their political choices. However, because the topic is the political choice to support laws forcing some to help others and the patriotic bias is based on an interest that all morally responsible people share, this lemma is a short step removed from the theorem asserting a duty of priority in attention to compatriots' needs in tax-financed aid. It shows a lack of respect for another to force her to do more than she must to do her fair share in the task of world-improvement. Because of the cost in social trust, someone would be forced to do more than her fair share if she were taxed according to laws violating patriotic priority. So support for such laws is wrong. On the other hand, such laws as are needed to sustain domestic social trust would be supported by every compatriot committed to equal respect for all: the better-off because of the social interest implicit in that commitment, the worst-off for material reasons, as well. If a political arrangement would be supported by every morally responsible participant, i.e., every participant committed to equal respect for all, then each has a moral duty to support it.

Like Rawls's discussions of "excusable envy," this first argument for patriotic bias appeals to a psychologically inevitable limit on trust and respect. Even if the domestic disadvantaged could overcome this limit, engaging in trusting, respectful political activity and avoiding both resentment and servility despite worldwide diffusion of concern, there would be a second basis for patriotic priority of attention, the need to give priority to compatriots' needs in order to avoid unjust domination.

Anyone engaged in political choice is engaged in projects which, if they succeed, will result in laws that all compatriots are forced to obey. Equal respect for all is incompatible with supporting the coercive enforcement of terms of self-advancement under which some are seriously burdened, regardless of their choices, in ways that could be alleviated at relatively little cost to the advantaged. More specifically, suppose that current laws enforce rules of peaceful private self-advancement that guarantee that some compatriots will be seriously burdened by inferior life-prospects unless their advantaged compatriots help to lift these burdens: losers in competition in one generation convey seriously inferior capacities to get ahead to their children. Suppose that there are measures through which suffering from inferior life-prospects could be alleviated without imposing losses on the advantaged, through taxation, that are at all as great as the alleviation. (The taxation used to improve the education of Carla's child will lower the life-prospects of Kevin's child, but the cost to the one is much less than the gain to the other.) In this situation, support for the status quo would show disrespect for the disadvantaged. After all, someone whose life-prospects are burdened by such laws could not willingly uphold a shared social standard allowing these burdens to be imposed in spite of the small costs of change, unless that sufferer lacked self-respect.

From the perspective of equal respect that I have described, the appropriate assessments of benefits and burdens would, surely, rule out support for laissez-faire capitalism in virtually all per-capita rich countries and require aid exceeding current measures, on any hypothesis about the efficacy of domestic aid that coheres with optimism about the efficacy of foreign aid. For, assuming such efficacy, there will be gains to the disadvantaged from wide-ranging policies requiring taxation of the rich that will be much more important than the costs in luxuries and comforts lost through such taxation. Someone rationally committed to foregoing all advantages depending on violation of rules that others could rationally, self-respectfully share must accord special importance to the prerequisites for participation in a social life regulated by rules rationally shared by self-respecting cooperators. Such a willing cooperator will regard it as extremely important to have resources for informed and rational reflection over how to live and what laws to support, to have an influence on a par with the influence of others' on laws and, more generally, on one's social environment, to have work that is valuable to oneself, under one's own intelligent control in important ways, and recognized as valuable by others, and to have opportunities for the leisure, affection, and whimsy that are needed for self-expressive living. These are all human requirements for taking part in a social life in which one's self-respect is displayed and supported. Because her commitment to rules sustaining such a social life is unconditional and because she regards everyone's life as equally valuable, a morally responsible person will express her special commitment to these values in comparing gains for some and losses for others. So she will take the burdens on people like Carla to be specially severe and costs for people like Kevin of relieving them to be relatively moderate.

Note that the domestic aid required by the broadly Kantian perspective is more demanding than relief required by considerations of mutual benefit. The standard of mutual benefit would legitimate a situation in which Kevin's and Carla's different life-expectations are proportional to expected differences in contribution, due to advantages of Kevin's that are not traceable to their choices. But Carla would display a lack of self-respect in accepting burdens due to these unchosen differences (such as the difficulties of growing up in a crime-ridden neighborhood, brought up by a single tired, distracted, ill-educated parent and taught by weary, cynical teachers). She would be like a slave who accepts the distribution of income between slaves and plantation-owners if it reflects the greater economic importance of plantation-owners' coordination of production and exchange, giving no weight to the facts that slaves are denied literacy and large networks of acquaintance and that major economic agents refuse to deal directly with them.

The sticking point in using this argument about unjust subordination to support patriotic bias is the resemblance between Kevin's relationship to Carla and Kevin's relationship to Khalid: the inferiority of Khalid's life-prospects is at least as stark, its burdens at least as severe, and, on optimistic views of the efficacy of foreign aid, it would be even easier to alleviate the burden at little cost to Kevin. However, because of two further differences, Kevin can favor Carla without showing disrespect for Khalid and Khalid can willingly accept such bias without showing a lack of self-respect.

First, Kevin takes part in a political process resulting in the coercive enforcement of laws governing compatriots, not foreigners. Because morally responsible people specially value relationships of mutual respect and trust, they regard it as specially important not to take part in the coercive imposition of arrangements that participants could not rationally, self-respectfully uphold. After all, in specially valuing a relationship, one both regards participation in it as providing a special reason for appropriate forms of concern *and* regards its opposites as relationships one has special reason to avoid—the more powerful the opposition, the stronger the reason. If I specially value friendship, I must be specially concerned not to tyrannize others—even more concerned than I must be to avoid benefiting from others' tyrannizing. Similarly, if I specially value relationships of mutual respect and trust, I must be specially concerned to avoid coercively dominating others in ways that they could not self-respectfully uphold, and this concern should take priority over my interest in alleviating inferior life-prospects due to rules for self-advancement in whose creation and coercive enforcement I do not participate. Kevin, then, expresses his commitment to equal respect for all, not his disrespect for Khalid, in Kevin's special concern for life-prospects determined by rules he helps to impose. And Khalid, for his part, shows no lack of self-respect in accepting a moral code requiring such special concern of the likes of Kevin. The endorsement of rules reflecting an attitude that makes it rational to have equal respect for all can entail no loss of self-respect.

In the second place, the different baselines appropriate to assessing the impact on life-prospects of domestic and of international interactions make the moral pressure to supplement transnational interactions with foreign aid much less than the pressure to add policies of aid to domestic economic arrangements. We can attribute domestic inequalities in life-prospects on the scale of those separating Kevin and Carla to their domestic institutions because, in the absence of enduring, effectively enforced domestic institutions, everyone's life-prospects would be virtually nil, as compared with their actual life-prospects. International inequalities in life-prospects are not attributable to transnational institutions to the same extent, since rich and poor economies would differ quite substantially in prosperity in the absence of interaction between them. Indeed, the miserable record of per-capita poor countries that have pursued autarky suggests that the benefit of current interaction to those affected in poor countries is an improvement in life-prospects on the scale of corresponding improvements in rich countries. In some cases, there is, no doubt, an exploitive inequality. Still, the difference in the relevant baselines makes it much easier for Khalid than for Carla to accept advantages of Kevin's without loss of self-respect.

Even though these arguments for patriotic bias have turned on the need to avoid certain negative phenomena of resentment and unjust domination, the underlying perspective of equal respect makes adequate provision for needy compatriots a legitimate source of pride. One should be all the prouder of improving the world because one has avoided insensitivity to morally relevant differences, in the process of world-improvement. In addition, a morality of equal respect for all has room for a positive appreciation of someone's supporting aid advancing patriotic goals because of her loyalty to her compatriots. A well-integrated person who is committed to the morality of equal respect will have a noninstrumental desire to play an active role in a community in which people care for one another and contribute to the flourishing of common projects whose success is important to the success in life of each. After all, it would not be rational to be so concerned to live by rules that others willingly share, if one were perfectly content to be a harmless isolate or to interact with others on the basis of utterly self-centered goals. This general aspiration to community can certainly be satisfied by international cooperation. Some of us have life-projects and resources permitting us to cooperate in cosmopolitan communities of university intellectuals, social democrats, music lovers, or whatever. However, for most people, the broadest form of communal interaction corresponding to their desires and resources is participation in a national community in which the enhancement of compatriots' well-being and the flourishing of a shared way of life are a source of collective pride. So proud engagement in a national community is a centrally important way of realizing an aspiration of anyone fully committed to the universalist morality of equal respect.

BUDGETARY BIAS

Suppose that a broadly Kantian morality of equal respect for all does require priority of attention to compatriots' needs. The remaining task is to compare the domestic aid and foreign aid columns in the ideal budgets of virtually all per-capita rich countries, to see whether the respective sums express the budgetary bias, according to which the total aid bill that morally responsible citizens must support is very largely devoted to compatriots.

In these ideal ledgers, two general considerations magnify the domestic sum or discount the foreign sum. The magnification is due to the special expensiveness of helping a poor person in a per-capita rich country successfully pursue interests that a morally responsible person will regard as centrally important. For example, in a per-capita rich country, making a valued contribution through interesting work in which one is not bossed around requires a relatively expensive education. Interactions in which one expresses one's personality in ways that are recognized and appreciated require relatively expensive housing and clothing. In a morality of equal *concern* for all, this higher cost of living decently would tend to reduce the amount of provision for the worst-off of per-capita rich countries, since provision for the poor in per-capita poor countries more efficiently satisfies needs. But the same cause has an opposite effect if priority must be given to sustaining social trust and providing incentives for supporting domestic institutions among poor compatriots.

The other general consideration, which systematically reduces the sum in the foreign column, is the sharing of responsibilities for worldwide needs. The arguments so far combine with Goodin's considerations of efficiency to sustain a conclusion that is, in any case, more or less obvious: the better-off people in per-capita rich countries have the only major responsibility to pay taxes to aid their needy compatriots. On the other hand, if there is no difference in benefit from international exploitation and no difference in the proportion of relevantly deprived compatriots, there will be no difference in the extent to which people in different per-capita rich countries have a duty to make sacrifices to help the poor in poor countries. This responsibility is shared among people in rich countries, while their domestic responsibilities are not.

In addition, the perspective of full and equal respect for all ascribes a substantial responsibility for poor compatriots to people in per-capita poor countries, a responsibility quite out of proportion to local resources, based on the moral importance of local autonomy. A self-respecting person will seek participation in control over her government, the coercive apparatus that dominates her life, and (if she would protect the self-respect of others) she will want this control to reflect the ongoing achievement of agreement based on appeals to shared principles. This preference for shared deliberation is served by substantial local responsibility for the poor of poor countries. Dependence on the benevolent will of others who are not bound by shared political deliberations is not to be avoided at all cost, even the cost of starving to death, but it is a form of dependence that a self-respecting person will seek to avoid at serious cost.

Against the background of these general factors magnifying the aid budget for domestic needs and reducing the budget for foreign needs, we must now assess the specific reasons why tax-financed aid to the poor in poor countries might be part of the fair share of world-improvement of people in a rich country. First, the international economic regime might give rise to inequalities in life-prospects that are burdensome to people in poor countries, burdensome in ways that beneficiaries in rich countries could alleviate at much less cost than the alleviation produced. This would be similar enough to the domestic situations dictating tax-financed aid to the disadvantaged to provide a reason for international aid if it entails no significant sacrifice of the domestic projects. However, because of the previously noted differences in baselines of noninteraction, the impact of the international economic regime does not seem dramatically unequal in its effects on life-prospects.

Because the distribution of natural resources is so clearly morally arbitrary and the imposition of barriers to access to natural resources is so obviously in need of justification, those who call for increased foreign aid (a proposal that I am *not* opposing) often emphasize the need to compensate for inequalities in the international division of control over natural resources.[10] However, this specific inequality seems to add little to a case for foreign aid based on unequal benefit from international economic interactions as a whole.

Materially based well-being in the world at large is almost entirely the consequence of what is done to work up raw materials, which are otherwise usually
as valueless as a cup of crude oil in a kitchen. So a case for transfer based on
inequality should largely depend on unequal net benefits of whole systems of
production and exchange, the argument from exploitive interaction that I have
been mitigating. Through this deemphasis on inequalities in natural resources
as such, one avoids the embarrassment of rating the pressure to give on
resource-poor Japan as less than the pressure on resource-rich Canada, and
one puts no pressure at all on the resource-rich Republic of the Congo.[11]

Another consideration, especially salient from a perspective of equal
respect, is the impact of closed borders. Poor foreigners who want to take
advantage of the better opportunities for honest self-advancement in rich
countries are usually kept out. This creates a duty of concern for consequent
increased burdens.[12] But the concern should be shared among rich countries
restricting immigration. Moreover, it does not attend to the poor whose local
ties and lesser resources make emigration an unattractive option. And it must
be balanced against both losses to the home country due to emigration and
losses the poor who currently live in per-capita rich countries can suffer when
poor immigrants become their compatriots, subjects of patriotic priority.

These are the main reasons for aid to the foreign poor that might be based
on specific kinds of interactions with them. With domestic magnification and
foreign discounting on the bases previously described, would they create a total
aid budget in which foreign aid was more than a small proportion of domestic
aid, in any remotely typical per-capita rich country? I have offered reasons to
suppose that the answer is no. There are factual presuppositions in this case for
budgetary bias — above all, in the assessment of exploitive international benefits — which cannot be justified quickly, perhaps cannot be justified in the final
analysis. But note that a conclusive empirical argument for these presuppositions is not needed to meet the particularist challenge. Many thoughtful people
committed to substantial domestic aid have a patriotic budgetary bias that is,
itself, conditional on these factual assumptions. For example, *if* they were to
conclude that an *un*biased budget could provide the domestic basis for social
trust and the adequate political incentive that I have described *and* that such a
budget would be needed to return their nation's proportionate share of benefits
of interaction with people in poor countries that are exploitive in the sense that
I described, then they would not take support for such a budget to violate a
moral duty. Their patriotic convictions do not conflict with a universalist
morality that makes budgetary bias conditional on their plausible view that the
actual extent of international exploitation is not that enormous.

In addition to duties to help the foreign poor that depend on the nature of
relationships and interactions with them, there is certainly a prima facie duty
to help others just because they are suffering. But the net impact on an ideal
budget of this prima facie duty to relieve world suffering is severely con-

strained, in any remotely typical per-capita rich country, by the combination of the domestic burdens of disadvantage and the limits of the sacrifice that moral responsibility requires as a means to aid the needy to whom one is not bound by morally significant relationships and interactions.

Given the patriotic priority of attention established in previous sections, provision for foreign poverty must not involve a significant departure from the project of relieving serious burdens of domestic inequality. With the possible exception of a few small and specially favored societies, all advanced industrial societies seem to require market-based economic arrangements generating burdensome inequalities, on pain of inefficiency that would make life even worse for the worst-off. On views of the efficacy of domestic aid that cohere with reasonably optimistic views of the efficacy of foreign aid, the totality of laws and policies that could relieve such burdens is diverse, extensive, and financially demanding.

Suppose that all that could be done to help the domestic disadvantaged was done. At that point, in virtually all per-capita rich countries, the burdens of domestic aid would have pushed many of the better-off to a margin at which further transfer on the same scale involves losses not required by equal respect for all (hence, losses that should not be coercively imposed). No doubt, the consequent marginal costs in fatigue, detachment, and nonfulfillment on the part of the better-off would, still, be less important than the associated gains for poor foreigners, on the scale of values of a morally responsible person. Giving up interesting vacations, teaching another class each semester, and moving to a smaller house on a noisy street would be a loss on my part smaller than the gain for someone in Mali benefiting from the improved sanitation that my sacrifices finance. Still, such a loss, willingly endured just to help the needy, is serious enough to exceed the demands of equal respect for all. Neither the refusal to cushion the falling man at the cost of a broken arm that takes three months to heal, nor the refusal to invite a very charming waif to join one's household for a year when he will otherwise starve, is an expression of the view that the needy one's life is less valuable than one's own. These are expressions of self-concern falling well short of contempt for others. The losses imposed on the better-off when the project of worldwide aid is pursued well beyond relief of the burdens of domestic disadvantage are as substantial. For example, a rational, responsible, self-respecting professor could choose to endure discomfort as great as suffering from a broken arm that takes three months to heal, or choose to take in a boarder for a year, in exchange for avoiding the losses I have described, losses of a sort that seem inevitable if the overall project of aid is pushed so far beyond its patriotic stage that there is no patriotic budgetary bias, overall.

I do not claim that it is certain that domestic needs are as hard to relieve as these arguments for budgetary priority suppose. But, again, this is not necessary to justify the patriotic bias that most humane people otherwise attracted to universalism actually share. *If* it were to turn out that the elimination of burdensome domestic life-prospects in per-capita rich countries would leave the better-off free to make a similar, additional sacrifice for the sake of foreign needs while still doing no more than equal respect for all demands, many of those now committed to budgetary bias would abandon this bias, with great joy. The pervasive bias is conditional on a plausible hypothesis about the daunting requirements of domestic aid.

Still, because of her special interest in social trust and in adequate incentives for political cooperation, someone who respects everyone, worldwide, will adopt this plausible pessimism as her working hypothesis. She will insist on budgetary bias until helping her poor compatriots proves to be easier than she fears.

NOTES

Earlier versions of this paper were presented to the New York Society for Philosophy and Public Affairs in 1997 and to the Philosophy Program at the City University of New York Graduate Center in 1998. I am indebted to the subsequent discussions, in which comments by Virginia Held, John Kleinig, William Ruddick, Sybil Schwarzenbach, and others advanced my thinking on these topics. I have also benefited from Henry Shue's incisive criticisms of an earlier draft, comments on related work by Greg Demirchyan, Thad Metz, David Phillips, and Robert Wallace, and suggestions by the Editors of *Philosophy & Public Affairs*.

1. David Miller develops a detailed and powerful version of this particularist challenge in *On Nationality* (Oxford: Oxford University Press, 1995), chap. 3. Other recent versions have been presented in criticisms of Martha Nussbaum's cosmopolitan ethic (see especially George Fletcher, "Get Serious," *Boston Review* [October/November 1994]: 30; and Sissela Bok, "From Part to Whole," in Martha Nussbaum et al., *For Love of Country* [Boston: Beacon Press, 1996], pp. 38–44), and in defense of communitarianism (see, for example, Michael Sandel, *Democracy's Discontent* [Cambridge, Mass.: Harvard University Press, 1996], especially p. 17).

2. See Robert Goodin, "What Is So Special about Our Fellow Countrymen?" *Ethics* 98 (1988): 663–86. He acknowledges that international inequalities can override patriotic restrictions on responsibility, on pp. 684–86.

3. Richard Dagger's appeal to reciprocity in "Rights, Boundaries and the Bonds of Community," *American Political Science Review* 79 (1985): 436–47, has been especially influential.

4. See especially Thomas E. Hill Jr., "Servility and Self-Respect" (1973) in his *Autonomy and Self-Respect* (Cambridge: Cambridge University Press, 1991).

5. See T. M. Scanlon, "Contractualism and Utilitarianism," in Amartya Sen and Bernard Williams, *Utilitarianism and Beyond* (Cambridge: Cambridge University Press, 1982), especially pp. 110–17.

6. See Judith Jarvis Thomson, "A Defense of Abortion," *Philosophy & Public Affairs* 1, no. 1 (fall 1971): 48f.

7. For a powerful and detailed portrayal of the trusting and respectful political practice in which participants seek common ground through principled persuasion, see Joshua Cohen, "Deliberation and Democratic Legitimacy," in A. Hamlin and P. Pettit, *The Good Polity* (Oxford: Blackwell, 1989), pp. 17–34.

8. The milieu that is jeopardized includes the "friendly civic relations" whose nature and value Sybil Schwarzenbach describes, with illuminating reference to Aristotle's account of *politike philia*, in "On Civic Friendship," *Ethics* 107 (1996): 97–128.

9. See Samuel Scheffler, "Relationships and Responsibilities," *Philosophy & Public Affairs* 26, no. 3 (summer 1997): 189–209, especially pp. 196, 206. However, in using a comprehensive morality of equal respect to balance special obligations to compatriots against obligations to the poor of the world, I am resisting Scheffler's pessimism about the availability of a single moral outlook which gives adequate scope both to special responsibilities and relationship-independent duties to help the disadvantaged (see pp. 207f.). I agree that no single moral outlook can integrate the proper valuing of special relationships with the pursuit of overall distributive fairness if the latter must express equal or impartial concern for all. But here, as elsewhere, the identification of moral equality with equal respect is a basis for cautious optimism about the capacities of universalist moral theory.

10. Thus, in "An Egalitarian Law of Peoples," Thomas Pogge's central proposal to reduce international inequality is a global resources tax, because this is "an institutional proposal that virtually any plausible egalitarian conception of global justice would judge to be at least a step in the right direction" (*Philosophy & Public Affairs* 23, no. 3 [summer 1994]: 199). Charles Beitz begins his pioneering argument for a global original position by noting that the unequal distribution of natural resources would create a Rawlsian reason to reduce international inequality regardless of the status of international interactions ("Justice and International Relations," *Philosophy & Public Affairs* 4, no. 4 [summer 1975]: 288–95).

11. Neither Pogge nor Beitz, I should add, regards the unequal distribution of natural resources as the centrally important aspect of international inequality in the final analysis, given the actual nature of worldwide economic activity.

12. As I argued in *Moral Differences* (Princeton: Princeton University Press, 1992), pp. 299f.

Chapter Ten
IGOR PRIMORATZ

PATRIOTISM
Morally Allowed, Required, or Valuable?

*A*fter a long period of neglect, patriotism is being discussed again by philosophers and political theorists. The renewed interest in the subject is due to the ongoing debates between impartialists and partialists in ethics and between liberals and communitarians in political philosophy. But it surely owes something to the resurgence of its close relation, nationalism, and the wish of some philosophers to say something helpful on the significance and moral status of a type of outlook that has made a considerable impact in politics in the last decade or so.

Patriotism has had its critics and its defenders. But neither have always been as precise as one might wish about the moral position they have been attacking or defending. This lack of precision is more damaging to a defense of patriotism than to its critique. If patriotism is morally unacceptable, that is all there is to it, morally speaking. But if it can be convincingly defended, if the claim about its moral unacceptability can be refuted, it is still not clear just what has been established. Patriotism may be merely morally permitted. Or it may be morally required, a moral duty. Then again, it may be neither: it may be morally good to be a patriot, although it is not something that can be enjoined as a duty. Patriotism would then be something to praise or admire, but the lack of it would not be a ground for moral condemnation.

In this paper I focus on this question. Before taking it up, I need to say a few words on the definition of patriotism.

From *Nationalism and Ethnic Conflict: Philosophical Perspectives*, edited by N. Miscevic (Chicago and LaSalle, Ill.: Open Court Publishing Co., 2000), pp. 101–13. Copyright © 2000 Carus Publishing Co. Reprinted by permission of the publisher.

1. WHAT IS PATRIOTISM?

The word "patriotism" is sometimes used in a sense that contrasts it with "nationalism." In ordinary usage in contemporary Western societies, "patriotism" normally has positive connotations, while "nationalism" does not and, indeed, often implies a measure of disapproval or criticism. Accordingly, people sometimes describe the way they relate to their country or nation as patriotism, while branding the same attitude of others to *their* country or nation as nationalism. Another way of contrasting the two is in terms of a defensive versus aggressive attitude. In "Notes on Nationalism," George Orwell portrays patriotism as devotion to a particular place or way of life one thinks best but has no wish to impose on anyone else; patriotism is thus essentially defensive. Nationalism is said to be bound up with the desire for power; a nationalist wants to acquire as much power and prestige as possible, not for himself, but for his nation, in which his individuality is submerged.[1]

This, of course, is not very helpful. If we aim at getting clear about the moral status of patriotism, we should rather define it in a way that is not question-begging. It might be useful to define both patriotism and nationalism in a morally neutral way and on the same level, as two partly similar, partly different attitudes. Patriotism is, basically, love of and concern for one's country. Nationalism might be defined analogously as love of and concern for one's people or nation (where the latter is meant in an ethnic, rather than merely political, sense). The subject of this paper is patriotism; although some of what I will be saying on patriotism, *mutatis mutandis*, also applies to nationalism, I wish to put the latter aside.

The definition of patriotism I will be assuming here requires two clarifications. As we are morally bound to show some concern for human beings in general and many if not most of us tend to feel a measure of such concern anyway, patriotism must involve *special* concern for one's country and compatriots. Patriotism is not the same as love of and concern for humanity; a patriot loves her country *more* than any other, and is *more* concerned for the interests of her country and compatriots than for the interests of other countries and their inhabitants.

So far I have mentioned the patriot's country and compatriots, but not the state and fellow-citizens. Such an apolitical definition does seem to capture a possible, minimal sense of patriotism. In this sense, a completely apolitical person can be a patriot. But the word is hardly ever used in this sense today. As a rule, the *patria* to which the patriot is devoted is not merely a geographical, but also a political entity; the people about whose interests she is particularly concerned are not only her compatriots, but also fellow-citizens. The special concern that defines patriotism in its contemporary sense is also a concern for one's state. It involves a degree of active participation in public, political life of the patriot's country, in which the common interests are articulated, discussed, and promoted. Accordingly, normally we would not describe a completely apolitical person as a patriot.[2]

2. IS PATRIOTISM MORALLY ALLOWED?

There is a tradition in moral philosophy that rejects patriotism in no uncertain terms. One type of objection presents patriotism as an irrational belief in the superiority of one's own country over all others and the willingness to promote its interests at the expense of other countries. Its typical manifestations are the absence of any critical assessment of one's country's policies, a knee-jerk support of those policies, an aggressive stance towards other countries, militarism, and jingoism. It makes for international tensions and leads to war. According to the other main line of argument, patriotism offends against the requirement of universality and impartiality of moral judgment. It is an arbitrary, morally illegitimate type of partialism, deriving its force from what William Godwin called "the magic in the pronoun 'my.'"

On the other hand, some philosophers have questioned the type of universality and impartiality of moral judgment which requires that, for the sake of morality, we renounce so many of those personal feelings, loyalties, and relationships that provide a large part of the value and meaning of our lives, and also that we learn to ignore certain highly important special moral commitments and attend exclusively to the impersonal, universal moral duties. In this context, some have defended the type of partiality enjoined by the love of one's country. In his seminal lecture "Is Patriotism a Virtue?" Alasdair MacIntyre has gone further, and maintained that patriotism constitutes the very foundation of morality and that, accordingly, patriotic considerations ought to override other, more abstract moral considerations that might come into conflict with them. If a person's love of country is not strong enough to trump love of humanity or respect for universal justice, it is not true patriotism, but merely its "emasculated" version that ultimately reduces to an empty slogan.[3]

Still other philosophers have tried for a middle-of-the-road position: one that safeguards the demands of universality and impartiality properly circumscribed, while making room for a constrained and thus morally acceptable type of patriotism. I am referring to the writings of Marcia Baron and Stephen Nathanson in defense of what Nathanson terms "moderate patriotism."[4] I find their arguments convincing, and do not propose to improve upon them. Nor will I summarize those arguments. I will merely briefly describe the type of patriotism they have defended.

Moderate patriotism is not exclusive. Its adherent is willing to universalize the judgment according to which she is allowed to prefer her country and compatriots to other countries and their inhabitants and grant that everyone is entitled to this sort of partiality to their country. This shows her claim that she is allowed to be partial to her country to be a genuine moral judgment; for universalizability is a defining trait of such judgments. An extreme patriot who is not willing to universalize his stand and denies that foreigners have the same right to be patriots of their countries thereby ceases to participate in moral discourse on the subject, and adopts the stance of a morally indefensible and intellectually suspect exclusivity.

Moderate patriotism is not exclusive in yet another sense. Its adherent shows special concern for her country and compatriots, but that does not prevent her from having a measure of concern for other countries and their inhabitants. Moreover, moderate patriotism allows for the possibility that under certain circumstances the concern for human beings in general will override the concern for one's country and compatriots. Such patriotism is compatible with a decent degree of humanitarianism. Extreme patriotism, by contrast, gives greater weight to the interests of one's country and compatriots than to those of other countries and their inhabitants whenever the two come into conflict.

Finally, moderate patriotism is not uncritical, unconditional, unlimited. Its adherent is not convinced in advance that her country is always in the right, and that any other country that stands in its way must be in the wrong. She is willing to submit to critical scrutiny her country's stance in international politics, its political and military objectives and the methods it uses in pursuing them. When the result of such scrutiny is unfavorable to her country, she will no longer support it in its conflict with another country simply because it is her country. An extreme patriot does not even entertain the idea of critically judging his own country. In general, a moderate patriot expects her country to live up to certain basic moral requirements and in that way, too, deserve her support, devotion, and special concern for its interests. When it fails to do so, she will support it no longer. Such a patriot, for instance, will not support the rule of her country over a territory to which it has no valid right and whose inhabitants are opposed to its rule over them, or in the waging of an unjust war. An extreme patriot, on the other hand, remains committed to the policies of his country in such cases.

This difference between the moderate and morally acceptable, and the extreme and morally illegitimate variety of patriotism, is nicely captured in two maxims—one short and widely popular, the other slightly longer and much less popular. One is: My country, right or wrong! The other is: My country, right or wrong; if right, to be kept right; and if wrong, to be set right.[5]

3. IS PATRIOTISM MORALLY REQUIRED?

To say that moderate patriotism is morally acceptable is not to say that it is morally valuable or even required. Philosophers who have discussed the moral standing of patriotism and defended its moderate variety, such as Marcia

Baron or Stephen Nathanson, do not distinguish between these three positions clearly and consistently enough.[6] But neither the second nor the third thesis follows from the first, and if we are to accept either the claim that patriotism is a duty, or the claim that it is morally valuable, its proponents need to provide further argument.

In line with the conclusion of the preceding section, "patriotism" will henceforth refer only to its moderate version. What type of argument could establish the thesis that patriotism is not only morally permitted but also positively valuable, or even obligatory?

One might be tempted to give short shrift to the latter idea. Patriotism is, by definition, *love* of one's country. But we cannot be duty-bound to love anyone or anything, since it is not within our power to choose to do so or not. Feelings are not a matter of free choice; therefore, they are not subject to moral prescription or proscription. This, however, is too quick. Many people talk about "the duty of patriotism," and criticize those they feel do not live up to it or even dare to renounce it. If we accepted this argument, we would not merely reject the claim of patriotic duty as unconvincing (as, in my view, we should); we would have to pronounce all such talk fundamentally, irreparably confused. What we need to do instead is to acknowledge that, when discussing whether patriotism is a duty, what we are referring to is not the *feeling* of special love of or concern for one's country, but rather the giving of special weight to the interests of one's country in one's *choices* and *actions*.

On one view, such choices and actions are enjoined by a rule justified by its acceptance utility. The rule of patriotism, calling for special concern for the interests of one's own country and compatriots, has the same basis and status as all other special duties: such duties mediate our fundamental, general duties and thus make possible their most effective discharge. They do so by providing for a division of moral labor, indispensable since our capacities for doing good are limited by our circumstances and each one of us can normally be of much greater assistance to those who are in some way close to us than to those who are not. Thus, for instance, charity begins at home because one will do much more good by attending to the needy at home than by traveling to the other end of the world in order to do good there.

However, the rule-utilitarian justification of the duty of patriotism will not be readily embraced by patriots. They will most likely find it much too weak, tenuous, and indeed alien to what they feel patriotism is all about. For—to explain the latter point first—what it says is that the duty of patriotism is a mere pragmatic device for assigning to individuals some of the universal duties. It owes whatever moral force it has to the moral weight of those universal duties. Accordingly, as a recent proponent of this understanding of patriotism grants, "it turns out that 'our fellow countrymen' are not so very special after all."[7] They merely happen to be the beneficiaries of the most effective way of expressing our concern for other human beings. And, on a practical level, the duty of patriotism construed in rule-utilitarian terms will be flawed in the way all special duties are when understood in this way. It will be overridden on each and every occasion when acting out of universal human concern would have even slightly better consequences.[8] That, obviously, will be much too often for any patriot worth his salt.

Another line of argument for the duty of patriotism ascribes intrinsic value to citizenship, and attempts to show that this value generates the duty of special concern for one's country and compatriots.[9] This has been cogently criticized by Friderik Klampfer, who confronts the adherent of this approach with a dilemma. If citizenship is to be valuable in itself, and to a degree that makes it possible to ground the duty of patriotic partiality, it must be conceived as a very rich and intrinsically significant relationship. But the notion of citizenship so conceived will leave out many compatriots. On the other hand, if the duty of patriotism is to have its proper scope, that is, to apply to all compatriots and only to them, it must be reduced to its formal, legal terms. But citizenship so defined can have, at best, some instrumental value, and is much too weak to generate the duty of patriotism.[10]

Still another line of argument, on which I wish to focus, is suggested by John Horton's attempt to justify political obligation by deploying the notions of positional obligations, membership, and identity.[11] Although the concept of patriotism is neither equivalent to, nor necessarily included in, that of political obligation, Horton's argument for the latter is relevant, since his conception of this obligation is considerably richer than the obligation to obey the laws and authorities of one's country. It also includes a concern for the interests of one's polity. What sort of concern? Obviously, it has to be a *special* concern for one's polity and its members, and not merely an instance of concern one has for all human beings and communities. This special concern for the interests of one's polity includes a concern for the interests of its members as one's compatriots, and participation in its political life in which the welfare of the community as a whole is articulated and promoted.

In attempting to determine one's proper relation to one's polity, Horton makes use of the concept of positional obligations. Family obligations are a standard example. The obligations one member of a family has to another cannot be explained by referring to a free and deliberate act of undertaking an obligation. Nor are they based on the feelings one family member has for another; for they also hold in the absence of such feelings. They are not in need of justification in terms of some fundamental moral principles such as justice or the common good, but rather obligate in their own right. "It is generally sufficient to point out that one does stand in a certain relationship to this or that member of one's family. . . . It is often sufficient to point out that a man is this boy's father to attribute certain obligations on the part of the man. It is both unnecessary and misleading to seek some further moral justification for the obligations."[12] These obligations follow directly from one's membership in the family; they are an integral part of our understanding of the institution of family, and this institution would not exist without them. An individual is in most cases born into a family, and finds herself obligated to other members of the family by virtue of being its member.

To be sure, a family and a polity differ in some important respects. But the similarities are more to the point. An individual is in most cases born into a polity, and finds himself under appropriate obligations to other members and to the polity as a whole by virtue of his membership. "Membership in a polity is rarely optional and, where it is, it may be so only by courtesy of that polity: it is normally acquired simply by being born into a political community and is frequently sustained through continued residence within its territory. These are the conditions which standardly characterise membership."[13]

Both family and polity membership are important parts of our identity. This explains the sense of identification with one's family and polity. This identification is given expression in various ways. One may value the achievements of one's own or any other polity; but one can only be proud of the achievements of one's own polity. One may condemn the crimes of one's own or any other polity; but one can only be ashamed of the crimes perpetrated by one's own polity. The reason for this is the way one relates to the deeds and misdeeds of one's own polity, a way in which one does not and cannot relate to actions of any other polity: the former, but not the latter, are experienced and considered as, in a sense, one's own. An individual can even oppose his country's policies, and yet feel shame or even guilt for them. For those policies, as the policies of *his* country, are implemented in his name too.

This identification is not merely subjective and one-sided; others too tend to identify the individual with her polity and what it does. The authorities and fellow citizens expect that the individual will identify with the polity and act accordingly. On the other hand, an individual is sometimes on the receiving end of acts of foreigners and policies of foreign states that give expression to the idea of collective responsibility. The idea of collective responsibility is much too often applied in ways that are irrational and morally indefensible; but that is not to say that the idea itself is morally untenable. The practice of war reparations, for instance, is generally considered both reasonable and morally appropriate in certain circumstances; but such reparations are for the most part paid by people who bear no individual responsibility for the war. To appeal to an individual's identification with his polity, therefore, is not to appeal to "merely subjective notions or feelings."[14]

It will be objected that positional or membership obligations are not necessarily *moral* obligations. If they were, the fact that a person is a member of the Mafia would imply that that person's obligations as a *mafioso* are moral obligations. Horton replies that positional or membership obligations are constrained by basic moral principles: membership in a morally illegitimate group such as the Mafia or the morally indefensible position of concentration camp

guard clearly do not entail any moral obligations. But the fact that fundamental moral principles set *limits* to obligations pertaining to institutions does
not show that moral legitimacy of those institutions and the obligations they
generate *derive* from those principles. At least some institutions, groups, positions that are not morally illegitimate do generate positional or membership
obligations as genuinely *moral* obligations, and those obligations are not in
need of any *further* justification. The position of father is one example; membership in a polity is another. Some of these groups or institutions play such a
central role in the life of the individual that they become part of the individual's
identity, an indispensable part of the answer to the question who he is. That
holds true of the obligations bound up with membership in those groups or
institutions. Membership in a polity, then, enjoins the obligations contained in
the concept of patriotism. Special concern for the welfare of one's polity and
its members and participation in its political life are indeed moral obligations;
they are based directly, and solely, on one's membership in the polity. To
acknowledge the membership is to acknowledge the moral obligations bound
up with it; to deny their moral force is to deny the membership.

Does this argument succeed in showing that patriotism is not only morally
allowed, but also required? It seems to me that it does not.

Patriotism is presented as an obligation bound up with the individual's
position that has not been freely and deliberately chosen, with membership
acquired by birth into a polity and continued residence in it. The nature of
such obligations is explained by using the example of family and obligations
bound up with membership in a family, with the position of a family member.
In the first step of the argument, then, there is a partial analogy between family
and polity. But this step fails—not, as one might expect, because the analogy
is only partial, but because family is not a good example of the type of moral
obligation Horton has in mind. His analogy seems plausible only at first sight;
its plausibility is due to its generality. When we take a closer look and start distinguishing between various types of family obligations, we get a rather different picture.

It is readily seen that obligations spouses have to one another are primarily obligations they undertook freely and deliberately by the act of contracting a marriage (in any relevant sense of "marriage").[15] Obligations parents have to their child, too, are primarily generated by the parents' choice to
beget a child, or to act in such a way that, whether they mean to beget a child
or not, they may do so. The bringing of a child into the world is bound up with
the moral obligation of nurturing and bringing up the child. (The trivial nature
of this remark sufficiently explains why, having said that a man is the father,
we feel no need for any further argument for the claim that he has certain
obligations to the child.) A child at first has no moral obligations to the parents
or to anyone else, as such obligations presuppose a certain degree of maturity.
Once that degree is reached, the child's obligations to the parents, if any,

would seem to be primarily those of gratitude. To be sure, in a normal, healthy family in all three cases there are also relations of friendship, and such relations involve certain mutual obligations. Finally, it seems that moral obligations between siblings can only be those of friendship.

Neither obligations of gratitude nor those of friendship are generated by some act of freely and deliberately undertaking such obligations. But these obligations are irrelevant to an analogy with patriotism. It is not and indeed cannot be maintained that the obligations one has to compatriots are obligations of friendship. Friendship is a personal relationship, while the relation between compatriots is not and cannot be personal in any polity we are likely to live in.[16] Nor is it claimed that moral obligations to compatriots are a case of obligations of gratitude; arguments against the gratitude theory of political obligation apply with equal force to an attempt to interpret patriotism as required by the duty of gratitude to one's polity.[17] Other moral obligations within the family—the obligations of spouses to one another and their obligations to children—are not obligations we find we have independently of our free and deliberate acts that express or imply commitment. Horton repeatedly points out that we are born into a family and a polity, and argues that this fact and the fact of our continuous residence generate our obligations to family members and compatriots. But this claim is mistaken. The fact of birth can, by itself, ground no moral obligations of the person born. If this fact is *all* that can be adduced in support of the claim that an individual has certain moral obligations, then it is not at all clear that the individual indeed has such obligations. If, for instance, one is a child of one's parents *only* in the biological sense, if the parents have never done anything in the way of nurturing and raising their child after bringing it into the world, it would seem that one has no filial moral obligation to them at all. It is said that blood is thicker than water; it may well be, but it is still not clear just how blood relationship can, by itself, generate moral obligations. The same holds of continuous residence, whether in a home or a homeland. The standard arguments against attempts to ground political obligation on one's continuous residence in one's country are equally damaging to an attempt to ground the obligations of patriotism in the same way.[18]

The second step of the argument, focusing on identity and membership, is no more successful than the first. I suspect that any plausibility it may have is a result of an ambiguity of these terms. Both terms can be used either in (a) a factual, morally neutral sense, or (b) in a sense that involves certain moral obligations. An individual can (a) reside continuously in the country since his birth, be registered as a citizen, and possess all the usual documents. He may speak the country's language and fully participate in its social and cultural life. He can even participate in its political life (perhaps only with a view to promoting the interests of his class or region). He can obey the country's laws and authorities (perhaps without ever giving the subject much consideration, perhaps because he figures that disobedience does not pay). That might include paying taxes, serving in the army, and so on. When asked who he is, what he is, his reply may include a reference to the country he lives in, the polity whose citizen he is, as an important item without which the reply would be significantly incomplete. In view of all this, he can refer to the country as *his* country. Of course, (b) he can also believe he has a moral obligation to show special concern for the welfare of his country and compatriots and to take part in the country's political life, in which its welfare is shaped, articulated, and promoted, and possibly even a moral obligation to obey its laws and authorities. In replying to the question who and what he is, he may mention these beliefs and the behavior to which they give rise, holding that otherwise the reply would remain significantly incomplete.

But (a) and (b) are two different accounts of membership, or two different (partial) accounts of identity, and although the latter may well accompany the former, it need not do so. If someone, in answering the question who and what she is, mentions (a), but expressly rejects (b), the answer will not be inconsistent. It will not be reason enough for us to say that her identity is incomplete, or that her talk of "her country" is a result of some misunderstanding, or an indication of hypocrisy. In other words, not everyone who intelligibly and sincerely speaks of "her country" is necessarily a patriot. A person who is not a patriot is not necessarily a person with flawed, incomplete identity or spurious membership, nor one who defaults on one of her moral obligations. On the other hand, a person who feels as a patriot and acts accordingly is not thereby carrying out a moral obligation. She is merely doing something she is morally allowed but not required to do. The argument aiming to establish patriotism as a moral obligation that focuses on positional obligations, membership, and identity does not succeed.

4. IS PATRIOTISM MORALLY VALUABLE?

If patriotism is not morally obligatory, that need not mean that it is morally neutral, merely morally allowed. There is a further possibility, a stance in between these two positions. One might grant that patriotism is indeed not morally required, but argue that it is more than merely morally permitted: it is morally valuable. It can be conceived as a moral virtue. Some moral virtues are obligatory: justice or truthfulness are not something we may choose to stick to, but are not bound to do so. But that does not hold of all moral virtues: some are not required, but it is good if we possess them. An example of the latter type is the sort of concern for those in extreme need or misery shown by Mother Teresa, or for people in great danger and distress exhibited by members of humanitarian organizations such as Doctors Without Borders. A person showing concern for others well beyond the degree of concern for others which is required of us all, is thought to be a morally better person than the rest of us (other things being equal). On the other hand, when we fail to follow the example set by such persons, that is no reason for moral condemnation. For what such persons are doing is *beyond* the call of duty. Patriotism is a *special* concern for the interests of one's country and compatriots, that is, a concern beyond what we owe other people and communities; is it not, then, one of such virtues?

The question to ask at this point is: Is a patriot a *morally* better person than a nonpatriot (other things being equal)? Is the special concern for one's country and compatriots, which defines patriotism, *morally* valuable? And if it is, just why? If we ask the analogous question about the kind of concern for other human beings shown by Mother Teresa or by members of Doctors Without Borders, the answer would seem to be that such concern is morally valuable for the same reason that makes a more modest degree of concern for other humans a duty falling on each one of us. The same moral value, sympathy for and assistance to people in need of it, grounds a certain degree of concern for others as a general moral duty and explains why a significantly higher degree of such concern is a moral ideal. This explanation, however, does not apply in the case of patriotism. Patriotism is not but another extension of the duty of concern for others; for it means a special concern for *my* country *because it is my country*, for *my* compatriots *because they are my compatriots*. Unlike Mother Teresa, who showed concern for every destitute, sick, dying person she could reach, and Doctors *Without Borders*, the concern of a patriot is by definition selective; and the selection is done by the word "my." But the word "my" cannot, by itself, play the critical role in an argument meant to prove that a certain line of action is *morally* valuable. If it could, one might deploy the same type of argument to establish that moderate tribalism (understood as love of and special concern for one's tribe) or moderate racism (understood as love of and special concern for one's race) are *morally* valuable too.

5. CONCLUSION

If what I have been saying is correct, then patriotism remains morally allowed, but no more than that. It is neither a morally obligatory position, nor one that is optional, but morally valuable if adopted. It may be a virtue in some nonmoral sense (a political virtue, perhaps), but it is not a moral virtue. And, other things being equal, a patriot is not a morally better person than one not given to this particular type of partiality.[19]

NOTES

1. *The Collected Essays, Journalism and Letters of George Orwell*, vol. 3, ed. S. Orwell and I. Angus (London: Secker & Warburg, 1968), p. 362.

2. Historically, "patriotism" is a political concept. See M. G. Dietz, "Patriotism," in T. Ball, J. Farr, and R. L. Hanson, eds., *Political Innovation and Conceptual Change* (Cambridge: Cambridge University Press, 1989).

3. A. MacIntyre, *Is Patriotism a Virtue?* (Lawrence: University Press of Kansas, 1984).

4. See M. Baron, "Patriotism and 'Liberal' Morality," in D. Weissbord, ed., *Mind, Value, and Culture: Essays in Honor of E. M. Adams* (Atascadero, Calif.: Ridgeview Publishing Co., 1989); S. Nathanson, "In Defense of 'Moderate Patriotism,'" *Ethics* 99 (1989/90); *Patriotism, Morality, and Peace* (Lanham, Md.: Rowman & Littlefield, 1993); "Nationalism, Patriotism and Toleration," *Synthesis Philosophica* 9 (1994).

5. The former is an abridged form of the words of Stephen Decatur, U.S. naval officer (1779–1820), in a toast made at Norfolk, Virginia, in 1816: "Our country! In her intercourse with other nations, may she always be in the right; but our country, right or wrong." The latter is from a speech of Carl Schurz, German-American politician (1829–1906), in the U.S. Senate in 1872.

6. Thus M. Baron first appears to be arguing that moderate patriotism is valuable ("Patriotism and 'Liberal' Morality," p. 272) or deserves to be regarded as a virtue (p. 284), but later says that the claim she is defending is more modest: patriotism is only "a plausible candidate for being a virtue" (p. 290). As she explains, her aim "is not the lofty one of showing that properly understood, patriotism is a virtue, but only that there is, for someone who accepts the 'morality of liberalism', at least one conception of patriotism which it is plausible for her to hold to be a virtue" (pp. 299–300 n. 37). But we are not told just why one should hold that moderate patriotism is indeed a virtue; and what Baron's arguments show is only that such patriotism is morally permissible.

S. Nathanson, too, vacillates between different claims for moderate patriotism. Sometimes he seems to be defending such patriotism as but a morally permissible preference for one's own country (*Patriotism, Morality, and Peace*, p. 169); sometimes he portrays it as a special duty, analogous to the duty one has to one's family (ibid., pp. 42–44, 65–66, 71); sometimes he seems to be suggesting that moderate patriotism is a virtue (ibid., p. 113); at other times still, he presents it as a moral ideal (ibid., pp. 48, 199, 209). But, again, there is no explicit argument for any of the positive claims for moderate patriotism; what Nathanson's arguments actually establish is only that this type of patriotism is morally allowed.

7. R. E. Goodin, "What Is So Special about Our Fellow Countrymen?" *Ethics* 98 (1987/88): 679.

8. On this see I. Primoratz, *Justifying Legal Punishment* (Amherst, N.Y.: Humanity Books, 1997), pp. 118–37.

9. For a sketch of this argument, see A. Mason, "Special Obligations to Compatriots," *Ethics* 107 (1996/97).

10. See F. Klampfer, "Can the Appeal to Intrinsic Value of Citizenship Really Help Us Justify Special Duties to Compatriots?" in P. Kampits, K. Kokai, and A. Weiberg, eds., *Applied Ethics: Papers of the 21st International Wittgenstein Symposium* (Kirchberg am Wechsel: Austrian Ludwig Wittgenstein Society, 1998), pt. 1.

11. J. Horton, *Political Obligation* (London: Macmillan, 1992), chap. 6.

12. Ibid., pp. 147, 156.

13. Ibid., p. 150.

14. Ibid., p. 154.

15. This is true even of arranged marriages, as long as the "arrangement" falls short of duress. In cases where it amounts to duress, such marriages may be thought by society to generate marital obligations, but they do not.

16. I am leaving aside the classical idea of "civic friendship," which is not a personal relationship and therefore does not count as friendship in the modern sense of the word. Aristotle describes it as "mere friendship of association," which "seems to rest on a sort of compact" (*The Nicomachean Ethics*, trans. D. Ross [London: Oxford University Press, 1963], 1161b, p. 212).

17. See A. J. Simmons, *Moral Principles and Political Obligations* (Princeton, N.J.: Princeton University Press, 1979), chap. 7; Horton, *Political Obligation*, pp. 100–102.

18. See Simmons, *Moral Principles and Political Obligations*, chap. 4; Horton, *Political Obligation*, chap. 2.

19. Thanks to John Horton, Friderik Klampfer, and Stephen Nathanson for helpful comments on a draft of this paper.

Chapter Eleven

MARY G. DIETZ

PATRIOTISM
A Brief History of the Term

I

Contemplating his retirement from political life in 1796, yet wishing to leave the American people with some sentiments vital to their identity, George Washington wrote: "Citizens by birth or choice, of a common country, that country has a right to concentrate your affections. The name of American, which belongs to you, in your national capacity, must always exalt the just pride of Patriotism" (Washington 1948, 631). Though the exact words of Washington's Farewell Address may be forgotten, the idea he exalted is not. So commonplace are appeals to patriotism—not only in the United States but in most nations—that the concept seems, everywhere, to be a timeless artifact, a spirit that transcends historical moment and is impervious to political change. In reality, however, patriotism is not an evanescent entity but a relatively new word of eighteenth-century origin whose linguistic life, brief though it is, involves dramatic change over time. When Washington appealed to "patriotism" in 1796, for example, he invoked a highly specific political virtue and a set of particular political practices barely remembered in the rush of subsequent American history. In telling the story of "patriotism," then, I wish not only to narrate changes of language, politics, and principle, but also to reveal that the "just pride" Washington urged Americans to exalt is almost extinct in these "nationalistic" times, and with it a conception of civic virtue is nearly lost as well.

From *Political Innovation and Conceptual Change*, edited by Terence Ball, James Farr, and Russell L. Hanson (Cambridge: Cambridge University Press, 1989), pp. 177–93. Copyright © 1989 Cambridge University Press. Reprinted with the permission of Cambridge University Press.

II

"Patriotism" is a relatively new word, but its cognate "patriot" is older and their etymological root, *patria*, is more ancient still. In Greek and Roman antiquity *patria* referred chiefly to the city. But for the Greeks, who thought of themselves as *politai* or citizens, and conceived of political membership in terms of participation in the life of the polis, *patriotai* were barbarians — foreigners named after their country, not citizens of distinctive city-states. Without question, the Greeks had deep emotional attachments to and pride in their native cities (one need only recall Homer's epics, Pericles' Funeral Oration, or Socrates' tribute to Athens in the *Crito*) but they did not primarily associate politics with the preservation of a "fatherland" or a moment of founding. Aristotle's remark that "the identity of a *polis* is not constituted by its walls" is at least partly indicative of the extent to which territory alone was not the focal point of Greek political identity or loyalty (Aristotle 1958, 98).

As Hannah Arendt (1958, 120–24) has observed, it was in Rome that the full meaning of the word *patria* and its emotional resonance came into being; the *patria*, Rome itself, was the site and symbol of all values — moral, religious, political, and ethical — for which a soldier or citizen might care to live and die. The powerful symbolism of heroic self-sacrifice for the glorious fatherland, so much a part of modern patriotism, had its roots in Roman history. Cicero asked, "What good citizen would hesitate to welcome death if it were profitable for the *patria*?" (Kantorowicz 1957, 242). He also declared *Patria mihi vita mea carior est*, "Fatherland is dearer to me than my life" (Kantorowicz 1957, 244). The most Roman of all conventions, the law, abounded with ethics concerning the *patria*. The Digest distinguished between two *patriae*, the individual city (*patria sua*) and the city of Rome (*communis patria*). In the empire, all subjects, regardless of their membership in a *patria sua*, recognized Rome as their common fatherland (Kantorowicz 1957, 246–47). As the empire expanded, allegiance to *patria* became an increasingly abstract matter. Love of fatherland was tied less to the specific locale of the city and more to an idea (e.g., the imperial *pater patriae*) which the empire represented and numerous political symbols and religious doctrine reinforced (Finley 1984, 50–70, 122–41).

Nothing, however, more systematically undermined the sense of *patria* as a specific locale and a political entity than Roman thought, particularly Stoicism, where the concept assumed a thoroughly philosophical and religious meaning. Epictetus's declaration, "You are a citizen of the universe," captured the Stoic understanding of *patria* as cosmos, the universal society to which all humans belonged (Wolin 1960, 77–82). Although the concept *patria* was still a part of the political language of citizenship, loyalty, and community, that political language was strained to its breaking point; for some time two conceptions of *patria* competed in Rome: the secular-political one of the Roman empire as fatherland, and the philosophical-religious one of the universe as the locus of human membership. In the end, material and intellectual events conspired to render the political meaning of *patria* virtually valueless by the time of the late empire. The growth of the large-scale, impersonal cosmopolis of Rome weakened all meaningful sense of "ties" to the fatherland; then Christianity demolished that understanding completely; for worldly territory had minimal relevance for the Christians' understanding of themselves as members of a shared community. The earthly city could not wrest from them the emotional commitment that characterized Cato's *pugna pro patria* or Cicero's devotion to Rome. Following the teachings of the Fathers, the Christians had become citizens of another world. The writer of the *Letter to Diognet* observed, "Every place abroad is their fatherland, and in their fatherland they are aliens," which is simply to say that, for the Christian, *patria* had lost all political significance (Kantorowicz 1951, 475).[1] They would "render unto Caesar" but they would not worship him or glorify the land of their birth. The transvaluation of *patria* from a secular to a spiritual entity was a part of the political task of early Christianity, one Hannah Arendt has characterized as the attempt "to find a bond between people strong enough to replace the world" (Arendt 1958, 53). And no one took up that task with more vigor and altered the concept of *patria* more decisively than St. Augustine. In his monumental effort to articulate the religious identity of Christianity, Augustine vividly transformed the conception of heroic self-sacrifice and with it the conception of the object of such sacrifice. More than any other work of late antiquity, The City of God loosened the concept of *patria* from its political moorings and rendered it spiritual, the object of devotion for the new models of self-sacrifice—the saints, the martyrs, and the holy virgins (Kantorowicz 1951, 474–75). No longer were those who pledged devotion and died for Rome the paragons of heroic glory, for in Augustine's theory of *ordo* Rome was but a minor part of a vast and hierarchically ordered cosmic whole. Those who looked to Rome as the fatherland, as the source of their identity and their life, were destined to remain helplessly trapped in the *civitas terrena*.[2] Hence, the political community diminished in importance; the celestial city and the soul of the communicant took on a grandeur unprecedented in the history of political thought, not to mention the life of the citizen.

If in the late empire the emergence of *patria* as a primarily spiritual entity was the result of the increasing influence of *ecclesia* and the depreciation of the political order, then the low Middle Ages and the rise of feudalism did nothing to reverse that trend; indeed, the centuries of Western feudalism exacerbated it. What we find following the collapse of the Roman empire is a shift in the nature and meaning of territorial identification. As civilized urban centers receded and medieval baronies and feudal estates developed, people no longer thought of themselves as members of anything larger than a town or village, and one's loyalty as knight, warrior, or vassal was offered up to the lord and master rather than in the name of a territory, an empire, or a "state" (Kantorowicz 1951, 476–77). Though the concept of *patria* itself still existed, it was almost always used in secular practice with reference to one's immediate locality. In the intellectual and theological life centered in the monasteries, *patria* retained its exalted Augustinian meaning.

As is so often the case in the history of conceptual change, the usage of the word is in part conditioned by the material conditions of the times. *Patria* had lost the emotional content and the rhetorical power it had in antiquity, much as the ancient city itself had ceased to exist. In its place stood the church, the only great source of institutional coherency throughout the low Middle Ages. The classical emotional values of *patria* were recovered, however, in the twelfth and thirteenth centuries, as new political territories developed. And the church itself, or at least church doctrine, played an important role in the recovery.

The story of how *patria* once again became identified with political-territorial loyalty—only now directed toward a national kingdom rather than an ancient city and legitimized by Christian doctrine—is a long and complicated one (Post 1953). The briefest of sketches will have to suffice. Two phenomena are of importance in understanding the revitalization of *patria*: the rise of national territories or "kingdoms" from about the ninth century onward, and the institution of the tax *ad defensionem natalis patriae*, "for the defense of the native fatherland" (or *pro defensione regni*, "for the defense of the king") (Kantorowicz 1951, 479).[3] By the early twelfth century, the concept *patria* was mobilized (most effectively in 1124 by Louis VI of France) for both religious and political purposes: to solicit the funds necessary for the waging of the Holy War and to recruit the services of potential defenders of the realm. The kings began to demand taxes and services in the name of the fatherland (*communis patriae*) and, by the late thirteenth century, *patria* acquired a recognizably modern sense, evocative not only of national territory but also of an emotional commitment to "fatherland" which itself was perceived of as sacred (*corpus mysticum*) and, most importantly, was associated with the person of the king.[4]

In short, the late twelfth and thirteenth centuries were decisive turning points in the Western world for the early beginnings of national consciousness and the reclamation of *patria* as an entity worthy of self-sacrifice. A theological standard of *amor patriae* was allied with the conception of an organic body politic; Cato's declaration was revived and reiterated time and again. Death *pro patria* was no longer considered a pagan act but rather a glorious sacrifice animated by Christian virtues.[5] Although it took some time before the claims of the jurists and the arguments of the scholastics found their equivalent in popular expression, the groundwork was now laid for a conception of *patria* that would flourish in the Renaissance, namely, the idea that the homeland (whether monarchic territory, princedom, or city-state) deserved a love and loyalty that took precedence over the family, the individual, and even the transcendent spirit of the Christian believer.[6] The expression, "I love my native city more than my own soul," common among the Renaissance humanists although brought most vividly to life in the political writings of Machiavelli, indicated the emergence of a new normative vocabulary. As human beings increasingly turned their attention toward the concrete political, social, and ideological manifestations of their allegiance to *patria*, they began to deliberate upon the nature of their obligation to act as "patriots." To no small extent these deliberations revolved around the coherence between court and country which the medieval world had certified in the form of the king (*pater patriae*). Early modern patriotism is primarily a story of emotional and political revaluation of this coherence — of the idea of the king as *pater patriae* and, correspondingly, of the conception of *patria* as the king.

III

"Patriot" came into early modern English around the sixteenth century, a verbal borrowing from the French *patriote*.[7] Originally, it referred simply to a fellow-countryman (in 1596 Lombarde wrote of "our honest patriote Richard Harrys") though it retained the appraisive character of its root in both popular literature and poetry. Thus in *Volpone* (1605) Ben Jonson observed, "such as were known patriots, sound lovers of their country" (*Oxford English Dictionary*). Until near the end of the seventeenth century, however, "patriot" lay relatively idle in English political discourse, including that of the Civil War. The Stuart kings staked no claim upon it, nor do we find the word appropriated by any of the opponents of the crown. Neither the regicides nor any of the host of lesser but no less voluble defenders of the law of freedom and the common weal declare themselves "patriots." There was, however, one exception, found in the popular press of the day. In 1643, following his death in battle against the king's Cavaliers, the parliamentarian John Hampden was memorialized in the *Weekly Account* as "that noble patriot of his country, whose losse is infinitely lamented in all places" (Karsten 1978, 23–24).[8] This seemingly minor moment of eulogistic history had immense significance for the role that "patriot" came to play in the political rhetoric of late-seventeenth- and eighteenth-century England. Beginning with the commendation of Hampden, the word was increasingly appropriated for various political purposes (i.e., not simply in reference to those who share a homeland and a romantic love of it) and so began a career of ambiguous and, at times, equivocal meaning.[9]

The site for the emergence of "patriot" as a fully fledged part of English political discourse was the radical Whig rhetoric of the late 1680s and 1690s, during and following the Glorious Revolution of 1688. Two events of rhetorical significance occurred. First, "patriot" was tied to a particular set of political principles: the defense of liberty and the rights of Englishmen against tyranny, the laws and constitution of England against the king and court, and "revolutionist" or Whig (as understood in 1688) as opposed to conservative or Tory sensibilities. Secondly, the word was linked in Whig rhetoric to political martyrdom, only now the defender of *patria* or "patriot" was he who opposed the tyranny and excesses of the king. Thus the link between king and *patria* was rhetorically severed, and the "patriot," at least in English political discourse, took his stand with country (or, more exactly, with the constitution) and against absolutist kings.

As examples of "patriot" self-sacrifice, the Whigs chose John Hampden and the republican Algernon Sidney, beheaded for treason under Charles II in 1683. Both were enshrined in poem, pamphlet, and private gatherings as martyrs to the cause of liberty in England.[10] Thus, beginning in 1693 yearly celebrations were held at the Calves Head Club to roast (the Stuart) calf and toast Hampden, Sidney, and other "patriots who killed the tyrant" (Karsten 1978, 21–24). In his tract *Sydney Redivivus* (1689) Humphrey Smith noted "the Blood of patriots is the seed of Asserters of the People's Liberty." Some years later the poet James Thomson extolled in a tribute to Sidney "the Patriot's noble Rage / Dashing corruption down through every worthless age" (Karsten 1978, 184, 40, 33).

The symbolic use of the "Twin Patriots" that extended into the eighteenth century in both England and America is truly remarkable, but the "patriotic" import of this exercise in hagiography should not be overlooked.[11] Though associated with certain founding principles—liberty, constitutional rights, and property—"patriot" became an ideological tool of legitimation forged in the fires of Whig and Tory animosity. During this episode, at least, the story of the concept turns less on radical shifts in its meaning than on what Quentin Skinner (1980, 566) calls its "specific moral light," or what we might term the specific *political* lights and allegiances the concept was enlisted to defend. In the turbulent politics of early modern Britain, "patriot" assumed an appraisive and an "existentially contested" character. It was appropriated as a political attribute by Whig and Tory alike but, more importantly, the conception was a part of two larger, competing perspectives on political reality. At stake, then, in the Whig and Tory debates, was not only the "right" to the title "patriot" but the legitimacy of one political vision, governmental program, and party over another. This contest for legitimacy was played out in the language of patriotism.

Thus in 1681, the poet John Dryden, an arch-Tory, discredited the parliamentarians' use of the term and seemed to reject it (at least in its new guise) altogether: "Gull'd with a Patriot's name, whose Modern sense / Is one that wou'd by Law supplant his Prince." But in 1699 he sought to reclaim it: "A patriot both the King and Country serves / Prerogative and privilege preserves" (*Oxford English Dictionary*). Dryden's poetic attempt at conceptual recovery was followed by Alexander Pope's in 1716: "An honest Courtier yet a Patriot too/Just to his Prince and his Country true"; although his comment "A patriot is a fool in ev'ry age" is perhaps better known (*Oxford English Dictionary*).

The poets and essayists were not the sole reliquaries of Tory patriotism, however. Perhaps the most determined theoretical effort to wrest the word from Whig control was Bolingbroke's pamphlet of 1738, *The Idea of a Patriot King* (1917b). Bolingbroke imagined a monarch who would "respect great principles," "lift no party" nor "list himself in any." The patriot king would avoid factions and rest his authority on "the spirit and the strength of the nation" (1917b, 53, 51). Like the Whigs, Bolingbroke fixed the "spirit of the nation" in the English constitution, and *The Idea of a Patriot King* had its impact.[12] In the middle of the eighteenth century at least, "patriot" was an appraisive term in both the Tory and Whig lexicon. Bolingbroke used it with great skill against Walpole, and the Tory Samuel Johnson defined it in the 1755 edition of his *Dictionary* as "one who maintains and defends his country's freedom and rights," while at the same time noting its use "ironically for a factious disturber of the government."[13] At least until the latter half of the nineteenth century, then, the term "patriot" retained a clear meaning and a favorable evaluation. Whigs and Tories might have disagreed as to whether one or the other truly *was* a patriot or not, but the association of the concept with the past, the defense of constitutional liberties, and the fight against corruption was not in dispute.

Not surprisingly, much the same set of usages attended the word "patriotism," an extension of "patriot" that came on the scene of English politics along with a host of other "-isms" in the eighteenth century. Although he did not coin the term, Bolingbroke wrote a series of letters in 1736–38 "on the spirit of patriotism" in which he invoked Cato and "the true principles of liberty" (Bolingbroke 1917a).[14] Shortly thereafter, in 1750, Bishop Berkeley published his "Maxims Concerning Patriotism," intended to disassociate the "fop," the "epicure," and the "factious man" from the "patriot" (1953). Yet the Tories' attempt to legitimize their position and secure their political goals by appealing to "patriotism" seems to have diminished in the last quarter of the century. It was almost as if they conceded the Whigs' hegemony of "patriot" rhetoric and then sought to turn a hitherto commendatory term into a condemnatory one. Contrary to the maxims of the good bishop, patriotism became the stock-in-trade of factious men. The reasons for this shift in rhetoric are not entirely clear (nor is the rhetoric itself entirely consistent), but perhaps the Tories' turn can be better assessed if we shift our historical gaze from British party politics toward America. For across the Atlantic, "patriot" and "patriotism" were taking on more radical connotations and acquiring more revolutionary force than anything in the standard fare of Whig and Tory discourse in England.

IV

Although the English colonists called themselves "Americans," referred to their country as "America," and exhibited, in prose and verse, a genuine love of the land long before the War of Independence, the concepts of "patriot" and "patriotism" did not come alive until the "Great Awakening" of the 1760s and 1770s. Only with the stirring of the movement for independence did the language of "patriotism" emerge in American life: the reality of a new land, the development of a distinct collective identity, and, most decisively, a growing perception of a "conspiracy against liberty," fueled by the revolutionary literature of the period, set the stage for the radicalization of "patriotism." At first the term was associated with the defense of liberty and property against tyrant kings and corrupt ministers, a legacy the colonists drew from the Whig symbolism of Hampden and Sidney. Hence, in 1770 John Adams declared: "If oppression is warranted by law, the Patriot is much more likely to fall victim than the pimp or the pander. Hampdens will stain the scaffold with blood" (Karsten 1978, 48). In the same year, Benjamin Franklin and James Burgh compared the resistance of the colonist to taxation without representation to "the conduct of the brave Hampden" (ibid.). American essayists and pamphleteers who increasingly opposed the crown venerated Sidney as "our patriot" and hailed him as a "martyr to liberty" (Karsten 1978, 42–46). But the appeal to "patriotism" did not end with references to the memory of the British "twins" and their fight against corrupt kings. Soon "patriotism" stood for opposition to any sort of king, especially an English one. By 1775, "patriot" rhetoric was enlisted in defiance of British authority in its entirety—king, parliament, England itself were declared corrupt, fallen from liberty, and no longer deserving of allegiance. Essays, pamphlets, newspapers, broadsides, songs, and poems took up the cause of revolution against the crown, and their authors either appropriated the name "patriot" for themselves or became known as supporters of the "patriot cause." So Sam Adams wrote of those who would fight for independence: "All are not dead, and where there is a spark of patriotik fire, *we* will enkindle it" (Davidson 1941, 5). No wonder that, back in Britain, Samuel Johnson declared patriotism "the last refuge of a scoundrel."

The term "patriot" and "patriotism" did not simply reflect a set of emerging political developments. The concepts themselves enkindled the political movement and fired the imaginations of the participants. The language of patriotism served at least two political purposes in America: first, it established the boundaries of revolutionary political practice in a far more decisive manner than in eighteenth-century England. None of the ambiguity that enveloped the use of the word in Whig and Tory discourse arose in the colonies. By 1776, the American revolutionary alone was a "patriot"; all others were "loyalists," defenders of the mother-country and the English constitution.[15] Secondly, the concepts of "patriot" and "patriotism" were clearly affixed to a particular set of ideological, constitutional, and political principles: a free republic, love of liberty, sanctity of property, limited government, and the foundation of a new body politic, and to a distinctively *political*, public spirit that evolved from the experience of a shared struggle and self-sacrifice for a common cause. It was precisely this political spirit, and not simply a romantic attachment to country, that Washington alluded to in his Farewell Address, which was, in essence, a meditation on patriotism. In short, if in eighteenth-century England the language of patriotism had become the hard currency of party rhetoric, then in

America (for a time, at least) "patriotism" was the vital consciousness of a revolutionary movement, the generative force of a new people and, as Tocqueville later wrote, a "reflective" spirit of self-government.

V

As we turn to the nineteenth century, we find that from 1790 until 1850 the language of patriotism in England was primarily appropriated not by Tories or Whigs but by Chartists, Dissenters, trade-unionists, and Anti-Corn Law Leaguers who defended "the rights of Englishmen" against a new set of social and economic conditions. They condemned the slavery of factory labor; pressed the rights of workers, the poor, and the unemployed; and warned against the encroachments of state power. More importantly, they viewed themselves, initially at least, not as Chartists or Dissenters, socialists or trade-unionists, but as "patriots" defending a familiar set of patriot concerns—liberty, property, and constitutional rights—only in an environment exceedingly different from that of their seventeenth-century counterparts and even of their American compatriots, from whom they drew inspiration. The "patriot cause" now involved opposition to the increasingly centralized state and the growing capitalist economic order. The patriots' call was for reform.[16]

Thus at the turn of the century, patriotic clubs were formed, *Patriot* newspapers appeared, and songs proclaimed the patriotism of the radical reformers. In 1843, the Chartist Henry Vincent lectured at Leeds and called for the awakening of "the patriotic feelings of every English heart" (Karsten 1978, 127). In 1853, the funeral of Ben Rushton was a major public event. The Chartist was eulogized as a "noble patriot" whose life had been spent in opposition to the power of the English church and state. All of this led the Tory Richard Oastler to coin a new definition: "He will be the greatest patriot who can produce the greatest dissatisfaction" (Cunningham 1982).

Of course it would be mistaken to assume that during this brief period of English radicalism and opposition to government the claim to "patriotism" was not heard in any other quarter. Radical patriotism was neither unopposed nor completely dominant during these years, but it did mark a moment, soon to be lost, when "patriotism" was firmly antistatist, *internationalist* in its leanings, and on the side of one of the largest social movements in modern history. The "patriot" stood for political equality and social justice in national life. What Karl Polanyi says of England after the decline of Chartism—that "[it] had become poorer by that substance out of which the Anglo-Saxon ideal of a free society could have been built up for centuries to come"—could equally be said of the concept of patriotism (Polanyi 1944, 167).[17]

By the late nineteenth century, a transformation of political and economic forces and the related rise of more potent "statist" symbols significantly diminished the meaning of patriotism in the special sense of constitutional reform and (in its Chartist manifestation) economic egalitarianism. As patriot rhetoric became increasingly assimilated into the emerging vocabulary of "state" and "nation," and its central idea underwent a transference to the national, party, and racial doctrines of the modern age, it lost its earlier, critical sting. Indeed, it seems that at a certain moment in history, patriotism ceased to be the springboard for opposition to a government's program or policies in the name of constitutional principles, and became instead the basis for uncritical support of the "my country right or wrong" variety.[18] At the root of this decisive shift in the meaning of patriotism is a phenomenon John Dunn (1979, 55) has called "the starkest political shame of the twentieth century," and John Schaar, "patriotism's bloody brother" (1981, 285). The phenomenon is "nationalism" and though its own distinctive history cannot be fully traced here, we must say something about it, for nationalism weighs heavily upon the meaning of patriotism in our age.

Nationalism did not become a part of our political discourse until the middle of the nineteenth century. As Ernest Gellner notes, "nationalism owes its plausibility and compelling nature only to a very special set of circumstances, which do indeed obtain now, but which were alien to most of humanity and history" (1983, 125). The material preconditions Gellner has in mind—the rise of the state, the growing power of national institutions, a developing world-market and centralized economies, imperialist expansionism, and new forms of social organization based on deeply internalized, education-dependent, high culture—all served to foster what might be loosely called "secular religions" of national identity. A collective spirit rooted in a sense of national supremacy and "ersatz greatness" (as Simone Weil once put it) reinforced the idea of the nation as the ultimate object of political loyalty, and of the state as the embodiment of the nation. This nationally predicated political sentiment was invigorated by mass education, in which the mystification of the nation's past played a significant role. Doctrines of particular political parties served to reinforce national loyalty as well, and to associate it with certain ideological (but rarely constitutional) principles. And, most ominously, warfare, "the great motor of nationalist expansion," used nationalist fervor as its generating force.[19]

The pervasiveness of these social and political conditions, which in fact prevail in the modern world and nowhere else, have had profound implications for our current understanding of patriotism. The transference of nationalistic sentiments into the language of patriotism is readily apparent in the contemporary discourse of politicians, presidents, and public relations experts, not to mention the ordinary language of the citizen.[20] Quite clearly, the older idea of the patriot as one who defends constitutional rights, reveres liberty, agitates for an end to corruption, and struggles against the outrages of centralized power, has been thoroughly eroded. What Tocqueville called "reflective patriotism" and characterized as self-government and the exercise of political rights seems no longer to be remembered as a virtue—if it is remembered at all. Likewise, the republican values that fired the insurgent imaginations of such diverse patriots as Algernon Sidney, Sam Adams, Tom Paine, or Ben Rushton have been largely drowned out in the shrill rhetoric of modern "patriotism." Indeed, patriotism itself has become more of an expression than a practice, but if at all a practice, surely not one informed by a reverence for public liberty or a skepticism toward the state, much less a proclivity for Adams's "enkindling" of revolutionary sentiments. The moral light of patriotism, along with its meaning, has been cast in drastically different hues: in terms of a sense of duty and service to the state, the uncritical support of government programs and policies, and the veneration of the nation as an absolute value. Without question, "patriotism" and "patriot" are still compelling parts of political rhetoric, but one need only consider their current usage and range of reference to understand how the "rhetoric of state" has absorbed them, and how far removed they are from their eighteenth-century roots in the radical defense of liberty, constitutional rights, reform, and revolution.

Ernest Gellner would assess this condition by having us think of nationalism as "a very distinctive species of patriotism" (1983, 138). But I believe this suggestion stands in danger of collapsing two historically rooted forms of political practice whose differences we ignore at our own peril. The blurring of patriotism into nationalism, or even the acknowledgment of nationalism as a "species" of patriotism, reveals that we have literally lost touch with history, with a very real past in which real patriots held to a particular set of political principles and their associated practices—to a conception of citizenship that bears scant resemblance to modern nationalism.

To put this another way, patriotism as a particular "way-of-being" in the world—as an active, and often radically participatory form of citizenship rooted in a concern for the good of one's own country—is nearly lost to us, and the damages that result from this failure of memory are not negligible. In this respect, maintaining a distinction between patriotism and nationalism is more than just an exercise in semantics or arid conceptual analysis. For the more patriotism's past recedes from our collective political imaginations the less are we able to "think what we are doing"—to evaluate the sort of citizens and "patriots" we are in the present and to assess the examples we set for the future. In fact, without some awareness of the attitudes and practices that constituted patriotism before the rise of the centralized nation-state, we are unlikely to appreciate the extent to which our contemporary patriotic discourse and practices are historically contingent (and in many ways demoralized) phenomena, not inherent attributes of humanity or universal necessities beyond reproach. Our failure to appreciate such things and thereby engage in the critical reappraisal of our own patriotic presuppositions and nationalist presumptions is nothing short of a failure of citizenship. That is why remembering patriotism's past can itself be understood as a patriotic act—as an attempt to revivify and perhaps restore a more virtuous understanding of the relation between self and country than our current conception allows and our current practices reflect.

Exactly how the practice of patriotism might be reconceptualized or reconstructed is a subject fit for the future labors of political theorists who are concerned with questions of civic virtue, loyalty, dissent, citizenship, obedience, liberty, and the manifold complexities associated with "love of country."[21] And while this brief conceptual history provides no final answers, it does serve to remind us that, at its root, the "problem of patriotism" is not simply a rhetorical or an analytical matter, but a historical reality, in need of our remembrance.

NOTES

1. The Christian's minimal attachment to an earthly home is perhaps no more vividly evident than in Augustine's account of his mother's death. In response to Augustine's brother's lament that she die not in a foreign land but in her own country, Monica says, "Put this body away anywhere . . . I ask only this of you, that you remember me at the altar of the Lord, wherever you may be" (Augustine 1960, 223).

2. Augustine does grant that Rome is or was a commonwealth. But he is also unambiguous about the "common interest" that binds the people of a political commonwealth—it is decidedly inferior to the love (*caritas*) which binds the Christian community to God, just as the political *patria* is but a shadow of the *patria aeterna* (1960, 478).

3. So, for example, in 1302 after the French defeat at Courtrai, Philip IV asked for aid from the clergy: "ad defensionem natalis patrie proqua reverenda patrum antiquitas pugnare precepit, eius curam liberorum preferens caritati" ("For the defense of the native fatherland which the venerable antiquity of our ancestors ordered to fight for, because they preferred the care for the fatherland even to the love for their descendants") (Kantorowicz 1951, 479).

4. The influence of popular songs, poetry, and prose cannot be underestimated—in the case of France, the *Chansons de geste* and, in England, Geoffrey of Monmouth's *History of the Kings of England* served as nationalistic literature and historiography, respectively, in the Middle Ages. We also find a related development, the differentiation of one's own land from others' and scorn for the latter, what Koht somewhat anachronistically calls the beginnings of "nationalism" during this era (1946–47, 276).

5. Tolomeo of Lucca even placed *amor patriae* in a rank of honor "above all other things," and St. Thomas asserted that *pietas* was the power animating devotion to both parents and *patria* (Kantorowicz 1951, 489; 1957, 243).

6. Expressions regarding the timelessness of national territory (e.g., *la France éternelle*) belong to the period of the late fourteenth and early fifteenth centuries. Expressions concerning the primacy of "the fatherland" emerge as well. Consider the humanist Coluccio Salutate's declaration: "[If] such would be expedient for the fatherland's protection or enlargement, it would seem neither burdensome and difficult nor a crime to thrust the axe into one's father's head, to crush one's brothers, to deliver from the womb of one's wife the premature child with the sword" (Kantorowicz 1957, 245).

7. The German *Patriotismus* and *Patrio* also come from the French *patriote*, at about the same time. From this point on, I will deal primarily with the development of patriotism in its Anglo-American context.

8. Cromwell also called Hampden (his cousin) "the Patriot," although Cromwell himself did not fare so well as a model for patriots; in both England and the colonies he was too closely linked with the danger of a standing army (Karsten 1978).

9. Consider Maxwell's derisive observation in 1644, concerning "the specious and spurious pretences of our glorious Reformers and zealous patriots" and, in 1677, Hicks's claim that patriots will be the ruin of the church (*Oxford English Dictionary*).

10. There is at this time a resurgence of interest in Cato, whose proclamation *pugna pro patria* is taken up by the Whigs. Trenchard and Gordon defended the cause in the *London Journal* under the byline "Cato" (Karsten 1978, 21–24).

11. For a helpful though apolitical treatment of the deluge of patriotic poetry in early-eighteenth-century England, see Bonamy Dobrée (1978). For the poets, patriotism had to do with love of the country as a natural environment.

12. The specifics of Bolingbroke's program (never accomplished) included: independent parliaments, frequent elections, no placemen, nonparty government, and a militia instead of a standing army. As Betty Kemp (1966, 40) notes: "[U]nder the patriot program 'the modern party system' could not have developed, in so far as its prerequisites were placemen and patronage." The Whigs, for all their patriot rhetoric, had no theorist comparable or superior to Bolingbroke writing on the meaning of "patriot." Their preeminent theoretical voice, Locke, made no reference to patriots or patriotism in the *Second Treatise*, an especially surprising omission, since Locke was a compatriot of Algernon Sidney and sympathetic to the cause for which Sidney was martyred and enshrined as a "patriot hero."

13. There is a substantial literature on Bolingbroke's opposition to Walpole's administration, and much of it concerns the ideological implications of his professions of patriotism. The debates (at least implicitly) raise a conceptual issue concerning the status of "patriotism" (was it a commonplace slogan, or did it represent a specific set of political ideas and principles? or was it both?) that has relevance for any historical interpretation of Bolingbroke's opposition to Walpole. See, especially, Quentin Skinner (1974).

14. The *Oxford English Dictionary* cites the first usage of "patriotism" as Bailey's definition (1726): "the acting like a Father to his country."

15. The "loyalists" themselves called the American revolutionaries "rebels," but with rare exceptions, like Chalmers's response to Paine, *Plain Truth*, they laid no claim to the title "patriot."

16. Prominent in the early Chartist movement was an identification with historical "patriots" elsewhere—including the American revolutionaries and the French *patriote* party of 1789. Many of those who called themselves patriots and argued that England had forfeited political liberty cited *La Patriote Françoise* as their model, following the French revolutionaries' own use of the term.

17. Karsten (1978, 133) also notes that with the passing of Chartism "neither Hampden nor Sidney served again as champions of the people."

18. The *Oxford English Dictionary* cites *Fraser's Magazine* (1844) with the earliest usage (a condemnatory one): "nationalism is another word for egotism." (The full reference to the quotation is: "Our country! In her intercourse with foreign nations may she always be right, but our country right or wrong," by Stephen Decatur in 1816.)

19. The phrase is John Dunn's (1979, 67). Equally cogent comments on the relationship between the state, the nation, war, and nationalist consciousness in the twentieth century can be found in Randolph Bourne (1977).

20. It seems, however, that the word has been officially obliterated from the vocabulary of social science. *The Encyclopedia of Social Sciences* makes no mention of it. Nor does Raymond Williams include it in *Keywords* (1983), though "nationalism" merits an entry. Even when "patriotism" is not obliterated, however, as in *The Blackwell Encyclopaedia of Political Thought* (Miller 1987), its political meaning is forgotten. The entry notes that patriotism "has often been confused with nationalism but it is a far older idea, and carries with it less theoretical baggage," and (even more dubiously), "Patriotism is really a sentiment rather than a political idea, but one that can be pressed into service by needs of many different sorts, most notably in times of war" (p. 369). Contrary to this view, I have argued that patriotism has long been a political idea, and that its "service" as a concept to various creeds is not an accidental, but an integral part of its public, political meaning. It is instructive—albeit disturbing—that even political theorists overlook this conceptual point.

21. Some political theorists (although not many) have taken up this issue with varying verdicts on whether or not "patriotism" can be revitalized. For a rare and particularly intriguing treatment of patriotism and the case of France in the 1940s, see Simone Weil (1952). Also see Schaar (1981), MacIntyre (1981), Janowitz (1983), and Anderson (1983).

REFERENCES

Anderson, Benedict. 1983. *Imagined Communities*. Thetford: Thetford Press.

Arendt, Hannah. 1958. *The Human Condition*. Chicago: University of Chicago Press.

Aristotle. 1958. *Politics*. Edited by Ernest Barker. Oxford: Oxford University Press.

Augustine of Hippo, St. 1960. *Confessions*. Edited by J. Ryan. New York: Doubleday.

Berkeley, Bishop George. [1750] 1953. "Maxims Concerning Patriotism." In *The Works of George Berkeley*, vol. 6, edited by A. A. Luce and J. E. Jessop, 251–55. London: T. Nelson and Sons.

Bolingbroke, Viscount Henry St. John. [1736] 1917a. *Letters on the Spirit of Patriotism*. Oxford: Clarendon.

———. [1738] 1917b. *The Idea of a Patriot King*. Edited by S. Jackman. Indianapolis and New York: Bobbs-Merrill.

Bourne, Randolph. 1977. *The Radical Will: Selected Writings 1911–1918*. Edited by O. Hansen. New York: Urizen Books.

Cunningham, Hugh. 1982. "Will the Real John Bull Stand Up, Please?" *Times Literary Supplement* 19 (February 19).

Davidson, Philip. 1941. *Propaganda and the American Revolution 1763–1783*. Chapel Hill: University of North Carolina Press.

Dobrée, Bonamy. 1978. "The Theme of Patriotism in the Poetry of the Early Eighteenth Century." *Proceedings of the British Academy* 25: 49–65.

Dunn, John. 1979. *Western Political Theory in the Face of the Future*. Cambridge: Cambridge University Press.

Finley, M. I. 1984. *Politics in the Ancient World*. Cambridge: Cambridge University Press.

Gellner, Ernest. 1983. *Nations and Nationalism*. Ithaca, N.Y.: Cornell University Press.

Janowitz, Morris. 1983. *The Reconstruction of Patriotism*. Chicago: University of Chicago Press.

Kantorowicz, Ernest. 1951. "*Pro Patria Mori* in Medieval Political Thought." *American Historical Review* 56: 472–92.

———. 1957. *The King's Two Bodies: A Study in Medieval Political Theory*. Princeton, N.J.: Princeton University Press.

Karsten, Peter. 1978. *Patriot-Heroes in England and America*. Madison: University of Wisconsin Press.

Kemp, Betty. 1966. "Patriotism, Pledges, and the People." In *A Century of Conflict*, edited by M. Gilbert, 37–46. London: Hamish Hamilton.

Koht, Thomas. 1946–47. "The Dawn of Nationalism in Europe." *American Historical Review* 52: 265–80.

MacIntyre, Alasdair. 1981. *After Virtue*. Notre Dame, Ind.: University of Notre Dame Press.

Miller, David, ed. 1987. *The Blackwell Encyclopaedia of Political Thought*. Oxford: Blackwell.

Polanyi, Karl. 1944. *The Great Transformation*. Boston, Mass.: Beacon Press.

Post, G. 1953. "Two Notes on Nationalism in the Middle Ages." *Traditio* 9: 281–320.

Schaar, John. 1981. *Legitimacy in the Modern State*. Brunswick, N.J.: Transaction Press.

Skinner, Quentin. 1974. "The Principles and Practice of Opposition: The Case of Bolingbroke versus Walpole." In *Historical Perspectives: Studies in English Thought and Society in Honour of J. H. Plumb*, edited by Neil McKendrick, 93–128. London: Europa Publications.

———. 1980. "Language and Social Change." In *The State of the Language*, edited by L. Michaels and C. Ricks, 562–78. Berkeley: University of California Press.

Washington, George. [1796] 1948. "Farewell Address." In *Basic Writings of George Washington*, edited by S. Commins, 627–43. New York: Random House.

Weil, Simone. 1952. *The Need for Roots*. Boston, Mass.: Beacon Press.

Williams, Raymond. 1983. *Keywords: A Vocabulary of Culture and Society*. Revised and expanded edition. London: Fontana.

Wolin, Sheldon. 1960. *Politics and Vision*. Boston, Mass.: Little, Brown.

Chapter Twelve
ATTRACTA INGRAM

CONSTITUTIONAL PATRIOTISM

I

We are hearing today of postnational and postconventional political identities, and of something called "constitutional patriotism" (Habermas 1992, 7). An idea of the state as an association of citizens bound together by certain rules and practices rather than shared ends, which was used in the first instance to detach civic identity within the state from tribal, ethnic, and confessional identities, is now being used to suggest that we can separate state and nation. In the context of the idea of European citizenship the possibility that we are being urged to explore is an idea of political union held together by willing subscription to a system of authority created and maintained by a constitution (Habermas 1992, 17).

The idea of postnational identity is of a political identity founded on recognition of democratic values and human rights as these are contextualized in a particular constitutional tradition. Citizens are thought of as bound to each other by subscription to these shared values rather than by the more traditional prepolitical ties that nation-states have drawn on as sources of unity. In a multinational context, the nation cannot be the basis of political unity. But the unity of a postnational state cannot be formed by forging a communal supranational identity, modeled on the myths of common heritage and culture that went into the construction of many current national identities. For the idea is to transcend nationalism as an outmoded political idea unsuited to the multiple identities that now increasingly characterize the more cosmopolitan social worlds that people in most Western democracies inhabit.

A postnational identity has to accommodate difference and plurality. So it has to be an identity in which membership is constituted by recognition of a

From *Philosophy & Social Criticism* 22, no. 6 (1996): 1–18. Copyright © Sage Publications. Reprinted by permission of Sage Publications.

common system of authority erected and maintained by a constitution. Unity and legitimacy come from the constitution and the formal tie that holds people together is their continuing voluntary recognition of the constitution, their constitutional patriotism.

The idea of a constitutional patriotism is not new. It has been around in one form or another as long as the idea of citizenship. For it is part of the idea that the creation of political community is a morally transformative act in which human beings develop relationships as citizens that tie them together independently of their prior associational ties to family, religion, and the like.

In the normative reconstructions of the modern state, political histories begin with a founding act, that of the lone founder in classical republicanism, or of the social contract in republicanism in the liberal mode. The significance of the founding myth is that it denies the relevance of any historical identity for claims on the state apart from the identity it constructs itself. These ideas turn on the belief that the state itself is the source of its own unity, the same idea we are now calling constitutional patriotism.

But while the idea is not unfamiliar, what is new is that the demands of constitutional patriotism are not seen as requiring a single undifferentiated political order, or as needing to assimilate all identities to a single ethno-cultural identity. Constitutional patriotism is meant to be compatible with the existence of a great deal of cultural and national pluralism, and with the claims of some cultural groups (nations like the Basques, Scots, Catalans) to a degree of political autonomy that they are currently denied within existing states. At the same time, nationalist claims are being thought of as claims to degrees of autonomy within wider political unions. They are being seen less as claims to political independence traditionally conceived (having a state of one's own), and more as claims to the conditions of self-expression within a wider order.

Opinions differ about the feasibility of constitutional patriotism. Some feel that the genius of sophisticated political regimes such as the United States has been to demonstrate that people can indeed find in a constitution a source of political unity that overarches their other identities. Others claim that the U.S. Constitution owes its unifying power to the fact that it "draws upon, defines, and upholds a national identity" (Scruton 1990, 79). Whatever the proper reading of "the nation" encompassed by the U.S. Constitution, the general point at issue is whether sharing universal values of democracy and respect for justice and rights is sufficient for shared political life, or whether, in addition, a political people needs shared identity, in the sense of shared language, associations, and culture (Norman 1994, 5). This is an empirical issue of great importance but I do not address it here, except to suggest that the particularity of shared political institutions may be no less conducive to solidarity than pre-political national identities. Instead, I want to look at some aspects of the more fundamental question of whether constitutional patriotism is even theoretically possible. I want to ask whether we can *conceive* the unity of the state apart from the unity of the nation. I will proceed as follows. In the next section I discuss the view that the idea of the modern state is incoherent and that it tacitly relies on the social idea of membership provided by the nation. The following section gives an alternative to the nationalist account of the existence of bounded communities and suggest why Habermasians and Rawlsians are right in thinking that the shared value of justice, as embodied in a historical set of institutions, can suffice for political identity. Finally, I give a brief indication of the relevance of this discussion to the idea of European Union.

II

The idea of a postnational political identity is a development of an idea of the modern state that is often associated with liberalism, though its most interesting twentieth-century articulation is in the writings of the conservative theorist Michael Oakeshott (Oakeshott 1975). This is the idea that the state itself is the source of the unity of the body politic, an idea that may be described as the liberal unity doctrine because it is usually defended and attacked as a liberal position.

As described by Bhikhu Parekh, the modern state is based on a purely political principle of unity. The modern state "is not to subscribe to, let alone to enforce, a specific body of moral, religious, or cultural beliefs, save those such as the rule of law which are inherent in its structure. Its job [is] to provide a framework of authority and a body of laws within which individuals and groups [are] at liberty to live the way they [want] . . . to be its member is to acknowledge the structure of its authority and to bide by its laws" (Parekh 1986, 39). Its structure of authority is the only source of unity the modern state has, or ought to have.

This idea of the state is criticized for basing the unity of the state on a purely political idea of membership, which is incapable of generating the ties of loyalty between citizens necessary for its own survival. Indeed the very neutrality of the liberal rule of law with respect to sources of unity such as religious or philosophical ideals of the good life is said to make it, more than any other, dependent on a national idea. As Roger Scruton puts it, "For a liberal state to be secure, the citizens must understand the *national* interest as something other than the interest of the *state*. Only the first can evoke in them the sacrificial spirit upon which the second depends" (Scruton 1990, 75).

Scruton sees two main problems within liberal theory which undercut the claim that the liberal state is the source of its own unity. First, by basing political obligation on consent the theory makes political partnership "rescindable, defeasible, and insecure." The problem seems to be that the liberal view of political obligation fails to generate the kind of obligations a state requires in order to survive over time—obligations that flow from common membership in a historical political community and that are accepted because citizens identify with that community.

> The liberal state has no home, and generates no loyalty towards generations which, being either dead or unborn, form no part of the contract. Without such a loyalty there is neither honourable accounting nor provision for the future, but only a squandering of resources in the pursuit of present goals. The liberal state must depend therefore upon some other loyalty than loyalty to itself. More than any other system of government, the liberal rule of law depends upon the renewal of public spirit, and therefore on patriotism. (Scruton 1990, 75)

Second, the theory has no way of excluding anyone from the contract that founds the state. "[I]f the contract is open to anyone it is open to all. Anything short of world government is therefore tainted with illegitimacy" (Scruton 1990, 76). So liberals must either deny the legitimacy of any existing boundaries or tacitly accept that they are rightly drawn on the basis of nonpolitical loyalties such as the nation supplies (Scruton 1990). (For the sake of argument, I assume, with Scruton, that we are talking about contractual liberalism throughout, though not all liberalism is contractual.)

Third, there is a problem for liberal unity, hinted at by Scruton, but also present as an undercurrent in much of what Charles Taylor has to say about the incoherence of atomism—which he says is "used loosely to characterise the doctrines of social contract theory" (Taylor 1985, 187). This is the problem of how a notion of individual contract can possibly give rise to a collective "we" for purposes of political actions and sharing. The point may be illustrated by considering what makes it the case that my playing the piano and your playing the violin constitutes "us" playing a duet. Even if each of us plays the same piece of music, *I am playing* and *you are playing* do not add up to *we are playing* without some prior understanding that *we are playing* is the reason that I am playing and you are playing. The point here is that the agreement to play together has to be seen as engaging the actions of each for the sake of the duo and what it can achieve rather than as a vehicle for each of the players to show off their skills as solo performers. It is not a matter of coordinating solo activities but of engaging in a single, complex, joint activity. Similarly, it may be said, no number of individual acts of consent to the formation of a political society can yield the collective "we" that is to share justice and because of which each of us is, or ought to be, willing to act in certain ways towards other members. Contract yields a society of individuals cooperating for the sake of their separate interests. It cannot produce the "we" identity that moves people to act in the common interest. Further, this defect in the contractual model is concealed because it implicitly relies on a "we" identity that has been formed by a national idea. Liberal unity is chimerical without identity, and this has to be supplied from prepolitical cultural sources.

The first problem for liberal unity, then, is that by conceiving political membership as voluntary, it sabotages political unity by making all thought of duty to other members subject to the tribunal of individual consent. The second problem is that liberal theory cannot justify boundaries and so renders all states illegitimate. Third, there is the problem of how collective political identities can be constructed out of a collection of individual identities. These problems support the claim that the liberal state relies, and must rely, on prepolitical loyalties.

I believe that these problems about liberal unity are misunderstandings and it may be useful to try to say why, before going on to say something about why liberal unity is and must be political.

The first problem rests on the misconception that the foundation of a liberal theory of the state is a doctrine of actual consent. That is an indefensible doctrine and no current version of contractual liberalism subscribes to it. It is indeed true that a liberal contractual view insists that political obligations are self-assumed, meaning that from the contractual standpoint within which the legitimacy of the state is assessed, the terms of membership must pass the test of being ones that all free and equal persons could in principle endorse. This is a hypothetical consent test. One might disagree with this test and the whole approach on which it rests. One might decry the fact that it fails to import into political life the unassumed obligations that people may recognize to those with whom they share a history and way of life. But if that disagreement is to be more than the disagreement about the desirability of Enlightenment over Counter-Enlightenment politics, if it is to cut to the heart of liberal politics, it has to be directed to showing the incoherence of supposing that contract is consistent with political unity. If the argument for that claim is that voluntary memberships are vulnerable to individual and arbitrary refusals of the burdens of membership, it is not true. For it is not part of the contract position that you and I can decide to withdraw from the obligations of liberal membership as suits us. From your and my real-world standpoint, wondering how best to discern our political obligations, the results of the hypothetical consent test are binding. We cannot refuse the obligations of a just contract, any more than our surrogates in a hypothetical original position can rationally veto terms of justice that they are led to by reasoning from their vital interests.

This argument, I should make clear, is intended to address the objection to the coherence of liberal contract as a theory of unity. It does not touch the *empirical* claim that shared political justice is insufficient for liberal unity, especially when we take into account the demand that the modern state should have a social welfare character. Liberal unity in a social justice regime, the claim goes, requires shared national identity. This empirical claim is about the capacity and willingness of populations to form multicultural or multinational political units. It might well be empirically true that populations in the grip of a national idea are unwilling to form a state with people who do not share their national culture. And there might be horrendous facts of history accounting for that unwillingness. But that does not tell us that liberal unity is always and everywhere impossible, or that it is never right, in principle, to try to educate people to abandon nationalism. In certain contexts, the moral case against political assertion of certain national identities may be very strong. After Auschwitz, Habermas holds, there is a good case for promoting postnational identity in Germany. And the successful experience of the former federal republic of living under a liberal constitution gives reason to suppose that further uncoupling of state and nation is empirically feasible. After twenty-five years of terrorism in Northern Ireland, there is a good case for cultivating postnational identity in Ireland as a whole. And there is an interest in peace and recognition of difference on the island that makes the project of postnational identity empirically plausible.

The second claim about liberal incoherence—the claim that it cannot justify boundaries and so renders all states illegitimate—is based on the mistaken idea that there is a theoretical solution to the boundary problem. The idea of an original voluntary union of free and equal citizens cannot specify how the citizen body is composed. The composition is a contingent matter of historical power and chance, but boundaries are not for that reason necessarily unjust. Nationalism itself does not provide a theoretical solution because there is no conceptual connection between the relationship of citizenship and that of nationality.

Boundary-setting is a matter not for theoretical but for practical reason but that does not mean that it is all arbitrary. From a contractual point of view borders follow the functions of government. This suggests the following test of the justice and legitimacy of contested boundaries: they are borders that demarcate populations whose members are capable of cooperating with one another in one state without undue strains on the efficient functioning of democratic government and political processes. This test looks to the stability of proposed borders from the point of view of democratic citizenship as the value to be realized. It holds that concern for the establishment and maintenance of democratic citizenship leads the search for political units in which that concern can be met most reliably. The test offers both a framework for practical deliberation about boundaries and also appropriate space for the contingent facts that are normally salient to a practical solution—facts of history, geography, language, and the desires of the inhabitants of an area to live politically with each other but not with certain neighbors.

Of course, these are the sort of facts seized on by the nationalist in defense of the claim that the liberal state presupposes prepolitical identity. But their significance for the liberal is quite different. The key factors here are the brute bureaucratic and social costs of political integration in a regime of democratic citizenship. In relatively homogeneous societies these may be expected to be less than in more heterogeneous societies. And where accommodating a diversity would put the cost in social, cultural, and special representation rights so high as to jeopardize the prospects of stable democratic order, the test favors borders that give the best prospects for democracy. In short, the ideal of democratic order seeks out its own supporting conditions in the context of the circumstances in which it is to be realized.

Liberal borders are marked in pencil on a map, not set out in indelible ink by the hand of God or nature. They are no more exclusionary or permanent than the circumstances that set them here rather than there in the first place. That is why they cannot exclude needy strangers knocking at the gate when there is room for them inside. Hence liberal immigration policy cannot exclude except on grounds having to do with the ability of current memberships to absorb the burdens of new members without serious loss of well-being. Nor can boundaries be maintained in the face of opportunities for wider political unions that more effectively meet the needs of members. The same grounds of democratic interests may sometimes argue for narrower political unions or for ones in which some functions of government belong to smaller groups, while others belong to a wider group.

But the claim that liberalism must rely on prepolitical national unities to establish boundaries is not true. What *is* true is that boundaries are set by all sorts of historical contingencies, including successful fights for national independence. It is also true that liberalism may sometimes sanction boundaries that follow national sentiment when that is to the advantage of individuals inside them as that is explicated by the test. Thus J. S. Mill and Henry Sidgwick give a role to national sentiment in the interests of securing representative political institutions and social justice (Mill 1975, 380; Sidgwick 1919, 309). But such arguments merely harness a sense of nationality, where it exists, to the service of more fundamental principles of liberal political morality. They identify a feature of the social world as it is which supports a nation-state as the vehicle for the delivery of the more important interests of individuals. They are not claims about the intrinsic importance of nations or about the perennial capacity of nation-states to provide effectively for the interests of their members.

Now, this way of thinking about borders as following function appears to neglect a fact that nationalism gets right—that people must be prepared to recognize each other as part of a collective "we" for purposes of common political action and sharing. The liberal state is suspected of relying on a hidden collective identity supplied by the nation because it cannot generate its own collective identity. Thus we encounter the third charge against liberal unity—the charge that a notion of individual contract cannot establish a collective identity. In fact, I hope to show, this charge rests on a mistaken belief (which nationalism itself cannot suppose to be true) that collectives can only be spawned by previous collectives.

Defenders of the nation have long recognized that it is an intentional kind, that is, one formed and kept in being by a collective belief (Scruton 1990, 71; Renan 1964, 9–10). This is the meaning of Ernest Renan's famous description of the nation as a daily plebiscite. To say that a social phenomenon is an intentional kind, according to John Searle, is to say that "the phenomenon in question can only exist if people believe it exists" (Searle 1991, 339). The fact about social phenomena that Searle is describing is that they are products of a form of mental causation which he calls "intentional" causation (Searle 1991, 335). For example, my desire to have a drink brings it about that I am drinking because my desire is a mental state the content of which represents the drinking that it brings about. On a larger scale, many social phenomena exist in response to a mental representation of themselves. This goes for marriage, divorce, property, money, elections, universities, doctoral theses, as well as states and nations. These and other cases can "only be the facts they are if the people involved think that they are those facts" (Searle 1991, 336). Of course you or I might be mistaken on a particular occasion. You may have a counterfeit lira bill in your pocket and not know it is counterfeit. But that certain bills are counterfeit is in general true because other pieces of paper are genuine currency and that is so because we all believe them to be so. Money exists if people think it exists. And it does not exist if no one thinks it exists (Searle 1991, 339). So too for many other social phenomena including nations. Where nations exist, it is in response to people believing in them. And if everyone thinks that they are a nation, then they are, and if not, then they are not.

The most important feature of this sort of account of social phenomena is that the intentionality that constitutes them is collective. Collective intentionality is characteristically displayed in forms of behavior where as Searle says "it is not the case that *I* am doing something and *you* are doing something but *we* are doing something together" (Searle 1991, 342). Now the constitution of social facts by the phenomenon of collective intentionality presupposes that we are certain sorts of beings; roughly, ones that can recognize each other as potential agents of collective intentional cooperation—of the sort manifested by playing as a team in the World Cup, or performing in the Birmingham Symphony Orchestra, or being a guest at a party, a marriage partner, or a party to a row. All of these involve mental states that make reference to "we" identities that act in concert. And none of the collective intentions involved can be analyzed into individual intentions that are entirely independent of the intentions and actions of others (Searle 1990, 403).

What we have to presuppose if Searle's analysis is right is that the capacity to share certain forms of mental life is a biological given (Searle 1990, 413). What we don't have to presuppose is anything as mysterious as a group mind. Individual minds and individual brains are the bases of intentionality, whether individual or collective (Searle 1990, 407).

What has all this to do with nations and states? I want to use Searle's analysis to suggest that both are phenomena produced by collective intentionality. We have already seen that defenders of the nation accept that it is an intentional kind. But I also want to suggest that neither nations nor states need the mediation of other collective identities before they can get going. We do not have to be a nation in order to be a state, any more than we have to be a tribe in order to be a nation. We have only to be individuals with the capacity to engage in acts involving collective intentionality. When the social contract theorists wrote of individuals coming together to form political society, they could neglect reference to any other identities of the individuals, not because they had none, but because the phenomenon of collective intentionality that explains individual ability to have prepolitical recognitional identities is of the same kind as explains the possibility of political society. Whether we talk of prepolitical or political identities, we are talking in the end about a product of collective intentionality that is rooted in a primitive individual capacity of identifying with others, similarly equipped, as parts of a collective "we." And this, of course, is something that can hold between strangers no less than already connected individuals. The issue is always what provokes the collective intentional recognitions and a good part of the answer has to be the classical social contract claim that civic cooperation is the answer to problems of securing individual life, liberty, and property.

So it is not true that the contractual model of political society cannot generate a "we" identity. What is true is that the collective unity of the state must originate in some prior *idea* of collective unity, before it can give itself a civil constitution. It is tempting to take this to mean that a population must have an independent consciousness of itself as a nation before it can give itself the constitutional order of the state. But this merely directs us to looking for the prior social unities on which the nation depends (clans, tribes, and families, perhaps) and gives us no explanation of how the more primitive unities could combine in any higher-order collective "we" without already being one. If the unity of the state is a problem in the sense that we are incapable of forming a collective "we" except on the basis of a prior collective "we," then appealing to the unity of the nation is no help because its unity raises the same problem.

This is not to deny the existence of nations as cultural phenomena or that states have sometimes originated from nations, or that the phenomenon we call the nation-state takes care to build a sense of identity which fuses recognition of certain political practices with a sense of cultural identity that is not only political. Nor is it to deny that there are sometimes overwhelming reasons for a nation to seek a state of its own.

But it is to say that the idea of the state as a collective identity is logically independent of the idea of the nation, and this permits us to consider the prospects for a constitutional patriotism apart from the prejudice of national unity. It allows us to see that whether the two ideas should be fused or separated in political practice is not something that admits of a single answer. What is appropriate in particular cases depends on facts of history and culture and basic political morality. In some cases, it may well be feasible and desirable to build political identities that overarch several national identities.

III

So far I have argued that we have seen no theoretical reason to suppose that the unity of the liberal state depends, or must depend, on the nation. The question we should ask, then, is why the liberal state has to be the source of its own unity. I want to look at one familiar type of argument having to do with diversity. Liberal unity, just to remind ourselves, is meant to be supplied by commitment to human rights and democratic values. "Although a well-ordered society is divided and pluralistic . . . public agreement on questions of political and social justice supports ties of civic friendship and secures the bonds of association" (Rawls 1980, 540).

The case from diversity to the need for liberal unity is that the latter allows for a reasonable pluralism of views about the good, individual liberty, and social experimentation. The argument may be founded on a claim about the ultimate moral significance of values such as autonomy or individuality as in the classical liberalisms of Kant and Mill. Alternatively, it may be developed as a response to the fact of pluralism, a response that is made possible and feasible by the existence of certain shared moral ideas in the public culture of democratic societies. This is the defense provided by Rawls's political liberalism (Ingram 1996). Both types of argument found the unity of the state on commitment to certain shared (liberal) values. What that commitment *means* is willingness to deal with other citizens on the basis of a just arrangement which gives priority to these values. For people with this commitment, as Rawls observes, liberal justice is a shared common aim among citizens and an important part of their identity (Rawls 1987, 10, n. 17). The point I am making here is a conceptual one. It is part of the idea of the liberal state that it is unified by certain shared values and the institutional structures that carry them over time. The idea involves willingness to view people, for purposes of politics, as generic individuals rather than as members of this or that clan, tribe, or nation.

This may be contested as empirically utopian. It may be argued that people in the real world call honor a liberal ideal of justice only insofar as they view themselves as having a prior social unity—what we now call a national identity. As a general thesis this is empirically rebutted by the existence of multicultural and multinational states. Nevertheless, it might be said that these are exceptions, and that, for the most part, peoples who think of themselves as historical nations adopt the liberal citizenship perspective only when they have a secure state of their own. I do not wish to contest this claim. But the fact, when it is a fact, that people view themselves as a historical nation, does not entail that their political unity is a form of cultural rather than constitutional patriotism, or that they do not, and cannot, adopt the standpoint of themselves as a political people who have become who they are by building and sustaining their version of political institutions governed by the principles of a liberal democratic order.

But if we say this, the problem is to explain how shared political values and constitutional patriotism are compatible with boundaries. The solution I want to outline is the one offered by Kant and recently revived by Jeremy Waldron (Waldron 1993). Kant argues that the natural duty of justice requires us to make political terms with whoever we can, and, in the first instance, this is with those adjacent to us. But the duty of justice does not require that we create a political union at any price. A Leviathan is not the solution. The appropriate form of political union is produced in response to an idea of it as a condition in which members are willing to offer each other, and abide by, terms that can be universally agreed. Thus both the character and the formation of political membership are matters of justice.

The argument from the natural duty of justice to membership is a strong version of the social contract argument for the state. The traditional form of that argument is that individuals form a state to secure themselves against war or the threat of war. In most versions, the formation of a system of coercive law to secure life, liberty, and property is seen as rational. In the strong version proposed by Kant, the formation of a state is not merely a matter of rationality. It is also a moral duty. "[I]f you are so situated as to be unavoidably side by side with others, you ought to abandon the state of nature and enter, with all others, a juridical state of affairs, that is, a state of distributive legal justice" (Kant 1965, 71). The same reasoning is used by Kant to argue for federal unions.

> Peoples who have grouped themselves into nation states may be judged in the same way as individual men living in the state of nature, independent of external laws; for they are a standing offence to one another by the very fact that they are neighbours. Each nation, for the sake of its own security, can and ought to demand of the others that they should enter along with it into a constitution similar to the civil one, within which the rights of each could be secured. This would mean establishing . . . a particular kind of league, which we might call a pacific federation. (Kant 1970, 102)

The reason in both cases is to avoid violence and war. Even if individuals are good-natured and righteous, Kant thinks that they can never be secure against violence from one another because "each will have his own right to do what *seems just and good to him*, entirely independent of the opinion of others" (Kant 1965, 76). So too for states.

Now while Kant believes that the human race has a common right to the earth's surface, and is for that reason a universal community, he does not think that we have to wait on universal consent before any state can be formed. Those with whom I am likely to come into conflict in the first instance are my neighbors. So I should enter into a political arrangement with them before some deadly conflict puts an end to my interest in anything.

Our first duty then is to address the issue of local conflicts by making just political and legal arrangements with all who are willing to do so. This inevitably institutes a special moral relationship between those who recognize each other as partners in a common state. As the undertakers of a shared political project we recognize each other as members of a society of mutual obligation, the specific terms of which are laid out, and of the institutions we construct over time. But the extent of membership is always revisable. Other candidates for inclusion appear as we broaden the range of our locality. Some of these will have separate arrangements, which we will have to deal with as corporate bodies at some stage, altering and revising the scope of our legal and political framework accordingly.

What is distinctive about this type of argument is that the formation of political community and the member/stranger distinction it embodies is a requirement of justice as is the formation of some level of wider political union. I want to draw attention to three points about the argument.

The first is that exclusion from membership has to be justified on grounds of justice to existing members and is essentially based on an existing membership's ability to fulfill the principles of political order that bind it together. This bears on immigration policy and federal or confederal political extensions. Exclusions based on race, color, religious belief, or cultural difference are not sanctioned, though willingness to abide by the basic terms of the host political association might well be among entry conditions. The duty to form wider political connections might be absolved in the face of politically significant differences. For example, it is difficult for a liberal democratic polity to envisage being able to broaden the range of political association to include civic partnership with political regimes that are not based on democratic values or an ideal of respect for human rights. It should also be said that the duty to expand, in whatever ways seem desirable, the range of political membership implies that it *can* be done. Where people are unwilling this is not the case and Kant insists that people should not be forced to join federal unions, or to concede aspects of their sovereignty that they need in order to honor their local commitments to justice and economic well-being.

The second point is that however provisional the boundaries of a political community, their purpose is to install political justice over a limited domain of the earth's surface. It is inconsistent with this aim to suppose that the membership thus brought together under just institutions has the same obligations to outsiders as to insiders. But the provisional character of the boundaries also suggests that the interests of outsiders cannot be wholly disregarded in favor of those of insiders, even when insiders practice no direct assault on them. Taxing the rich to further raise the welfare condition of the worst off in our society may be less desirable morally than taxing the rich to send aid to the Third World when our poorest members are incomparably better off than people fighting for bare survival.

The third point is that political communities with revisable Kantian borders may have all sorts of identities including the possibility of overlapping plural political identities. What matters is the existence of shared political culture, and this depends only on willingness to install and defend common institutions, not on cultural singularity. Within the nation-state framework that is familiar to most of us, our political identity flows from our practice of sharing and improving a particular historical set of political and legal institutions. Our particular identity is constituted by *our* effort to institutionalize principles of justice. And that effort has a different history and a different shape in different bounded communities. Thus there is a clear sense in which I may have political duties to a particular population, you to another, and each of these duties flows from the way in which our natural duty of justice has to be institutionalized in the kind of world we live in. We, or our ancestors, have to establish local institutions to handle local conflicts in advance of encountering all possible sources of conflict in the world as a whole.

But the boundaries need not be regarded as containers within which all of a standard set of governmental tasks are performed. *We*, who identify ourselves as a historical society carried forward by our institutions, may join with others in wider political unions in which some of the tasks of government are performed across boundaries. Thus we may create overlapping political memberships corresponding to our interests in having wider and narrower realms of political power devolved on functional lines. Though I cannot develop this point here, the argument is not for gradual advance to a world state—for there to be no boundaries—but for a network of criss-crossing boundaries established on the basis of functions people need rather than on lines of prepolitical identities.

Reflection on the Kantian explanation of particular boundaries helps to clarify how shared political values, such as democracy and human rights, are compatible with boundaries. What differentiates one state from another is the particular institutional expression those values receive in different historical efforts in different places, to build the liberal state. In turn, this points us to all understanding of constitutional patriotism as loyalty to a particular constitutional tradition and helps detach patriotism from nationalism. Liberal unity does indeed require a certain kind of citizen solidarity. But its source need not be the cultural nation. It can be supplied by common recognition of ourselves as members of a historical political association committed to the constitution we made and continue to remake through the generations.

So the solidarity that is needed to make the liberal state work is not utopian in presupposing that liberal citizens are moved by a global regard for justice that permits no partiality towards particular historical polities. It is a solidarity rooted in regard for the concrete institutions that belong to our distinct political heritage and may be no less deep than a solidarity founded on the prepolitical ties of a nation. As citizens of liberal democratic states, some of us are already fundamentally identified with political societies which conceive themselves, if somewhat uncertainly, in this way. We think of our identity as rooted in a political group in which an essential part of our self-expression as individuals is catered for by rights to participate in the continuing self-definition and development of the group.

IV

I want to return briefly to the issue of postnational identity in the context of European Union. In the terms of my argument, a postnational identity is a form of consciousness of institutional belonging and obligation that comes from identification with a particular political project of modern state-building. Liberal unity, I have argued, is theoretically coherent and can provide a deep enough collective identification to motivate people to meet the obligations of a liberal state. But I do not know whether the peoples of Europe can develop the sense of obligation to the European common weal that Habermas has identified as crucial (Habermas 1992, 9). Much depends on how successful we are in developing institutions that accommodate existing national and subnational identities, at the same time as providing an overarching system of social justice acceptable to all. But since civic belonging in Europe has to "pass through" membership of national states, the problem of reconciling obligations to the European common weal and obligations to our own states cannot be solved institutionally without leaving a great deal more autonomy to member states than is usual in federal arrangements. This is not because member states are merely self-serving, but rather because their citizens are, and are likely to remain, fundamentally identified with their own political societies. And this fact is a reason for thinking that citizens will continue to be motivated to put the well-being of their own state ahead of others, thereby reproducing the divisions of national interests that make integration desirable but incredibly difficult in the first place.

Citizens of Europe may eventually come to embrace a postnational identity in which the perspective of their own state loses its power to overwhelm a sense of wider obligation. We may be inclined to think of this common sense of European obligation as coming about through the operation of European institutions, especially ones that develop a sense of European citizenship as the means to primary goods that secure forms of life people actually want for themselves. But the social welfare thrust of such institutions has to compete with the undeniable preference for putting one's own country first. So, it may be more realistic to envisage the gradual development of a degree of democratically endorsed European internal sovereignty as coming about in consequence of the development of a sense of postnational identity that is developed first within current nation-state boundaries. Only if we can link democratic citizenship more securely with social justice in the smaller communities can we expect people to learn of a worthwhile solidarity that transcends the cultural nation, and then, perhaps, the civic nation.

NOTE

I wish to thank the participants of the working group on pluralism, sovereignty, and citizenship at the IVR conference in Bologna in 1995 whose comments have helped me improve this paper. It has also benefited from an earlier outing at a conference of the Irish Philosophical Society in University College, Cork. I am grateful to the participants, especially Garret Barden and Dolores Dooley, for their valuable suggestions on that occasion. I am deeply indebted to Wayne Norman who sent me useful and encouraging comments on an earlier draft, and to John Baker who provided detailed and incisive written comments that helped me see the many holes I had dug for myself.

REFERENCES

Habermas, Jürgen. 1992. "Citizenship and National Identity: Some Reflections on the Future of Europe." *Praxis International* 12, no. 1: 1–19.

Ingram, Attracta. 1996. "Rawlsians, Pluralists, and Cosmopolitans." In *Philosophy and Pluralism*, edited by Dave Archard. Cambridge: Cambridge University Press.

Kant, Immanuel. 1965. *The Metaphysical Elements of Justice.* Indianapolis, Ind.: Bobbs-Merrill.

———. 1970. "Perpetual Peace: A Philosophical Sketch." In *Kant's Political Writings*, edited by Hans Riess. Cambridge: Cambridge University Press.

Mill, J. S. 1975. "Representative Government." In *Three Essays.* Oxford: Oxford University Press.

Norman, Wayne. 1994. "Towards a Normative Theory of Federalism." In *Group Rights*, edited by Judith Baker. Toronto: University of Toronto Press.

Oakeshott, Michael. 1975. *On Human Conduct.* Oxford: Clarendon Press.

Parekh, Bhikhu. 1986. "The 'New Right' and the Politics of Nationhood." In *The New Right: Image and Reality*, edited by N. Deakin. London: Runnymede Trust.

Rawls, John. 1980. "Kantian Constructivism in Moral Theory." *Journal of Philosophy* 77, no. 9: 515–72.

———. 1987. "The Idea of an Overlapping Consensus." *Oxford Journal of Legal Studies* 7, no. 1: 1–24.

Renan, Ernest. 1939. "What Is a Nation?" In *Modern Political Doctrines*, edited by A. Zimmern. London: Oxford University Press.

———. 1964. "Qu'est-ce qu'une nation?" In *The Dynamics of Nationalism*, edited by Louis L. Snyder. New York: Van Nostrand.

Scruton, Roger. 1990. "In Defence of the Nation." In *Ideas and Politics in Modern Britain*, edited by J. C. D. Clark. London: Macmillan.

Searle, John. 1990. "Collective Intentions and Actions." In *Intentions in Communication*, edited by P. Cohen. Cambridge, Mass.: MIT Press.

———. 1991. "Intentionalist Explanations in the Social Sciences." *Philosophy of the Social Sciences* 21, no. 3: 332–44.

Sidgwick, Henry. 1919. *The Elements of Politics.* 4th ed. London: Macmillan.

Taylor, Charles. 1985. *"Atomism."* In *Philosophical Papers*, vol. 2, *Philosophy and the Human Sciences*. Cambridge, Mass.: Harvard University Press.
Waldron, Jeremy. 1993. "Special Ties and Natural Duties." *Philosophy and Public Affairs* 22, no. 1: 3–30.

Chapter Thirteen

JOHN H. SCHAAR

THE CASE FOR COVENANTED PATRIOTISM

I intend to write something of a plea for patriotism. That intention is so uncongenial to almost everybody who is likely to read the essay that I want to spell it out with some care. In doing this, I wish not to disarm the critics, but to help them find the right target.

Consider first the state of opinion and sentiment on the subject.

Patriotism is unwelcome in many quarters of the land today, and unknown in many others. There is virtually no thoughtful discussion of the subject, for the word has settled, in most people's minds, deep into a brackish pond of sentiment where thought cannot reach. Politicians and members of patriotic associations praise it, of course, but official and professional patriotism too often sounds like nationalism, patriotism's bloody brother. On the other hand, patriotism has a bad name among many thoughtful people, who see it as a horror at worst, a vestigial passion largely confined to the thoughtless at best: as enlightenment advances, patriotism recedes. The intellectuals are virtually required to repudiate it as a condition of class membership. The radical and dropout young loathe it. Most troublesome of all, for one who would make the argument I intend to make, is the fact that both the groups that hate and those that glorify patriotism largely agree that it and nationalism are the same thing. I hope to show that they are different things—related, but separable.

Opponents of patriotism might agree that if the two could be separated then patriotism would look fairly attractive. But the opinion is widespread, almost atmospheric, that the separation is impossible, that with the triumph of the nation-state, nationalism has indelibly stained patriotism: the two are warp and woof. The argument against patriotism goes on to say that, psychologically considered, patriot and nationalist are the same: both are characterized by exaggerated love for one's own collectivity combined with more or less contempt and hostility toward outsiders. In addition, advanced political opinion holds that positive, new ideas and forces—e.g., internationalism, universal humanism, economic interdependence, socialist solidarity—are healthier bonds of unity, and more to be encouraged, than the older ties of patriotism. These are genuine objections, and they are held by many thoughtful people. I shall try to respond to them toward the end of the essay.

The obstacles to speaking for patriotism do not end with brackishness of opinion. For if some people favor patriotism, largely for the wrong reasons, and some oppose it, largely for the wrong reasons, others hardly think about it at all. Millions of Americans are simply without patriotism, and this large group includes all classes and kinds of persons. They do not think unpatriotic thoughts, but they do not think patriotic thoughts either. The republic for them is a vague and distant thing, absent from their hearts, lost to their eyes. Reflecting this indifference, our great patriotic holidays, now administratively arranged to provide long weekends, are less occasions for shared remembrance and renewal of the political covenant than boosts to the consumer economy. That modern compendium of man's knowledge of man, the *International Encyclopedia of Social Sciences*, apparently agrees that patriotism is a nonthing, for it is silent on the subject.

There is another obstacle to discussion. The word "patriotism" is a member of a family of words and largely takes its meanings from its membership. Some other members of the family are "legacy," "covenant," "reverence," "loyalty," "nurture," "roots," "citizen," "debt," "gift," and "republic." These words, which once clarified the matter, today encounter the same barrier of mystification-distrust-indifference as does patriotism itself. All these words must appear in the discussion: there are no satisfactory alternatives. Furthermore, these words cannot be cut out of our political lives as easily as they have been dropped from our encyclopedia. If we lose them, it will not be easy to find replacements, and we may learn too late that the loss was grievous. Still, many people do not now share this view of the matter, and this sets a difficult obstacle in the path of discussion.

Patriotism has certainly declined in the United States. Nor is this decline the result of recent or transient causes. Most of the widely known patriotic associations were formed in the last decade of the nineteenth century, which suggests that as the natural springs of patriotic sentiment dried up, the land had to be irrigated. By now the land is so parched that even when American participation in the war in Southeast Asia comes to an end, along with all the reports of American corruption and exploitation at home and abroad, I doubt whether we shall love this country any the more, although we might despise it less.

I have little hope that my plea for patriotism will succeed, and much anxiety that it will be heard by many as fatuous or wrong-headed. Citizens would not need the argument, and noncitizens probably cannot hear it. Still, I shall make the argument. I do so partly out of blockheadedness, partly out of a wish to repay a welcome debt to patriotic predecessors and contemporaries, and partly for two reasons that might carry more weight. The first reason stems from my affection and respect for fellow-citizens, and from my wish to see them even more respectable than they are. We have lost patriotism. Although many count the loss small, and many others do not know it has occurred, I believe that the loss is great. The second reason stems from my wish to see a revitalized radical politics in this country, and from my conviction that Susan Sontag is correct when she says that "probably no serious radical movement has any future in America unless it can revalidate the tarnished idea of patriotism."[1] The radicals of the 1960s did not persuade their fellow-Americans, high or low, that they genuinely cared for and shared a country with them. And no one who has contempt for others can hope to teach those others. A revived radicalism must be a patriotic radicalism. It must share and care for the common things, even while it has a "lovers' quarrel" with fellow-citizens.

NATURAL PATRIOTISM

Since patriotism is a complex and dangerous word, we must give some care to definition. But not too much care, for like all the important political words, it cannot be protected against the vicissitudes of history and passion; and not the wrong kind of care either, for the word comes not from the laboratory but from life. The word will not hold still while we attach a single, universal meaning to it, but we can describe a nucleus of meanings.

At its core, patriotism means love of one's homeplace, and of the familiar things and scenes associated with the homeplace. In this sense, patriotism is one of the basic human sentiments. If not a natural tendency in the species, it is at least a proclivity produced by realities basic to human life, for territoriality, along with family, has always been a primary associative bond. We become devoted to the people, places, and ways that nurture us, and what is familiar and nurturing seems also natural and right. This is the root of patriotism. Furthermore, we are all subject to the immense power of habit, and patriotism has habit in its service. Even if we leave the homeplace for a larger world, finding delight in its variety and novelty, we delight as much in returning to familiar things. The theme of homecoming is the central motif of patriotic discourse, as old and as deep as the return of Odysseus from Troy, and the feeling is always the same:

> When we saw the top of the mountain from Albuquerque we wondered if it was
> our mountain, and we felt like talking to the ground, we loved it so, and some
> of the old men and women cried with joy when they reached their homes.[2]

The other side of the case is the melancholy figure of the lone wanderer, or of the Stoic whose "my home is everywhere" meant he had a home nowhere.

To be a patriot is to have a patrimony; or, perhaps more accurately, the patriot is one who is grateful for a legacy and recognizes that the legacy makes him a debtor. There is a whole way of being in the world, captured best by the word *reverence*, which defines life by its debts: one is what one owes, what one acknowledges as a rightful debt or obligation. The patriot moves within that mentality. The gift of land, people, language, gods, memories, and customs, which is the patrimony of the patriot, defines what he or she is. Patrimony is mixed with person; the two are barely separable. The very tone and rhythm of a life, the shapes of perception, the texture of its hopes and fears come from membership in a territorially rooted group. The conscious patriot is one who feels deeply indebted for those gifts, grateful to the people and places through which they came, and determined to defend the legacy against enemies and pass it unspoiled to those who will come after.

But such primary experiences are nearly inaccessible to us. We are taught to define our lives not by our debts and legacies, but by our rights and opportunities. Robert Frost's stark line, "This land was ours, before we were the land's," condenses the whole story of American patriotism. We do not and cannot love this land the way the Greeks and the Navaho loved theirs. The graves of some of our ancestors are here, to be sure, but most of us would be hard pressed to find them: name and locate the graves of your great-grandparents. The land was not granted to us in trust by a Great Spirit, nor are there in this land a thousand places sacred to lesser deities. Having purged ourselves of pantheism, we do not dwell in a realm alive with sacred groves and fountains.[3] We are all doctrinal monotheists and our only patriotic god is the god of battles. We took the land from others whom we regarded as of no account. The land itself we saw as a resource for comfort and power available to all who had the strength to take it. Among us, only persons (artificial as well as natural) have rights. The homestead has none. We may buy, sell, and use it as we wish. It has no claims we need heed or even hear. Still today, and even in the ecology movement, the same attitude prevails: Save *Our* Coast. Still possession, not union and stewardship.

Perhaps this lack of natural patriotism is some part of the explanation of American restlessness and rootlessness.[4] When Europeans first came to this land they saw nothing but savages in a howling wilderness, both of which had to be conquered. Seeking neither welcome nor permission from those already here, they imposed their alien god and ways on the "new land." That original act of conquest and sacrilege was repeated innumerable times as the wave rolled west, until now the very land accuses the intruders. There can be no experience of homecoming without welcome, and we shall not feel welcome here until we learn how to ask it of those who alone have it to give. That we may be slowly coming to understand this is one of the few hopeful signs for American patriotism.[5]

Perhaps it is impossible to know whether the nature of the conquest helped produce American restlessness and rootlessness, but it is certain that the restlessness and rootlessness in their turn make a natural patriotism nearly possible. The seeds of patriotism can germinate on even the stoniest ground, but they must have time to put down roots. We are a nation on the go, always moving, and always with somewhere left to move to. Many of us now even have mobile homes, with no roots in the earth at all. The purpose of life is to get ahead, and getting ahead means leaving others behind—an outlook which makes us distinctive among the nomadic peoples. There is little piety toward the past and the future is something to be conquered. Ages and generations of care are required for the nurturing of that primary patriotism of place which has been a treasured and defining experience of most of humankind. In recent American letters, perhaps only William Faulkner, Robert Frost, and Edmund Wilson wrote in the language of natural patriotism—and Wilson became querulous toward the end. We are a people to whom the experience of displacement is so natural that we do not know we are displaced, and it is hard for us to appreciate how desolating the experience can be for others. The following words were written by a Laotian poet pleading for a way of life now destroyed by American bombs:

> Pity—our houses, ricefields, inheritance—we must abandon. The ricefields will grow jungles. They will become a wild place filled with tigers. Have pity; the lands, the ponds with fish, everything; pity the bathing hole where no one will come to swim and muddy the cool waters. Pity the crabs, fish, game, bamboo shoots; our kind of food. Sorrow for the fruit trees we planted in the garden and around the village, the clumps of large and small bamboo; have pity! . . . The day does not exist when we will forget.[6]

Can we for whom "relocation" means moving elsewhere in pursuit of income and opportunity understand this? Have we found satisfactory substitutes for it in batting averages, or color television, or flights to the moon?

In sum, then, that kind of patriotism which Tocqueville called instinctive is not available to us.[7] There is no way to measure the weight of this loss, but if instinctive patriotism is the basic urge I think it is, then the loss is heavy. Surely, human beings can feel the lack of something they need even though they might never have had it. To feel the loss of something, it is not necessary first to have had that thing. (Consider "love," for example, which many psychologists say we all need, even though many of us have never had it.) The trouble is, that when a deprivation is of this sort the victim may not interpret his condition correctly: people attempted all sorts of cures for goiter before they learned about iodine. Not knowing what it is one needs, one mistakes symptoms for cause, and tries to fill the need through harmful substitutes for the real thing. Perhaps this is the case with us.

Just one step removed from land patriotism is patriotism of the city. Both center on the idea and sentiment of home and nurture. Both acknowledge that the foundation of life is debt. Both shape individual life by reference to the common and familiar things. Their only important difference is in the object of attachment. The city is the creation of human beings and is in that obvious sense artificial, the image of an ideal, while the land, even when altered by labor and love, remains fundamentally the work of nature. The supreme expression of city patriotism is to be found in Pericles' eulogy for the Athenian dead, and a study of that discourse will teach one all that can be learned about the subject.

Certainly city patriotism can be as intense as patriotism of the land. Machiavelli cared more for his city than for his own soul. And Fustel de Coulanges' book on *The Ancient City* describes how much of human life could be founded on the city's gods, exhibited in the city's temples and public spaces, and protected by the city's walls. Each family had its private home and hearth, but the city was a second home, made by all and common to all. City patriotism was profoundly "social" in its orientations: Socrates did not like to leave Athens for even a day in the country, because he could not talk with trees.

City patriotism, then, is not profoundly different from land patriotism, though it is a step beyond it in the direction of the artificial and the ideal. Like land patriotism, it too is declining. In the times when cities were few, they were precious to their citizens by reason of their very artificiality. A small man-made thing protected by its walls from the vast wilderness without, the city nourished a life which was distinctively human. As time went on, the works of the human kind appeared everywhere, becoming less valuable as they became more common. That is true the world over. In the United States, in addition, cities have been from the beginning products largely of the impulse of profit and hustle, owing little to the sacred and the traditional. Hence, there is as little of city patriotism among us as there is of the ancient patriotism of place. Furthermore, the people and shapes, as well as the monuments and traditions, of our cities change so rapidly that citizens have no time to form solid and enduring attachments. Even the sports teams, closest modern equivalent to the gods of the ancient city, can be moved by a few million dollars.

COVENANTED PATRIOTISM

But if instinctive patriotism and the patriotism of the city cannot be ours, what can be? Is there a type of patriotism peculiarly American; if so, is it anything more than patriotism's violent relative, nationalism?

Abraham Lincoln, the supreme authority on this subject, thought there was a patriotism unique to America. Americans, a motley gathering of various races and cultures, were bonded together not by blood or religion, not by tradition or territory, not by the walls and traditions of a city, but by a political

idea. We are a nation formed by a covenant, by dedication to a set of principles and by an exchange of promises to uphold and advance certain commitments among ourselves and throughout the world. Those principles and commitments are the core of American identity, the soul of the body politic. They
make the American nation unique, and uniquely valuable, among and to the
other nations. But the other side of this conception contains a warning very
like the warnings spoken by the prophets to Israel: if we fail in our promises
to each other, and lose the principles of the covenant, then we lose everything,
for they are we. This makes it quite clear that we are dealing here with a conception very different from Rousseau's advocacy of a civil religion as the bond
of political community. For Lincoln, the principles of the covenant set the standard by which the nation must judge itself: the nation is righteous and to be
honored only insofar as it honors the covenant. For Rousseau, the civil religion
is designed to induce the individual to venerate the nation itself. I shall hope
to show that the best way to define the failure of American patriotism is to see
it as a decline from the noble example and promise of Lincoln's conception, to
the banal performance of Rousseau's.

Lincoln developed and expounded his conception of the national covenant
over a number of years and on a number of significant occasions. One of his
fullest statements of the idea came when he was about to enter the highest office
in the land. On his way to Washington to take up the presidency, Lincoln was
invited to speak in Independence Hall, Philadelphia. Deeply moved by the place,
he expressed his understanding of America's meaning and mission in a handful of
memorable words—and half-consciously revealed his own and the nation's
future. The whole speech should be read. Here are some critical passages:

> I am filled with deep emotion at finding myself standing here in the place
> where were collected together the wisdom, the patriotism, the devotion to
> principle, from which sprang the institutions under which we live . . . . I can
> say . . . that all the political sentiments I entertain have been drawn . . . from
> the sentiments which originated, and were given to the world from this hall
> in which we stand. I have never had a feeling politically that did not spring
> from the sentiments embodied in the Declaration of Independence . . . . I have
> often inquired of myself, what great principle or idea it was that kept this con-
> federacy so long together. It was . . . something in that Declaration giving lib-
> erty, not alone to the people of this country, but hope to the world for all
> future time. It was that which gave promise that in due time the weights
> should be lifted from the shoulders of all men, and that *all* should have an
> equal chance. . . .
>
> Now, my friends, can this country be saved upon that basis? If it can, I
> will consider myself one of the happiest men in the world if I can help to save
> it. If it can't be saved upon that principle, it will be truly awful. But, if this
> country cannot be saved without giving up that principle—I was about to say
> I would rather be assassinated on this spot than to surrender it.[8]

In this discourse Lincoln asserted that the articles of the political covenant are both perfectly clear and grounded in the firmest authority. Three years later, on land consecrated by blood, he repeated the same themes. The nation born in 1776 was "conceived in liberty, and dedicated to the proposition that all men are created equal." Continuing in unbroken line, generation was tied to generation by that common birth and promise. In a fragment written early in 1861, but not published, Lincoln stated his understanding of the relation between covenant and people—between the Declaration of Independence on the one side and the Constitution and Union on the other. He expressed the connection by a luminous metaphor drawn from the Book of Proverbs. The principle announced in the Declaration he called an "apple of gold," while "the Union and the Constitution are the pictures of silver, subsequently framed around it. The picture was made, not to conceal, or destroy the apple; but to adorn and preserve it. The picture was made for the apple—not the apple for the picture" (IV, 240).

One more statement, this time from the young Lincoln. Again the occasion is significant. Lincoln had just been elected to the Illinois legislature, and he accepted an invitation to address the Young Men's Lyceum of Springfield: an occasion of beginning, then, like the speech in Independence Hall. Lincoln chose as his theme "the perpetuation of our political institutions" (I, 108–15).

He opened the discourse by reminding his listeners that the men of the Revolution had fought to found a polity dedicated to liberty and self-government. Those principles were safe while the founders lived for they knew the price that had been paid for them. The scenes and memories of the struggle were visible to their eyes and lively to their memories. Many individuals and families treasured and retold the stories of sacrifice and danger. But now those scenes are distant. We who came after the struggle and had no part in it cannot see it in the scars on our bodies, cannot even relive it through the eyes and voices of the actors. Being distant, we easily forget why those others fought and died, and we cannot justly value the gift they gave to us. Our forgetting opens the path to talented persons of great ambition who, if they cannot gain fame by preserving the principles of the founding, will gain fame by wrecking them. Only if the founding principles are kept alive and pure in the minds and hearts of the citizenry shall we be safe from perverted ambition—or, indeed, safe from ourselves. We must, then, see as the chief task of political life the task of political education: inculcate respect for valid laws as a "political religion"; retell on every possible occasion the story of the struggle; teach tirelessly the principles of the founding. The only guardian of the compact is an informed citizenry, and the first task of leadership is the formation of such a citizenry.[9]

This is a conception of patriotic devotion that fits a nation as large and heterogeneous as our own. It sets a mission and provides a standard of judgment. It tells us when we are acting justly and it does not confuse martial fervor with dedication to country. Lincoln also reminded us that the covenant is not a static legacy or a gift outright, but a burden and a promise. The nation exists only in repeated acts of remembrance and renewal of the covenant through changing circumstances. Patriotism here is more than a frame of mind. It is also activity guided by and directed toward the mission established in the founding covenant. This conception of political membership also decisively transcends the parochial and primitive fraternities of blood and race, for it calls kin all who accept the authority of the covenant. And finally, this covenanted patriotism assigns America a teaching mission among the nations, rather than a superiority over or a hostility toward them.[10] This patriotism is compatible with the most generous humanism.[11]

Now, only the willfully blind could fail to see that American patriotism in practice has failed to live up to Lincoln's teaching of the ideal. Most of the reasons are obvious; others are more subtle.

First of all, certain peoples were excluded from the covenant, some from the beginning, some later on: Indians, Negroes, Mexican Americans, Orientals. Then too, from early on, liberty was largely interpreted as private liberty, and equality soon came to mean equal opportunity to compete for the prizes of wealth and power. There was little teaching of liberty as public liberty—the power of acting with others to shape the conditions of the common life. (Henry Adams thought the political age had ended by 1816, supplanted by the economic age.) The activity of politics was seen as but another of the instrumentalities by which self-interested individuals advanced toward private goals. The very notion of a public good dissolved into an aggregate of particular goods, and Lincoln's conception of the patriotic citizen as one who treasures and upholds the basic principles of the political covenant dissolved along with it.[12]

Today our skepticism toward all notions of disinterested, public-regarding behavior is so thoroughgoing that the patriot can hardly appear. We are inclined to regard all professions of public-spirited and altruistic motive as the blandishments of a charlatan or the deceptions of a schemer—and we are largely right, for over time, a people gets the politics it expects and asks for. When these political conceptions were added to the ethic of competition and mastery in the economic sphere, the ground was prepared for the full flowering of that individualism which Tocqueville diagnosed as the deadliest enemy of civic virtue. In sum, liberalism and capitalism corrupted the covenant, while racism denied it to large groups of the population.

Other forces completed the work which liberalism, capitalism, and racism had begun. The idea and experience of a covenanted community have deeper roots in the American past than those exposed by Lincoln. The Puritan Commonwealth of New England was exactly such a community. Individuals became members of the community only upon acceptance of certain articles of religious faith and morals. That acceptance had to be proved in practice, and to the satisfaction of the guardians of the covenant. Social institutions were designed to encourage performance of the covenant. The Puritans discouraged the formation of isolated, private farmsteads and tried to keep all persons in the towns, in sight of each other, and with life centered in the meetinghouse. In sum, membership was not a right of birth. It had to be earned, and was the reward of choice and effort. Institutions were designed to encourage the choice and supervise the effort.

That idea of earned membership still forms the center of American nationality, but time and circumstances have worked strange changes on it.[13] As time went on, America opened its doors to the stranger on easy terms. Only one restriction remained: the strangers had to become republicans. They had to accept the fundamental terms of the founding covenant. The Constitution even specifies that each state shall have a republican form of government We imposed no religious tests for membership, no tests of cultural or linguistic background, no tests—with well-known exceptions—of blood or race. But we did require a profession of republican faith. In that decisive way, the New England idea of earned membership in a covenanted community persisted. It is a fascinating idea, at once universal and generous and parochial and narrow: universal and generous in that it is willing to embrace as members a great variety of human and cultural types, rejecting neither Turk nor Greek *qua* Turk or Greek, blind to divisions that had for centuries brought the Old World to repression and war; narrow in that it reduced the person to official beliefs, denying the significance of all those other things that go to make up character and style, all those things that human conversation is about.

As time went on, the narrowness prevailed against the generosity. First of all, the social institutions that provided the nursery and school for learning and following the covenant declined. The close New England town gave way to the isolated homestead, or to the city of recent immigrants. No longer was life lived and tested under the eyes of familiars. Then, the forgetting that Lincoln so feared took its toll so that the gift of public liberty seemed a small one. Our teachers began to teach, and we to value, private life and liberty above all. The growth of capitalist enterprise and the spread of the competitive ethic hastened the work of isolation and privatization. And then, during the last third of the nineteenth century, capitalism became equated with America itself. At the very time when the free enterprise system was being swallowed by the corporate system, the ideology of free enterprise became identified with the spirit of Americanism. Finally, with the huge immigrations of 1890–1920, and with the emergence of the United States as a world power, efforts to assimilate the foreign-born and assure their loyalty were greatly accelerated. More and more we turned to propaganda and to one or another form of loyalty test. An American became one who would not profess certain beliefs or who would not do certain things: from belief in anarchism, to the practice of polygamy, to joining the Communist Party, and on to disavowing the use of revolutionary force and violence. A nation of strangers, ignorant of the most important things about the folks next door, we attempted to assure predictable behavior by requiring ritual disavowals of feared beliefs and practices. The quest for consensus in national politics followed almost naturally—as though patriots were persons who did not disagree, as though patriotism were a matter of professing certain doctrines and supporting the party policies of the day, rather than a steadfast devotion to the founding principles and a disinterested search for the good of the whole.

The "apple of gold" tarnished, while we polished the "picture of silver." Rousseau's conception of a civic religion drove out Lincoln's conception of a covenanted citizenry whose patriotism was exercised in active dedication to the promises and goals of the republic.

Even so, Lincoln's idea remains alive as possibly the only saving conception of patriotism possible for us. It is surely the understanding of patriotic duty that inspired the civil rights activity of the 1960s, and that for one glorious moment called more Harvard seniors to the Peace Corps than to the Business School. It is the only idea of civic obligation that can provide a full defense for civilly disobeying laws or orders circumscribing liberty or violating the principle of equal justice for all. The idea was expressed by many of the young men who publicly refused conscription during the late 1960s on the grounds that the Vietnam War violated America's obligations to itself and to the nations — expressed not by those who fled or hid, or who used the labyrinth of the law to avoid the burdens of moral choice and political action, but by those who publicly resisted and publicly paid the penalties of resistance.

Lincoln's conception of covenanted patriotism also offers the noblest rationale for active citizenship (government of, by, and for the people) resident in our tradition. Virtually every other argument for participation familiar to Americans starts from the premise of self-interest and sees political participation in exclusively instrumental and economistic terms. Seen in this light, SDS's "Port Huron Statement" of 1962, with its conviction that the individual should "share in those social decisions determining the quality and direction of his life," is the finest expression of the Lincolnian idea in recent times. The Port Huron Statement offers a vision of an active and cooperative citizenry who see the political system as *their* system, and who understand that if the system is to survive according to its own principles, it will survive only by their efforts, and not by the ministrations of an elected monarch and an elite of managers, no matter how benign and competent. Such an elite might be able to keep order and distribute comfort, and might even be able to defend the populace against external enemies and help it to adjust to the strains of incessant change at home, but it cannot preserve the system on its own principles. It cannot do that because one of those principles is that the system belongs to the citizens. It is theirs; and at the moment an elite "saves" it for them, at that moment it dies.

Finally, Lincoln's idea proposes a strictly political definition of our nationhood, one which liberates us from the parochialisms of race and religion, and one which severs patriotic devotion from the cult of national power. It is, in my estimation, a calamity that this idea of patriotism has been so corrupted and subverted among us. The work of reviving, purifying, and establishing it is the supreme task of American political education.

NATIONALISM

A covenanted polity might be our finest tradition and best hope. It is not our reality. That reality is nationalism.

Even natural patriotism has a face less attractive than the one drawn above. Our preference for our own home and ways is easily understandable, and on the whole, admirable. Understandable too, but less admirable, is the easy step from preference to pride. Our peculiar characteristics easily come to seem not just the best for us, but the best. And they remain the best because they are ours. The logic may be weak, but the psycho-logic is very strong. Furthermore, the strange ways of others may seem to us not merely inferior to our own, but dangerous and threatening. Fear and distrust of the stranger are the dark force of patriotism, and they are as potent and flammable as the saving force of love for one's own.

The moral thrust of patriotism, then, is inherently ambivalent. It simultaneously unites and divides, encourages both concord and discord. There is no way to eradicate that ambivalence. It is this feature of the sentiment that has brought many to yearn for its disappearance. But that is a mistaken yearning, based on failure to see that not just patriotism but every human devotion both unites and divides. Every devotion draws a magic circle around some people and things, excluding others, and thereby automatically divides the world into those within and those outside the circle. Love does that, and so do faith and loyalty. Division and conflict are built into the dialectic of devotion.

The real trouble enters with the recognition that patriotism is not just a moral devotion but also a political passion, an attachment to political objects. From a group's political history come most of the points of pride, the revered heroes, the memories of sacrifice and courage, and the goals and values which form the ordinary member's sense of shared identity and shape his conception of patriotic duty. Through that history one becomes a participant in the corporate life, sharing its destiny, appropriating its triumphs and defeats, making its will one's own. Socrates called the laws of Athens his parents.

That corporate life is organized. It has a focus and a structure. And when that organization takes the form of the state, patriotism is easily warped to destructive ends. States are in their very nature combat organizations. They claim a monopoly of the legitimate use of force, and they employ propaganda to shape the thoughts and emotions of members. Through propaganda, the state incessantly tries to convince citizens that the support and enlargement of state power is their first duty, even to the point of overriding all other duties, even to the point of excusing lies and murder. The state may be, as Nietzsche called it, the coldest of cold monsters, but it knows well how to heat up the passions of its subjects. That is the elementary and invaluable political knowledge of the statesmen of our day, right or left: Fidel Castro's exploitation of the theme of anti-Americanism has been a more valuable resource in the consolidation of the Cuban state than any amount of material aid the United States could possibly provide; the architects of the Cold War, using anticommunist propaganda, gave the Pentagon a stronger foundation than could ever have been built from tradition and prudence.

In our time the nation-state has successfully claimed itself to be the sole legitimate object of patriotic attachment, with results that have been on the whole disastrous. Many lesser loyalties fell before the surge of nationalism, and patriotism, too, had to be reduced in its objects and meanings. In earlier times, when people were enclosed in narrow circles of experience and devotion, the proper vocation of education was to call them out of the parochial, urging them toward higher and more general loyalties. But now the situation is different, and perhaps the task of education is different too. E. M. Forster spoke the untimely words appropriate to our time when he said that if ever it became necessary to choose between betraying his country or his friend, he hoped he would have the courage to betray his country.

Because nationalism is so pervasive today, it seems to be almost in the order of nature. But that is wrong. It is patriotism of the kind described at the outset of this essay that is natural. Nationalism is artificial. It is the product of specific social, economic, and intellectual forces and just as it was born only yesterday, it could die tomorrow. Nationalism takes sentiments basic to the nurture of human life, welds them to a certain political structure, and warps them in an almost entirely bellicose direction. It appeared in the states of the West at a definite stage of history and it filled definite needs. Nationalism could triumph only when liberalism had proceeded so far in its work of breaking the bonds among men that new ones were needed to provide at least a minimum of warmth and some measure of connectedness and direction. In all the liberal states, the same two myths were forged to replace the broken links: nationalism was one; the cult of progress the other. Outside the West, nationalism has typically flared up in response to humiliations imposed by Western states on traditional cultures and regimes.

Feelings of nationality existed long before the modern age, to be sure, but they were largely inarticulate and unorganized. They were not shaped and sharpened by propaganda into a unity of emotion, thought and will: Machiavelli's appeal for a prince to unify Italy and liberate it from the foreigners had to wait three hundred and fifty years for an answer. But patriotism and nationalism were not the same, and nationality was not regarded as the foundation of the political order. In the classical age, for example, those who called themselves Greeks had a strong sense of common nationality which distinguished them from non-Greeks. Greeks spoke the same language and had many gods and ceremonies in common, but they gathered themselves politically into a large number of city-states, each autonomous and with its distinctive regime. The Greek treasured his unique city as much as he treasured his common Greekness, and did not think that common nationality required a single political organization encompassing and commanding the loyalty of all Greeks. Similarly, for nearly the whole of recorded history, right up until quite recent times, most wars took place not between different national groups, but either between great empires or between tribes, regions, and cities of kindred nationality. Struggles were either cosmopolitan or local, not nationalistic. Admittedly, the war between the Jews and the Philistines provides an early example of nationalist conflict—complete even to the use of inflammatory propaganda—but the case is anomalous.

We live so fully enclosed in the circle of nationalism that we can hardly see beyond it. Hence, it is useful to emphasize just how recent the phenomenon is. Up until only yesterday in China, family and clan set the horizons of loyalty. What we call Italy and Germany have been unified states for less than a century. When George Washington said "my country," he meant Virginia, a usage which persisted until some time after the revolution of 1776. Our own civil war was the greatest nationalist struggle of the nineteenth century.[14] The South surely had the better of the Constitutional argument, and only arms could clear the way for the definition of the American polity as an "indestructible Union, composed of indestructible States" (*Texas* v. *White*, 1869).

Vast changes in the foundations of social life were required for the appearance and triumph of nationalism, changes that in sum amount to a characterization of modernity. The decline of religious faith as the basic bond among people and as the primary source of cultural life prepared the way. So too did the breakdown of cultural isolation consequent upon the development of improved means of travel and communication. These gave persons experience of others who before had hardly been present. Up until very recently, the whole territory inhabited by what we would today call a nationality, a territory often characterized by great variety of climate, land forms, and customs, was practically unknown to ordinary persons. It could become known only through travel or instruction, and these were restricted to a tiny minority. Another force decisive in the production of nationalism was the (still continuing) consolidation and growth of centralized state power. By imposing the same laws and officers on large numbers of people, by subjecting those people to the same historical experiences, the great monarchies of England, France, Sweden, and Prussia, and the huge republic of the United States were instrumental in producing common attitudes and traits among a large population. In time, this formed what is loosely called a national character—a thing real enough, though hard to define, and by no means immutable: the French used to think the English riotous. The centralized state simultaneously molded national character and claimed to be its sole legitimate defender and spokesman.

Another factor in the production of nationalism was the dissolution of the monarchical and dynastic principle of political legitimacy. Modern nationalism is inconceivable without the idea of popular sovereignty as the base of political legitimacy, and without the breakup of the feudal and monarchical orders. Popular sovereignty promised that the ruled would henceforth be the rulers. When the disintegration of the old order was completed, and societies became aggregates of individuals, then nationalism became the cement which held these particles together, and popular sovereignty the myth that told them they were now in charge of their own futures.

In our own day, a number of forces have given nationalism new vitality, and further corrupted the primary meanings of patriotism. One such force is the fiction that blood or race is the biological source of nationality and the basic bond among human groups. Another is the doctrine that sees the *Volks-geist* as the ever-welling fountain of nationality in all of its cultural and political manifestations. Still a third is the conviction on the part of certain nations—a conviction fostered by propaganda always and by terror and repression when necessary—that they are the bearers of precious cultural and biological seeds which must be safeguarded against enemies and planted among the unconvinced and the ignorant. Under the crusading impact of these ideas, nationalism in recent times has been a force almost wholly productive of death and exploitation.

We are still in the middle of the story of nationalism. No one can say where it will end, how long it will last, or whether it is even compatible with the survival of civilization. Two contrary tendencies vie at the moment. On the one hand, the formation of dozens of new states since World War II has meant the spread of nationalism on a world scale. On the other hand, in the older states of Europe and to a lesser degree in the United States, nationalism is ebbing. State centralization continues apace, certainly, but more under the cool logic of technology and rationalization than under the hot ideology of nationalism. But no new cohesive or cementing forces which might take the place of nationalism are yet visible (even such supranationalist ideologies as socialism and race are bent to nationalist ends), and it is doubtful whether nationalist faiths will disappear until other faiths arise to replace them.

The task of the patriot today, I think, at least in the United States, is to work to weaken the principle of nationalism and to cut its connections with the state. Nationality can be severed from nationalism, and nationalism can be depoliticized—just as religion was. No one can say if or when that day will arrive, but the struggle to hasten it is perhaps the most worthy political struggle of our time. Through that struggle, people might begin to rebuild the conditions for patriotism, and to revitalize the life-giving devotion for the things of the homeplace, a devotion whose absence now leaves us all displaced persons—tribeless, homeless, heartless ones bounced between a narrow egotism on the one side and an unsustaining universalism on the other, to be caught by a fierce nationalism in the middle.[15]

SOME OBJECTIONS:
HISTORICAL, MORAL, PSYCHOLOGICAL

At the outset, I described certain obstacles in the path of an argument for patriotism, acknowledged their severity, and promised to return to them.

1. Some will object to the word itself. It is a fact that the word does not appear in English usage until 1726 (though all the "ism" words are relatively recent; *nationalism*, for example, does not appear until 1844). Thus, it seems risky to associate the term with primitive emotions and ancient political experiences, as I have done. Furthermore, the banner of patriotism has been waved by at least as many scoundrels as noble men: for every Lincoln there is a Stalin. Hence, it seems risky to recommend a revival of the word and the emotion.

I admit these troubles with the word, but no other will do. Just because the word is new is no evidence that the thing is: there were viruses before there was a word for them. Besides, when Lincoln (and he was not the only one) said "patriotism" he meant something noble and interesting.

It won't do to banish words because we dislike some of their associations. Most rich words are a little rank. Of course language is often confusing, but it is also the most wonderful expression of our humanity. When we banish a word or truncate its meaning, we also truncate ourselves. There is a good bit of evidence that our humanity is today being abbreviated by this process.

It might also be politically dangerous to banish the word, because we may need it someday. Suppose the president were to suspend the writ of habeas corpus for persons opposed to his Court appointments. We might consider it our patriotic duty to resist; and if we did, we would probably see ourselves as acting in the tradition set by patriotic forefathers—taking the mantle of Jefferson, for example, who called upon his countrymen to fight for the ancient rights of Englishmen. We would be much weaker politically if that patriotic argument and tradition were not available to us.

Hence, it is right and prudent to keep the word alive, and to recommend the experience. Ben Johnson called patriots "sound lovers of their country." I want to restore that sense of the word.

2. Readers might be willing to let me use the word as I want, but they might still argue that the taint of history cannot be removed from it. Specifically, patriotism has been so tied up with nationalism and all its horrors in the modern age that the two can never be separated. Prussian officers served the Nazi state out of patriotism. General Curtis B. LeMay proposed bombing Vietnam into the Stone Age out of patriotism. In recent American politics, the only man who talks more about patriotism than President Nixon is Governor Wallace. Patriotism and nationalism are inextricably linked in modern history, and both spell ignorance and hate.

In response, one would say first that it is not satisfactory here to reel off the names of monsters: for every scoundrel who called himself a patriot one could name a good man who also claimed the name. The enemies of nationalism, fighting against the state and for their families, their city, their land, or their conception of a just society—such have called themselves patriots, too.

Certainly some ignorant and cruel people have claimed the name of patriot, but that does not mean that ignorance, cruelty, and patriotism are all the same. We really do use different words for the different phenomena. Few today would call Senator Joseph McCarthy a patriot—vicious perhaps, a fool possibly, but not a patriot. As for ignorance, there are of course ignorant patriots as well as ignorant nationalists. But there are also sophisticated versions of each. It does not help thought to collapse the words or the things.

Moreover, I think that the modes of knowledge and ignorance characteristic of nationalism and patriotism are different. The knowledge of the patriot, especially of the natural patriot, is rich in memory or history and is solid and sensuous in its texture. This kind of knowledge is concrete and conservative. Its emotional tone is made up of reverence mixed with nostalgia. Such knowledge has little of the abstract about it and is not easily packaged for export. Hence, its main military expression is characteristically defense against invaders. It does not claim universality, and patriots do not comfortably support wars of expansion or wars of "principle." Edmund Burke, whose writings embody all these characteristics of patriotic thought, defended one revolution and opposed another, precisely on the grounds that the one was conservative and concrete while the other was abstract and universalist in its claims. What is today called "people's war" can only succeed when the military fish can swim in the sea of the people. That is to say, people's war is defensive and local. I think this is the kind of war characteristic of patriotism. Should it turn out that people's war, rightly conducted, has the capacity to endure and prevail against huge invading forces, that could show the way to tremendous change in world history—a real shift in the balance between nationalism and patriotism.

Nationalism, on the other hand, is rich in the knowledge of instrumental rationality, the knowledge needed to define the properties of the world as resources and to convert those resources into power. The organization of the nation-state is the political expression of the process of technique, as Jacques Ellul calls it, the process of systematically converting the things of the world into resources of power. Consider this passage from Karl Polanyi's discussion of the early stages of the modern nation-state:

> Politically, the centralized state was a new creation . . . which . . . compelled the backward peoples of larger agrarian countries to organize for commerce and trade. In external politics, the setting up of sovereign power was the need of the day; accordingly, mercantilist statecraft involved the marshaling of the resources of the whole national territory to the purposes of power in foreign affairs. In internal politics, unification of the countries fragmented by feudal and municipal particularism was the necessary by-product of such an endeavor.[16]

That is to say, nationalism was specifically built out of the rubble of patriotism, and the chief tool in the destruction was instrumental rationality systematically employed to convert the world into resources for economic and political power.

Very early in its progress the nation-state added ideology to its armory of weapons for aggression and expansion. Those ideologies have been many, but each claims that it is not partial, so that the expansion of the nation-state can be presented as something other than the victory of the stronger. Ideology lets the nation-state parade its might and cloak its ambition as the embodiment of a universal principle. From G. W. F. Hegel to W. W. Rostow the process has been the same. "Modernization" is our version of Hegel's idealization of the Prussian State. Like very good nationalist ideology, it ranks the U.S. number one on a universal scale of values and is made for export to other countries.

Patriots make no such claims to universality, and, in that way at least, are wise in their ignorance.

Certainly there can be a patriotism more "advanced" than devotion to place alone, more devoted to ideals and principles, which is still not aggressive and expansionist. That kind of patriotism can even believe its own principles superior and yet feel no missionary urge to impose them on others. The New England Puritan intention to build a "city on a hill" is one example; Lincoln's vision of America as a promise and hope to the oppressed everywhere is another; Bourne's idea of a transnational America based on mutual respect and acceptance of variety is a third. This patriotism can have a teaching mission, but the teaching is done by example: others will see the shining city and take from it such light as they need.

We need a principle of political loyalty that can keep alive a noble tension between love for one's own place and respect for the places of others. It is very difficult for either the militant nationalist or the promiscuous universalist to honor that tension. Both of them smash through the complexities of cultural diversity, reducing them to a principle: for the nationalist, the principle is "ours is superior to the others"; for the universalist, the principle is "all are equal." The obscurantism and aggressiveness of the former obviously produce injustice. So does the eclecticism which rejects nothing, though here the injustice is less obvious. If a group within a foreign society which we will not judge protests against an injustice within its own social order, shall we still not judge? Suppose the same injustice should exist among ourselves. Have we any right to oppose it at home if we kept silent when we saw it abroad? The position of critic at home but conformist elsewhere, and the position of conformist at home but critic elsewhere, are equally contradictory and productive of injustice.

I think the patriotic mentality has a fair chance of keeping the noble tension alive. To be a patriot means to live out of a recognition that one is a member of a particular society and culture. But so are all other human beings, and their particular memberships are as important to them as ours are to us. Hence, there is no contradiction—only a tension—between taking up one's particular place and acknowledging one's condition as a member of humanity, for each member of humanity has a local habitation. We may believe that other societies, or some other society, are not as good as our own. But even if we believe that, we have no method for proving it. Recognizing that no society can be judged absolutely good or absolutely evil, it is still possible to treasure our own, even while criticizing it, and to judge others', even while respecting them. Toward all other societies than one's own one may take up a privileged position, as it were, liking them or not, as one wishes. One's own society is the only one in which one must be involved, and from which one must struggle for disengagement: there is no privileged position possible here, only the necessities of social existence. The patriot, I think, easily grasps this lesson, and easily applies it to his thinking about other peoples. Patriots know, for example — and the knowledge is almost instinctive — that only residents, not outsiders, can radically change a society's ways and customs without wrecking the society, for the changes are made from within, and that makes all the difference. This attitude by no means denies, though it admittedly does not indiscriminately encourage, borrowing from other cultures to improve one's own. At the same time, the patriotic orientation is basically conservative. Indeed, the emotion itself seems a throwback to what Rousseau called that "middle ground between the indolence of the primitive state and the questing activity" of the expansionist and technological states. Perhaps that middle condition really was, as Rousseau held, the "best for man." Perhaps too the emotions peculiar to it were healthier than the emotions associated with both the nationalism and the universalism of our day.[17]

So, it is possible and important to distinguish between patriotism and nationalism; or, more specifically, to break the confused connection between patriotism and the modern nation-state. If the whole world were to become American territory (or Russian, or Japanese, etcetera) the conception of the American state as we know it would become unnecessary. But the conception of the community will never be discarded. The word "state" represents (usually) hostile divisions of the earth, and signifies the progressive formation of connections among villages, cities, and regions. This development occurs in response to the need of all men to live together, and in response to the urge of some men to dominate that living together. But if all the boundary lines representing states were erased, and the state as we know it disappeared, the conception of the community would not be threatened. It will exist as long as mankind exists. Patriotism is the emotion and bond characteristic of community. Hence, it too will exist, in more-or-less pure form, as long as humanity exists. Nationalism is an aberration.[18]

3. Why bother to separate patriotism from nationalism, its bloody brother? Why not let both die their historical deaths, while we look and work toward other modes of unity? Today, we are called to be neither patriots nor nationalists, but something more cosmopolitan and more hopeful than both.

The two most frequently recommended alternatives are international (socialist) class consciousness, and internationalism as such. I shall deal with the former only in passing, because I believe it to be a feckless alternative, and that for two reasons. First, World War I showed the weakness of the dream of international class solidarity when confronted by the reality of nationalism. Secondly, there are many kinds of socialists, and there is no inherent incompatibility between being a socialist and being a patriot. Eugene V. Debs was a profound patriot, and so was Ho Chi Minh. Mao Tse-Tung is a patriot, and so is Fidel Castro. I am inclined to judge, on the evidence, that any socialist who thinks his socialism has nothing to do with any special place or special people is either foolish, or dangerous, or both. The examples are legion, beginning with Robert Owen's villages of cooperation, each a tidy parallelogram, relentlessly projected across all the spaces of the New and Old Worlds, even into the backcountry of Bolivia, where they might bump against the *focos* of Che Guevara and Regis Debray. The history of the Comintern provides a particularly instructive chapter.

Internationalism, however, seems more promising. Some varieties of it are very old, e.g., the cosmopolitanism of the ancient Stoics and Epicureans. Others, of greater interest and importance today, are newer. Examples here are the projects of Kant and the Abbé de Saint-Pierre for world peace achieved through international administrative institutions. There is a direct line of descent from those proposals to the United Nations Organization and the World Federalist movement of our day, with certain contemporary "functionalist" theorists of integration not far off to the side.

These are the responses of humane and enlightened people to the horrors of war and the complexities of living in an ever-shrinking and more crowded world. The great dangers we face if we do not become more international are strong reasons for trying to become so. Obviously, we must have nuclear disarmament. With the threat of annihilation removed, we might then go on to deal with the problems of disease, hunger, crowding, sane and equitable use of world resources, and so forth. Simple patriots, many will say, are not equal to such tasks. They are too narrow in their loyalties, too old-fashioned in their outlooks. We need people of broader views and sharper skills. Patriots, indeed, are part of the problem, rather than part of the solution.

These are serious points. Patriotism obviously costs too much if its price is world peace and justice. I have no arguments that will convert the internationalist—none, even, that satisfy myself. Only a few thoughts that might put the debate on a sounder footing.

First of all, I am not sure that patriots by their nature oppose treaties of disarmament or arms regulations. Nationalists are more likely to do that, if their state is one of the mighty ones. One who rightly loves his country is not eager to see it blown up. Secondly, there are forms of internationalism that are entirely congenial to patriots. An American patriot can enjoy French wine and Russian novels and Greek philosophy as much as anyone else can. More than that, a patriot can have genuine toleration and even respect for other peoples, and an earnest wish that they share equally with him in the blessings of justice and liberty. Thomas Jefferson and Tom Paine, devoted American patriots, were also in this sense devoted internationalists, and saw no clash between the two. They were right, and they might still serve as models of enlightened patriotism.

Those points are worth making, but they do not go to the heart of the matter. That is found in the basic character of the actual internationalizing forces of today, and of the internationalist schemes that are proposed as responses to those forces.

It is a *fact* that the world today is small, crowded, and explosive. But what has produced that fact? Regardless of one's political outlook, the basic answer has to be technology, with some help from imperialism and cupidity. The main expressions and agents of internationalization today are the multinational corporation, propaganda, neocolonialist development and exploitation of weak countries, expansion of the technological mode of production into new territories, highly technologized military systems capable of dealing death at a distance, ruthless destruction of "backward" peoples and cultures, the increasing standardization of life, and meaningless tourism. These are not lovely things. Let's agree to call them, at best, mixed blessings. Surely they have not made the world more peaceful. Nor have they improved the quality of life. On the contrary. The forces that are pushing us toward international uniformity are sterile and life denying. It is not clear to me that we should enlist under this banner.

Patriotism, I have tried to argue, is less a program and a set of forces than a way or style of being in the world. The patriot keeps his eye on the past, on places and things, on traditions. For these reasons, patriotism is often called conservative. It *is* conservative, although it is perfectly possible for a conservative patriot to be a revolutionary. Today, a care for roots is genuinely revolutionary and is connected with freedom: it can slow down the rush toward chaos powered by the innovating, internationalizing forces of our time. I am of course aware that innovations can be rich and human, but it is obvious that most of them today are not. Rather, they partake of the machines whose children they are. Compared to the technological outlook, patriotism is a complexly human and rich idea, connected with life, supportive of liberty and diversity.

In sum, I am suggesting that most internationalism today has utterly confused humanity and its possibilities with technology and its possibilities. No doubt, technology has unified the world in a thousand ways, producing a call on the part of many humane people for world law and the brotherhood of man. But it would be more straightforward for the internationalist to speak less about the brotherhood of man and more about the standardization of the technological order, for it is a brute fact that technology has destroyed and is destroying hundreds of forms of human life. It is a cruel confusion to call that brotherhood, unless one holds that brotherhood can appear only after those who were different are dead.[19]

There are, of course, a few actual tribes and primitive peoples left on the planet, and a handful of older cultures not yet hopelessly debauched. My patriotic recommendation is to leave them alone. No aid; no anthropologists; no tourists.

A MODEST PROGRAM

I have argued throughout that patriotism is a way of being in the world, rather than a doctrine or program of action. Still, one might suggest a few programmatic steps which, to recall Susan Sontag's words, might help to "revalidate the tarnished idea of patriotism."

The main thing is to strengthen the bonds among ourselves, specifically the bonds of common projects and participation in common situations. Given our reality, that strengthening will require a huge effort to decentralize and to simplify the gigantic structures that now dominate every sector of society — work, education, communications, government. "All Power to the Fragments!" — that, I think, is the right watchword. Everywhere we look today the tendency of power to autonomize itself, to cut itself off from its subjects and become an alien force over them, grows apace.[20] That tendency is always basic to complex social systems and may even be an inevitable law of their nature. We must struggle to devise institutions capable of checking power without canceling it. On the theoretical level, that will require the development of conceptions of authority and community appropriate to our time, and able to supplant the alienating conceptions and practices which now prevail. On the practical level, it will require endless experimentation with and reflection on new ways of living and working together, especially ways that emphasize community, simplicity, and stability.

Education must be approached as a task of preparing persons for freedom and participation. Local and ethnic history should have a large place in the curriculum, and history should be taught not as the flow of some process, but as accounts of decision, action, and conflict, stories of times when people rose above the ordinary and tried to take charge of their lives, thereby doing something memorable in the world. Nothing should be done to encourage on the part of the individual the sense that "someone else is in charge, and I just live here." Everything possible should be done to dismantle the educational bureaucracy and break the stranglehold of officialdom on education. Encourage nonpublic educational ventures: let a hundred flowers bloom.

We must also begin to move toward what must almost be called a revolution of competence in the arts of daily living, so that we no longer stand helpless among our machines and organizations, stupefied by our own productions. This will require a disciplined austerity in material things, the reduction of luxury, and the suppression by moral and educational means of idle consumption and display. We must reduce the intricacies and rigidities of the division of labor, and we must reject the gods of efficiency and comfort. Everything that teaches us to regard the earth as a home, rather than as a mine, must be encouraged. Simplify. Stabilize. Develop personal and small community landscapes. Combat consumerism.

On a more theoretical level, we must formulate new answers to the question, under what conditions does inequality of power and status not pave the way to—or even mean the same as—exploitation and domination? Our slogan of equality of opportunity has shown itself to be a false answer to this question, setting persons against each other as it does, falsifying and obscuring the real grounds of the inequalities among us. But that must not mean throwing out the question with the answer, thereby sinking into the squalid promiscuity that says anything goes and all desires are equal.

Finally, we must rework the swarm of questions around the troubled theme of the relations between vanguard and main army in the struggle for radical change. It is a rock-bottom fact of our condition that if opinions are consulted and votes counted, there will be no radical change. The forces that are transforming the United States today are so basic and pervasive—the chaotic release of energy, the exploitative disruption of all natural and human networks—that they cannot be formulated or mastered in narrowly political terms. What is needed is a new social mind, as Henry Adams called it, a social mind centered on conservation, variety, and balance. That kind of change cannot be deliberately and rapidly introduced and supervised by the few, nor implemented from the top down. A supervised revolution can only enlarge police and administration.

The main activity, then, must be educational. But the education cannot be limited to the writing and speaking of alternative views. The most powerful political-moral teaching combines action and knowledge. Resistance, for example, opens up a space in the political world which would not otherwise have been there. Once open, it remains forever after a possibility, a course which once was taken and which might once again be taken. Action becomes part of history, and is thus available for rediscovery in the future. Nor is the scope of the action the most important factor here: consider the importance in American—even world—history of Thoreau's night in jail. It is enormously important to keep intact the memory of such actions of resistance. One of the greatest weaknesses of the New Left in the 1960s was that the thread had been broken. There really was a silent generation cutting off the 1960s from the 1930s. No matter how thin the thread becomes, it must never be permitted to break. Keeping it intact does not of course assure or constitute success, but it is sufficient reason for acting. Without memory, there is no identity. ("The seat of mind is in memory," as St. Augustine said.) Patriots, I have argued, specialize in that form of knowledge which is memory of action. That is part of their radicalism, especially in an age which grows more and more mindless.

Finally, if political education is to be effective it must grow from a spirit of humility on the part of the teachers, and they must overcome the tendencies toward self-righteousness and self-pity which set the tone of youth and student politics in the 1960s.[21] The teachers must acknowledge common origins and common burdens with the taught, stressing connection and membership, rather than distance and superiority. Only from those roots can trust and hopeful common action grow.

NOTES

1. Susan Sontag, *Trip to Hanoi* (New York: Farrar, Straus and Giroux, 1968), p. 82.

2. The words are Manuelito's, a chief of the Navaho, describing the return of his people to their ancestral lands. Quoted here from Dee Brown, *Bury My Heart at Wounded Knee* (New York: Holt, Rinehart and Winston, 1971), p. 35.

3. The early Christians were poor patriots. Their monotheism killed the lesser gods, denuding the land of sacred groves and local shrines. Machiavelli also thought that the Christians were poor patriots.

4. See chapter 1, "The Spirit of Place," in D. H. Lawrence's *Studies in Classic American Literature* for a suggestive development of this theme.

5. These lines were written on Thanksgiving Day, one of the purest of American holidays. And yet, there are complexities to be remembered here as well. The Puritans had not only days of thanksgiving but days of penance too, and they were reluctant to routinize high occasions. They remembered that their plenty was a gift. And what of the Indians? There is not enough whiskey in the land to drown their pain on this day when the conquerors feast.

6. Fred Branfman, *Voices from the Plain of Jars: Life Under an Air War* (New York: Harper and Row, 1972). Quoted here from *New York Review of Books* 19, no. 2 (August 10, 1972): 20.

7. *Democracy in America*, vol. 1 (New York: Schocken, 1961), p. 282.

8. Roy P. Basler, ed., *Collected Works of Abraham Lincoln*, vol. 4 (New Brunswick, N.J.: Rutgers University Press, 1953), p. 240.

9. Lincoln returned time and again to this theme of forgetting, nowhere more powerfully than in his great speech at Peoria (October 16, 1854) where he argued that the Nebraska bill was but one more step along the path whereby "little by little, but steadily as man's march to the grave, we have been giving up the *Old* for the *New* faith." Ibid., vol. 2, p. 275.

10. This mission used to matter to others elsewhere in the world. A report from Russia: "On the morning of the Fourth of July, 1876 . . . hundreds of small, rude American flags or strips of red, white and blue cloth fluttered from the grated windows of the [political prisoners] around the whole quadrangle of the great St. Petersburg prison. . . ." Reported in Ira Woods Howerth, "Patriotism, Instinctive and Intelligent" (1912); quoted here as reprinted in Maurice G. Fulton, ed., *National Ideals and Problems* (Freeport, N.Y.: Books for Libraries Press, 1968), p. 213.

11. I want to call the reader's attention to Randolph Bourne's essay "Trans-National America" in Bourne, *War and the Intellectuals*, ed. and with introduction by Carl Resek (New York: Harper Torchbooks, 1964), pp. 107–24. It is the only American writing on patriotism known to me that is not shamed by Lincoln's understanding of the matter.

12. For a more sanguine account of the development of American patriotism than the one which follows, see Merle Curti, *The Growth of American Thought*, 3d ed. (New York: Harper and Row, 1966), chap. 16.

13. The seed of the following analysis comes from G. K. Chesterton's crotchety and brilliant essay in his *What I Saw in America* (London: Hodder and Stoughton, 1922), chap. 1.

14. See Edmund Wilson's introductory essay in his *Patriotic Gore* (New York: Oxford University Press, 1962).

15. The patriot who needs texts for this work might find them in Abraham Lincoln and Mary Parker Follett: Lincoln for the principles of the covenant; Follett for the practices of organization and action. I shall return to this matter of program at the end of the essay.

16. Karl Polanyi, *The Great Transformation* (Boston: Beacon Press, 1957), p. 65.

17. Claude Levi-Strauss, *Tristes Tropiques*, trans. John Russell (New York: Atheneum, 1967), pp. 381–93, makes a powerfully suggestive argument that Rousseau really was right on this matter. I am indebted to Levi-Strauss for many of the ideas in the foregoing paragraphs.

18. I owe this argument to C. Douglas Lummis, who drew it from Gondo Seikyo, a Japanese agrarian anarchist of the prewar period.

19. R. Buckminster Fuller is a great internationalist and a great prophet of technological unification. Anyone who thinks I have overstated the deadly confusion of technological with human possibilities should read his works. Start with *Operating Manual for Spaceship Earth* (Carbondale, Ill.: Southern Illinois Press, 1969). (Lewis Mumford thinks the place of publication must be an editorial error, for "such a manual could come only from Heaven.")

20. See Maurice Merleau-Ponty, *Signs*, trans. Richard C. McCleary (Evanston, Ill.: Northwestern University Press, 1964), p. 223.

21. "God we were smug and self-righteous," Dotson Rader has recently said of the Freedom Riders, "no wonder the crackers hated us." (*I Ain't Marchin' Anymore*, 1969, p. 16.) And no wonder they still do, when the author, professing a new self-knowledge, can still call them crackers. The cracker has little reason for trying to distinguish between high-minded and low-minded carpetbaggers. SNCC soon reached the same conclusion. The ecology movement, largely upper-middle-class in composition, has been insufferably high-minded and self-righteous, and unwilling even to consider the economic impact of their proposals on the lower classes. The lower classes have lived with pollution for a long time. The upper middle classes became aware of it when their playgrounds were threatened.

Chapter Fourteen
MICHAEL WALZER

CIVILITY AND CIVIC VIRTURE IN CONTEMPORARY AMERICA

*D*ecline and fall is the most common historical perception, even among intellectuals. I want to examine this perception in its most important contemporary form, which is also a recurrent form. "We have physicists, geometers, chemists, astronomers, poets, musicians, painters," wrote Rousseau in 1750, "we no longer have citizens. . . ."[1] Here in the United States we still do have citizens, but it is frequently said of them that their commitment to the political community is less profound than it once was, that there has been a decline of civic virtue and even of ordinary civility, an erosion of the moral and political qualities that make a good citizen. It is hard to know how to judge statements of this kind. They suggest comparisons without specifying any historical reference point. They seem to be prompted by a variety of tendencies and events which are by no means uniform in character or necessarily connected: the extent of draft resistance during the Vietnam War, the domestic violence of the middle and late 1960s, the recent challenges to academic freedom, the new acceptance of pornography, the decline in the fervor with which national holidays are celebrated, and so on.

Perhaps one way of judging these (and other) phenomena is to ask what it is we expect of citizens — of citizens in general but also of American citizens in particular, members of a liberal democracy, each of whom represents, as Rousseau would have said, only 1/200,000,000th of the general will. What do we expect of one another? I am going to suggest a list of common expectations; I shall try to make it an exhaustive list. Working our way through it, we shall see that we are the citizens we ought to be, given the social and political order in which we live. And if critics of our citizenship remain dissatisfied, then it will be time to ask how that order might be changed.

From *Social Research* 41 (1974): 593–611. Copyright © 1974 New School of Social Research. Reprinted by permission of *Social Research*.

LOYALTY, SERVICE, CIVILITY

1. We expect some degree of commitment or loyalty—but to what? Not to *la patrie*, the fatherland; that concept has never captured the American imagination, probably because, until very recently, so many of us were fathered in other lands. Not to the nation; the appearance of an American nationality was for a long time the goal of our various immigrant absorption systems, but this goal has stood in some tension with the practical (and now with the ideological) pluralism of our society. Most of those who mourn our lost civility would not, I think, be happy with an American nationalism. Not to the state, conceived abstractly, but to a particular kind of state: our allegiance is to the republic. Now that is a very special kind of commitment, stripped of the mystical connotations of loyalty in Old World countries. We stand, partly by necessity, partly by choice, on narrower ground. Ours is a political allegiance, and our politics is Judaic or puritan in character; it does not lend itself to ritualistic elaboration. Our holidays are occasions for speeches, not for ceremonial communions; our inaugurations are without sacramental significance. We are (rightly) unwilling to make spectacles of our celebrations, and for that reason it has been virtually impossible to adapt them to the needs of a mass society. There is a certain cynicism today about the symbolic expressions of American loyalty—perhaps because no one can imagine 200,000,000 people celebrating the Fourth of July, simultaneously and together, in some way that isn't repellent to liberal sensibilities. Surely it is a commendable feature of our public life that we do not press the occasion upon our citizens.

Our passivity in this regard probably has something to do with the triumph of secularism in the republic. The content of many American celebrations— Memorial Day and Thanksgiving, for example—is or was markedly religious in character and must lose much of its resonance as religion loses its hold. On the other hand, we have always denied that any particular religious belief or even religious belief in general was necessary in an American citizen. Now that denial is being tested, not as to its justice, but as to its practicality. Understandably, people are worried, for it is often said that loyalty has to be collectively symbolized and acted out if it is to be sustained. The appropriate symbols and actions, however, must grow naturally out of our common life; they cannot be invented, conjured up, pulled out of a politician's hat. If we have not tried to substitute the goddess Reason for the Christian God, as Robespierre tried to do in France, surely that too is to our credit. But the symbols and actions don't grow naturally, and liberal loyalty seems to be sustained in some other way— not through communal celebrations but through private enjoyments, as writers like John Locke undoubtedly intended. One gets a different kind, and perhaps a different degree, of loyalty then, but there is no reason to think that one doesn't get the kind and degree a liberal republic requires.

2. We expect citizens to defend their country, even to risk their lives in its

defense. In American lore, the minuteman, who rushes to arms when his country is in danger, long ago came to represent the citizen at his best. But it has to be said that this colonial hero and his successors, the militiamen of the nineteenth century, were essentially volunteers who did not always agree with the politicians in the capital or even with their local commanders as to when the country was in danger. They claimed a kind of local option which was for years the despair of American military planners.[2] Nor is it, after all, any sign of civic virtue merely to rush to arms. In August 1914, Austrians and Germans, Frenchmen and Englishmen, flooded the enlistment offices, but we would not want to explain their military enthusiasm by reference to the quality of their citizenship. Indeed, in an earlier America, the readiness of the inhabitants of the Old World to die at the behest of their states and sovereigns would more likely have been understood as a sign of the poverty of their lives and their lack of moral independence. The same attitude explains the old American hatred of conscription. It was thought an infringement of individual liberty and a sure sign of tyrannical government when family and home were invaded and young men dragged off to war. When James Monroe, then Secretary of War, first proposed a draft in 1814, Daniel Webster assured him that the country would not stand for it:

> In my opinion, Sir, the sentiments of the free population of this country are greatly mistaken here. The nation is not yet in a temper to submit to conscription. The people have too fresh and strong a feeling of the blessings of civil liberty to be willing thus to surrender it. . . . Laws, Sir, of this nature can create nothing but opposition. A military force cannot be raised, in this manner, but by the means of a military force. If the administration has found that it cannot form an army without conscription, it will find, if it ventures on these experiments, that it cannot enforce conscription without an army.[3]

We have come a long way since those days, a way marked as much by changes in the external world as in our domestic society. The domestic changes have been made only gradually and, as Webster predicted, in the face of constant opposition. It is worth remembering how recent a creation the docile draftee is before we mourn his disappearance (has he disappeared?) as a loss of American virtue. In 1863, the first conscription law was fiercely resisted — over one thousand people died in the New York draft riot of that year — and it was massively evaded during the remainder of the Civil War. The draft was still being evaded on a large scale in World War I, particularly in rural areas where it was easy to hide. And who can say that the young men who took to the woods in 1917 were not reaffirming the values of an earlier America? They would have grabbed their rifles readily enough had the Boche marched into Kentucky. Perhaps that is the only true test of their citizenship.

The citizen-soldier defends his hearth and home, and he also defends the political community within which the enjoyment of hearth and home is made possible. His fervor is heightened when that community is in danger. Armies of citizens, like those of Rome or the first French Republic or Israel today, are born in moments of extreme peril. Once the peril abates, the fervor declines. The armies of great powers must be sustained on a different basis, and the long-term considerations that lead them to fight here or there, in other people's countries, when there is no immediate or visible threat to their own, can hardly be expected to evoke among their citizens a passionate sense of duty. Perhaps these citizens have an obligation to fight, in obedience, say, to laws democratically enacted, but this is not the same obligation that American publicists meant to stress when they made the minuteman a mythic figure. It has more to do with law-abidance than with civic courage or dedication.

3. We expect citizens to obey the law and to maintain a certain decorum of behavior—a decorum which is commonly called civility. That word once had to do more directly with the political virtues of citizenship: one of its obsolescent meanings is "civil righteousness." But it has come increasingly to denote only social virtues; orderliness, politeness, seemliness are the synonyms the dictionary suggests, and these terms, though it is no doubt desirable that they describe our public life, orient us quite decisively toward the private realm. Perhaps this shift in meaning is a sign of our declining dedication to republican values, but it actually occurred some time ago and does not reflect on ourselves and our contemporaries. For some time, we have thought that *good behavior* is what we could rightly expect from a citizen, and the crucial form of good behavior is everyday law-abidance. Has this expectation been disappointed? Certainly many people write as if it has been. I am inclined to think them wrong, though not for reasons that have much to do with republican citizenship.

If we could measure the rate and intensity of obedience to law—not merely the nonviolation of the penal code, but the interest, the concern, the anxiety with which citizens *aim* at obedience—I am certain we would chart a fairly steady upward movement in every modernizing country, at least after the initial crisis of modernization is past. Contemporary societies require and sustain a very intense form of social discipline, and this discipline is probably more pervasive and more successfully internalized than was that of peasant societies or of small towns and villages. We have only to think about our own lives to realize the extent of our submission to what Max Weber called "rational-legal authority." It is reflected in our time sense, our ability to work hard and methodically, our acceptance of bureaucratic hierarchies, our habitual orientation to rules and regulations. Consider, for example, the simple but surprising fact that each of us will, before April 15, carefully fill out a government form detailing our incomes and calculating the tax we owe the United States—which we will then promptly pay. The medieval tithe, if it was ever a realistic tax, was socially enforced; our own tax is individually enforced. We ourselves are the calculators and the collectors; the tax system could not succeed without our conscientiousness. Surely the American income tax is a triumph of civilization. There are very few political orders within which one can imagine such a system working; I doubt that it would have worked, for example, in Tocqueville's America.

But I want to turn to two other examples of our relative civility which speak more directly to the concerns of our recent past, which have to do, that is, with violence. In 1901, David Brewer, an associate justice of the U.S. Supreme Court, delivered a series of lectures on American citizenship at Yale University, in the course of which he worried at some length about the prevalence of vigilante justice and lynch law.[4] This was the peculiarly American way of "not tarrying for the magistrate." "It may almost be regarded," Brewer said, "as a habit of the American people." Clearly, our habits have changed; in this respect, at least, we have grown more law-abiding since the turn of the century. The police sometimes take the law into their own hands, but they are our only vigilantes; ordinary citizens rarely act in the old American way. This is not the result of a more highly developed civic consciousness, but it is a matter of improved social discipline, and it also suggests that, despite our popular culture, we are less ready for violence, less accustomed to violence, than were earlier generations of American citizens.

We are also less given to riot; if nineteenth-century statistics are at all reliable, our mobs are less dangerous to human life. The most striking thing about the urban riots of the 1960s, apart from the surprise which greeted them, for which our history offers no justification, is the relatively small number of people who were actually killed in their course. By all accounts, riots were once much bloodier: I have already mentioned New York's "bloody week" of 1863. They also seem to have been more exuberantly tumultuous, and the tumult more accepted in the life of the time. Here, for example, are a set of newspaper headlines from New York in 1834:[5]

A Bloody Fight
Mayor and Officers Wounded
Mob Triumphant
The Streets Blocked by Fifteen Thousand Enraged Whigs
Military Called Out

These lines describe an election riot, not uncommon in an age when party loyalties were considerably more intense than they are now and a far higher proportion of the eligible voters were likely to turn out on election day. The accompanying news story does not suggest that the rioters or their leaders were extremists or revolutionaries. They apparently were ordinary citizens. Our own riots were also the work of ordinary citizens, but not of the contemporary equivalents of Whigs, Orangemen, or even Know-Nothings. They seem to have been peculiarly disorganized, each of them less a communal event than a series of simultaneous acts of individual desperation. They were more frightening than the earlier riots and also less dangerous. Perhaps this change is appropriate to a liberal society: if civility is restrained and privatized, then so must incivility be.

This last example suggests a certain tension between civility and republican citizenship. Indeed, in the early modern period, one of the chief arguments against republicanism was that it made for disorder and tumult. Faction fights, party intrigue, street wars; instability and sedition: these were the natural forms of political life in what Thomas Hobbes called "the Greek and Roman anarchies," and so it would be, he argued, in any similar regime.[6] He may have been right, in some limited sense at least. The improvement in social discipline seems to have been accompanied by a decline in political passion, in that lively sense of public involvement which presumably characterized the enraged Whigs of 1834 and other early Americans. I shall have more to say about this when I turn to the general issue of political participation. But first it is necessary to take up another aspect of our new civility.

TOLERANCE, PARTICIPATION

4. We expect citizens to be tolerant of one another. This is probably as close as we can come to that "friendship" which Aristotle thought should characterize relations among members of the same political community. For friendship is only possible within a relatively small and homogeneous city, but toleration reaches out infinitely. Once certain barriers of feeling and belief have been broken down, it is as easy to tolerate five million people as to tolerate five. Hence toleration is a crucial form of civility in all modern societies and especially in our own. But it is not easily achieved. Much of the violence of American history has been the work of men and women resisting its advance in the name of one or another form of local and particularized friendship or in the name of those systems of hierarchy and segregation which served in the past to make pluralism possible. It's probably fair to say that resistance has grown weaker in recent years; the United States is a more tolerant society today than at any earlier period of its history. Of course, we need to be more tolerant; it's as if, once we commit ourselves to toleration, the demand for it escalates; it is no longer a question of a recognized range of religious and political dissidence, but of the margins beyond the range. Even the margins are safer today; more people live there and with less fear of public harassment and social pressure. It is precisely these people, however, who seem to pose a problem for us, who lead us to worry about the future of civic virtue. A curious and revealing fact, for their very existence is a sign of our civility.

The problem is that many Americans who find it easy (more or less) to tolerate racial and religious and even political differences find it very hard to tolerate sexual deviance and countercultural lifestyles. One day, perhaps, this difficulty will be remembered only as a passing moment in the painful development of an open society. But it doesn't feel that way now; it feels much more drastic, so that intelligent people talk of the end of civilization, all coherence gone, the fulfillment of this or that modernist nightmare. For surely (they say) political society requires and rests upon *some* shared values, a certain spiritual cohesion, however limited in character. And a commitment to moral laissez-faire does not provide any cohesion at all. It undermines the very basis of a common life, because the ethic of toleration leads us to make our peace with every refusal of commonality. So we drift apart, losing through our very acceptance of one another's differences all sense of kinship and solidarity.

This is undoubtedly overstated, for the fact is that we do coexist, not only Protestants, Catholics, and Jews; blacks and whites; but also Seventh-day Adventists, Buddhists, and Black Muslims; Birchers and Trotskyites; sexual sectarians of every sort, homo and hetero. Nor is it a small thing that we have made our peace with all these, for the only alternative, if history has any lessons at all, is cruelty and repression. Liberalism may widen our differences as it widens the range of permissible difference, but it also generates a pattern of accommodation that we ought to value. It would be foolish to value it, however, without noticing that, like other forms of civility, this pattern of accommodation is antithetical to political activism. It tends to insulate politics from group conflict, to promote among citizens a general indifference toward the opinions of their fellows, to freeze the intolerant out of public life (they are disproportionately represented, for example, among nonvoters). It stands in the way of the personal transformations and new commitments that might grow out of a more open pattern of strife and contention. It makes for political peace; it makes politics less dangerous and less interesting. And yet our notions about citizenship lead us to demand precisely that citizens *be interested* in politics.

5. We expect citizens to participate actively in political life. Republicanism is a form of collective self-government, and its success requires, at the very least, that large numbers of citizens vote and that smaller numbers join in parties and movements, in meetings and demonstrations. No doubt, such activity is in part self-regarding, but any stable commitment probably has to be based and is in fact usually based on some notion of the public good. It is, then, virtuous activity; interest in public issues and devotion to public causes are the key signs of civic virtue.

Voting is the minimal form of virtuous conduct, but it is also the easiest to measure, and if we take it as a useful index, we can be quite precise in talking about the character of our citizenship. Participation in elections, as Walter Dean Burnham has shown, was very high in the nineteenth century, not only in presidential contests, but also in off-year congressional and even in local elections.[7] Something like four-fifths of the eligible voters commonly went to the polls. "The nineteenth century American political system," writes Burnham, ". . . was incomparably the most thoroughly democratized of any in the world."

A sharp decline began around 1896 and continued through the 1920s, when the number of eligible voters actually voting fell to around two-fifths. Rates of participation rose in the 1930s, leveled off, rose again in the 1950s, leveled off again—without coming close to the earlier figures. Today, the percentage of American citizens who are consistent nonparticipants is about twice what it was in the 1890s. By this measure, then, we are less virtuous than were nineteenth-century Americans, less committed to the public business.

The reasons for this decline are not easy to sort out. Burnham suggests that it may have something to do with the final consolidation of power by the new industrial elites. The triumph of corporate bureaucracy was hardly conducive to a participatory politics among members of the new working class or among those farmers who had been the backbone of the Populist movement. Some workers turned to socialism (Debs got a million votes in 1912), but far more dropped out of the political system altogether. They became habitual nonvoters, at least until the CIO brought many of the men and women it organized back into electoral politics in the 1930s. If this account is right—and other accounts are possible—then nonvoting can be seen as a rational response to certain sorts of social change. No doubt it was also functional to the social system as a whole. The decline in participation during a period of increasing heterogeneity and rapid urbanization probably helped stabilize the emerging patterns of law-abidance and toleration. Certainly American society would have been far more turbulent than it was had new immigrants, urban dwellers, and industrial workers been actively involved in politics. That is not to argue that they shouldn't have been involved, only that people who set a high value on civility shouldn't complain about their lack of civic virtue.

A recent study of political acts more "difficult" than voting—giving money, attending meetings, joining organizations—suggests that there was a considerable increase in participation in the course of the 1960s.[8] Not surprisingly, this increase coincided with a period of turmoil and dissension of which it was probably both cause and effect. One might impartially have watched the events of that time and worried about the loss of civility and rejoiced in the resurgence of civic virtue. The connection between the two is clear enough: people are mobilized for political action, led to commit themselves and to make the sacrifices and take the risks commitment requires, only when significant public issues are enlarged by the agitators and organizers of movements and parties and made the occasion for exciting confrontations. These need not be violent confrontations; violence draws spectators more readily than participants. But if the issues are significant, if the conflict is serious, violence always remains a possibility. The only way to avoid the possibility is to avoid significant issues or to make it clear that the democratic political struggle is a charade whose outcome won't affect the resolution of the issues—and then rates of participation will quickly drop off.

The civil rights and antiwar agitations of the 1960s demonstrate that there are still dedicated citizens in the United States. But the activity generated by those movements turned out to be evanescent, leaving behind no organizational residue, no basis for an ongoing participatory politics. Perhaps that is because not enough people committed themselves. The national mood, if one focuses on the silence of the silent majority, is tolerant and passive—in much the same way as it was tolerant and passive in the face of prohibitionists or suffragettes or even socialists and communists in the 1930s: that is, there is no demand for massive repression and there is no major upsurge in political involvement. It is also important, I think, that the two movements of the sixties did not link up in any stable way with either of the established parties. Instead of strengthening party loyalty, they may well have contributed to a further erosion. If that is so, even rates of electoral participation will probably fall in the next few years, for parties are the crucial media of political activism. These two failures—to mobilize mass support, to connect with the established parties— may well suggest the general pattern of political life in America today. For most of our citizens, politics is no vocation. They think it a duty to vote, but they have no deep commitment to a creed or party, and only about half of them bother to vote. Beyond that, they are wrapped up in their private affairs and committed to the orderliness and proprieties of the private realm. Though they are tolerant, up to a point, of political activists, they regard politics as an intrusion and they easily resist the temptations of the arena. This makes life hard for the smaller number of citizens who are intermittently moved by some public issue and who seek to move their fellows. It may help explain the frenetic quality of their zeal and the way some of them drift, in extreme cases, into depression and madness. The institutional structures and the mass commitment necessary to sustain civic virtue simply don't exist in contemporary America.

PARTICIPATORY POLITICS

The ideals of citizenship do not today make a coherent whole. The citizen receives, so to speak, inconsistent instruction. Patriotism, civility, toleration, and political activism pull him in different directions. The first and last require a kind of zeal—that is, they require both passion and conviction—and they make for excitement and tumult in public life. It is often said that the worst wars are civil wars because they are fought between brethren. One might say something similar about republican politics: because it rests on a shared commitment, it is often more bitter and divisive than politics in other regimes. Civility and tolerance serve to reduce the tension, but they do so by undercutting the commitment. They encourage people to view their interests as fragmented, diverse, and private; they make for quiet and passive citizens, unwilling to intrude on others or to subject themselves to the discipline of a creed or party. I am not going to argue that we need choose in some absolute way one or the other of these forms of political life. What exists today and what will always exist is some balance between them. But the balance has changed over the years: we are, I think, more civil and less civically virtuous than Americans once were. The new balance is a liberal one, and there can be little doubt that it fits the scale and complexity of modern society and the forms of economic organization developed in the United States in the twentieth century. What has occurred is not a decline and fall but a working out of liberal values—individualism, secularism, toleration—and at the same time an adjustment to the demands of capitalist modernity.

The new citizenship, however, leaves many Americans dissatisfied. Liberalism, even at its most permissive, is a hard politics because it offers so few emotional rewards; the liberal state is not a home for its citizens; it lacks warmth and intimacy. And so contemporary dissatisfaction takes the form of a yearning for political community, passionate affirmation, explicit patriotism. These are dangerous desires, for they cannot readily be met within the world of liberalism. They leave us open to a politics I would find unattractive and even frightening: a willful effort to build social cohesion and political enthusiasm from above, as it were, through the use of state power. Imagine a charismatic leader, talking about American values and goals, making war on pornography and sexual deviance (and then on political and social deviance), establishing loyalty oaths and new celebrations, rallying the people for some real or imagined crisis. The prospect is hard to imagine without the crisis, but given that, might it not be genuinely appealing to men and women cut off from a common life, feeling little connection with their neighbors and little connection with the past or future of the republic? It would offer solidarity in a time of danger, and the hard truth about individualism, secularism, and toleration is that they make solidarity very difficult. The recognition of this truth helps explain, I think, the gradual drift of some American intellectuals toward a kind of communal conservatism. Thus, the fulsome debate, some years ago, about our "national purpose" (a liberal nation can have no collective purpose) and the new interest in the possibilities of censorship, both of which suggest the desire to shape citizens in a common mold and to raise the pitch of their virtue.

Even assuming these are the right goals, however, that is the wrong way to reach them. It begins on the wrong side of the balance, with an attack on the heterogeneity of liberal society, and so it poses a threat to all our (different) beliefs, values, and ways of life. I want to suggest that we start on the other side, by expanding the possibilities for a participatory politics. In the liberal world, patriotic feeling and political participation depend on one another, it seems to me, in a special way. For Rousseau and for classical republicans generally, these two rested and could only rest on social, religious, and cultural unity. They were the political expressions of a homogeneous people. One might say that, for them, citizenship was only possible where it was least necessary, where politics was nothing more than the extension into the public arena of a common life that began and was sustained outside. Under such conditions, as John Stuart Mill wrote of the ancient republics and the Swiss cities, patriotism is easy; it is a "passion of spontaneous growth."[19] But today, society, religion, and culture are pluralist in form; there is no common life outside the arena, and there is less and less spontaneous patriotism. The only thing that we can share is the republic itself, the business of government. Only if we actually do share that are we *fellow* citizens. Without that, we are private men and women, radically disjoined, confined to a sphere of existence which, however rich it can be and is in liberal society, can never satisfy our longing for cooperative endeavor, for *amour social*, for public causes and effects.

Among people like ourselves, a community of patriots would have to be sustained by politics alone. I don't know if such a community is possible. Judged by the theory and practice of the classical republics, its creation certainly seems unlikely: how can a common citizenship develop if there is no other commonality—no ethnic solidarity, no established religion, no unified cultural tradition? When I argued that the contemporary balance of civility and civic virtue is appropriate to a liberal society, I was making the classical case for the connection of society and state, of everyday life and political commitment. I did not mean, however, to make a determinist case. One can always strain at the limits of the appropriate; one can always act inappropriately. And it is not implausible to suggest that social circumstance, like Machiavelli's fortune, is the arbiter of only half of what we do. Given liberal society and culture, certain sorts of dedication may well lie beyond our reach. But that's not to say that we cannot, so to speak, enlarge the time and space within which we live as citizens. This is the working principle of democratic socialism: that politics can be opened up, rates of participation significantly increased, decision making really shared, without a full-scale attack on private life and liberal values, without a religious revival or a cultural revolution. What is necessary is the expansion of the public sphere. I don't mean by that the growth of state power—which will come anyway, for a strong state is the necessary and natural antidote to liberal disintegration—but a new politicizing of the state, a devolution of state power into the hands of ordinary citizens.

Three kinds of expansion are required. They add up to a familiar program which I can only sketch in the briefest possible way: a radical democratization of corporate government, so that crucial decisions about the shape of the economy are clearly seen to be the public's business; the decentralization of governmental activity so as to alter the scale of political life and increase the numbers of men and women able to play an effective part in everyday decision making; the creation of parties and movements that can operate at different levels of government and claim a greater degree of individual commitment at every level than our present parties can. All this is needed if patriotism is to be nourished, in the absence of social and cultural cohesion, by what Mill calls "artificial means," that is, "a large and frequent intervention of the citizens in the management of public business."[10]

How such an intervention might actually be achieved, I cannot consider here. It is more important for my present purposes to acknowledge that achieving it (or trying to) will significantly raise the levels of intensity and contention in our politics, and even the levels of intolerance and zeal. Militancy, righteousness, indignation, and hostility are the very stuff of politics. The interventions of the people are not like those of the Holy Ghost. For the people bring with them into the arena all the contradictions of liberal society and culture. And the political arena is in any case a setting for confrontation. Politics (unlike economics) is inherently competitive, and when the competition takes place among large groups of citizens rather than among the king's favorites or rival cliques of oligarchs, it is bound to be more expressive, more feverish, and more tumultuous.

And yet it is only in the arena that we can hope for a solidarity that is spontaneous and free. *E pluribus unum* is an alchemist's promise; out of liberal pluralism no oneness can come. But there is a kind of sharing that is possible even with conflict and perhaps only with it. In the arena, rival politicians have to speak about the common good, even if they simultaneously advance sectional interests. Citizens learn to ask, in addition to their private questions, what the common good really is. In the course of sustained political activity enemies become familiar antagonists, known to be asking the same (contradictory) questions. Men and women who merely tolerated one another's differences recognize that they share a commitment—to *this* arena and to the people in it. Even a divisive election, then, is a ritual of unity, not only because it has a single outcome, but also because it reaffirms the existence of the arena itself, the public thing, and the sovereign people. Politics is a school of loyalty, through which we make the republic our moral possession and come to regard it with a kind of reverence. And election day is the republic's most important celebration. I don't want to exaggerate the awe a citizen feels when he votes, but I do think there is awe, and a sense of pride, at least when the issues being decided are really important and the political order is built to a human scale. There can be even civility in the arena, courtesy, generosity, a concern for rules (especially, as in war, among professionals and veterans) —though one must expect something else much of the time.

In saying all this, I am repeating an argument that Lewis Coser made in the 1950s in his book *The Functions of Social Conflict*. The argument is worth repeating since the conflicts of the 1960s do not seem to have confirmed it for most Americans. Nor would it be irrational to recognize, with Coser, the "integrative functions of an antagonistic behavior" and decide, nonetheless, to live with some lesser degree of integration.[11] I am inclined to think that we can have civility and law-abidance without any intensification of patriotism and participation. No doubt, the present balance is unstable, but so is every other; we have to choose the difficulties we shall live with. What we cannot have, and ought not to ask of one another, under present conditions, is civic virtue. For that we must first create a new politics. I have tried to suggest that it must be a socialist and democratic politics and that it must not supersede but stand in constant tension with the liberalism of our society.

NOTES

1. Jean Jacques Rousseau, "Discourse on the Sciences and Arts," in *The First and Second Discourses*, ed. Roger D. Masters (New York: St. Martin's Press, 1964), p. 59.

2. See Marcus Cunliffe, *Soldiers and Civilians: The Martial Spirit in America, 1775–1865* (Boston: Little, Brown, 1968), especially chaps. 6 and 7.

3. Speech in the House of Representatives, December 9, 1814, reprinted in Lillian Schlissel, ed., *Conscience in America* (New York: E. P. Dutton, 1968), pp. 70–71.

4. David Brewer, *American Citizenship* (New York: C. Scribner's Sons, 1902), pp. 102 ff. From the same period, see also James E. Cutler, *Lynch-Law: An Investigation into the History of Lynching in the United States* (New York: Longmans, Green, 1905).

5. Quoted in Cunliffe, *Soldiers and Civilians*, p. 93.

6. *De Cive* 12.3.

7. Walter Dean Burnham, "The Changing Shape of the American Political Universe," *American Political Science Review* 59 (March 1965): 7–28.

8. Sidney Verba and Norman H. Nie, *Participation in America: Political Democracy and Social Equality* (New York: Harper & Row, 1972), especially chap. 14.

9. John Stuart Mill, "M. de Tocqueville on Democracy in America," in *The Philosophy of John Stuart Mill*, ed. Marshall Cohen (New York: Modern Library, 1961), p. 158.

10. Mill, *The Philosophy of John Stuart Mill*, p. 159. I should stress that I believe these "artificial means" to include economic as well as political self-management. I don't think this is an unfair extension of Mill's meaning. A natural patriotism for him was one generated by all those social qualities that we possess, so to speak, without having to make them for ourselves; an artificial patriotism derives from conscious activity.

11. Lewis A. Coser, *The Functions of Social Conflict* (Glencoe, Ill.: Free Press, 1956), chap. 7.

Chapter Fifteen

MARGARET CANOVAN

PATRIOTISM IS NOT ENOUGH

A national identity which is not based predominantly on republican self-under-standing and constitutional patriotism necessarily collides with the universalist rules of mutual coexistence for human beings.

—Jürgen Habermas, *Die Zeit*, 30 March 1990[1]

The title of this article alludes to the words of Edith Cavell, the British matron of a Red Cross hospital in German-occupied Belgium during the First World War. Arrested in 1915 and shot for helping to smuggle wounded British and Allied soldiers out of the country, she became a convenient symbol of British heroism and Hunnish brutality. But Nurse Cavell had also cared for wounded German soldiers, making no national distinctions in her devotion to those in need of help. Her last words, widely reported, were: "I realize that patriotism is not enough. I must have no hatred or bitterness towards anyone." She therefore became for many in the postwar period a symbol of revulsion *against* patriotism in the sense of an exclusive and militaristic loyalty to one part of humanity.

I begin by invoking this ambiguous figure, symbol both of heroic patriotism and of the ideal of universal humanity, because my subject is the tense and ambiguous relationship between patriotism and universalism. For most of this century Western political philosophy has been dominated by universalist principles and unsympathetic to the claims of particular, limited loyalties. But in the past decade or so there has been a novel and interesting development. An increasing number of political thinkers with internationalist sympathies have begun to defend a form of patriotism, understood as something decisively different from nationalism. This article undertakes a critical examination of this new form of patriotism, sometimes called "constitutional" or "postnational"

From the *British Journal of Political Science* 30 (2000): 413–32. Copyright © 2000 Cambridge University Press. Reprinted with the permission of Cambridge University Press.

patriotism. I shall argue that despite its attractions the notion is open to a number of objections. I shall conclude (though my point will be different from Cavell's) that patriotism is indeed not enough.

WHY DO SOME UNIVERSALISTS DEFEND PATRIOTISM?

In view of patriotism's association with war and enmity, it may seem strange that any political theorist with universalist sympathies should advocate it. During the past half century internationalists have more often been wary of any kind of partial solidarity that might divert people from a sense of their common humanity. But although that suspicion continues to be powerfully voiced,[2] there has recently been a perceptible change of mood. Developments in theory and in practice have combined to make political theorists more aware of the attractions of particular loyalties. One reason for this is the impact of communitarianism in political philosophy. Communitarians have pointed out that the abstract and apparently rootless individuals who figure in much liberal political philosophy do not correspond to real human beings, to whom matters of communal identity, heritage, and loyalty are vitally important.[3] A number of political philosophers have taken such arguments as a foundation on which to build more or less qualified defenses of nationalism.[4]

Alongside those theoretical arguments, practical politics has turned the spotlight more dramatically on to matters of identity and loyalty. For one of the most striking recent political developments has been the resurgence of national claims and conflicts. That is not in itself an argument against universalist political theory: on the contrary, confronted by events in the Balkans and elsewhere, many internationalist liberals have been confirmed in their belief that nationalism is in all circumstances an evil, to be transcended by concentrating on universal human rights. But others have drawn a different and more complicated conclusion. For them, the lesson is that (at any rate for the present) the grand ideal of universal human community is too ambitious, being too distant to mobilize popular support. People may be able to extend their sympathies to take in their fellow-countrymen, but few of them are capable of consistent solidarity with the entire human race.[5] It follows that if one is appalled by nationalist conflicts and "ethnic cleansing," if one is concerned for minority rights and multicultural harmony, then denunciations of nationalism are not enough. It is necessary also to theorize and foster an alternative form of loyalty that will be compatible with universal values but will be able to attract the people of a particular territory, perhaps as a stage on the way to world citizenship.[6]

The conceptions of patriotism currently being developed by a number of political theorists are intended to fill this gap: to describe a form of loyalty different from and superior to nationalism, but able (in the words of Maurizio Viroli) "to fight nationalism on its own ground."[7] This reformulated patriotism is offered (to quote Viroli again) as an "antidote" to nationalism, sufficiently akin to it to attract popular loyalty, but sufficiently different to be compatible with respect for universal human rights and to be more tolerant of ethnic and cultural differences. Clearly, current thinking about patriotism, and particularly the attempt to establish a distinction between "patriotism," which is desirable, and "nationalism," which is not, is more than a matter of intellectual curiosity. It also represents a rhetorical[8] and political strategy. This in itself should prompt us to look rather carefully at what we are being offered.

PATRIOTISM VERSUS NATIONALISM

What is it, then, that is supposed to differentiate "patriotism" (which is desirable) from "nationalism" (which is not)? As we shall see later, the distinction is used in subtly different ways to express a range of views, but for the sake of clarity it can be stated in ideal-typical form. The central claim is that patriotism means the political loyalty of citizens to the free polity they share, whereas nationalism is a matter of ethnicity and culture.[9] While nationhood is taken to be a "prepolitical" matter depending on ties of birth and blood, the bond that unites citizens in a patriotic polity is a matter of will, the free consent of citizens united by their commitment to liberal democratic principles. The distinction is among other things a contrast between art and nature.[10] Its defenders point out that republican political thought from the ancient Greeks to the French Revolution conceived of free politics as human foundations, deliberately built, whereas the postrevolutionary romantic nationalists introduced a deterministic model of national polities growing organically out of the nation's blood and soil.

According to its advocates the distinction has particular relevance for a modern world in which matters of ethnic identity are increasingly politicized, but in which the economic and demographic realities of globalization contradict the traditional nationalist ideal that each nation should have its own state. Faced with the problems of holding multicultural societies together in harmonious tolerance, supporters claim that patriotic loyalty to the principles and practices of a free state can provide a functional substitute for nationalism, with all its advantages by way of mobilizing loyalty, but none of its disadvantages. Unlike nationalism (it is argued), patriotism is not exclusive, uncritical, or bellicose, and is therefore compatible with commitments to universal humanity. Unlike nationalism, patriotism does not expect or demand ethnic and cultural homogeneity, and is therefore tolerant of diversity.[11]

This is a composite portrait of a "new patriotism" which has not so far undergone much theoretical elaboration. It is important because it chimes in well with a prevailing intellectual mood, but there are some difficulties in coming to grips with it. Not only are we concerned with a variety of statements by writers who have their own preoccupations; more interestingly, this new discourse of "patriotism" covers a spectrum between positions that differ a good deal. At one end of the spectrum, heavily influenced by Kantian liberalism and most closely approximated by Jürgen Habermas, lies what I shall call "cosmopolitan constitutional patriotism," the vision of a new form of loyalty to a new, supranational polity.[12] This is balanced at the other end by what I shall call "rooted republicanism," best represented by Maurizio Viroli's book, *For Love of Country*. Drawing on the classical republican tradition of patriotism which was displaced by nationalism from about 1800,[13] this version focuses on loyalty to one's own particular polity, but calls for this to be interpreted in terms of freedom rather than ethnicity.[14]

In practice, none of the theorists concerned can be located at any fixed point on this spectrum between Kantian universalism and classical republicanism, for there is a good deal of shifting back and forth in the middle ground. For example, although Viroli aims at a revival of patriotism in particular free polities and sets out explicitly to recover classical republican values, his reading of the republican tradition is censored by his modern liberal humanitarian and cosmopolitan conscience and by revulsion against Italy's Fascist past. As a result the stridently chauvinist and militaristic nature of classical patriotism drops out of view.[15] At the other end of the spectrum, too, appearances can be misleading, for Jürgen Habermas's apparently abstract and universalizable "constitutional patriotism" is traceable to a very specific situation and a particular national history, raising questions about its wider relevance. The German term, *Verfassungspatriotismus*, was coined to denote attachment to the liberal democratic institutions of the postwar Federal Republic of Germany. Patriotism in those circumstances meant loyalty to a polity that was nonnationalist or even *anti*nationalist in its structure. It was a truncated state, including only part of the nation, with a set of liberal democratic institutions imposed from without and designed to run counter to the political traditions predominant in Germany for the previous century. Furthermore, the Nazi past made the whole topic of loyalty (patriotic or nationalist) uniquely sensitive. Behind Habermas's abstract formulations, in other words, lies an attempt quite as specific as Viroli's to influence the political identity of a particular polity.[16]

One reason for the blurring between republican and liberal influences on the one hand, and cosmopolitan and local aims on the other, is that all concerned form a united front against a common enemy: ethnic nationalism. Another reason is that as well as sharing an enemy they share a model. The United States is frequently cited by new patriots as an example of a nonnational polity held together by patriotism, and different aspects can be stressed according to taste: its classical republican elements or the liberal principles built into its constitution; its unique heritage or its universal significance as a gathering-place for immigrants from all ethnic groups. Later on we shall consider reasons for doubting the suitability of the United States as a model, at any rate for the more cosmopolitan versions of new patriotism. But the existence of this all-purpose example does much to bolster the plausibility of new patriotism's antinationalist discourse.

In order to deal with this rather amorphous discourse I shall concentrate most critical attention on the end of the spectrum where the most ambitious claims are located, that is to say on the notion of a universalistic and universalizable "constitutional patriotism." Having looked at its problems I shall turn to the other end of the spectrum, where we can find the more modest position identified here as "rooted republicanism." I shall argue that although this is more defensible it cannot actually solve the problem to which it is addressed.

COSMOPOLITAN CONSTITUTIONAL PATRIOTISM

Although the terminology of "constitutional patriotism" arose out of the unusual circumstances of postwar West Germany, the notion has been generalized by Habermas, who suggests in his 1990 essay on "Citizenship and National Identity" that multicultural and multinational societies might be unified at the level of politics by a liberal political culture supported by a *constitutional* patriotism." Patriotism of this kind, he says, gives its loyalty to the universal principles and practices of democracy and human rights. He concedes that in a future Federal Republic of Europe, "the *same* legal principles would also have to be interpreted from the perspectives of *different* national traditions and histories," but adds that,

> One's own tradition must in each case be appropriated from a vantage point relativized by the perspectives of other traditions, and appropriated in such a manner that it can be brought into a transnational, Western European constitutional culture. A particularist anchoring of *this kind* would not do away with one iota of the universalist meaning of popular sovereignty and human rights. The original thesis stands: democratic citizenship need not be rooted in the national identity of a people. However, regardless of the diversity of different cultural forms of life, it does require that every citizen be socialized into a common political culture.[17]

Perhaps characteristically, Habermas's discussion is complex, qualified, and somewhat opaque. Those influenced by him tend to be less cautious, and a useful expansion of these ideas has been offered by the Irish philosopher Attracta Ingram.[18] In an essay entitled "Constitutional Patriotism," she observes:

> The idea of post-national identity is of a political identity founded on recognition of democratic values and human rights as these are contextualized in a particular constitutional tradition. Citizens are thought of as bound to each other by subscription to these shared values rather than by the more traditional prepolitical ties that nation-states have drawn on as sources of unity. . . .

> A post-national identity has to accommodate difference and plurality. So it has to be an identity in which membership is constituted by recognition of a common system of authority erected and maintained by a constitution. Unity and legitimacy come from the constitution and the formal tie that holds people together is their continuing voluntary recognition of the constitution, their constitutional patriotism.[19]

Both Habermas and Ingram connect constitutional patriotism with hopes for the transcendence of existing nation-states. Besides looking towards supranational citizenship and constitutional patriotism at the level of the European Union, Habermas speaks of this as a stage on the way to "world citizenship."[20] Ingram suggests that "it may well be feasible and desirable to build political identities that overarch several national identities," and develops a Kantian argument according to which liberal states actually have a duty to unite with their neighbors and extend the area within which peace and political justice can be enjoyed.[21]

There is in both cases a certain lack of clarity about the relation between these universalist projects and the particular polities and specific political identities that exist. Ingram makes greater concessions to particularism, suggesting that a common set of liberal democratic values can be customized within particular traditions: "Our particular identity is constituted by *our* effort to institutionalize principles of justice. And that effort has a different history and a different shape in different bounded communities."[22] We shall need to return later to that tell-tale possessive language ("our," along with "we" and "us"), for although it helps to give plausibility to the project of constitutional patriotism, it also signals far-reaching confusions about the implications of collective political identity. For the moment, however, let us concentrate on the vision of a postnational polity united by this new sort of loyalty. It is not difficult to understand its attraction, for in it the conflicting demands of universal liberal principles and particularistic communities appear to be satisfied. In what follows I shall argue that this triumph is illusory, for a number of reasons:

1. The project of avoiding the illiberal effects of nationalism by basing the state upon shared liberal values is self-defeating.

2. The claim that citizens can share loyalty to the polity rather than to their nation begs vital questions about the state.

3. The cases cited to show the plausibility of this kind of patriotism do not in fact do so.

4. The notion that constitutional patriotism can provide a substitute for ties of birth and blood is incoherent.

CRITICISMS OF COSMOPOLITAN CONSTITUTIONAL PATRIOTISM

The Civic Faith

In their concern to replace the bond of nationhood with something less visceral and exclusive, constitutional patriots often suggest that citizens are better bound together by shared principles or values: for Habermas, a loyalty to "abstract procedures and principles"[23] that amounts to a shared political culture into which every citizen will need to be socialized.[24] Despite the Kantian inspiration of constitutional patriotism, this acceptance of the need for deliberate political socialization echoes much older classical republican traditions. For unlike romantic nationalists (who believed that citizens of a true nation-state belong together by nature) earlier republicans always thought of polities and their citizens as creatures of artifice. Citizens were formed through patriotic education, and republicans were prepared to go to disconcerting lengths to achieve this. Adrian Oldfield, undertaking an "exploration of what it would mean to take civic republicanism seriously in the modern world," observes that many of its aspects would be unpalatable to modern liberals, for the appropriate civic education means that "minds have to be manipulated."[25]

That may seem a rather highly colored description of what constitutional patriots would see as inculcation of universal truths. But it underlines the point that if shared political principles are actually to become the unifying bond of the state, then the principles in question must be authoritatively agreed and serious efforts must be made to inculcate them into the citizens. Just as earlier generations of political theorists took for granted that states had an interest in the religious beliefs of their citizens, so the patriotic polity seems also to be envisaged as a kind of confessional state.

Constitutional patriots may object that such socialization is not only politically necessary but philosophically justifiable, since the "common political culture" is built upon the universal principles of democracy and human rights, which Habermas evidently regards as being of a kind to which "all who are possibly affected could assent as participants in rational discourse."[26] But the difficulties of achieving practical consensus on such principles should not be underestimated. Although the patriotic project is hailed by its advocates as an answer to the problems of increasingly multiethnic and multicultural societies, it may be precisely in such societies that dissent from liberal democratic principles is likely to occur.[27] Religious minorities are particularly liable to find themselves in disagreement with liberal orthodoxy. Such tensions are symbolized by the French "affair of the headscarves," the controversy caused by Muslim schoolgirls whose determination to cover their heads was taken to conflict with the republican principles of secularism expressed within that vital agency of political socialization, the state school system.[28] French experience is relevant here because the French republican version of nationalism has a good deal in common with constitutional patriotism.[29]

Loyalty to principles, then, may not necessarily be an improvement on national loyalty as a basis for a multicultural polity. But some constitutional patriots may object that this discussion of beliefs misses the point; that despite talk of "principles" by Habermas and others, what is crucial is a more practical loyalty to the constitution itself, in other words shared allegiance to the institutions and procedures of a liberal democratic state.[30] The important thing is that citizens should share a polity without sharing a nation. Unfortunately, this version of the patriotic project also has flaws, as I hope to show in the next section.

Whose State Is It?

Build a liberal democratic state that protects the rights of all its people and welcomes them on equal terms into a shared public arena, and national or ethnic differences can be transcended in what Habermas has called an "abstract, legally mediated solidarity among strangers."[31] Theoretical aspirations of this kind translate into visions of a future United States of Europe, of a nonsectarian polity of all Ireland, even of solutions to more intractable conflicts in the Balkans and further afield. Notice that this ideal goes well beyond more pragmatic schemes for coping democratically with the tensions between potentially hostile groups. In the face of communal conflicts in many parts of the world, a variety of ingenious constitutional arrangements have been devised to induce such groups to accept accommodation rather than confrontation, and some such attempts have been successful: the latest (its fate still in the balance at the time of writing) is the 1998 Good Friday Agreement in Northern Ireland. The hallmark of such arrangements is that communal divisions and mutual suspicions are not expected to go away, but the institutional mechanisms are designed to reward political bargaining rather than violence. Approaching the problems of South Africa in this spirit, Donald Horowitz speaks of "harnessing self-interest to the cause of peace," stressing that his approach "does not seek or need to change hearts or minds in order to succeed."[32] Going beyond that kind of modus vivendi, constitutional patriots have higher hopes, aiming to lift individuals above their ascriptive identities into a shared public sphere where all are equal citizens with a shared loyalty to an impartial state.

The trouble with this appealing vision is its circularity. Supposing that a polity really does live up to Habermasian standards, then its citizens may seem to have such an obvious interest in supporting it that they may perhaps be expected to give it their loyalty regardless of national ties that pull them in a different direction.[33] But a polity needs to be strong and well integrated to be able to manifest those liberal virtues, and the states that come nearest to the ideal are in fact underpinned by something too easily taken for granted: a "people," a transgenerational political community, members of which recognize the state as "our" state and thereby confer upon it the legitimacy and power it needs.[34] The history of Northern Ireland illustrates the difficulties where this cannot be taken for granted. For Catholics, the state has not historically been "ours" but "theirs," and its corresponding lack of legitimacy has gravely weakened its authority and power, hampering attempts at impartiality in recent decades. The vicious circle is that a state is unlikely to be powerful enough to demonstrate the liberal democratic virtues that can attract constitutional patriotism unless it is very widely regarded by its population as our state rather than someone else's. Those who support patriotism against nationalism as a unifying bond dodge such questions of power and legitimacy, tending to assume that "the modern state" per se will deserve the loyalty of its subjects, even if they are not bound to it by ties of nationhood.[35] But many actually existing states are feeble or unworthy of loyalty, while those that are powerful and most like the Habermasian model are overwhelmingly nation-states, the possession of a specific historic people. The institutions of the European Union are notoriously weak precisely because they lack that tie to a "people."[36] The claim that an impartial state can form a benign umbrella soaring above rival national or ethnic identities and attracting patriotic loyalty ignores the most crucial political question. Where is the state to draw its power from? What holds up the umbrella?[37]

Misleading Examples

Constitutional patriots may respond by pointing to a small number of effective states which (they claim) prove their point that nationalism can be replaced by constitutional patriotism. The implication is that if this can be done successfully in one place it should also be possible in others. Postwar West Germany, where the language of *Verfassungspatriotismus* was coined, is held by Attracta Ingram to show "that a further uncoupling of state and nation is empirically feasible."[38] But there is room for skepticism here. A more plausible conclusion to be drawn from German experience would be that this apparent "uncoupling" was misleading, and that behind the handful of constitutional patriots who talked about the nature of their loyalty were a great many German nationalists who did not.[39] When the opportunity for unification arrived the political significance of that tacit identity became apparent. West Germans took for granted that they had a collective responsibility for the people of the German Democratic Republic (and not, of course, for Poles, Czechs, Hungarians, and so on). Whatever the subsequent disillusionment in both parts of Germany, the power generated in 1989 by the sense of being *Ein Volk* was enough to transform the map of Europe.[40] The German example therefore tends to undermine rather than to support the new patriots' case. But what of the two prize exhibits always cited in this connection, Switzerland and the United States of America?[41] Do not they support the case for constitutional patriotism, demonstrating that loyalties that are political and universalistic can be constructed to hold together a multinational or multicultural society? I will try to suggest briefly why these examples should be treated with caution.

Within the Swiss Confederation, German, French, Italian, and Romansch-speaking segments have long shared a political system and managed their disputes remarkably harmoniously. Indeed, the Swiss political scientist Wolf Linder claims that his country "provides a model for finding political institutions and patterns of behaviour that enable peaceful conflict resolution in a multicultural society." It turns out, however, that Swiss experience is not as encouraging as it might seem. For, as Linder goes on to point out, success in this field requires a lot more than a set of well-designed institutions, let alone a set of universal principles. "Democracy and peaceful conflict-resolution . . . need the social development of a political culture. Unlike technical innovation, this takes a long time to develop."[42] Although Swiss political institutions owe a good deal to deliberate design, their success has had at least as much to do with special circumstances and a highly contingent series of historical events. One important point is that the component parts of Switzerland are deeply rooted communities defined by birth and blood as well as geography. These have grown together in the course of a shared history, producing a strong sense of pride in distinctive Swiss-ness, but local autonomy and local loyalties continue to be strong. The deeply historical and contingent character of Swiss unity gives little support to the project of cosmopolitan constitutional patriotism, and this unique polity might be better considered a candidate for the category of "rooted republicanism" we shall be considering later.

The United States is a more plausible example, in that its political identity is indeed inextricably intertwined with the Constitution, and even with the political principles this articulates. To quote Benjamin Barber, "The American trick was to use the fierce attachments of patriotic sentiment to bond a people to high ideals."[43] This unusually ideological understanding of what it is to be American has no doubt helped the country to cope relatively successfully with immigration from all round the globe.[44] In one of the most eloquent defenses of patriotism as distinguished from nationalism, John Schaar has analyzed its specifically American form, finding in the speeches of Abraham Lincoln what he calls a "covenanted patriotism," "actively guided by and directed toward the mission established in the founding covenant." To adopt it is to accept one's inheritance from the Founding Fathers and one's obligation to carry on their work. According to Schaar, "This conception of political membership . . . decisively transcends the parochial and primitive fraternities of blood and race, for it calls kin all who accept the authority of the covenant."[45]

It is easy to see why cosmopolitan liberals reacting against European experiences of nationalism might wish to emulate this kind of patriotism. But we should think twice before accepting the claim that it amounts to a nonnational form of loyalty. For it does not really mean a gathering of all those across the world who are willing to commit themselves to Lincoln's principles. In the same breath as speaking of transcending those "primitive fraternities of blood," Schaar articulates an almost Roman sense of ancestral piety towards the inherited "mission established in the founding covenant." The point is that the principles of the constitution are not just liberal principles but (for Americans) "our" principles, handed down to us by our forefathers, biological or adopted.[46] To think of the United States as a society bound together by constitutional patriotism rather than by nationhood is to overlook inheritance — inheritance not only of citizenship, but of the Constitution, the principles, the national mission, the American Way of Life. Despite immigration in each generation, most Americans are so not because they willingly accept the Constitution, but because being American is in their blood. For many this is an inheritance of only one or two generations' depth, and if the United States were a less powerful and prosperous country, their simultaneous inheritance of diverse ethnic ancestries might pose greater political problems. But the fact remains that, like other nations, Americans are defined and united primarily by birth and inheritance,[47] and it is to these neglected considerations that we must now turn.

Ours by Right of Birth

As we have seen, some new patriots believe that they have discovered a form of solidarity founded upon acceptance by citizens of a liberal democratic constitution. Stressing the political links between individuals, they give the impression that "subscription to shared values" and "voluntary recognition of the constitution" can be disconnected from the "prepolitical ties" thought to be characteristic of nation-states,[48] and thereby brought into harmony with "the universalist rules of mutual coexistence for human beings."[49] But this appealing vision owes its plausibility to a tacit reservation that undermines universalist aspirations. For despite the liberal language of individual commitments and abstract legal status, constitutional patriots (like everyone else) take for granted the existence of historic political communities, and therefore that the populations whom they seek to bind with political loyalties already owe their common citizenship to the most fundamental of "prepolitical" ties: familial inheritance. To the vast majority of citizens, even the most Habermasian polity is "ours" because it was our parents' before us. One of the main purposes of the discourse of "constitutional patriotism" is of course to play down this obvious point and to lay stress on the kinds of solidarity that settled populations can share with the increasing number of immigrants in their midst. But this leads Habermas and others to exaggerate the contrast between supposedly "prepolitical" ties of birth on the one hand and political relations between citizens on the other. Despite its prominence in the discourse, this dichotomy is in fact so implausible that even constitutional patriots themselves do not consistently stick to it. The confusion involved can perhaps be illustrated through a reductio ad absurdam on a Habermasian theme: citizenship of that purportedly postnational entity, the European Union.

European citizenship (something envied and desired by a great many people, especially in North Africa and Eastern Europe) is at present a secondary status added on to national citizenship within one of the component states. Some of these states are more generous than others in admitting immigrants to citizenship, but in all cases the vast majority of citizens simply inherit their status from their parents: it comes to them as a matter of birth, like a title to family property. Now imagine that "prepolitical ties" were really to be devalued in favor of "voluntary recognition of the constitution." Why should being born into a family of European citizens—a Spanish family, say, or a British family, or a German family—give one a privileged claim on European citizenship? Would not considerations of equal human rights imply that one should take one's chance alongside applicants from Albania and Algeria, from Slovakia and Sudan, perhaps by taking a competitive examination at the age of eighteen to determine which of the applicants showed greatest understanding of and devotion to the constitution?

There may be some internationalists prepared to defend such an arrangement in principle, on the grounds that it is morally repugnant for rights to depend on the lottery of birth.[50] So far as I am aware, however, none of the theorists attracted by constitutional patriotism has advocated such an arrangement, and it is clear that despite their rejection of "prepolitical ties" they take for granted (just as nationalists do) that citizenship is part of the ancestral endowment that makes "us" a "people" in collective possession of a polity.[51] Since constitutional patriots know very well that fusion of "political" and supposedly "prepolitical" ties is inseparable from the continuing existence of a democratic polity, why are they so reluctant to acknowledge this? The explanation lies, I believe, in a fear of racism that makes them gloss over the political significance of family membership and present us with a false dichotomy. We are warned that unless the polity is understood as a community of liberal patriots, constituted and bound together by the individual choice of its members, then it must be a "nation" defined by a particular kind of supposedly pure blood. Either we insist on a nonnational, patriotic polity to which birthright is irrelevant, or we open the door to a national polity understood in racist terms.

But this analysis of the alternatives is misleading. The fact is that any polity, however liberal its ethos, is and must be an inheritance passed on from generation to generation. Indeed, one of the best recipes for a stable liberal democracy is a widespread sense among the population that the polity is a collective inheritance belonging to a "people."[52] Whether or not that "people" is conceived in terms of theories about genetic makeup is a separate issue, but the crucial significance of collective political inheritance is undeniable, and is implicitly conceded by the constitutional patriots themselves. As we saw ear-

lier, Attracta Ingram falls back on collective language (as in "our political identity," "our distinct political heritage," "the constitution we made and continue
to remake through the generations")[53] that reveals assumptions about the existence of political collectivities inherited through families. Even Habermas,
while arguing for a "liberal immigration policy" that would pave the way for
world citizenship, concedes "the right to preserve one's own *political* culture,"[54]
a formulation which assumes that the liberal democratic polity to which immigrants are seeking entry belongs initially to those who inherit it by right of
birth. For the new patriots, in other words, just as for nationalists, the (supposedly nonnational) "people" is constituted and bound together primarily by
birth. As we observed in the U.S. case, even if such a "people" welcomes immigrants into citizenship, the newly naturalized citizens themselves pass on their
membership of the people to their children in the traditional manner. It is misleading for new patriots to assert that their polity can dispense with "prepolitical" ties. But this raises a further question. Must "the people" who inherit the
polity form a "nation"? Is it not possible for the inherited bonds that unite
them to their political heritage and to one another to be patriotic without being
national? That is the claim explicitly made by another group of new patriots,
those I have referred to as "rooted republicans."

ROOTED REPUBLICANISM

Even within the discourse of the new patriotism, the Habermasian version has
come in for criticism on the grounds that it is too abstract and too ambitious.[55]
Conceding the arguments advanced above, such critics might maintain that the
real strength of the discourse lies with those who set themselves a more limited
task, counterposing to nationalism a type of patriotism drawing on the classical
tradition of love for one's own inherited polity. The most prominent
spokesman for this strand in the discourse, Maurizio Viroli, advocates a "patriotism of liberty" that is explicitly particularistic, but nevertheless free of illiberal characteristics because it is a "patriotism without nationalism."[56] This sort
of patriotism has two particularly salient characteristics. In the first place,
although it may arise out of "ethnocultural unity," it is a "political culture of
liberty" which puts its stress squarely upon the republican tradition of active
citizenship and civic virtue.[57] Secondly and in consequence of this, it is a critical love of country, dedicated to making sure that one's polity lives up to its
highest traditions and ideals, if necessary at the cost of unity.[58]

These are attractive sentiments: the obvious question they raise, however,
is why they should be regarded as exclusively patriotic rather than national. It
is interesting that Stephen Nathanson, who argues in favor of what he calls a
"moderate patriotism" that would be "worthy of support by morally conscientious people," does not make a sharp distinction between (good) patriotism

and (bad) nationalism, observing instead that each of them comes in different versions, some acceptable to modern liberals and some not.[59] It is hard to avoid the suspicion that the sharp distinction offered by new patriots has more to do with rhetorical impact than with cool analysis, and that it is convenient to call particularistic sentiments one approves of "patriotism," while heaping all the blame on to nationalism, "patriotism's bloody brother."[60] In Viroli's account, for example, nationalism is taken to mean "unconditional loyalty or an exclusive attachment," contrasted with the "charitable and generous love" of country that is patriotism.[61] When an example of nationalism seems to show liberal characteristics, it turns out to have been patriotism all along.[62] This propensity to blacken the name of nationalism goes along with an inclination to play down the more illiberal aspects of patriotism. Either these are admitted sotto voce,[63] or else they are dismissed with the implication that bad patriotism is virtually equivalent to nationalism.[64]

The weakness of the "rooted republican" version of the new patriotism is therefore that it trades on a caricature of nationalism as a bigoted and racist commitment to ethnic and cultural homogeneity. That caricature ignores the huge complexity of national loyalties, the differences between different national traditions and changes within specific traditions over time. This is not the place to explore those complexities,[65] except to point out that while there is plenty of evidence of racist versions of nationalism (as of chauvinist versions of patriotism), there is also a long-standing association between some nationalisms and liberal democracy.[66] The most distinguished recent defender of liberal nationalism, David Miller, denies that national loyalty has to imply ethnic or cultural homogeneity, and envisages an open-minded, inclusive national political culture that seems virtually indistinguishable from Viroli's conception of patriotism.[67]

It is relevant here that (to quote David Miller) "national identities are not cast in stone."[68] One reason for the convergence between the more liberal recent statements of nationalism and the more particularistic versions of new patriotism is that (at any rate among Western intellectuals, though not among militants elsewhere) nationalist discourse has been shifting further away from the nineteenth-century Romantic conception of nations as natural entities, towards the belief that nations are (in Benedict Anderson's indispensable phrase) "imagined communities."[69] A charge traditionally raised against nationalism is that it teaches the false doctrine that human beings are naturally divided into separate (and probably unequal) nations. But sophisticated nationalists have recognized for a long time that their nations are in fact contingent outcomes of historical events, and that the sense of naturalness is largely mythical, part of the way in which nations are imagined. The understanding of nations as "imagined communities" is currently attracting attention not only because it chimes in well with the postmodern sense of the shifting, kaleidoscopic quality of "reality," but also because if nationhood is something imagined, then (so its supporters often believe) it can be reimagined in a more palatable form. Instead of trying to replace national identities with patriotic loyalties, therefore, some political theorists moved by very similar concerns are suggesting the reinvention of existing national identities to make them more consonant with liberal concerns. The implication of this may seem to be that the new patriots are actually pushing at an open door: that their fear of nationalism is exaggerated and their concern to distinguish patriotism from it unnecessary, since nationalism can itself be reinvented in a form that all good liberals can endorse. But any such conclusion would be simplistic, for two reasons. In the first place, political identities cannot be made to order; and in the second place, even if they could be, that would still not solve the dilemmas of liberal patriots.

On the first point, some writers suppose that (as Richard Kearney says) "nations and states are of our own making and can be *remade* according to other images."[70] But this reasoning commits the fallacy (pointed out by Hannah Arendt) of mistaking "action" for "work."[71] As Arendt showed, politics is not a matter of molding passive material. Free politics means action engaged in by plural actors, and no one can control or predict its outcome. Encouraging citizens to debate matters of common identity[72] *may* generate more enlightened and cosmopolitan views, but it could just as well provide opportunities for populist mobilization that might reinforce entrenched conceptions of "us" and "them," or lead to reimagined identities of an even less palatable kind. The increasing success in Western Europe and elsewhere of political parties hostile to immigration is a reminder of these possibilities. Faced with the wilderness of contingency that is the real world of politics, liberals cannot find a short cut to universal harmony through new concepts of patriotism or nationalism.

Suppose, however (to move on to our second problem) that we really *could* remold a political identity within a given territory to conform to the best new patriotic or civic nationalist model: would that solve the problem we started from? Remember that our problem was the tension between particular loyalties and universal principles. In the uncompromisingly cosmopolitan words of Martha Nussbaum,

> To count people as moral equals is to treat nationality, ethnicity, religion, class, race, and gender as "morally irrelevant" — as irrelevant to that equal standing. . . . What I am saying about politics is that we should view the equal worth of all human beings as a regulative constraint on our political actions and aspirations.[73]

Traditionally it was in warfare that patriotism clashed most stridently with such commitments: the soldier could not treat his country's friends and enemies as moral equals.[74] It is highly characteristic of the new discourse of patriotism (bearing witness to changed political conditions in the West) that the military concerns that loomed so large in the past have almost dropped out of view. The first duty of a patriot is no longer to lay down his life for his country;

in the eyes of new patriots it may instead be to campaign actively to make that country live up to its pretensions by respecting human rights. But the demilitarization of borders in many parts of the developed world does not overcome the tension between particular and universal commitments and loyalties. Instead, a dramatic new source of conflict (still focused upon borders) has replaced the old one: immigration and the problem of its limits. Given the never-ending streams of would-be immigrants to prosperous parts of the world such as the United States and the European Union, there is an apparently irreconcilable contradiction between universalist humanitarianism on the one hand, and commitment on the other to the persistence of a polity (national or patriotic) belonging to a privileged subsection of humankind—"our people."[75] New patriotism does nothing to help solve this dilemma. As we saw, even the most apparently cosmopolitan constitutional patriotism does not alter the fundamental truth that citizenship is first and foremost an inherited privilege, and must be so if a democratic body politic is to be able to persist.

CONCLUSION

Despite the claims made for it, new patriotism does not provide a coherent solution to the problem of reconciling universal humanitarian principles with limited and particularistic political commitments, and has no advantages in this respect over nationalism of the more liberal sort.[76] The dilemmas to which it is addressed do not yield to philosophical solutions, and can be managed only by more or less messy political compromises. That said, there is no doubt that the discourse of new patriotism can on occasion aid such political compromises, and may in some circumstances make up in political effectiveness for its deficiencies in philosophical cogency. It is evident (as I suggested earlier) that variants of this discourse have been elaborated and adopted at least in part for rhetorical reasons, as political moves intended to gather support for liberal humanitarian commitments. Consciously or not, its supporters are employing the traditional tactics of the rhetorician, such as using familiar terms in altered senses, redescribing the political situation and shifting the battle lines to maximize support for their own position.[77] The German discourse of *Verfassungspatriotismus*, for example, should be seen as a way of managing tensions between traditional understandings of national loyalty and the postwar constitutional arrangements of the Federal Republic. As a rhetorical response to that situation it seems to have been quite successful, partly no doubt because its local resonances were decently clothed in the language of unpolitical generality. Habermasian abstraction can make it possible to talk about highly specific problems while apparently not talking about them.

There is nothing particularly unusual about this situation, for it is in the nature of political thinking to be on the one hand the elaboration of a general theoretical position and on the other a move in a political game.[78] Further-more, it sometimes happens that arguments that are intellectually weak are rhetorically effective and politically constructive. The large issues raised by the overlaps and tensions between political rhetoric and philosophical argument cannot be discussed here. Faced with the discourse of new patriotism, how-ever, it is possible to sympathize with the intentions it embodies (and even to commend its use as a political strategy in some circumstances), while still con-cluding that as a coherent theoretical solution to the problems its adherents claim to confront, patriotism is not enough.

NOTES

Earlier versions of this article were presented to seminars at the universities of Keele and Exeter, and at the Universidad Autónoma de Madrid, and I benefited greatly from the discussions. John Horton and David Miller read the draft and made particularly helpful comments and suggestions, as did the Editor and referees of the *British Journal of Political Science*.

1. Jürgen Habermas, "D-Mark Nationalism," *Die Zeit*, 30 March 1990, trans-lated in R. T. Gray and S. Wilke, eds., *German Unification and Its Discontents: Documents from the Peaceful Revolution* (Seattle: University of Washington Press, 1996), pp. 186–205 at p. 198.

2. See, for example, Martha Nussbaum's "Patriotism and Cosmopolitanism," printed with sixteen responses in Martha C. Nussbaum et al., *For Love of Country: Debating the Limits of Patriotism* (Boston, Mass.: Beacon Press, 1996), pp. 2–17.

3. Charles Taylor, "Cross-purposes: The Liberal Communitarian Debate," in Nancy L. Rosenblum, ed., *Liberalism and the Moral Life* (Cambridge, Mass.: Harvard University Press, 1989), pp. 164–78; Alasdair MacIntyre, "Is Patriotism a Virtue?" (Lawrence: The E. H. Lindley Memorial Lecture, University of Kansas, 1984).

4. David Miller, *On Nationality* (Oxford: Oxford University Press, 1995); Yael Tamir, *Liberal Nationalism* (Princeton, N.J.: Princeton University Press, 1993); Neil MacCormick, "Is Nationalism Philosophically Credible?" in William Twining, ed., *Issues of Self-Determination* (Aberdeen: Aberdeen University Press, 1991), pp. 8–19; Avishai Margalit and Joseph Raz, "National Self-determination," *Journal of Philosophy* 87 (1990): 439–61.

5. This point is made in many of the replies in Nussbaum, *For Love of Country*.

6. Habermas, "Citizenship and National Identity," p. 514. The essay is incorpo-rated as Appendix II in Jürgen Habermas, *Between Facts and Norms: Contributions to a Dis-course Theory of Law and Democracy* (Cambridge, Mass.: MIT Press, 1996). Cf. Benjamin R. Barber, "Constitutional Faith," pp. 30–37 at p. 36, and Charles Taylor, "Why Democ-racy Needs Patriotism," pp. 119–21 at p. 121, both in Nussbaum, *For Love of Country*.

7. Maurizio Viroli, *For Love of Country; An Essay on Patriotism and Nationalism* (Oxford: Clarendon Press, 1995), p. 15. Cf. Attracta Ingram, "Constitutional Patriotism," *Philosophy and Social Criticism* 22 (1996): 1–18; Stephen Nathanson, *Patriotism, Morality,*

and Peace (Lanham, N.Y.: Rowman and Littlefield, 1993); Mary G. Dietz, "Patriotism," in Terence Ball, James Farr, and Russell L. Hanson, eds., *Political Innovation and Conceptual Change* (Cambridge: Cambridge University Press, 1989), pp. 177–93. One of the earliest examples was Schaar, "The Case for Patriotism," in John H. Schaar, *Legitimacy in the Modern State* (New Brunswick, N.J.: Transaction Books, 1981), pp. 285–311.

8. A sharp contrast between "patriotism" and "nationalism" has more rhetorical impact than the more defensible claim (made, for example, by Stephen Nathanson) that there are liberal and illiberal versions of both. Nathanson, *Patriotism, Morality, and Peace*, pp. 185–86.

9. Habermas, "Citizenship and National Identity," pp. 500, 507.

10. According to Attracta Ingram, "constitutional patriotism . . . is part of the idea that the creation of political community is a morally transformative act in which human beings develop relationships as citizens that tie them together independently of their prior associational ties to family, religion and the like" (Ingram, "Constitutional Patriotism," p. 2). Cf. Viroli, *For Love of Country*, p. 121; Schaar, "The Case for Patriotism," pp. 290–91; Dietz, "Patriotism," p. 189.

11. Viroli, *For Love of Country*, pp. 1–2, 13–17, 183–85; Schaar, "The Case for Patriotism," p. 293.

12. Habermas, "Citizenship and National Identity," pp. 500, 514; Ingram, "Constitutional Patriotism," p. 14.

13. Viroli and Dietz place themselves within this tradition. On the European transition (about 1800) from republican to nationalist discourses, see Martin Thom, *Republics, Nations and Tribes* (London: Verso, 1995).

14. Viroli, *For Love of Country*, pp. 16, 183–84.

15. On this aspect of ancient republicanism, see Paul A. Rahe, *Republics Ancient and Modern: Classical Republicanism and the American Revolution* (Chapel Hill: University of North Carolina Press, 1992). For Viroli the key feature of ancient Roman patriotism was "compassion" (*For Love of Country*, p. 20).

16. This comes out clearly in Habermas's essay on "D-Mark Nationalism," cited above.

17. Habermas, "Citizenship and National Identity": all quotations in this paragraph are from p. 500, emphasis in the original. See also Jürgen Habermas, *The New Conservatism: Cultural Criticism and the Historians' Debate* (Cambridge: Polity, 1989), pp. 256–61.

18. Like Habermas, Ingram comes from a national tradition that has been heavily contested.

19. Ingram, "Constitutional Patriotism," p. 2.

20. Habermas, "Citizenship and National Identity," pp. 507, 514. Cf. interviews with M. Haller in Jürgen Habermas, *The Past as Future* (Lincoln: University of Nebraska Press, 1994), pp. 163–65.

21. Ingram, "Constitutional Patriotism," pp. 11, 12–15.

22. Ibid., p. 14

23. Habermas, *New Conservatism*, p. 261.

24. Habermas, *Between Facts and Norms*, pp. 500, 514. Writing more recently about the "transition of the European Community to a democratically-constituted, federal state," Habermas has stressed again the need to deliberately forge a new kind of "abstract, legally mediated solidarity among strangers" through the development of EU-wide political communication. His answer to the linguistic barriers that at present stand

in the way of any such shared public sphere is the promotion of English "as a second first language." Given Europe's existing level of integration, he maintains that, "Given the political will, there is no *a priori* reason why it cannot subsequently create the politically necessary communicative context as soon as it is constitutionally *prepared* to do so" (J. Habermas, "Comment on the Paper by Dieter Grimm: 'Does Europe Need a Constitution?'" *European Law Journal* 1 [1995]: 303–307, emphasis in the original).

25. Adrian Oldfield, *Citizenship and Community—Civic Republicanism and the Modern World* (London: Routledge, 1990), pp. ix, 6, 146, 153, 164.

26. Habermas, *Between Facts and Norms*, p. 458.

27. The controversy generated by John Rawls's parallel attempt to articulate a strictly "political" liberalism illustrates the difficulty of settling even on an "overlapping consensus" that can in practice be shared by the denizens of plural societies (John Rawls, *Political Liberalism* [New York: Columbia University Press, 1993]).

28. See Norma C. Moruzzi, "A Problem with Headscarves: Contemporary Complexities of Political and Social Identity," *Political Theory* 22 (1994): 653–72. Precisely because the dominant French version of nationhood is strongly imbued with elements of constitutional patriotism, it may be in some respects less tolerant of multicultural difference than less principled and more untidy versions.

29. The tradition has been lucidly restated by Dominique Schnapper, who maintains that Habermasian constitutional patriotism (in so far as it is feasible at all) amounts to a belated German discovery of the true (French) idea of nationhood (Dominique Schnapper, *La Communauté des Citoyens: Sur l'Idée Moderne de Nation* [Paris: Gallimard, 1994], p. 182). Habermas himself evidently believes that socialization into citizenship does not imply French-style assimilation, contrasting this with U.S. experience (Habermas, "Comment on Grimm," p. 306). It may be objected, however, that unlike France, the United States has not yet had to face the challenge of deep ideological diversity presented by Islam.

30. Ingram, "Constitutional Patriotism," p. 2.

31. Habermas, "Comment on Grimm," p. 305.

32. Donald L. Horowitz, *A Democratic South Africa? Constitutional Engineering in a Divided Society* (Berkeley: University of California Press, 1991), p. 155. The large literature on constitutional engineering in divided societies contains some sharp disagreements, notably between supporters on the one hand of "consociational" solutions that institutionalize group differences, and on the other side advocates of forms of majoritarian democracy that give politicians incentives to recruit voters across ethnic divides. For classic treatments, see Arend Lijphart, *Democracy in Plural Societies: A Comparative Exploration* (New Haven, Conn.: Yale University Press, 1977); and Donald L. Horowitz, *Ethnic Groups in Conflict* (Berkeley: University of California Press, 1985). Levels of optimism also vary, with Horowitz in particular stressing the very great difficulty of achieving stable democracy in the face of differences between ascriptive communities (Horowitz, *A Democratic South Africa?* pp. 162, 241).

33. Even this apparently modest assumption is cast into doubt by the strength of nationalist sentiment in Scotland and Québec, despite the relatively civilized political structures of Britain and Canada.

34. For arguments that liberal democratic political theory has regularly taken for granted the existence of that collective power without acknowledging that its basis was

nationhood, see Margaret Canovan, *Nationhood and Political Theory* (Cheltenham, Glos.: Edward Elgar, 1996).

35. Cf. Bhikhu Parekh, "Politics of Nationhood," in Keebet von Benda-Beck-mann and Maykel Verkuyten, eds., *Nationalism, Ethnicity and Cultural Identity in Europe: Comparative Studies in Migration and Ethnic Relations I* (Utrecht: European Research Centre on Migration and Ethnic Relations, 1995), pp. 139–40.

36. On the "democratic deficit" see Jack Hayward, ed., *The Crisis of Representation in Europe* (London: Frank Cass, 1995).

37. Failure to confront this question is a serious flaw in Yael Tamir's attempt to marry cultural nationalism with something like constitutional patriotism (Tamir, *Liberal Nationalism*, pp. 165–66).

38. Ingram, "Constitutional Patriotism," p. 7. Surprisingly, this was written after unification.

39. For evidence of the topic's sensitivity see the documents collected in *Forever in the Shadow of Hitler?* trans. J. Knowlton and T. Cates (Amherst, N.Y.: Humanity Books, 1993), especially Habermas's contributions.

40. David Miller makes the point in a private communication that while East German enthusiasm for unification could at a pinch be read as commitment to liberal democratic principles and squeezed into the model of *Verfassungspatriotismus*, the actions and motivations of West German politicians and people cannot be understood in terms of that model.

41. Habermas, "Citizenship and National Identity," p. 500.

42. Wolf Linder, *Swiss Democracy: Possible Solutions to Conflict in Multicultural Societies* (New York: St. Martin's Press, 1994). Both quotations are from page xviii.

43. Barber, "Constitutional Faith," p. 32.

44. Note, however, that a strong commitment to the United States on the part of many immigrants may have more to do with what John Harles calls "the politics of the lifeboat"—relief and gratitude at finding sanctuary—than with understanding of or belief in the actual principles of the constitution, as in the case of the Laotian immigrants Harles studied (John C. Harles, *Politics in the Lifeboat: Immigrants and the American Democratic Order* [Boulder, Colo.: Westview Press, 1993], pp. 144–98).

45. Schaar, "Case for Patriotism," p. 293.

46. Michael W. McConnell, "Don't Neglect the Little Platoons," in Nussbaum, *For Love of Country*, pp. 78–84 at p. 82; Taylor, "Cross-purposes," pp. 166, 280.

47. Schaar, "Case for Patriotism," pp. 291–93.

48. Ingram, "Constitutional Patriotism," p. 2; Habermas, "Comment on Grimm," p. 306.

49. Habermas, "D-Mark Nationalism," p. 198.

50. Cf. Brian Barry and Robert E. Goodin, eds., *Free Movement: Ethical Issues in the Transnational Migration of People and of Money* (New York: Harvester Wheatsheaf, 1992).

51. On Burke's articulation in *Reflections on the Revolution in France* of this fusion of the political with the familial, see Canovan, *Nationhood and Political Theory*, pp. 69–70.

52. Other kinds of polities have been less dependent on family inheritance among the subject population. Monarchies could preserve dynastic continuity even though territories and subjects were lost and gained, while organizations like the Catholic Church and the Communist Party survived wide-ranging recruitment of personnel. It is democratic polities that need lasting collective identity on the part of their citizens.

53. Ingram, "Constitutional Patriotism," pp. 14–15.

54. Habermas, "Citizenship and National Identity," p. 514, emphasis in original. Cf. Bernard Yack, "The Myth of the Civic Nation," *Critical Review* 10 (1996): 193–211 at p. 200.

55. Viroli, *For Love of Country*, pp. 172–75.

56. Ibid., pp. 17, 161. "Patriotism without Nationalism" is the title of his epilogue.

57. Ibid., pp. 175–76, 184.

58. Ibid., pp. 178, 183–84; cf. Dietz, "Patriotism," pp. 187–89.

59. Nathanson, *Patriotism, Morality, and Peace*, pp. 185–86, 197.

60. Schaar, "Case for Patriotism," p. 285.

61. Viroli, *For Love of Country*, p. 2.

62. Ibid., p. 7.

63. Schaar, "Case for Patriotism," p. 296.

64. Viroli, *For Love of Country*, pp. 184–85.

65. See, for example, Benedict Anderson, *Imagined Communities: Reflections on the Origin and Spread of Nationalism* (London: Verso, 1983); Canovan, *Nationhood and Political Theory*; Liah Greenfeld, *Nationalism: Five Roads to Modernity* (Cambridge, Mass.: Harvard University Press, 1992); Miller, *On Nationality*; Anthony D. Smith, *National Identity* (Harmondsworth, Middx.: Penguin, 1991).

66. As Habermas admits in "Citizenship and National Identity," p. 493. It may be argued that without nationhood (which can incorporate a population into a single "people") liberal democracy would never have come about (Greenfeld, *Nationalism*, e.g., p. 10). Cf. Canovan, *Nationhood and Political Theory, passim*.

67. For example, see Miller, *On Nationality*, p. 127. Cf. Schnapper, *Communauté des Citoyens, passim*.

68. Miller, *On Nationality*, p. 127.

69. Anderson, *Imagined Communities*. This does not imply that they are imaginary.

70. Richard Kearney, *Postnationalist Ireland: Politics, Culture, Philosophy* (London: Routledge, 1997), p. 69.

71. Hannah Arendt, *The Human Condition* (Chicago: University of Chicago Press, 1958), pp. 220–30.

72. As proposed, for example, by David Miller in *On Nationality*, pp. 179, 181.

73. Martha C. Nussbaum, "Reply," in Nussbaum, *For Love of Country*, pp. 131–44 at p. 133.

74. Alasdair MacIntyre has written provocatively that because of the particularistic demands of patriotism, "good soldiers may not be liberals" (MacIntyre, "Is Patriotism a Virtue?" p. 17).

75. Cf. Barry and Goodin, *Free Movement*; W. Rogers Brubaker, ed., *Immigration and the Politics of Citizenship in Europe and North America* (London: University Press of America, 1989); Thomas Hammar, *Democracy and the Nation State: Aliens, Denizens and Citizens in a World of International Migration* (Aldershot, Hants.: Avebury, 1990).

76. The critique of new patriotism offered here does not imply an endorsement of nationalism, which has problems of its own that cannot be addressed here. Cf. Canovan, *Nationhood and Political Theory*, chaps. 9 and 10.

77. For an exhaustive survey of the traditional rhetorical techniques, see Quentin Skinner, *Reason and Rhetoric in the Philosophy of Hobbes* (Cambridge: Cambridge University Press, 1996), pt. 1.

78. Cf. Margaret Canovan, "The Eloquence of John Stuart Mill," *History of Political Thought* 8 (1987): 505–20.